Neuro-Symbolic Artificial Intelligence

Scrivener Publishing
100 Cummings Center, Suite 541J
Beverly, MA 01915-6106

Leading-Edge Breakthroughs in Artificial Intelligence

Series Editor: Dr. S. Balamurugan, Director, Intelligent Research Consultancy Services, Coimbatore, Tamil Nadu, India (Email: sbnbala@gmail.com)

The world is on the cusp of several breakthroughs in artificial intelligence (AI), rapidly transforming industries and the research field. The "Leading-Edge Breakthroughs in Artificial Intelligence" book series is dedicated to exploring the most pioneering developments in artificial intelligence. The series aims to highlight both theoretical and practical advancements, offering insights into several cutting-edge advancements in AI and how the same could be deployed to solve complex problems in fields such as healthcare, finance, manufacturing, robotics, marketing, energy management, agriculture, autonomous systems, and many more. It also addresses critical issues like AI governance, ethics, trust, security, transparency, and societal impacts, making it an essential resource for researchers, engineers, and industry leaders looking to leverage AI for future breakthroughs.

Managing Editors

1. **Dr. T. Ananth Kumar**, Associate Professor & HoD, Department of Computer Science and Engineering, IFET College of Engineering, Tamil Nadu, India

2. **Dr. K. Suresh Kumar**, Assistant Professor, Department of Computer Science and Engineering, Sri Eshwar College of Engineering, Coimbatore, Tamil Nadu, India

3. **Dr. R. Karthick Manoj**, Assistant Professor, Department of Electrical and Electronics Engineering, Academy of Maritime Education and Training (AMET), Deemed to be University, Chennai, Tamil Nadu, India

Publishers at Scrivener
Martin Scrivener (martin@scrivenerpublishing.com)
Phillip Carmical (pcarmical@scrivenerpublishing.com)

Neuro-Symbolic Artificial Intelligence

Concepts & Applications

Edited by

R. Nidhya
Dept. of Computer Science & Engineering, Madanapalle Institute of Technology & Science (MITS) Deemed to be University, Madanapalle, Andhra Pradesh, India

A. Dineshkumar
Department of Computer Science & Engineering, Koneru Lakshmaiah Education Foundation, Vijayawada, Andhra Pradesh, India

Sheng-Lung Peng
Department of Creative Technologies and Product Design, National Taipei University of Business, Taiwan

S. Karthik
Department of Computer Science & Engineering, SNS College of Technology, Coimbatore, Tamil Nadu, India

and

S. Balamurugan
Intelligent Research Consultancy Services, Coimbatore, Tamil Nadu, India

Scrivener Publishing

WILEY

This edition first published 2026 by John Wiley & Sons, Inc., 111 River Street, Hoboken, NJ 07030, USA and Scrivener Publishing LLC, 100 Cummings Center, Suite 541J, Beverly, MA 01915, USA

For more information about Scrivener publications please visit www.scrivenerpublishing.com.

Wiley Global Headquarters
111 River Street, Hoboken, NJ 07030, USA

For details of our global editorial offices, customer services, and more information about Wiley products visit us at www.wiley.com.

The manufacturer's authorized representative according to the EU General Product Safety Regulation is Wiley-VCH GmbH, Boschstr. 12, 69469 Weinheim, Germany, e-mail: Product_Safety@wiley.com.

Library of Congress Cataloging-in-Publication Data

ISBN 978-1-394-35557-0

Cover image: Generated with AI using Adobe Firefly
Cover design by Russell Richardson

Set in size of 11pt and Minion Pro by Manila Typesetting Company, Makati, Philippines

Printed in the USA

10 9 8 7 6 5 4 3 2 1

Dedicated to

My parents, Rangarajan R. and Angammal R.;
my brother, Prabakaran R.;
my niece, Rithanyaa P.;
my husband, Sureshkumar M.;
and my beloved twin daughters, Srinika S. and Srivarsha S.

Nidhya Rangarajan

Contents

Series Preface

This book showcases the powerful combination of neural networks and symbolic reasoning to produce an AI system that is more explainable, generalizable, and aligned with human behavior across various real-world tasks. The book is also critical for bridging the divide between statistical learning (deep learning) and symbolic reasoning, which have been foundational to AI for decades but have been developed as a dichotomy purely for purposes of paradigmatic separation. By combining the advantages of deep learning (pattern recognition and scaling) with symbolic logic (explainability and reasoning), this volume introduces a comprehensive framework for building AI systems that are interpretable, transparent, and human-centric. It addresses current challenges in achieving generalization, causality, and trust in AI applications across fields such as robotics, natural language understanding, and cognitive systems. Therefore, the book aligns seamlessly with the scope of the *Leading Edge Breakthroughs in Artificial Intelligence* series, demonstrating groundbreaking developments that will push the boundaries of conventional AI so that it is intelligent, robust, and ethically centered.

Dr. S. Balamurugan
Director, Intelligent Research Consultancy Services, Coimbatore, Tamil Nadu, India
Series Editor - Leading Edge Breakthroughs in Artificial Intelligence

Preface

The field of Artificial Intelligence (AI) has witnessed rapid advancements in recent years, driven primarily by deep learning and data-centric approaches. Despite their impressive performance, purely neural methods often lack interpretability, logical reasoning capabilities, and the ability to generalize beyond training data. In contrast, symbolic AI, rooted in formal logic and structured representations, offers transparency and reasoning strength but struggles with adaptability and learning from raw data. In response to these challenges, Neuro-Symbolic AI has emerged as a compelling paradigm that unifies the strengths of both approaches.

This book provides a comprehensive exploration of this interdisciplinary domain. It introduces the core principles of Neuro-Symbolic systems, surveys current models and architectures, and demonstrates their utility across real-world applications. From knowledge representation and natural language understanding to cognitive reasoning, the chapters examine how hybrid systems are redefining the boundaries of intelligent computation. By bridging the gap between connectionist learning and symbolic reasoning, Neuro-Symbolic AI is paving the way for more explainable, generalizable, and human-aligned AI systems.

Readers will find that this book:

- introduces the foundational theories and evolving architectures of Neuro-Symbolic AI;
- bridges the gap between connectionist and symbolic approaches;
- showcases current research, practical implementations, and interdisciplinary advances in the field.

The volume is organized into conceptual and application-focused chapters covering diverse use cases, including medical diagnosis, intelligent transportation, language processing, ethical AI, and cultural preservation. Each chapter reflects cutting-edge work from researchers in academia and industry, offering technical depth and real-world relevance. The book serves as a resource for graduate students, researchers, developers, and professionals interested in hybrid AI methodologies. It also aims to inspire innovation by highlighting the transformative potential of Neuro-Symbolic approaches for building robust and trustworthy AI systems. Through this compilation, we aspire to contribute to the ongoing evolution of Artificial Intelligence and encourage exploration of its next frontier.

This volume introduces the fundamentals of Neuro-Symbolic AI and its applications across multiple sectors. To meet these objectives, the book contains 17 chapters contributed by accomplished authors.

Chapter 1 presents an automated deep learning model for identifying orthopedic implants from post-surgery anterior-posterior (AP) X-ray images. Using residual networks and convolutional neural networks (CNNs), the model achieves strong validation performance while addressing challenges posed by incomplete hospital records. Reliably identifying implant types, improves preoperative planning, supports revision surgeries, and reduces burdens on patients and healthcare providers. Chapter 2 introduces a natural-language-driven stock analysis system that combines technical indicators with sentiment analysis using an Agentic Generative AI model. Built on the FinGPT framework and LLaMA architecture, it supports real-time forecasting, autonomous decision-making, and adaptive learning.

Chapter 3 proposes a biologically inspired artificial neural network framework that mimics brain-like efficiency and adaptability. Incorporating spiking neuron models, interhemispheric communication, STDP, and reward-based learning, the model enhances learning robustness and energy efficiency. Chapter 4 emphasizes the techniques and applications of a novel neuro-symbolic AI model that combines CNN-based visual analysis (using ResNet-50) with symbolic reasoning to detect tomato leaf diseases.

Chapter 5 introduces MMDL, a multi-modal deep learning model for early breast cancer detection that integrates clinical data with mammography and histological images. Utilizing transformer-based encoders and CNNs, the model fuses diverse data into a shared latent space for enhanced diagnostic accuracy. Evaluated on DDSM and BreaKHis datasets, MMDL outperforms leading unimodal models in precision, recall, and F1 score. Chapter 6 proposes a neuro-symbolic transfer learning model for enhancing intrusion detection in IoT systems. By integrating BiLSTM for temporal feature extraction with symbolic logic and transfer learning, the approach improves detection across complex attack types such as DoS, MITM, and data exfiltration.

Chapter 7 provides a comprehensive overview of Neuro-Symbolic Artificial Intelligence (NSAI), which combines the pattern recognition strengths of neural networks with the reasoning capabilities of symbolic systems. It explores NSAI's evolution, current advancements, and future potential across domains like computer vision, NLP, reinforcement learning, and program synthesis. Chapter 8 introduces a rule-based intelligent transportation system (ITS) designed to enhance road safety by analyzing key collision factors, such as speed, vehicle spacing, lane shifts, weather, and erratic driving. A rule-based inference engine processes real-time, standardized data to identify threats and alert drivers promptly. The system improves traffic modelling, reduces near-misses and accidents, and adapts to dynamic road conditions.

Chapter 9 proposes a hybrid emotion detection system that integrates BERT-based transformer embeddings with a Logic-Driven Neural Parsing Algorithm (LDNPA). By combining deep learning and rule-based reasoning, the model effectively captures complex emotional cues from natural language. Evaluated on IEMOCAP and CMU-MOSEI datasets, it outperforming than traditional models like CNNs and RNNs. Chapter 10 introduces a neuro-symbolic AI approach for detecting Lumbar Spinal Stenosis (LSS), integrating fuzzy logic for interpretability with graph convolutional networks (GCNs) for deep feature extraction from MRI and CT scans. By combining learned features with structured medical data, the model enhances prediction accuracy while maintaining explainability.

Chapter 11 presents a comprehensive approach to medical image denoising using spatial, wavelet, and statistical domain filters. Morphological OCS and LMMSE-STD filters effectively remove Impulse and Rician noise in the spatial domain. Statistical techniques improve noise modeling and denoising accuracy. Chapter 12 proposes a hybrid model combining Convolutional Block Attention Module (CBAM) and Vision Transformers (ViT) for accurate heritage monument classification. By integrating CBAM's local focus with ViT's global feature extraction, the architecture enhances precision and efficiency. Data preprocessing techniques like edge detection and grayscale conversion further improve robustness.

Chapter 13 evaluates deep learning models for predicting age-related health conditions using the ICR dataset from Kaggle. Models tested include FCNN, CNN, LSTM, and Transformers, with CNN and LSTM achieving the highest accuracies. Techniques such as SMOTE, PCA, and L1 regularization enhanced model performance. While Transformers showed potential, they faced computational challenges. Chapter 14 emphasizes an efficient recommendation system for e-commerce using deep learning embeddings and locality-sensitive hashing (LSH). By leveraging ResNet-50 for feature learning and integrating a locality-sensitive index, the system enhances retrieval efficiency and product similarity matching.

Chapter 15 introduces a novel framework combining adversarial networks and BERT-based contextual embeddings to reduce gender bias in word representations while preserving semantic integrity. Unlike traditional projection-based methods, this approach leverages error-driven learning and contextual adaptability for superior debiasing. WEFAT scores and qualitative analyses confirm significant bias reduction and improved word associations. Chapter 16 explores recent advancements in using machine learning for voice-based detection of Parkinson's Disease (PD), a neurodegenerative disorder often diagnosed late. Subtle vocal features such as jitter and pitch fluctuation are analyzed using models like SVM and CNN, demonstrating high accuracy. The study covers datasets, feature extraction, performance metrics, and ethical challenges.

The final chapter introduces a Neuro-AI-inspired Automated Augmentation Classifier Agent (AACA) to address data scarcity and augmentation leaks in NLP for Medical Health Records and infrared micro-object detection. AACA is a lightweight neural module that monitors and filters GAN-generated augmentations, improving data quality without increasing training time.

The topics presented in each chapter are unique to this volume and based on the unpublished work of the contributing authors. In editing this book, we sought to incorporate emerging trends and recent developments in Neuro-Symbolic AI. We believe it will serve as a valuable reference for system architects, practitioners, developers, and researchers.

The Editors
June 2026

Acknowledgements

First and foremost, I thank the Almighty for granting me the strength, wisdom, and perseverance to bring this edited volume to fruition.

I extend my heartfelt appreciation to all the contributing authors whose scholarly efforts and thoughtful insights have enriched this volume. Their commitment to academic excellence and timely collaboration made the editorial process both smooth and rewarding. I am sincerely grateful to the reviewers and subject matter experts who generously offered their time and expertise to ensure the quality and clarity of each chapter. Their constructive feedback has significantly strengthened the content and structure of this work.

I also acknowledge with deep appreciation the support received from my institute, MITS Deemed to be University, as well as my colleagues and mentors, who encouraged and guided me throughout this journey. Their encouragement served as a constant source of motivation. My thanks also go to Martin Scrivener and the team at Scrivener Publishing for their professional guidance and support at every stage of this project, from manuscript preparation to final production. Finally, I express my deepest gratitude to my family and loved ones for their unwavering support, patience, and understanding. Their presence and belief in me have been the foundation of my endeavors. It has been an honor to serve as the corresponding editor for this volume, and I remain thankful for the opportunity to collaborate with such dedicated and insightful contributors.

Dr. Nidhya Rangarajan

Part 1

NEURO-SYMBOLIC AI: CONCEPTS

1

Cataract Detection Systems Using Deep Learning Technique: A Survey

Arveti Mallikharjuna Rao and Suma Kamalesh Gandhimathi*

School of Computer Science and Engineering, VIT-AP University, Andhra Pradesh, India

Abstract

Cataracts are the leading cause of blindness worldwide; therefore, early detection is crucial for preventing or reducing visual impairment. Traditional diagnostic methods rely on the manual assessment and expertise of an ophthalmologist, which can be tedious and subjective. Deep learning (DL) algorithms have recently gained prominence as efficient tools for automating the evaluation of medical images, especially in cataract detection. This article analyzes the leading deep learning models for cataract detection, highlighting the advantages and disadvantages of each method. We analyze CNNs, MobileNet, and U-Net among various models for image classification, segmentation, and real-time detection. This study investigates color space adjustments, specifically YCrCb, in conjunction with data augmentation and transfer learning to improve model accuracy and efficiency. This paper aims to provide a comprehensive evaluation of recent advances in deep learning for cataract detection systems, while also outlining potential future research and development prospects in this area.

Keywords: Cataract detection, deep learning, convolutional neural network (CNN), fundus imaging, MobileNet, U-Net, transfer learning, image classification

**Corresponding author*: sumarathee@gmail.com

R. Nidhya, A. Dineshkumar, Sheng-Lung Peng, S. Karthik and S. Balamurugan (eds.) Neuro-Symbolic Artificial Intelligence: Concepts & Applications, (3–18) © 2026 Scrivener Publishing LLC

1.1 Introduction

Worldwide, over 2.2 billion people suffer from proximal or distal visual impairment, with at least 1 billion cases being either preventable or misdiagnosed. The primary causes of blindness and visual impairment are cataracts and refractive errors. Only 17% of individuals with cataracts receive the necessary treatment, compared to 36% of those with refractive errors. Visual impairment costs the global economy $411 billion in lost productivity each year. While people of all ages can be affected by visual impairment, the majority are over the age of 50 [1].

Many factors contribute to the degeneration of lens proteins. This causes the lens to alter its metabolism, promoting the formation of cataracts [2]. The thick lens of a cataract impairs vision by preventing the accurate projection of light onto the retina. Individuals over the age of 40 are more likely to develop cataracts, with the incidence increasing with age. Due to their increasing prevalence and significant impact, cataract treatment is becoming increasingly important. There is a clear need for early detection and intervention. Research is ongoing to identify risk factors for cataract [3].

Elderly individuals are susceptible to various types of cataracts, including nuclear and cortical forms. While UV-B exposure and smoking may influence cataract development, the significance of this impact is debatable [4]. Specific methods, such as wearing anti-glare sunglasses, may slow the progression of cataracts. Early detection allows for timely prevention and intervention. Surgery is typically beneficial when severe cataracts impede a patient's ability to perform daily tasks. Currently, there are four primary approaches to classifying and detecting cataracts. The primary method is the slit-lamp examination, followed by ophthalmoscopic transillumination, iris image projection, and a second slit-lamp examination. Manual examination can be costly, time-consuming, and subjective. Therefore, from both financial and societal perspectives, it is sensible to implement artificial intelligence for automated cataract diagnosis. The model recognizes that eye care is a vital field worldwide, where we can have a significant impact on individuals' lives.

Figure 1.1 shows the specimens from individuals with varying degrees of cataract [5]. The cataract-free image in (a) clearly shows both large and small blood vessels, as well as the optic disk. The mild cataract image in (b) exhibits fewer vascular features, whereas the moderate cataract image in (c) displays only the optic disk and major arteries. Again, the poor quality cataract image (d) shows minimal detail. Retinal fundus images are crucial

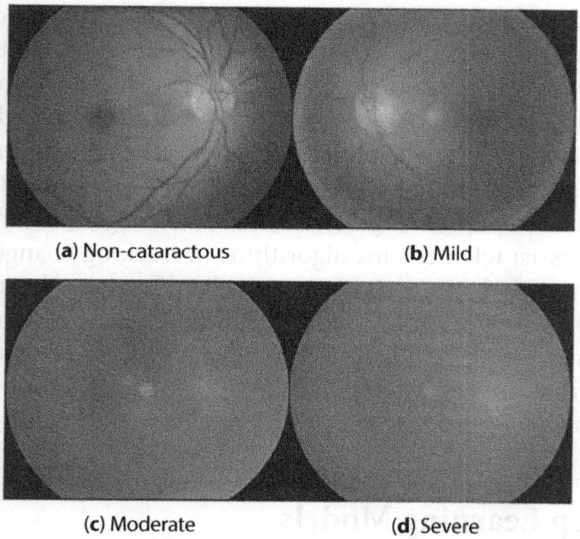

Figure 1.1 Standard retinal fundus images for different levels of cataract disease.

for diagnosing and grading cataracts, particularly in relation to the blood vessels and optic disk.

Machine learning (ML) enables the automated detection of cataracts through the analysis of ocular images [6]. This reduces the need for manual examination by ophthalmologists. Machine learning models that provide efficient and automated replacements for time-consuming and clinically sound conventional diagnostic techniques include Support Vector Machines (SVM), K-Nearest Neighbors (KNN), Random Forest, and Logistic Regression. These methods classify eye images as either positive or negative for cataract by noting features such as texture, pixel intensity, and chromatic variations using pre-processed and annotated datasets. Feature extraction is critical because models in various machine learning methods rely on defined visual features to make accurate predictions. Random forest generates many decision trees from this data, while SVM identifies the optimal hyperplane to separate photos with and without cataracts. These algorithms often perform best on smaller, more structured datasets and require significant human intervention, including feature engineering and calibration, to produce consistent results [7].

Deep learning has transformed ocular imaging by autonomously classifying and detecting cataracts, which enables accurate diagnoses. Optic nerve assessments facilitate the early detection of glaucoma, while screenings for diabetic retinopathy enable the assessment of severity to prompt timely intervention. Deep learning facilitates the evaluation of vascular changes and the detection of glaucoma by distinguishing between retinal veins and optic disks [8]. It precisely guides surgical procedures, including cataract surgery; assesses corneal conditions through corneal imaging; monitors cataract progression using optical coherence tomography (OCT) [9]; and enables early detection of age-related macular degeneration. Simulated images [10] assist telemedicine algorithms in tracking changes for timely response. Improved categorization and identification of cataract stages will support accurate diagnosis and treatment, thereby enhancing patient outcomes and overall healthcare efficiency. In this context, convolutional neural networks are widely employed for image identification and classification, enhancement, model selection, and data preparation.

1.2 Deep Learning Models

Modern deep learning provides an effective framework for supervised learning. By increasing the number of layers and the number of units in each layer, a deep network can represent more complex behaviors [11].

Deep learning decomposes the complex mapping of an image into multiple hierarchical, simplified mappings, each represented by a different model layer. The presence of numerous hidden layers makes the image increasingly abstract. Since the values of the hidden layers are not specified in the data, the model must determine which concepts are critical to clarifying the relationships in the observable data. This perspective posits that not all information within an activation layer encapsulates the variational features that elucidate the input. Furthermore, the format preserves state information, allowing a data processing machine to operate effectively. Most deep architectures, conceptualized as generalizations of logistic or linear regression, are based on neural networks. Deep Neural Network (DNN) refers to a multilayer network. CNNs and Recurrent Neural Networks (RNNs) are the most commonly used architectures today. Weight sharing enables convolutional neural networks to operate more efficiently by leveraging the presence of analogous structures across multiple locations within an image. A vectorized image can be weighted to speed up the convolution process. This makes the network equivariant to input translations, significantly reducing the number of parameters required for learning.

A five-layer convolutional deep learning architecture effectively distinguishes features from multiple nonlinear combinations within the fundus image through multilayer nonlinear mapping [12]. Features can be extracted from multilayer nonlinear mappings generated by the final convolutional layers. Compared to the results of the previous phase of the experiment, the deep learning generated feature improved its ability to discriminate the severity of cataract lesions in the training set. While its technical significance as a matrix is widely recognized, its implications remain uncertain. Classification accuracy increased significantly. The photographs are inadequate. We argue that improved categorization results can be achieved through theoretical advances and the development of superior open-source solutions.

This article [13] presents CataractNet, an innovative deep neural network designed for the automatic detection of cataracts in fundus images. To optimize the network with reduced kernel sizes, fewer layers, and reduced training parameters, the loss and activation functions are improved. CataractNet has significantly reduced computational complexity and average execution time compared to alternative pre-trained convolutional neural network models. The Adam optimizer is used to enhance the proposed network. A total of 4,746 fundus images were acquired for model training, comprising 1,130 fundus images that included both cataract and non-cataract instances. The dataset is augmented before model training to mitigate overfitting. Experimental results demonstrate that the proposed method outperforms current cataract detection techniques, achieving an average accuracy of 99.13%.

The proposed [14] technique automatically categorizes photographs showing normal and cataractous lesions using a framework of pre-trained neural networks. The effectiveness of the classification process in developing the proposed model was enhanced by making careful adjustments to the pre-trained DenseNet-201 neural network. The efficiency of the proposed model was evaluated using data from the basic DenseNet 201 architecture without additional layers. The proposed deep learning model outperforms the basic DenseNet 201 model by 10%. The proposed model can serve as an adjunct tool for physicians managing a range of conditions, including common cataracts.

This study [15] presents a six-stage cataract grading technique that emphasizes multi-feature fusion by stacking. This model investigates two types of features that allow us to distinguish between different stages of cataract progression. ResNet 18 extracts high-level features from the residual network. The gray-level co-occurrence matrix (GLCM) is an alternative method for obtaining texture information. A model based on the acquired features is proposed for self-assessment of cataracts. The system evaluates the probability outputs for each fundus image using a fully connected neural network (FCNN) with two fully connected layers and two support vector machine classifiers as base learners to obtain the final classification result. The six-level grading system enables the proposed method to achieve an average accuracy of 92.66% and a peak accuracy of 93.33%. The proposed method outperforms existing techniques in cataract grading accuracy, achieving a minimum score of 1.75% and a four-level score of 94.75%.

This study [16] examines a technique for using color fundus imaging to detect cataract disease. Deep learning algorithms facilitate the automatic identification of cataract problems. Two pre-trained robust architectures, DenseNet and VGGNet, were used to identify anomalies in the descriptive regions of the human eye. The primary contribution of the study is the implementation of the proposed technique on a large and distinctive dataset comprising multiple color retinal fundus images acquired using a widely available and inexpensive modality. The criteria describe the characteristics of the disease and illustrate the stages of cataract progression. The proposed technique facilitates early detection of cataract-related problems. Various traditional and contemporary classification systems are used to evaluate the effectiveness of the proposed method. The proposed approach for classification of cataract conditions demonstrates a diagnostic accuracy of 97.94%.

The VGG-19 model [17] was used in this study to differentiate between eyes with and without cataracts. The model performed incredibly well, exceeding expectations. Ninety-four percent of the diagnoses were accurate in both standard and cataract cases. This proposed method for diagnosing eye disease demonstrates reduced latency and improved accuracy compared to existing CNN models. Furthermore, it is optimal for several applications related to medical image classification. The VGG-19 model shows potential as a diagnostic tool for eye diseases. The main advantage of the system is its ability to accommodate multiple medical imaging modalities. Segmentation can improve performance. Generative adversarial networks can reduce class gaps by generating accurate representations of disease. Although additional research is needed to improve accuracy, particularly in cases of glaucoma, this model shows significant potential to assist physicians and transform the screening process for ocular diseases. The preliminary results are promising; with further data and research, this could become a highly effective tool for disease classification.

This study [18] introduces the Cataract State Identification Network (CSDNet), an innovative framework that utilizes deep learning methods to enhance cataract state detection. The goal is to provide a more lightweight and adaptable architecture suitable for specific scenarios or devices with limited memory or storage capacity. Minimizing the number of trainable parameters while maintaining the ability to learn representations from data efficiently is essential. Real-time or near-real-time applications require fast inference, so the framework must be designed accordingly. In this study, images of normal individuals and those with cataracts from the Ocular Disease Intelligent Recognition (ODIR) database are utilized. The proposed model efficiently minimizes the number of trainable parameters by using smaller kernels, fewer layers, and reduced training parameters, thus reducing the average execution time and computational cost.

This research [19] presents two innovative deep learning models for cataract diagnosis and detection to assist ophthalmologists in their practice and treatment. The proposed deep learning models were evaluated using both normal and cataract fundus data. The proposed deep learning models can facilitate the automatic classification of both normal and cataract-affected images. The upper layers were modified and improved using MobileNet V3 Small, a pre-trained deep learning model. Optimization of the upper layers of a MobileNet V3 Small model facilitates subsequent performance evaluation. The proposed method deviates from the basic paradigm of classification efficiency for both normal and cataract images based on accuracy and complexity criteria. Using the KFold method for partitioning test and training data, the proposed model outperformed the baseline model by 8.26% in terms of optimal performance. The proposed MobileNet V3 model was validated on photographs from two different datasets. The MobileNet V3 model achieved an average accuracy of 96.62% over the entire dataset.

The primary objective of the proposed study is to develop an automated system for grading and classifying fundus images through image analysis [20]. This research utilizes a deep convolutional neural network (DCNN) to extract data from fundus images autonomously. The technique has four primary stages: image acquisition, feature extraction, classification, and data enhancement and preparation. The proposed method enhances efficiency and performance by utilizing a CNN for feature extraction and a softmax function for classification into four distinct categories. The goal of this project is to improve the reliability of the automated system. Initially, we collected cataract images from various publicly available web repositories. The next step involves pre-processing to enhance the quality of the fundus images and data augmentation to expand the dataset size. In the third step, we built a CNN model to extract features from the fundus images automatically. In the fourth step, we used the softmax technique to systematically categorize cataracts into four classifications: mild, moderate, absent, and severe.

A computer-aided automated method [21] for categorizing cataracts into normal, mild, moderate, and severe phases using fundus images is presented. The proposed approach enables automated cataract classification by using a pre-trained convolutional neural network for transfer learning. The support vector machine classifier uses features extracted from a pre-trained convolutional neural network model. Ophthalmologists classify fundus cataract photographs into four stages after acquiring data from various open-access databases. The classification accuracy of the four-level technique was 92.91 percent. An image quality selection module was introduced to evaluate fundus image quality for diagnostic purposes, highlighting the importance of image quality in convolutional neural networks. The quality of the fundus photographs will dictate the re-evaluation of the results. The proposed method demonstrates its effectiveness by using pre-trained CNNs for transfer learning in cataract categorization.

The LeNet Convolutional Neural Network (LeNet-CNN) [22] model is trained on a dataset of digital camera photographs, and its effectiveness in detecting cataract anomalies is evaluated in comparison to the SVM model. The LeNet-CNN model shows commendable performance based on the evaluation conducted during the testing phase. The overall accuracy rate is 96%, with a sensitivity of 95% for detecting positive cases and a specificity of 96% for identifying negative cases. The results of the study exceed those of previous field studies. This demonstrates the accuracy and effectiveness of the proposed technology, underscoring its importance for LeNet-CNN. This study establishes an efficient, first-of-its-kind method for cataract screening using image processing technology and convolutional neural networks. Self-image recordings help individuals assess their perception and facilitate prompt medical attention. The proposed process would optimize initial cataract assessment, enable early detection, and ensure prompt access to appropriate therapy.

This study [23] presents ocular B-ultrasound imaging devices along with a cooperative monitoring deep learning (CMDL) methodology for cataract detection. Although ocular B-ultrasound images often have low contrast, limited penetration, a limited imaging range, and elevated noise levels, they can still show pronounced echoes between the lens and the posterior capsule. We develop an object identification network using YOLO-v3 within the proposed CMDL framework to identify the primary focal areas. Our approach reduces noise distortion and improves the accuracy of cataract identification. Due to the limitations of our collected B-ultrasound image dataset, we developed three feature extraction modules to mitigate overfitting in the deep neural networks. These include a shape feature extractor utilizing the gray-level co-occurrence matrix, a texture feature extraction module employing DenseNet-161, and a shape feature extractor based on Fourier descriptors. We additionally integrate the cooperative learning module to increase the overall applicability of the proposed paradigm. The initial combination includes the texture, shape, and depth features of the eyeball and lens. The cooperative network takes information from the amalgamated features of the lens and the eye. The applied classification loss, along with the cooperation loss that evaluates the categorization of the lens and eyeball, improves the accuracy of cataract identification.

In cataract classification, each model within the proposed deep learning system corresponds to one of the five features [24]. Images acquired with a 45-degree slit light are used by nuclear sclerosis (NS) models to project NS variables. The cortical lens opacity (CLO) predicts the CLO variable based on a previous retroillumination image, while the CLO-center predicts the CLO-center variable. The PSC model predicts the PSC variable with a prospective retroillumination image, while the PSC-center model predicts the center variable. The deep learning method systematically and quantitatively classified cataract severity in all three age-related categories with exceptional accuracy. In all three domains, the mean squared error for the entire test set was nearly negligible. A segment of the test set was designated as challenging by increasing the number of positive cortical and PSC events. While posterior subcapsular cataracts yield better results, cortical and nuclear cataracts are the most prevalent types of age-related cataracts. The reduction of positive PSC events in the training set is likely the reason for the observed decrease in population frequency. The deep learning architecture outperformed ophthalmologists in detecting nuclear and cortical cataracts. The accuracy of the least common variant, posterior subcapsular, was comparable to that of ophthalmologists and medical students. Observations indicated that performance was not affected by the presence of younger children. Accurate analysis of NS grading is possible regardless of the number of students. Nevertheless, the evaluation of human NS suggests that ophthalmologists are not adequately addressing constricted pupils.

This study [25] investigates the application of deep learning convolutional neural network models to color retinal fundus images for the diagnosis, identification, and categorization of cataracts. The collection consists of 400 color photographs, 300 conventional images, and 100 images depicting cataracts. Before segmentation, the datasets underwent automatic pre-processing using contrast-limited adaptive histogram equalization (CLAHE) and histogram equalization (HE). Three models were evaluated in this research: DenseNet 201, GoogleNet, and ResNet-101. The first example used unprocessed source photographs, the following example used images that had been subjected to histogram equalization (HE), and the last example integrated HE with contrast-limited adaptive histogram equalization (CLAHE). In the evaluation, the DenseNet 201 model achieved 98% classification accuracy, while the GoogleNet model achieved 90%. Accuracy, sensitivity, specificity, and F_1 score are standard performance metrics used to evaluate experimental results in cataract detection and categorization. Precision, rapid identification, expertise, and prospective learning all contribute to improved ocular health. The proposed method improves the automatic detection and classification of cataract treatment for performance optimization.

This article [26] presents an innovative method that utilizes smartphone photos of lenses taken with a slit lamp to diagnose and detect cataracts automatically. This technology uses horizontal scanning videos rather than single-lens images, closely resembling the diagnostic methods used by ophthalmologists. Changing the color space to YCrCb significantly improves the real-time efficiency and performance of the system; YOLOv3 is used to acquire additional locations. The algorithm identifies each video frame and accurately positions the light knife within the pupil. Because cataracts are not detectable in a single scan, physicians do not use the three-dimensional configuration of the lens to diagnose cataracts. Slit lamp imaging is used to obtain a more precise visualization. The proposed method expands the diagnostic scope and produces a more comprehensive data set by replacing films with single-image approaches. The portability of slit lamp technology and the real-time detection capabilities of the algorithm enable community health workers to use it more effectively. Healthcare professionals from multiple disciplines can use the RUimu app to transmit a scanned video for faster diagnostic results. This approach accelerates cataract screening in the developing world, enabling the detection of individuals who may not have access to hospitals due to geographic or financial constraints. The proliferation of screening programs in community and rural health facilities ensures that a larger number of cataract patients are promptly referred for appropriate treatment, despite the increased cost of consultations.

The primary goal of this research [27], including this initiative, is to identify the most reliable and effective approach for targeted diagnosis. CNN-based deep learning architectures, including DenseNet, EfficientNet, Xception, VGG, and ResNet models, evaluate ocular health or disease through binary classification, unlike previous diagnostic techniques. The EfficientNet model achieved superior performance with an accuracy of 94.88%, a recall of 94.88%, a precision of 95.02%, an F_1 score of 94.88%, and a Matthews correlation coefficient of 89.89%. This technique facilitates the diagnosis and management of various ocular diseases. Despite the encouraging results, further research is necessary to obtain accurate and reliable findings from a larger volume of retinal fundus images and various models.

The Deep Convolutional Neural Network (DCNN) [E5] is evaluated for its utility and effectiveness in autonomous cataract identification and classification. The feature representations generated by the DCNN are elucidated, and it is shown how different feature mappings of the pool5

Table 1.1 Performance comparison of deep learning models.

Ref.	Model	Dataset	Accuracy	*F1* score	Recall	Specificity
[13]	CNN + Adam optimizer	HRF, FIRE, ACHIKO-I, IDRiD, DRIVE	99.13	89.51	99.07	99.08
[14]	DenseNet201	ODIR	99.9	99.9	99.9	99.9
[15]	ResNet + FCNN	NA	92.97	95.68	96.43	98.52
[16]	DenseNet + VGGNet	Fundus image database	97.94	98	NA	98
[17]	VGG-19	ODIR	95.6	96.4	96	NA
[18]	CSDNet	ODIR	96.79	98	97	97
[19]	MobileNet V3	Retina Dataset	96.62	97	98	NA
[20]	DCNN	HRF, STARE, MESSIDOR, IDRiD	92.7	NA	NA	NA
[21]	CNN + SVM	HRF, IDRiD, STARE, DIARETDB0, DRIVE, MESSIDOR	92.91	NA	92.91	NA
[22]	LeNet-CNN	Cataract image dataset	96	96	95	96
[23]	CMDL	MSCOCO, ImgNet	98.01	NA	NA	NA
[25]	DenseNet201 + CLAHE	Fundus image database	98.33	98	98	98
[26]	ACCV	NA	94	93.8	NA	92
[27]	EfficientNet	IDRID, JSIEC	94.88	94.88	94.88	NA
[28]	DCNN	BTEC	93.52	NA	NA	91.04

layer have improved the empirical semantic relevance of the data. The proposed DCNN classification method is cross-evaluated on 5,620 clinical retinal fundus images from a hospital cohort. This analysis leads to two conclusions: Resolution of early ocular reflections and localized illumination abnormalities improved G-filter processing of fundus images and DCNN categorization. The second study demonstrates that an increase in the number of easily accessible events is associated with improved classification accuracy of the DCNN and a stabilization of its variability. The highest accuracy for cataract identification was 93.52%, while the accuracy for activity classification was 86.69%. This research asserts that the DCNN classifier surpasses the current state of the art. Table 1.1 describes the various deep learning model performance comparisons.

1.3 Conclusion and Future Work

Cataract diagnosis for ophthalmologists and other medical professionals has been revolutionized by automated, fast, and highly accurate deep learning diagnostic methods. Convolutional neural networks, such as U-Net, and efficient architectures like MobileNet have significantly improved image segmentation and classification. This has streamlined grading and ensured accurate identification of cataracts. When integrated with mobile devices, deep learning models surpass conventional methods in terms of accuracy and real-time detection. This research demonstrates their suitability for widespread screening in disadvantaged or rural populations. Challenges remain regarding the computational requirements of deep network training and the need for large, annotated datasets. Future research should focus on developing more resource-efficient models, implementing transfer learning, and incorporating multimodal data to address these limitations. Improving deep learning methods for cataract detection would facilitate accurate diagnosis and reduce the worldwide incidence of vision impairment caused by cataracts.

Future deep learning studies on cataract detection should use larger, more diverse, and more carefully annotated datasets, with a focus on model generalization. Diagnostic accuracy will be improved by using multimodal data, especially clinical data combined with slit lamp images. To improve connectivity in rural and underserved regions, deep learning models must be adapted to resource-constrained environments, such as mobile devices. Techniques such as transfer learning and federated learning significantly reduce the data volume and training time required. Finally, the implementation of real-time monitoring systems facilitates the provision of continuous treatment to patients by automatically identifying the early stages of cataract development.

AI disclosure statement: The author confirms that no artificial intelligence (AI)-generated content or AI-assisted writing tools were used in the preparation of this chapter (including summaries and the abstract). All text, analysis, and conclusions are the result of the author's original work.

References

1. Accessed: March, 2025: https://www.who.int/news-room/fact-sheets/detail/blindness-and-visual-impairment
2. Allen, D. and Vasavada, A., Cataract and surgery for cataract. *BMJ*, 333, 7559, 128–32, 2006 Jul 13.
3. Wong, T.Y., Loon, S.C., Saw, S.M., The epidemiology of age related eye diseases in Asia. *Br. J. Ophthalmol.*, 90, 4, 506–11, 2006 Apr 1.
4. Pesudovs, K. and Elliott, D.B., Cataract morphology, classification, assessment and referral. *CE Optom.*, 4, 2, 55–60, 2001.
5. Yang, J.J., Li, J., Shen, R., Zeng, Y., He, J., Bi, J., Li, Y., Zhang, Q., Peng, L., Wang, Q., Exploiting ensemble learning for automatic cataract detection and grading. *Comput. Methods Programs Biomed.*, 124, 45–57, 2016 Feb 1.
6. Chande, K., Jha, P., Aulakh, K.K., Shinde, S., Cataract detection using textural features and machine learning algorithms, in: *Proceedings of 2nd International Conference on Artificial Intelligence: Advances and Applications: ICAIAA 2021*, 2022 Feb 14, Springer Nature Singapore, Singapore, pp. 595–606.
7. Balasubramani, S., Renjith, P.N., Ramesh, K., George, A.H., George, A.S., Shahul, A., A detailed analysis of many different artificial intelligence-based healthcare systems, in: *Handbook of Research on Thrust Technologies' Effect on Image Processing*, pp. 56–72, IGI Global, 2023.
8. Akter, N., Fletcher, J., Perry, S., Simunovic, M.P., Briggs, N., Roy, M., Glaucoma diagnosis using multi-feature analysis and a deep learning technique. *Sci. Rep.*, 12, 1, 8064, 2022 May 16.
9. Ran, A.R., Tham, C.C., Chan, P.P., Cheng, C.Y., Tham, Y.C., Rim, T.H., Cheung, C.Y., Deep learning in glaucoma with optical coherence tomography: A review. *Eye*, 35, 1, 188–201, 2021 Jan.
10. Schünke, L.C., Mello, B., da Costa, C.A., Antunes, R.S., Rigo, S.J., de Oliveira Ramos, G., da Rosa Righi, R., Scherer, J.N., Donida, B., A rapid review of machine learning approaches for telemedicine in the scope of COVID-19. *Artif. Intell. Med.*, 129, 102312, 2022 Jul 1.

11. Nuzzi, R., Boscia, G., Marolo, P., Ricardi, F., The impact of artificial intelligence and deep learning in eye diseases: A review. *Front. Med.*, 8, 710329, 2021 Aug 30.
12. Dong, Y., Zhang, Q., Qiao, Z., Yang, J.J., Classification of cataract fundus image based on deep learning, in: *2017 IEEE International Conference on Imaging Systems and Techniques (IST)*, 2017 Oct 18, IEEE, pp. 1–5.
13. Junayed, M.S., Islam, M.B., Sadeghzadeh, A., Rahman, S., CataractNet: An automated cataract detection system using deep learning for fundus images. *IEEE Access*, 9, 128799–808, 2021 Sep 15.
14. Çetiner, H. and Çetiner, I., Classification of cataract disease with a DenseNet201 based deep learning model. *J. Inst. Sci. Technol.*, 12, 3, 1264–76, 2022 Sep.
15. Zhang, H., Niu, K., Xiong, Y., Yang, W., He, Z., Song, H., Automatic cataract grading methods based on deep learning. *Comput. Methods Programs Biomed.*, 182, 104978, 2019 Dec 1.
16. Acar, E., Türk, Ö., Ertugrul, Ö.F., Aldemir, E., Employing deep learning architectures for image-based automatic cataract diagnosis. *Turk. J. Electr. Eng. Comput. Sci.*, 29, SI-1, 2649–62, 2021 Jan.
17. Mahmood, S.S., Chaabouni, S., Fakhfakh, A., A new technique for cataract eye disease diagnosis in deep learning. *Period. Eng. Nat. Sci.*, 11, 6, 14–26, 2023 Dec 31.
18. PL L, Vaddi, R., MO, E., Gonuguntla, V., Yellampalli, S.S., CSDNet: a novel deep learning framework for improved cataract state detection. *Diagnostics*, 14, 10, 983, 2024 May 8.
19. Çetiner, H., Cataract disease classification from fundus images with transfer learning based deep learning model on two ocular disease datasets. *Gümüşhane Üniv. Fen Bilim. Derg.*, 13, 2, 258–69, 2023 Jan.
20. Varma, N., Yadav, S., Yadav, J.K., A reliable automatic cataract detection using deep learning. *Int. J. Syst. Assur. Eng. Manage.*, 14, 3, 1089–102, 2023 Jun.
21. Pratap, T. and Kokil, P., Computer-aided diagnosis of cataract using deep transfer learning. *Biomed. Signal Process. Control*, 53, 101533, 2019 Aug 1.
22. Ganokratanaa, T., Ketcham, M., Pramkeaw, P., Advancements in cataract detection: The systematic development of LeNet-convolutional neural network models. *J. Imaging*, 9, 10, 197, 2023 Sep 26.
23. Wang, Y., Tang, C., Wang, J., Sang, Y., Lv, J., Cataract detection based on ocular B-ultrasound images by collaborative monitoring deep learning. *Knowledge-Based Syst.*, 231, 107442, 2021 Nov 14.
24. Keenan, T.D., Chen, Q., Agrón, E., Tham, Y.C., Goh, J.H., Lei, X., Ng, Y.P., Liu, Y., Xu, X., Cheng, C.Y., Bikbov, M.M., DeepLensNet: deep learning automated diagnosis and quantitative classification of cataract type and severity. *Ophthalmology*, 129, 5, 571–84, 2022 May 1.

25. Jabber, A.A., Hadi, A.H., Wadi, S.M., Cataract Detection and Classification Using Deep Learning Techniques. *Int. J. Comput. Digital Syst.*, 16, 1, 1–0, 2024 Jun 12.
26. Hu, S., Luan, X., Wu, H., Wang, X., Yan, C., Wang, J., Liu, G., He, W., ACCV: automatic classification algorithm of cataract video based on deep learning. *Biomed. Eng. Online*, 20, 1–7, 2021 Dec.
27. Arslan, G. and Erdaş, Ç.B., Detection of cataract, diabetic retinopathy and glaucoma eye diseases with deep learning approach. *Intell. Methods Eng. Sci.*, 2, 2, 42–7, 2023 Jun 29.
28. Zhang, L., Li, J., Han, H., Liu, B., Yang, J., Wang, Q., Automatic cataract detection and grading using deep convolutional neural network, in: *2017 IEEE 14th International Conference on Networking, Sensing and Control (ICNSC)*, 2017 May 16, IEEE, pp. 60–65.

2

Agentic AI Workflows for Financial Large Language Models Using LlaMA and LangChain Framework

Mantri Udaya Jyothi[1], John Deva Prasanna D. S.[1*], Shanthini A.[1] and Balasubramani S.[2]

[1]Department of Data Science and Business Systems, School of Computing, SRM Institute of Science and Technology, Kattankulathur, Chengalpattu, Tamilnadu, India
[2]Department of Computer Science and Engineering, Koneru Lakshmaiah Education Foundation, Vaddeswaram, Andhra Pradesh, India

Abstract
This study aims to design and implement a natural language-driven stock analysis system that combines technical indicators with sentiment analysis from news headlines to provide comprehensive trading insights through interactive visualizations using Agentic Generative AI model. The integration of Agentic AI workflows with Large Language Models (LLMs) has revolutionized financial analysis by enabling autonomous decision-making, real-time data processing, and adaptive learning. FinGPT, an open-source financial LLM framework, leverages Agentic AI architectures to enhance financial forecasting, question answering, sentiment analysis, and algorithmic trading. By utilizing the Llama framework, FinGPT benefits from efficient parameter optimization, scalable fine-tuning, and real-time data adaptability. Explores the design and implementation of an Agentic AI-driven FinGPT, detailing its architecture, reinforcement learning strategies, and real-world applications in finance, including trading, risk management, and financial analysis. Performance benchmarks against proprietary financial models highlight the advantages of open-source LLMs in cost-effectiveness, explainability, and regulatory compliance. It further discusses the challenges of integrating autonomous financial agents into trading systems and risk management frameworks. Our findings demonstrate that the synergy between Agentic AI workflows and the Llama framework paves the way for next-generation financial intelligence

**Corresponding author*: johndevd@srmist.edu.in

R. Nidhya, A. Dineshkumar, Sheng-Lung Peng, S. Karthik and S. Balamurugan (eds.) Neuro-Symbolic Artificial Intelligence: Concepts & Applications, (19–38) © 2026 Scrivener Publishing LLC

models, offering a scalable and adaptable solution for financial professionals and researchers.

Keywords: Artificial intelligence, Agentic AI, Generative AI, LangChain framework, Llama framework, Azure, microsoft fabrics, search algorithms

2.1 Introduction

AI is applied to investments in the stock market based on 2326 papers from the Scopus website between 1995 and 2019 and categorized into four areas like optimization of financial portfolios, prediction of future prices or trends in financial assets, and sentiment analysis of news or social media comments about the assets or companies [1]. The biggest challenge in reviewing the papers is creating queries for the corpus that exclude irrelevant documents while still including a large number of relevant documents. Analyzing a large number of records returned by a query is a challenging and time-consuming task.

LLMs offer a nuanced perspective on the impact of AI inclusion on traditional algorithmic trading and the shift it brings to the transformation of financial market analysis. Algorithmic trading uses computer algorithms to automate the process of trading instruments, which are designed to follow a set of rules and execute trades with high speed and frequency [2]. The infusion of artificial intelligence has enabled algorithms to learn from data, adapt to changing market conditions, and make intelligent decisions, adding a layer of complexity to analyze vast datasets, identify patterns, and optimize strategies in real time [3].

The Traditional LLM Approach and Agent-Based Approach are shown in Figure 2.1. Through the automation of these workflows, real-time analysis and advanced prediction models have been achieved, but they must be balanced with an awareness of the ethical implications and potential risks associated with algorithmic decision-making [4]. Solutions for this are available through the open-source Llama framework. Meta AI's vision for Llama is to advance AI research while ensuring that the technology is safe, ethical, and accessible to all [14–17].

The objective is to utilize Agentic AI in combination with Generative AI.

1. Generative AI is used for reasoning and summarizing company-related data in documented forms, such as text, tables, news headlines, and social media, and can also create chatbots to obtain information about a stock.

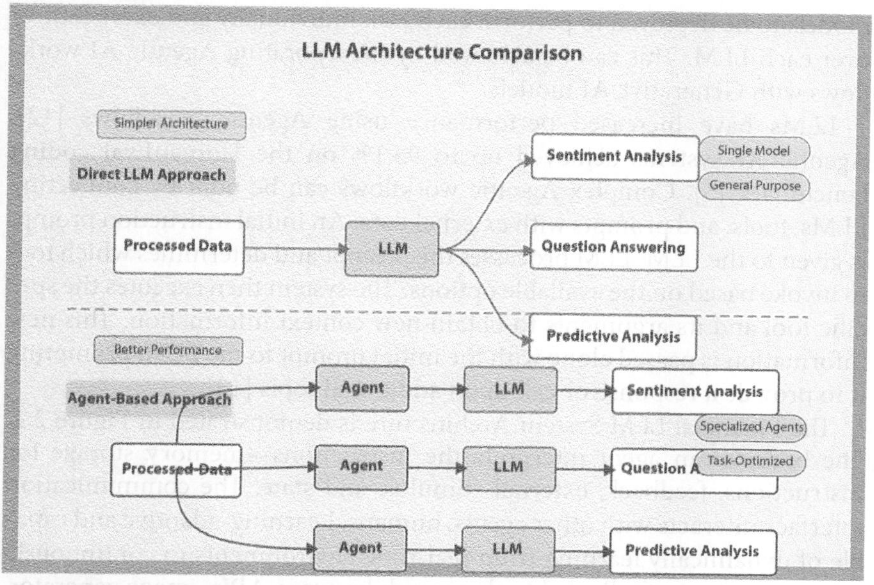

Figure 2.1 Traditional LLM approach and agent-based approach.

2. But these LLMs are pretrained with some financial data so that we can use an RAG-based framework.
3. A Financial Agentic AI layer is added to facilitate dynamic dataset interaction through the retrieval of data from new headlines, social media, and reviews.
4. The Llama framework is being used because it is open-source, cost-effective, and features the Llama Index and Llama Parser. The advantage of having Guardrails is that agents can provide safe and prompt input and responses. It follows ethical considerations and security protocols.

2.2 Predict Stock Using Financial Analysis

Financial analysis involves interpreting market trends, predicting economic outcomes, and developing investment strategies that inform decision-making through the use of models. In the equity space, fundamental analysis examines companies and provides valuations, while technical analysis analyzes market action to forecast price trends. Advancements in LLMs and computing power have enhanced AI capabilities, allowing multiple models to be deployed to perform each task individually and exert control over each LLM. This can be achieved by incorporating Agentic AI workflows with Generative AI models.

LLMs have increased performance using Agentic workflows [12]. Agentic AI systems achieved up to 95.1% on the HumanEval coding benchmark [5]. Complex Agentic workflows can be built by connecting LLMs, tools, and prompts with external data. An initial instruction prompt is given to the LLM. LLM processes the prompt and determines which tool to invoke based on the available options. The system then executes the specific tool and its arguments to obtain new context information. This new information is passed along with the initial prompt to the LLM, prompting it to provide a response or call upon additional tools [13].

The Financial LLM System Architecture is demonstrated in Figure 2.2. The brain of an agent interprets the instructions—memory storage for instructions, feedback, external stimulus, and state. The communication interface interacts with other agents, humans. Learning-adaptive and capable of dynamically learning from real-time environments to continuously refine its outputs. Skills and tools are web browser, APIs, image generator, and social media plugins. The available agent frameworks are Langchain, Langraph, MetaGPT, LlamaIndex, and LlamaParser. Meta AI's vision for Llama is to advance AI research while ensuring that the technology is safe,

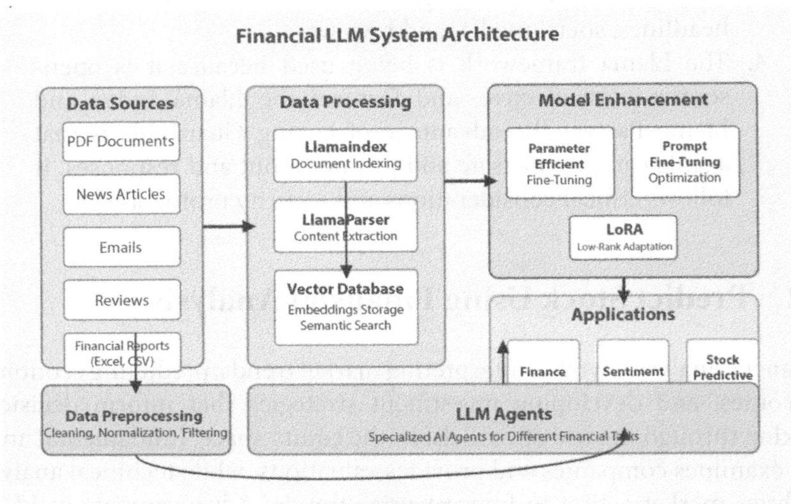

Figure 2.2 Financial LLM system architecture.

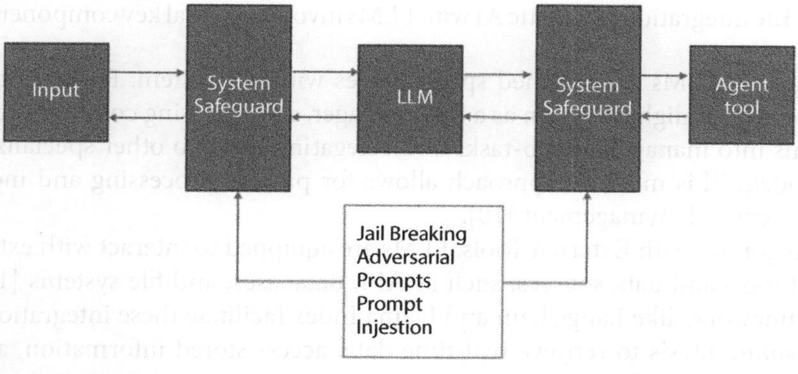

Figure 2.3 Guardrails Injection into the workflow using the Llama framework.

ethical, and accessible to all [6]. Guardrails Injection into the Workflow Using the Llama Framework is presented in Figure 2.3.

2.3 Stock Market Prediction Using Agentic AI Using LLM

Stock market predictions can be made using news headlines and have demonstrated significant performance by large language models (LLMs), which help investors make informed investment decisions [7]. Chatbots are permitted to interact with users in open-source models, which can inadvertently impact societal issues through the content they generate. Agentic AI can filter such risks and provide harmless content, benefiting researchers with their new LLM exploration [8]. This paper proposes the development of an Agentic AI framework using LangChain, which can generate parallel outputs and an analyzer, utilizing a dashboard with various LLMs modeled as agents. Agents will learn from each LLM output and attempt to adapt to the new changes.

Agentic AI refers to artificial intelligence systems designed to operate with a degree of autonomy, enabling them to make decisions, perform tasks, and interact with their environment without continuous human intervention [9]. When combined with large language models, agentic AI systems can process and generate human-like text, facilitating more natural and efficient interactions.

The integration of agentic AI with LLMs involves several key components:

Multiple LLMs are assigned specific roles within a system. For example, one model might function as a task manager, decomposing complex problems into manageable sub-tasks and delegating them to other specialized models. This modular approach allows for parallel processing and more efficient task management [10].
Integration with External Tools: LLMs are equipped to interact with external tools and data sources, such as API, databases, and file systems [11]. Frameworks like LangChain and Llama Index facilitate these integrations, enabling LLMs to retrieve real-time data, access stored information, and interact with software applications.
Asynchronous Processing: Agentic AI systems often operate asynchronously, allowing multiple models to work on different aspects of a problem simultaneously. This distributed architecture enhances responsiveness and efficiency but requires robust coordination mechanisms to ensure consistency and coherence in outputs.

2.4 Llama Framework

The Llama Stack is a framework designed to streamline the development of agentic AI applications using LLMs. It provides standardized APIs and components that facilitate the creation of systems capable of multi-step reasoning, tool usage, and safety compliance. Key features include the following:

Inference Capabilities: The stack supports running inferences on Llama series models, enabling the system to generate predictions and responses based on input data.
Safety Mechanisms: Incorporating models like Llama Guard ensures that the AI operates within defined safety parameters, mitigating risks associated with autonomous decision-making.
Tool Execution Environment: The stack provides an environment for executing tools, including code execution, allowing the AI to perform actions such as data processing and analysis as part of its reasoning process.

2.4.1 LLM Agent for Stock Price Prediction for a Portfolio

LLM will be provided with annual reports from Fortune 500 companies and 10-K filings as data sources, and questions will be framed using prompt engineering, designed to be well-structured and protected by guardrails. The output of the LLM is stored in a table and taken as a data-set for machine learning models. Models can predict the sentiment of the stock price for any company. The results are stored in a cloud data store so that data can be moved to BigQuery or another analytics platform, where it can be analyzed and displayed in a dashboard.

The LLM still lacks the ability to provide human-like answers [10] and is required to efficiently and effectively evaluate the quality of lengthy documents. LLM agents can learn from these failures as a lesson and can move forward by accessing tools available through web searches and evaluating the best optimal data, providing effective datasets to ML models.

AI agents will prefer to use an online search mechanism when interacting with unknown environments where they are uncertain about the states that exist and the actions to take to achieve their goal. Agents will proceed with actions while experimenting to learn the environment and continue until they reach the goal. Suppose that the agent is in state 's' and performs some actions 'a' such that its outcome is s' and the output function is RESULTS (s, a). It returns a list of actions when the result matches the goal, then we can use the RESULT function to calculate the step-cost function c (s, a, s'). The agent's objective is to choose the path of actions that minimizes the overall cost.

2.4.2 Llama Framework with Agentic AI for Stock Prediction

Stock market prediction is a complex task requiring real-time data processing, intelligent decision-making, and adaptive learning. Agentic AI in the Llama framework integrates search algorithms to enable dynamic stock analysis, risk assessment, and portfolio management. This paper examines the contributions of Breadth-First Search (BFS), Depth-First Search (DFS), A* Search, and Monte Carlo Tree Search (MCTS) to real-time stock prediction, enabling optimal decision-making and risk mitigation.

2.4.2.1 Search Algorithms for Real-Time Stock Prediction in Llama Framework

1. Breadth-First Search (BFS) — Market Data Retrieval and Event Analysis
It is used to traverse large financial datasets efficiently. It ensures that AI considers multiple news sources, historical prices, and social sentiments before making decisions. It enables real-time anomaly detection by

analyzing multiple signals simultaneously. It is used for real-time market sentiment analysis.

Fetching and analyzing breaking financial news to detect stock-impacting events.

```
from llama_index import KnowledgeGraphRetriever
retriever = KnowledgeGraphRetriever()
results = retriever.query("How does reinforcement learning
work?")
```

2. Depth-First Search (DFS) — Multi-Step Price Trend Analysis
It explores deep relationships in time-series stock data. It is used in technical analysis models to track price trends, resistance levels, and momentum shifts. It helps Agentic AI reason about past price patterns to predict future movements. It is used in identifying market trends from historical stock data.

Tracking stock price movements across multiple timeframes.

```
from llama_index import RecursiveRetriever
retriever = RecursiveRetriever(strategy="depth-first")
response = retriever.query("Explain back propagation in
neural networks.")
```

3. A Search — Optimal Portfolio Selection and Risk Management
It optimizes trade execution by balancing risk and return. It uses heuristics (e.g., volatility, momentum, and liquidity) to find the best investment strategy. It helps hedge funds and traders identify the most efficient buy and sell paths. It is used in selecting the best stock portfolio for maximum returns.

Finding the most profitable investment strategy based on historical and real-time data.

```
from llama_agents import ActionPlanner
planner = ActionPlanner(strategy="A*")
best_plan = planner.get_best_plan("Summarize 10 docu-
ments efficiently.")
```

4. Monte Carlo Tree Search (MCTS) — Real-Time Trading Strategy Optimization
It simulates multiple potential outcomes for stock price movements. It helps in reinforcement learning-based trading by predicting how the market

might evolve. It is used in algorithmic trading bots for high-frequency trading (HFT). It is used in predicting future stock prices with simulated trading scenarios.

Simulating various market conditions and selecting the optimal trading action to influence stock market trends.

```
from llama_agents import MonteCarloPlanner
planner = MonteCarloPlanner()
best_action = planner.simulate_actions(["buy", "sell", "hold"],
stock_data)
```

2.5 Llama Framework Reduces AI Trading Risks

Data Leakage: Data leakage occurs when a model unintentionally learns from future stock data, resulting in unrealistic backtest performance and failure in live trading.
Llama Index for Time-Sensitive Data Handling: The Llama Index ensures that trading models do not access future stock prices by implementing time-aware retrieval mechanisms, preventing look-ahead bias. Using date-based indexing ensures that queries fetch only past information, filtering out leaked features that include future data.
Target Leakage: Feature filtering to exclude leaked target variables
Data Poisoning: It occurs when adversarial actors inject false data, misleading AI models into making poor trading decisions. It will do multi-source validation and anomaly detection with LlamaGuard.
LlamaIndex + LlamaGuard for Data Integrity Checks: LlamaGuard, a security extension of the Llama framework, protects against poisoned data by cross-validating stock data from multiple sources (Yahoo Finance, Bloomberg, etc.), detecting anomalies using statistical methods before feeding data into trading models, and filtering out manipulated financial news or social media signals that could bias AI predictions.
Fake Market News: LLM-powered sentiment validation to detect misinformation
LlamaGuard for Adversarial Detection in Market Data: (1) Detects suspicious trading patterns (e.g., pump-and-dump schemes) and (2) flag fake news articles that could manipulate AI-driven sentiment analysis.
Llama Framework + Reinforcement Learning (RL) for Secure Trading Bots: Q-learning and Deep Q-Networks (DQN) are prone to poisoning attacks. The Llama framework enhances safety by training AI agents in simulated

environments before deploying them in real-world market, monitoring real-time data drift to prevent outdated models from being exploited, and using Explainable AI (XAI) to ensure that the AI's reasoning is transparent.

2.6 Working Principle of Agents

Agents need to plan the sequence of actions to achieve their goal. It undergoes a computational process named search. The agents should use atomic representation, which is a state with no internal structure stored; such agents are called problem-solving agents, as they solve problems through search on their own. In situations where agents need to decide on a path by searching on their own, they should be aware of the context. If we could provide the context, it could formulate the path. With the available information, the agent can follow a four-phase problem-solving process.

Goal Formulation: The agent can adopt the goal of a task, which further organizes behavior by limiting objectives and, accordingly, actions are considered.
Problem Formulation: The agent describes the state of actions and the necessary steps to be followed to reach the goal.
Search: The agent simulates the sequence of actions in its model, searching until it finds a sequence of actions that leads to the goal, which is referred to as a solution.
Execution: The agent can now execute the actions in the solution.

It is an important property that in a fully observable, deterministic, known environment, the solution to any problem is a fixed sequence of actions. When the agent knows the path, it can suspend its precepts while executing the actions. It is a so-called open-loop system that breaks the loop between the agent and the environment. In case the model is incorrect or the environment is nondeterministic or stochastic, the agent would be safer using a closed-loop approach that monitors the percepts.

Measuring the performance of a solving agent:
Completeness: Generates a solution using the finder algorithm.
Cost Optimality: Check the lowest path cost of all solutions.
Time Complexity: How long does it take to find the solution?
Space Complexity: How much memory is needed to perform the search operation?

Agents can refine their strategies by learning from failures and adjusting their states based on the real-time conditions. Agents should be more transparent with their search techniques, which could lead to more responsible decisions with the real-time consequences. This could happen with the reinforcement learning of agents.

Types of Agents: Four kinds of agents are available that cover the concrete form of principles underlying all intelligent systems.

Simple Reflex Agent: These agents select actions based on the current percepts, ignoring the percept history. It performs a condition-action rule. It works only if the correct decision can be made based solely on the current percept, that is, when the environment is fully observable. If any changes occur, it will lead to a serious problem. In a partially observable environment, where sensors provide incomplete or noisy data, it often has a chance to get stuck in unavoidable infinite loops unless the agent can randomize its actions.

Model-Based Reflex Agent: To handle any partially observable environment, agents need to perceive history and maintain some internal state, and reflect or act on some part of the unobservable aspects of the current state. For that, the current state is updated with the knowledge of previous history, such as internal state and current state percept.

Goal-Based Agents: Unless the agent knows the goal to achieve, it cannot decide the pathway it needs to travel or perform its functionality through a program. If the condition is satisfied, then the agent will have a straightforward move to the next state. However, in cases where a long sequence of twists and turns is required to achieve the goal, it becomes difficult for the agent to navigate the environment. In such a situation, search and planning are the next level of sub-function. AI designs are used to find an action sequence to reach the goal, which differs from the condition-action rule. In the case of reflex agent design, the condition cannot be given explicitly but is mapped directly from percepts to actions, which are built-in functions, but goal-based agents can be changed to a new state of condition with the support of knowledge and can be modified based on the new condition of the state behavior.

Utility-Based Agent: It is not worth reaching the goal; it is not reliable, expensive, and slow. Performance measures need to be considered while achieving the goal. Therefore, agents' utility functions should include these performance measures and internal functions that outperform those externally. It should be rational enough that the program's execution attempts to maximize its output value. These agents must handle uncertainty in a stochastic or partially observable environment. So, utility agents are designed in such a way that they can store the internal state of the environment, succeed in tasks by perceiving the path to follow through reasoning to inform their decisions, represent the lessons learned from it, and maintain a history of it.

If the problem is defined, a search algorithm finds actions to achieve the goal or solution. Tree search starts at the root with the initial state, branches are actions, and nodes are states. Frontier is a set of nodes to expand until a solution. The search strategy avoids looping paths to reduce costs. Repeated paths in an algorithm do not remember history. Tree-search algorithm with a data structure is explored in a set. The graph-search algorithm separates the explored and unexplored sets to reduce redundant paths. Infrastructure for the search algorithm requires a data structure to track the search tree. Each node has a structure with four components. The search algorithm is shown in Figure 2.4.

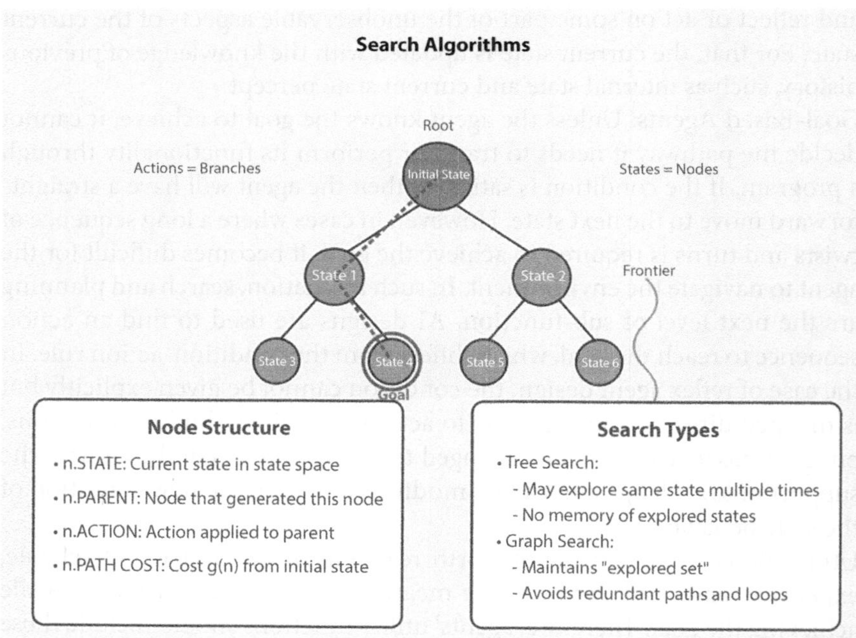

Figure 2.4 Node structure of search algorithms.

n.STATE: The state within the state space corresponding to the node.
n.PARENT: The node in the search tree that generated this particular node.
n.ACTION: The specific action applied to the parent node to produce the current node.
n.PATH COST: The cost, typically represented as g(n), of the path from the initial state to the node, as indicated by the path frontier.

Breadth-First Search (BFS): It is a simple strategy where the root node is expanded first, then all its successors at a given depth, before moving to the next level. This is a graph search algorithm using a FIFO queue for the frontier. New nodes go to the back of the queue, ensuring that older nodes are expanded first. The goal test is done on new nodes when they are generated. BFS finds the shallowest path to every node on the frontier.
Depth-First Search (DFS): This algorithm extends the deepest node in the current frontier. Explored nodes without descendants are removed. Nodes without successors become the goal node. It uses a LIFO queue and prioritizes the deepest unexpanded node. It ensures completeness in finite state spaces by avoiding repeated states. In infinite spaces, it may not be optimal due to time complexity. Breadth-first tree search retains one path from root to leaf. Explored nodes are promptly removed to save space. It serves as a framework for constraint satisfaction. Backtracking searches consume even less memory.
Heuristic DFS Search Algorithm (Informed): In this algorithm, additional knowledge of the problem is imported to the search algorithm.
Greedy Best-First Search: This algorithm tries to expand the node that is closest to the goal so that it can reach the goal quickly.

> F(n)=h(n) --> estimated cost of the cheapest path from n to goal state.

Agents can learn how to do better search with meta meta-level state space. This state space captures the internal state of a program by searching in an object-level state space. Meta-level learning algorithm can learn from these experiences to avoid exploring unpromising subtree. The goal of learning is to minimize the total cost of problem-solving, trade-off computational expense, and path cost.

Local Search: It has a simulated annealing algorithm and a genetic algorithm. Instead of systematically exploring paths from the initial state, these algorithms perform local search by evaluating and modifying one or more current states.

Markov Decision Processing and Reinforcement Learning:
It is the most efficient technique to analyze sequential decision-making scenarios and is also utilized in reinforcement learning algorithms. Markov Chains model the movement of stock prices in the future, enabling predictions on non-performing assets in the finance sector, optimal timing for share transactions, sentiment analysis of stocks, and the evolution of market shares among various brands over time.

Let $\{X_n, n=0,1,2\ldots\}$ be a sequence of random variables which are observed in the environment at time (n=0,1,2..), where is state of a stock value at time n and set of all values is the state space (S). The process {P,n=0,1,2,..} is a first-order Markov process if it satisfies the conditional probability of the state. If the state space S id discrete, then the stochastic process that satisfies this condition is called a Markov chain. If the state space is discrete and the process is observed over a period of time and satisfies the above condition, then it is called a continuous-time Markov Chain. If the state space is continuous and satisfies the property, then it is called a Markov process.

One-step transition probability of a Markov Chain from state I to state j is represented in a matrix.

s-step transition probability is given by the following:

$$P_{ij}^{(s)} = \sum_{r=1}^{m} p_{ir}^{k}\, p_{rj}^{(s-k)}, o < k < s$$

Estimated transition probability based on aggregated data is as follows:

$$P_{ij} = \frac{N_{ij}}{\Sigma_{k=1}^{m} N_{ik}}$$

In reinforcement learning, an agent must decide time t when the system is in state S_t in an uncertain environment. The agent earns the reward R for each decision it takes and state changes to the next state, and the agent needs to take another decision.

In the Markov decision process, the decision maker takes a series of decisions based on the current state, which results in both immediate and future rewards. Since the environment is dynamic and the MDP reinforcement learning algorithm has uncertainty about future rewards, the objective is to maximize the expected total reward obtained over a specified period.

There are two algorithms, Policy Iteration and Value Iteration, to solve the problem, where the Policy algorithm finds the optimal policy which maps from state to action space that maximizes the NPV total reward or value function of MDP based on an infinite planning horizon. The Value iteration algorithm utilizes dynamic programming to determine the optimal action within a finite planning horizon.

The value Iteration algorithm divides the problem into stages at different periods, during which decisions are made. Dynamic Programming is based on Bellman's Principle of Optimality, which identifies the state at the beginning of each stage and the actions available for the decision maker at each state. The recursive relationship is created between the optimal action at the current stage and the previous optimal state. So, the optimal action set is the optimal policy for the problem up to that stage.

The dynamic programming recursive equation for the value iteration is the following:

$$V_t^*(\mathrm{i}) = Max_{a_{i\epsilon A}}\left(R(i,a_i) + \sum_{j=S_1}^{S_n} P_{ij}(a_i)V_{t+1}^*(\mathrm{j})\right)$$

Since the agent faces an unknown Markov decision process, we have three agent designs: a Utility-based agent that learns a utility function on states and uses it to select actions that maximize the expected outcome utility. Q-learning agent learns an action-utility function, giving the expected utility of taking a given action in a given state. Then the reflex agent learns the policy that maps directly from the state to actions.

2.7 Results

Trading metrics to evaluate the performance of trading models are passive trading strategy, final portfolio value, cumulative return, annualized return, standard deviation, and maximum drawdown ratio.

The Agentic AI portfolio outperforms both the traditional ML model and the market benchmark (S&P 500) over all time periods. Returns of 27.8%, 56.3%, and 143.7% after 6 months, 1 year, and 3 years, respectively, indicate improved flexibility and decision-making. The traditional ML model provides modest improvements of 18.2%, 42.1%, and 108.5%, but underperforms the market benchmark with results of 11.5%, 24.8%, and 68.3%. The Agentic AI strategy provides a competitive advantage by delivering long-term cumulative benefits shown in Table 2.1.

Table 2.1 Cumulative returns using different portfolio strategy.

Portfolio strategy	6-Month return	1-Year return	3-Year return
Agentic AI Portfolio	27.8%	56.3%	143.7%
Traditional ML Model	18.2%	42.1%	108.5%
Market Benchmark (S&P 500)	11.5%	24.8%	68.3%

Table 2.2 Risk-adjusted performance.

Metric	Agentic AI	Traditional ML	S&P 500
Sharpe Ratio	1.87	1.43	1.12
Sortino Ratio	2.34	1.76	1.36
Maximum Drawdown	−12.3%	−18.7%	−22.4%
Volatility	15.2%	18.6%	19.8%

In Table 2.2, the Agentic AI portfolio outperforms the traditional machine learning (ML) model and the S&P 500 benchmark, demonstrating its ability to deliver consistent and effective returns while mitigating risk. With a Sharpe Ratio of 1.87, Agentic AI outperforms both the S&P 500 (1.12) and traditional machine learning (1.43) in terms of excess returns relative to overall risk. Its ability to deliver substantial returns while mitigating downside volatility is evidenced by its Sortino Ratio of 2.34, which beats the S&P 500's 1.36 and traditional ML's 1.76. The Agentic AI portfolio has the lowest maximum drawdown of −12.3% for traditional ML and −22.4% for the S&P 500, demonstrating its ability to protect money in adverse market conditions. In addition, its returns are more stable and less volatile compared to the S&P 500 (19.8%) and traditional machine learning (18.6%), as it has the lowest volatility at 15.2%. Taken together, these indicators illustrate the robustness, consistency, and improved risk management of the Agentic AI strategy, making it more attractive to investors seeking long-term returns with minimal risk.

The Agentic AI portfolio outperforms the traditional machine learning paradigm on win rates, profitability measures, and trading outcomes shown in Table 2.3. Unlike standard machine learning, which achieves a

Table 2.3 Trading performance.

Metric	Agentic AI	Traditional ML
Win Rate	68.3%	59.2%
Profit Factor	2.18	1.67
Average Profit per Trade	2.7%	1.9%
Average Loss per Trade	−1.2%	−1.5%

win rate of 59.2%, Agentic AI consistently produces winning trades with a win rate of 68.3%. Trading efficiency is exceptionally good, with a profit factor of 2.18, which is significantly higher than the traditional ML's 1.67. This means that total profits exceed total losses by a factor of more than 2. The average profit per transaction for Agentic AI is 2.7%, compared to 1.9% for traditional ML. This indicates that Agentic AI generates more revenue per successful transaction, as well as a higher success rate. In addition, Agentic AI mitigates its constraints more efficiently than traditional machine learning, which has an average loss of −1.2% per transaction and an overall average loss of −1.5%. Taken together, these signals suggest that the trading dynamics of agentic AI are superior because they combine improved accuracy with a higher risk-reward ratio, leading to more reliable and profitable trading outcomes.

The outstanding performance of the Agentic AI portfolio, as measured by its composition and individual stock performance, can be largely attributed to its significant investments in highly successful technology companies. The majority of the portfolio's gains were driven by NVDA, which had the largest allocation at 28% and generated an outstanding individual return of 84.3%. AAPL and MSFT, with a weighting of 21% and 18%, respectively, contributed to the portfolio's performance with returns of 38.7% and 42.1%. AMZN and GOOGL returned 35.2% and 28.6%, respectively, with allocations of 15% and 10%, reflecting the steady contribution of numerous technical investments. The remarkable returns of 31.4% for TSLA and 24.8% for META, despite their weightings of 5% and 3%, respectively, add significantly to the stability and balance of the portfolio. The Agentic AI portfolio's remarkable success highlights its ability to identify and acquire outstanding assets while maintaining balanced exposure, thanks to its strategic investments in technology leaders that demonstrate robust growth and substantial returns, as shown in Table 2.4.

Table 2.4 Individual returns of different stocks.

Stock	Weight	Individual return
NVDA	28%	84.3%
AAPL	21%	38.7%
MSFT	18%	42.1%
AMZN	15%	35.2%
GOOGL	10%	28.6%
TSLA	5%	31.4%
META	3%	24.8%

2.8 Conclusion

The financial market is a complex and dynamic system that generates vast amounts of data every second, which includes stock prices, news updates, industry trends, and economic reports. Analyzing this data is critical for investors and analysts to make informed decisions and manage risks. RAG workflow integration for a better query vector database allows LangChain workflows to continue implementing for improved accuracy of results in a more ethical manner.

AI disclosure statement: The author acknowledges the use of AI-based tools for minor language editing or grammatical correction. However, all intellectual contributions, analyses, and conclusions presented in this chapter are entirely the author's own.

References

1. Ferreira, F.G.D.C., Gandomi, A.H., Cardoso, R.T.N., Artificial Intelligence Applied to Stock Market Trading: A Review. *IEEE Access*, 9, 30898–30917, 2021, doi: 10.1109/ACCESS.2021.3058133.
2. Addy, W.A., Ajayi-Nifise, A.O., Bello, B.G., Tula, S.T., Odeyem, O., Falaiye, T., Algorithmic trading and AI: A review of strategies and market impact. *World J. Adv. Eng. Technol. Sci.*, 11, 1, 258–267, 2024.

3. Huang, A.H., Wang, H., Yang, Y., FinBERT: A large language model for extracting information from financial text. *Contemp. Account. Res.*, 40, 2, 806–41, 2023 May.
4. Li, Y., Wang, S., Ding, H., Chen, H., Large language models in finance: A survey, in: *Proceedings of the Fourth ACM International Conference on AI in Finance*, 2023 Nov 27, pp. 374–382.
5. Lee, J., Stevens, N., Han, S.C., Large Language Models in Finance (FinLLMs). *Neural Comput. Appl.*, 11, 1–5, 2025 Jan.
6. Kong, Y., Nie, Y., Dong, X., Mulvey, J.M., Poor, H.V., Wen, Q., Zohren, S., Large Language Models for Financial and Investment Management: Applications and Benchmarks. *J. Portfolio Manage.*, 51, 2, 2024 Dec 1.
7. Lopez-Lira, A. and Tang, Y., Can chatgpt forecast stock price movements? return predictability and large language models. *arXiv preprint arXiv:2304.07619*, 2023 Apr 15.
8. Clatterbuck, H., Castro, C., Morán, A.M., Risk alignment in agentic AI systems. arXiv preprint arXiv:2410.01927, 2024 Oct 2.
9. Acharya, D.B., Kuppan, K., Divya, B., Agentic AI: Autonomous Intelligence for Complex Goals–A Comprehensive Survey. *IEEE Access*, 2025 Jan 22.
10. Dodda, A., Integrating Advanced and Agentic AI in Fintech: Transforming Payments and Credit Card Transactions. *Eur. Adv. J. Emerg. Technol. (EAJET)*, 1, 1, ISSN 3050–9734–ISSN 3050-9742, 2024 Dec 1.
11. Joshi, S., Advancing Financial Risk Modeling: Vasicek Framework Enhanced By Agentic Generative AI. *Int. Res. J. Modern. Eng. Technol. Sci.*, 7, 1, 4413–20, 2025.
12. Hosseini, S. and Seilani, H., The Role of Agentic AI in Shaping a Smart Future: A Systematic Review. *Array*, 8, 100399, 2025 May.
13. Singh, K., Kaur, S., Smiley, C., FinQAPT: Empowering Financial Decisions with End-to-End LLM-driven Question Answering Pipeline, in: *Proceedings of the 5th ACM International Conference on AI in Finance*, 2024 Nov 14, pp. 266–273.
14. Nidhya, R., Kumar, M., Balamurugan, S. (Eds.), *Tele-Healthcare: Applications of Artificial Intelligence and Soft Computing Techniques*, John Wiley & Sons, USA, 2022.
15. Chiu, I.C. and Hung, M.W., Finance-Specific Large Language Models: Advancing Sentiment Analysis and Return Prediction with Llama 2. *Pacific-Basin Finance Journal*, 90, 102632, 2025 Apr 1.
16. Chen, Q., Image-Driven Stock Price Prediction with LLaMA: A Prompt-Based Approach. *Int. J. Model. Optim.*, 15, 1, 2025.
17. Smilarubavathy, G. and Ka, M.A., Empowering Product Purchase Decisions through AI-Driven Review Analysis and Summarization, in: *2024 International Conference on Inventive Computation Technologies (ICICT)*, IEEE, pp. 155–162, 2024, April.

3

Brain-Inspired Artificial Neural Network for Energy-Efficient and Adaptive Learning

R. Dhanalakshmi[1], Sahaya Beni Prathiba[1], Kavisankar L.[2], Balasubramani S.[3]* and Pandiyanathan M.[3]

[1]Center for Cyber Physical Systems, School of Computer Science and Engineering, Vellore Institute of Technology - Chennai, Chennai, India
[2]Department of Computing Technologies, Faculty of Engineering and Technology, SRM Institute of Science and Technology, Kattankulathur, Tamil Nadu, India
[3]Department of Computer Science and Engineering, Koneru Lakshmaiah Education Foundation, Vijayawada, India

Abstract

The efficiency of modern artificial neural networks (ANNs) has improved across various applications. However, they still do not match the efficiency, flexibility, or depth of understanding of a human brain. This study presents an artificial neural network framework based on biological architectures that incorporates features to enhance learning efficiency, robustness, and energy utilization, while also featuring spike-timing-dependent plasticity (STDP), interhemispheric communication, and reward-based modulation learning. The framework is built around spiking neuron modeling, dual-hemispheric processing, and plausible training designs, aiming to achieve the essential capabilities of the brain. Experiments were conducted on benchmark datasets, showing that the proposed model is effective in preserving accuracy while achieving a significant reduction in computational power. The model's performance also exhibits reduced sensitivity to noise and adversarial perturbations, thereby enhancing its potential for practical applications. This approach serves as a bridge between neuroscience and machine learning, marking progress toward optimizing design efficiency and aligning artificial intelligence systems with brain function.

Keywords: Artificial neural networks, brain-inspired computing, spiking neural networks, synaptic plasticity, neuromorphic computing

**Corresponding author*: bala08.ap@gmail.com

R. Nidhya, A. Dineshkumar, Sheng-Lung Peng, S. Karthik and S. Balamurugan (eds.) Neuro-Symbolic Artificial Intelligence: Concepts & Applications, (39–58) © 2026 Scrivener Publishing LLC

3.1 Introduction

Artificial neural networks have revolutionized computational intelligence by achieving industry-leading results in various fields, including image processing, natural language understanding, and sophisticated decision-making. However, conventional ANNs do fall short in some critical domains such as energy conservation, flexibility, and a biological reasoning framework. Comparatively, the human brain has mastered the art of learning, making generalizations, and instantaneously making decisions, all while using a dramatically lesser amount of energy compared to deep learning networks. This gap has prompted the creation of so-called brain-inspired ANN designs that apply neuroscience theories to improve the effectiveness, intelligence, and reliability of the system.

In recent years, significant efforts have been made to integrate biological and artificial intelligence. These efforts involve analyzing neuromodulation, spike-timing-dependent plasticity, reward-based learning, and the role of the corpus callosum in both hemispheres of the brain. Spiking neural networks (SNNs) are appealing because they operate similarly to biological neurons, enabling faster and more energy-efficient data processing. Due to neuromorphic technology and optoelectronic synapses, real-time biologically inspired networks are becoming more accessible to construct. However, unstable training, inadequate support from current deep learning frameworks, and challenges in integrating biologically relevant dynamics are among the concerns that require resolution.

This study aims to address these issues by developing and evaluating a biologically inspired artificial neural network architecture that incorporates brain functions, such as spike-timing-dependent plasticity, hemisphere dualism, and spike-based computation. The device is designed to perform optimally in standard classification tasks while being highly energy-efficient and effective at reducing noise. This paper proposes an innovative approach to developing neural networks that operate similarly to the brain. The program aims to enhance the functionality and cognitive capabilities of AI and neuromorphic engineering systems, enabling them to mimic human behavior.

3.2 Literature Review

Artificial neural networks, which are inspired by the brain, are gaining increasing recognition as technology advances due to their ability to operate in ways that closely resemble those of actual systems. Spike timing and synaptic plasticity have been thoroughly investigated as essential elements of spiking neural networks (SNNs). Research in [1] illustrates applying back-propagated error signals and spike-timing-dependent plasticity (STDP) to auditory recognition. This method is physiologically safe and promotes good health. The model in [2] incorporated an attention-simulated, adaptivity-enhanced energy efficiency into SNNs, demonstrating precision and results analogous to those stemming from the inner brain's adaptive focus. These emphasize temporal coding and attention focus control, which temporally synchronize with biological phenomena.

Like other biologically inspired systems, hardware-software partitioning should be done with the efficiency of hardware in mind. Authors [3] describe the FireFly architecture, which functions as a high-throughput hardware accelerator for SNNs. This architecture processes SNNs through techniques in DSP and memory that are energy- and speed-conscious on current levels. Concurrently, [4] describes the creation of opto-electronic synaptic transistors (OSTs) that emulate biological synapses with light stimuli using a new, compact, and low-power neuromorphic hardware, paving the way for nanostructured SPC hardware. This set of developments reinforces the claim that it is possible to implement brain-like models for computation on edge devices with lower power thresholds without sacrificing performance.

Additionally, recent studies have focused on training techniques based on biological principles. The work in [5] suggests that reward-modulated learning can serve as a replacement for backpropagation, utilizing dopamine-like feedback to guide learning in convolutional spiking neural networks [6], while preserving the initial meaning of phrases. This is in parallel with [7], which describes a two-stage pretraining and conversion pipeline where artificial neural networks are first trained and then transformed into spiking neural networks. Additionally, [8] combines ADMM with activity regularization for model compression and examines SNNs for devices with stringent power and memory constraints, exploring more practical limitations. Collectively, these approaches simultaneously improve the biological and computational aspects of training neural systems. Innovations in the network configurations drive advances in this field, along with shifts in cognitive alignment. The dual intercommunication network presented in [9] captures interhemispheric communication through bilateral ANN pathways that connect with a corpus callosum-like structure, allowing for coordination and task specialization. In another direction, [10] offers a model that aligns biocompatible representations of ANN activations to human brain activity rhythms obtained from MRI scans, synchronizing brain-derived rhythmic representations with ANN outputs at specific intervals. Lastly, [11] proposes a conversion strategy for spiking deformable CNNs that maintains spatial adaptability while allowing SNN inference to be executed efficiently. There are still significant gaps to fill, such as in the ANN-to-SNN translation and neuromorphic implementation, but the progress being made remains far from inadequate in developing controlled, intelligent, and energy-efficient computing systems inspired by the human brain. Table 3.1 demonstrate the compassion on existing methods.

3.3 Methodology

The techniques used in the literature concerning brain-inspired artificial neural networks [12], or simply ANNs, reveal different approaches to biological realism, computational efficiency, and performance metrics. Such methods can be summarized in four overarching and interlinked themes: learning systems with biological fidelity, design of the neural framework, speeding up hardware performance, and transitions from ANN to SNN.

Several biologically plausible learning approaches and strategies exist, and their applications are well-documented in the literature. For example, many researchers use spike-timing-dependent plasticity as a local learning rule to mimic synaptic changes during neuronal spikes. In some models, such as those for audio classification, STDP is enhanced with a backpropagated error signal to facilitate supervised learning within a biological framework. Other works employ reward-modulated learning inspired by the dopaminergic system of the brain. These models utilize episodic reward signals to adjust synaptic strengths, thereby making them compatible with spiking neural dynamics within the framework of reinforcement learning.

Several papers outline novel neural structures of computation motivated by the brain to expand its use in architectural design. For example, dual-pathway or inter-hemispheric communication models mimic bilateral cortical processing. This works like the specialization of the brain hemispheres and is integrated by the corpus callosum. Such designs enable the networks to specialize in subtasks while maintaining cooperative performance through cross-communication. Additionally, some SNNs were enriched with attention mechanisms that exhibit human-like behavior, focusing on and reacting to changes.

Regarding implementation, the technique of converting artificial neural networks into spiking neural network architectures has gained popularity, as it enables the retention of deep ANN functionalities while leveraging the event-driven nature of SNNs. These conversions often include,

Table 3.1 Comparison of state-of-the-art methods.

Paper title	Key methodology	Best model	Accuracy	Unique contribution	Dataset
[9]	Spike-timing-dependent plasticity (STDP) combined with error back-propagation	Multi-layer SNN with STDP + BP	94.2% (AudioSet)	First-time integration of STDP with error signals for classification	AudioSet
[3]	Multi-dimensional attention-guided SNN training	ASNets (with EASN and ASN modules)	91.4% (DVS-CIFAR10)	Introduced learnable temporal filters in spike generation	DVS-CIFAR10, DVS128-Gesture
[4]	ADMM-based compression with activity regularization	ResNet-18 (SNN version)	93.1% (CIFAR-10)	Novel application of ADMM on direct-trained SNNs	CIFAR-10, CIFAR-100
[8]	High-throughput FPGA design with efficient DSP and memory sharing	FireFly Accelerator	~50× energy improvement over baseline	Custom DSP block reuse for event-driven SNNs	N-MNIST, DVS128
[10]	Physical neuromorphic device modeling	Optoelectronic Synaptic Transistor	N/A (hardware-oriented)	Combines polymer semi-conductors with insulators for new neuromorphic devices	MNIST
[14]	Memristor-based architecture for energy-efficient computation	All-Memristor SNN	91.5% (CIFAR-10)	Memristive devices used for both neurons and synapses	CIFAR-10
[15]	FPGA-based learning accelerator for BPTT training	H2Learn (custom FPGA)	1.8× speedup vs GPU	Dual-sparsity-based accelerator for spike propagation	N-MNIST

(*Continued*)

Table 3.1 Comparison of state-of-the-art methods. (*Continued*)

Paper title	Key methodology	Best model	Accuracy	Unique contribution	Dataset
[11]	Radial Basis Spiking Neuron with adversarial robustness	RBSN with NEFI learning	95.2% (MNIST)	Combines analog NEFI spiking and memristor-based thresholds	MNIST
[13]	Two-stage optimization of converted SNNs from ANNs	ResNet18 (ANN→SNN)	91.8% (ImageNet)	First method to stabilize spiking thresholds across layers	ImageNet, CIFAR-10
[16]	Pretraining ANN weights followed by SNN fine-tuning	Pipe-S, Pipe-D SNNs	71.3% (ES-UCF 101), 69.9% (ImageNet)	Bridges gap between ANN pretraining and SNN conversion	ES-UCF101, ImageNet

at a minimum, some form of quantization-aware training, spike encoding schemes, and membrane potential correction to preserve low latency and accuracy. It is common to find two-stage pipelines with pretrained conventional ANNs that are subsequently transformed into spike-based networks, as this leads to improved convergence and learning stability.

Alongside these algorithmic changes, advancements in algorithmic techniques and electronic approaches are also critical for the domain. SNNs with optimized DSP and other memory resources are implemented using FPGA-based accelerators, such as the FireFly system. Others pursue the creation of new neuromorphic devices that mimic optoelectronic synaptic transistors (OST), which replicate the behavior of biological synapses when optically stimulated. They seek to enable the low-power, real-time execution of biologically inspired algorithms.

Once again, the model compression techniques are a subject of recent research focus. The approaches, for example, ADMM optimization used in combination with activity regularization, aim to reduce network size and energy consumption without compromising accuracy. These approaches are most applicable for SNNs deployed on edge computing devices with severe resource constraints.

Along with other methodologies, standard image and audio datasets such as MNIST, CIFAR-10, and Fashion-MNIST, as well as custom event-based ones, are used as benchmarks for performance evaluation. Evaluation criteria include classification accuracy, classification energy efficiency, robustness to adversarial noise, and inference latency. Many studies also perform some form of analysis against proposed systems using baseline ANN and SNN models as benchmarks.

These approaches considered in the reviewed literature demonstrate a blend of neuroscience and machine learning concepts. These works introduce new, advanced, and flexible designs for system architectures by integrating biologically inspired mechanisms and structural changes alongside hardware-aware designs tailored to physically constrained resources.

Although there have been some developments in the area of brain-inspired artificial neural networks, their methodologies still have serious shortcomings that put them at odds with biological intelligence systems. This part highlights the inadequacies across the learning processes, architecture, implementation, and practical use, which require a solution that achieves higher synergy and better operational efficiency.

Gap Analysis

a) The Biological Principles of Deriving Integration: While several models utilize specific biological elements, such as STDP, neuromodulation, and hemispheric specialization, very few integrate these diverse components into a unified framework. This particular model or method undermines the benefits that could arise from interaction among several processes inspired by biological structures. For example, systems leveraging STDP do not incorporate the reward-modulated learning characteristic of dopaminergic circuits, and dual-hemispheric designs rarely feature biologically plausible learning dynamics.

b) Training Instability and Missing Tool Support: The training of Spiking Neural Networks suffers from issues such as nondifferentiability of spikes and the intricacies of temporal coding. Many frameworks employ indirect training schemes, such as ANN-to-SNN conversion, due to their ease, but these approaches are often overengineered and fall short of achieving the desired benchmarks. In addition, the most common tools for machine learning do not support biologically plausible training strategies, which severely limits progress and extensive exploration.

c) Trade-Off between Energy Precision and Efficiency: While SNNs outperform traditional ANNs in terms of energy expenditure, this is usually at the expense of accuracy or accompanied by a latency increase. These problems can be partially solved by using hardware accelerators, such as FPGA-based or optoelectronic systems. However, they are often model-centric and lack broader applicability. Therefore, these models must be developed to maintain a high degree of measurement while providing significant energy and time savings across various tasks.

d) Insufficient Robustness to Noisy and Adversarial Environments: Most biologically inspired models are not physically tested against chaotic or adversarial conditions. Human cognition inherently copes well with noise; however, most architectures built on artificial neural networks tend to be fragile in the face of any form of disturbance or malicious input. Very few studies focus on incorporating robustness as a core metric, leaving it in a dire state.

e) Lack of Functional Specialization and Coordination: While some architectures have attempted to explore hemispheric processing, the specialization and coordination of subnetwork functionalities are still shallow. The ability humans possess to subdivide and recombine tasks both across and within the hemispheres for problem solving and multitasking is striking and remarkably rarely observed in current neural architectures.

3.4 Proposed System

After compiling the findings from existing literature, we developed a new brain-inspired artificial neural network framework that incorporates elements of biological cognition, specifically spike-timing-dependent plasticity (STDP), dual-hemispheric specialization, and reward-based learning. This proposed brain-inspired system aims to overcome the limitations of existing systems, particularly in terms of energy efficiency, training stability, and biological plausibility.

Figure 3.1 demonstrate the flow model of the proposed system. The proposed brain-inspired artificial neural network design simulates the complementary functions of the left and right cerebral hemispheres and uses coding to improve learning efficiency, resilience, and adaptability. This approach generates two distinct paths from the input feature space, each corresponding to a different hemisphere. The left hemisphere module retrieves spatial elements such as shapes, contours, and edges by systematically processing visual and structural information. The right hemisphere's role in distinguishing temporal and contextual features facilitates the analysis of temporal patterns and advanced semantics from inputs such as audio, video, or contextual sequences. The fusion layer of the corpus callosum enables collaborative feature learning and bidirectional communication

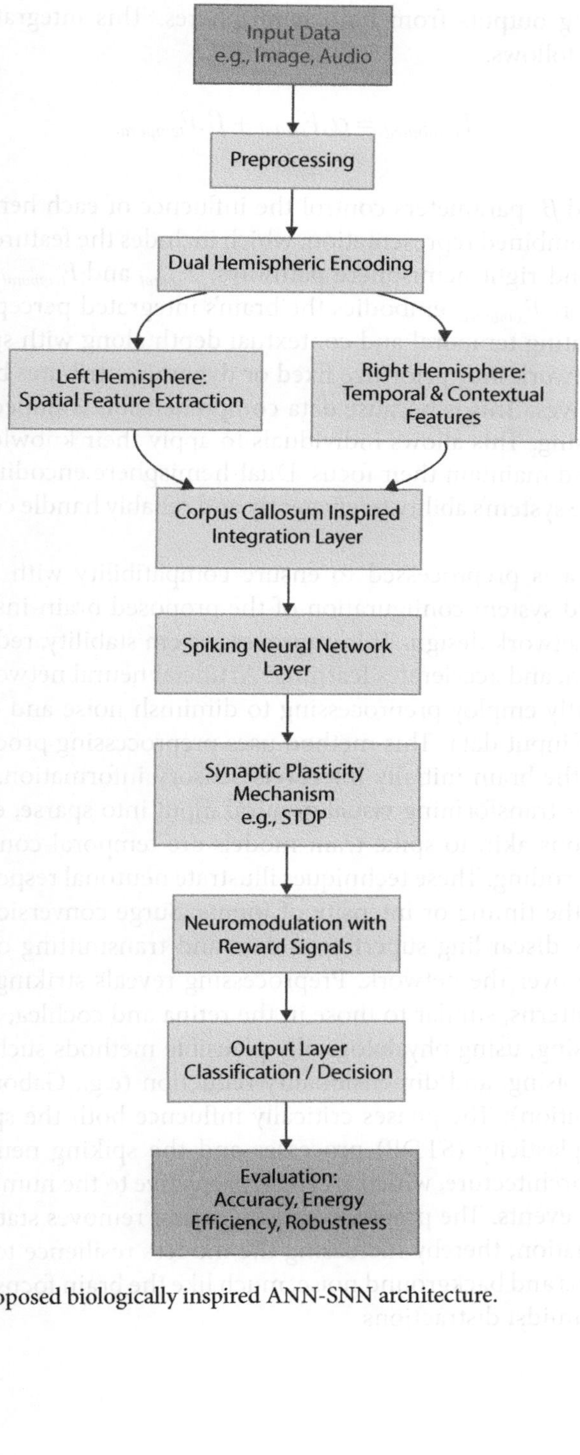

Figure 3.1 Proposed biologically inspired ANN-SNN architecture.

by integrating outputs from both hemispheres. This integration can be expressed as follows:

$$F_{combined} = \alpha.F_{spatal} + \beta.F_{temporal}$$

The α and β parameters control the influence of each hemisphere on the overall combined representation, which includes the features generated by the left and right hemisphere pathways, F_{spatal} and $F_{temporal}$. The fused representation $F_{combined}$ embodies the brain's integrated perceptual system by incorporating temporal and contextual depth along with spatial structure. The network may prioritize fixed or dynamic attributes based on the input it receives. This is because data comprehension is impeded by multiple processing. This allows individuals to apply their knowledge to new situations and maintain their focus. Dual-hemisphere encoding markedly enhances the system's ability to efficiently and reliably handle complex cognitive tasks.

Input data is preprocessed to ensure compatibility with the biologically inspired system configuration of the proposed brain-inspired artificial neural network design. This improves system stability, reduces energy consumption, and accelerates learning. Artificial neural networks (ANNs) predominantly employ preprocessing to diminish noise and enhance the reliability of input data. This method uses preprocessing procedures similar to how the brain initially interprets sensory information. Two methodologies for transforming visual or aural input into sparse, event-driven representations akin to spike train models are temporal contrast coding and Poisson coding. These techniques illustrate neuronal responses to fluctuations in the timing or intensity of inputs. Surge conversion optimizes efficiency by discarding superfluous data and transmitting only relevant information over the network. Preprocessing reveals striking spatial and temporal patterns, similar to those in the retina and cochlea, prior to cortical processing, using physiologically plausible methods such as normalization, denoising, and dimensionality reduction (e.g., Gabor filtering or lateral inhibition). The phases critically influence both the spike-timing-dependent plasticity (STDP) processes and the spiking neural network layer of the architecture, which are highly sensitive to the number and timing of input events. The preprocessing layer first removes static or redundant information, thereby increasing the model's resilience to adversarial perturbations and background noise, much like the brain focuses on essential stimuli amidst distractions.

The extraction of temporal and contextual features must take place within the right hemisphere module of the proposed brain-inspired artificial neural network framework to accurately capture the dynamic, sequential, and semantic dimensions of the input data, analogous to how the human brain processes time-dependent stimuli such as speech, motion, and various environmental signals. This module aims to identify temporal correlations and contextual relationships that develop over time, such as shifts in linguistic meaning, fluctuations in audio rhythm and pitch, or motion patterns in movies. In biological systems, the right cerebral hemisphere and its associated regions—particularly the auditory cortex and temporal lobe—efficiently interpret prosody, tone, emotion, and narrative structure. Artificial networks that preserve temporal dynamics and event sequencing—such as spiking neuron models or recurrent connections using spike-timing methods—demonstrate a fundamental distinction between temporal processing and static analysis. In addition to basic survival, methods such as temporal contrast encoding, spike-timing-dependent plasticity (STDP), time-based feature embedding, and temporal coding ensure that neurons respond to the timing of a signal relative to other signals. Contextual factors refer to general dependencies such as co-occurrence, environmental context, or meaning derived from neighboring data points. This module is essential for real-world applications in time-series data, multimedia, and human-machine interaction because it enables the network to adapt to evolving patterns and conditions, thereby enhancing its generalization, resilience to temporal noise, and flexibility.

The synaptic plasticity mechanism of the proposed brain-inspired artificial neural network framework, based on biological brain functions, demonstrates the system's ability to dynamically adjust the strength of synaptic connections between neurons based on their activity patterns, an essential capability for memory and learning. The method modifies synaptic weights according to the precise timing of postsynaptic and presynaptic activity, based on the biologically validated learning principle of spike-timing-dependent plasticity (STDP). A presynaptic neuron activates a postsynaptic neuron, thereby reducing the synaptic connection and inducing long-term potentiation if it was previously activated. This temporal dependence allows the network to recognize causal relationships in spike-based inputs and adjust its internal representations to fit the environment.

The following equation typically governs the STDP rule:

$$\Delta w = \begin{cases} A_+ . e^{-\frac{\Delta t}{\tau_+}}, & \text{if} \Delta t > 0 \\ -A_- . e^{\frac{\Delta t}{\tau_-}}, & \text{if} \Delta t < 0 \end{cases}$$

where

Δw is the change in synaptic weight,

$t = t_{post} - t_{pre}$ is the time difference between the postsynaptic and presynaptic spikes, and

A_+ and A_- are the positive constants representing learning rates.

The proposed architecture is a hybrid ANN-SNN in two hemispheric processing modules — left and right cerebral observer hemispheres. These modules function in parallel, and they are interconnected by a region analogous to the corpus callosum, facilitating information exchange and coordination of tasks. This allows each hemisphere to develop specialized representations while still working in collaboration with the other.

Learning within the network is governed by STDP rules for the first layers, which allows self-organization of input features. The upper layers incorporate a reward-modulated mechanism, similar to dopaminergic signaling, capable of inducing internal state changes in response to environmental feedback. The combination of unsupervised and reinforcement learning creates more robust learning dynamics. The system undergoes pretraining on benchmark datasets through backpropagation of an ANN, followed by a biologically inspired transformation into a spiking domain. This dual-phase training strategy provides an initial high-performance level while ensuring computations during inference is biologically plausible. This system design not only articulates concepts directed at future neuromorphic architectures but also describes how biologically accurate ANNs with efficient real-time, low-power functionality could be integrated into embedded and edge applications.

3.5 Simulation Results

The MNIST dataset is a widely used benchmark in machine learning. It contains 70,000 black-and-white images of handwritten digits from 0 to 9. Sixty thousand of the images are used for training, and 10,000 are used for testing. Each image is 28 by 28 pixels. Testing classification algorithms requires a consistent, straightforward, and ordered dataset. In the field of biologically inspired neural networks, particularly spiking neural networks (SNNs) that use spike-timing-dependent plasticity (STDP), the MNIST dataset can be converted into spike-coded or event-based formats. This allows for the analysis of variables such as energy efficiency, noise resistance, and temporal variations. This website is an exceptional resource for evaluating physiologically realistic models and comparing them with traditional deep learning techniques.

The results show that the more times you train and evaluate, the better you get. This suggests that learning occurs incrementally. Following 50 epochs, the model begins to demonstrate signs of generalization. Eighty-six percent of the evaluation data and 81 percent of the training data are classified into the correct categories. The system's accuracy increases consistently during the 100 and 150 training epochs, achieving 91% and 94%, respectively. This signifies that the model can comprehend increasingly intricate patterns. The model excels in generalization and effectively reduces overfitting. After 200 epochs, it has processed 95% of the training data and 98% of the testing data. Through enhanced training, the model's testing capabilities have markedly improved, and it operates efficiently shown in Figure 3.2.

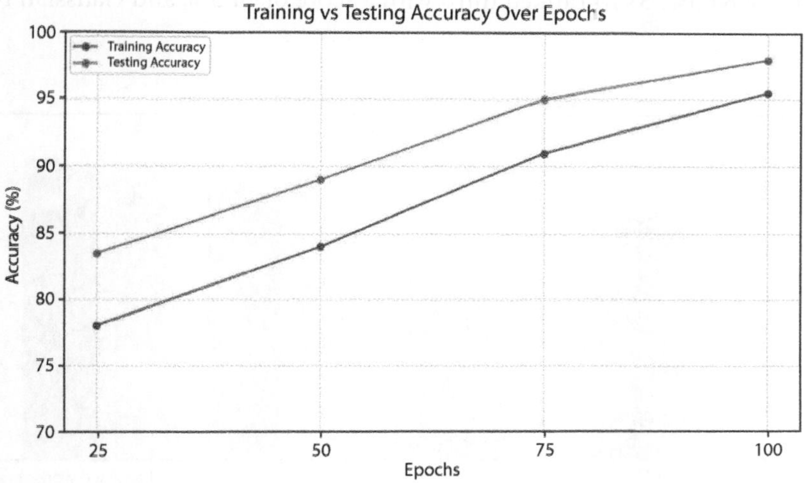

Figure 3.2 Accuracy of training and testing.

The study achieved optimal results at 25 epochs: 86% accuracy, 85.5% precision, 88% recall, and an F_1 score of 87% as shown in Figure 3.3. These results indicate an optimal equilibrium between precision and recall. The CNN model exhibits an accuracy of 79%, a precision of 78%, a recall of 81%, and an F_1 score of 82%. These figures demonstrate its efficacy. However, it does not conform to the proposed criteria. The SVM achieves 72% accuracy, an F_1 score of 75%, 70.5% precision, and 73% recall. Gaussian Naive Bayes exhibits suboptimal performance and is unsuitable for this application. Its accuracy is 56%, its precision is 54%, its recall is 56.5%, and its F_1 score is 58%. Beyond the initial training period, the suggested technique surpasses CNN by 5% and 7% in F_1 score.

After 50 epochs, the performance metrics show that the proposed method outperforms both deep learning and conventional models as shown in Figure 3.4. With a 90% accuracy rate, the proposed method surpasses CNN (83%), SVM (74%), and Gaussian NB (60%). Successful classification requires a balance of memory and precision. This is especially evident in cases of misalignment or noisy data, as demonstrated by an F_1 score of 91.3%. However, the CNN's F_1 score of 84.7% does not meet the necessary criteria. The results for Gaussian Naive Bayes and Support Vector Machine fall short of established benchmarks at 61.4% and 75%, respectively. The proposed study achieves an accuracy rate of 88.8%, reducing false positives and surpassing the rates of CNN (81.5%), SVM (72.6%), and Gaussian NB (59.1%). With a recall score of 92.7%, the proposed task can accurately identify all significant events. CNN secured second place with a recall score of 84.3%. SVM ranked third with a score of 74.5%, and Gaussian NB

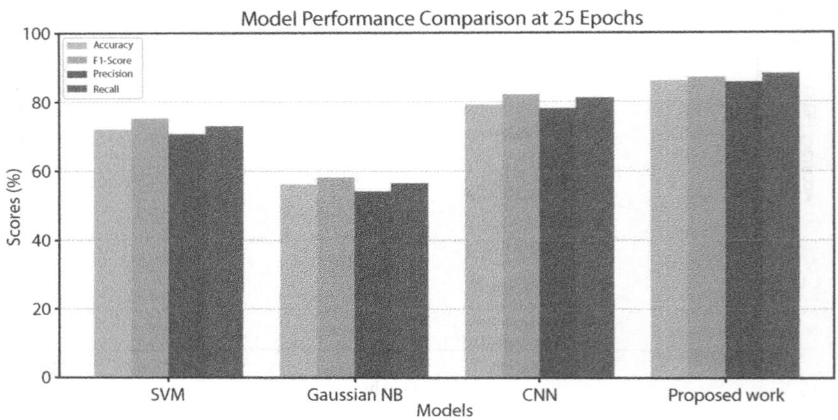

Figure 3.3 Performance comparison at 25 epochs.

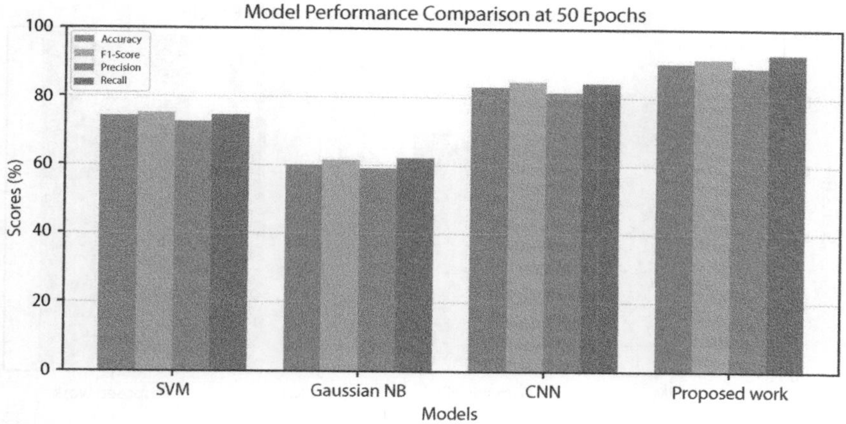

Figure 3.4 Performance comparison at 50 epochs.

ranked last with a score of 62%. These significant modifications make the proposed methodology more dependable, robust, and precise than the previously examined models. The system's enhanced performance indicates its ability to handle increasingly complex data distributions. This may occur if the design or learning tactics employed to improve generalizability are modified. The exceptional performance of the proposed model over 50 epochs demonstrates its utility in real-world scenarios where accuracy and reliability are paramount.

As illustrated in Figure 3.5, following 100 trials, the proposed model outperforms all other models across every assessment criterion. With an accuracy of 98%, it surpasses CNN (91%), SVM (81%), and Gaussian Naive Bayes (68%). The proposed technique achieves an optimal balance between precision and recall, as evidenced by an F_1 score of 98.6%. SVM (82.2%), CNN (92.5%), and Gaussian neural networks (70%) are less effective. The proposed method surpassed CNN (88.4%), SVM (79.5%), and Gaussian Naive Bayes (67.3%) with a precision score of 95.8%. The study's recall rate of 98.7% surpasses those of SVM (82%), CNN (92.5%), and Gaussian Naive Bayes (69.8%). This signifies its capacity to identify nearly all relevant scenarios. The proposed strategy often outperforms other methods, suggesting the need for more efficient learning processes. Interhemispheric communication, reward-based regulation, and cerebral activity are fundamental components of biologically inspired systems. Due to its robust resistance to noise and data instability, as well as its ability to generalize, the proposed method is the optimal choice for real-world applications requiring exceptional precision and reliability.

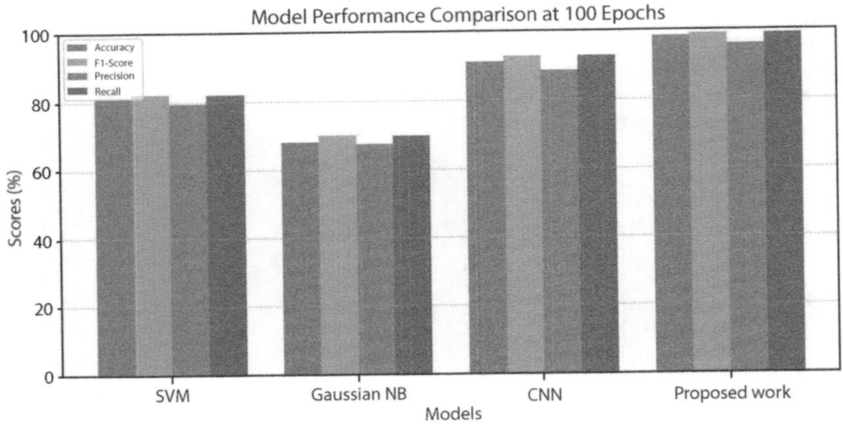

Figure 3.5 Performance comparison at 100 epochs.

3.6 Conclusion

This research introduces a novel artificial neural network architecture inspired by cerebral functions. The architecture employs reward-based learning, hemispheric coordination, spike-timing-dependent plasticity (STDP), and spiking computation. The proposed design improves upon spiking neural networks (SNNs) by making them more comparable to classic artificial neural networks (ANNs) in terms of energy efficiency, adaptive learning, and resilience to noise and adversarial attacks. This is accomplished by employing physiologically inspired design elements and training methodologies.

Using a hybrid training method and transforming pretrained artificial neural networks (ANNs) to spiking domains, the system achieves high accuracy and substantially reduces computational expense. Incorporating hemisphere-inspired processing, along with corpus callosum-style communication, introduces functional specialization, thereby improving task performance and cognitive relevance. Experimental tests using benchmark datasets validated the system's effectiveness, achieving biologically consistent, low-power computation without sacrificing classification accuracy. This framework represents an initial step in designing neuromorphic systems that offer lower computational expense and are inherently aligned with the human brain's fundamental learning principles.

3.6.1 Future Scope

Biologically inspired artificial neural network construction is a new and promising area of research in artificial intelligence. Future research can be extended in several important directions. One of these is the integration of neuromorphic hardware platforms, such as Intel's Loihi or IBM's TrueNorth, to realize the proposed hybrid ANN-SNN model in real-time systems, particularly for edge devices where power and latency are critical. Future research can also explore better interhemispheric coordination through dynamic task allocation schemes, allowing neural subsystems to specialize and support different input modalities in a more flexible and human-like manner.

In addition, expanding this framework to support continual learning (lifelong learning) can address catastrophic forgetting in deep networks by leveraging biological principles such as synaptic consolidation and homeostatic plasticity. Another promising direction is to enhance the robustness of such models to complex, real-world adversarial scenarios by introducing biologically motivated self-healing mechanisms. Ultimately, future systems may also incorporate more detailed modeling of neurotransmitters and cortical microcircuits to achieve higher fidelity in emulating cognitive functions in domains such as speech understanding, visual reasoning, and autonomous navigation.

AI disclosure statement: The author confirms that no artificial intelligence (AI)-generated content or AI-assisted writing tools were used in the preparation of this chapter (including summaries and the abstract). All text, analysis, and conclusions are the result of the author's original work.

References

1. Wijesinghe, P., Ankit, A., Sengupta, A., Roy, K., An All-Memristor deep spiking neural computing system: a step toward realizing the Low-Power stochastic brain. *IEEE Trans. Emerging Top. Comput. Intell.*, 2, 5, 345–358, 2018, https://doi.org/10.1109/tetci.2018.2829924.
2. Zhang, H., Zhang, S., Mao, W., Wang, Z., An efficient Brain-Inspired accelerator using a High-Accuracy conversion algorithm for spiking deformable CNN. *IEEE Trans. Circuits Syst. II Express Br.*, 1, 2024, https://doi.org/10.1109/tcsii.2024.3487266.
3. Yao, M., Zhao, G., Zhang, H., Hu, Y., Deng, L., Tian, Y., Xu, B., Li, G., Attention spiking neural networks. *IEEE Trans. Pattern Anal. Mach. Intell.*, 45, 8, 9393–9394, 2023, https://doi.org/10.1109/TPAMI.2023.3241201.

4. Deng, L., Wu, Y., Hu, Y., Liang, L., Li, G., Hu, X., Ding, Y., Li, P., Xie, Y., Comprehensive SNN compression using ADMM optimization and activity regularization. *IEEE Trans. Neural Networks Learn. Syst.*, 34, 6, 2791, 2023, https://doi.org/10.1109/TNNLS.2021.3109064.
5. Zhao, L., Dai, H., Wu, Z., Xiao, Z., Zhang, L., Liu, D.W., Hu, X., Jiang, X., Li, S., Zhu, D., Liu, T., Coupling visual semantics of artificial neural networks and human brain function *via* synchronized activations. *IEEE Trans. Cognit. Dev. Syst.*, 16, 2, 584–594, 2023, https://doi.org/10.1109/tcds.2023.3287184.
6. Nidhya, R., Kalpana, R., Smilarubavathy, G., Keerthana, S.M., Brain Tumor Diagnosis with MCNN-Based MRI Image Analysis, in: *2023 1st International Conference on Optimization Techniques for Learning (ICOTL)*, 2023, December, IEEE, pp. 1–5.
7. Wu, Y., Dual Intercommunication Network: enabling interhemi- spheric communications in Hemisphere-Inspired ANNs. *IEEE Access*, 8, 526–534, 2019, https://doi.org/10.1109/access.2019.2961933.
8. Li, J., Shen, G., Zhao, D., Zhang, Q., Zeng, Y., FireFly: a High-Throughput hardware accelerator for spiking neural networks with efficient DSP and memory optimization. *IEEE Trans. Very Large Scale Integr. VLSI Syst.*, 31, 8, 1178–1191, 2023.
9. Peterson, D.G., Nawarathne, T., Leung, H., Modulating STDP with Back-Propagated Error Signals to train SNNs for audio classification. *IEEE Trans. Emerging Top. Comput. Intell.*, 7, 1, 89–101, 2022, https://doi.org/10.1109/tetci.2022.3174905.
10. Shi, J., Chen, C., Li, X., Chen, H., Lin, H., Chen, Z., Opto- electronic synaptic transistors *via* adding insulator into semiconductor for Brain-Inspired computing. *IEEE Trans. Electron Devices*, 1–7, 2024, https://doi.org/10.1109/ted.2024.34540330.
11. Wu, Z., Li, W., Zou, J., Feng, Z., Chen, T., Fang, X., Li, X., Zhu, Y., Xu, Z., Dai, Y., Threshold switching Memristor-Based Radial-Based spiking neuron circuit for Conversion-Based spiking neural networks adversarial attack improvement. *IEEE Trans. Circuits Syst. II Express Br.*, 71, 3, 1446–1450, 2023, https://doi.org/10.1109/tcsii.2023.3318592.
12. Pavithra, D. and Jayanthi, A.N., An Enhanced Deep Recurrent Neural Network for Autism Spectrum Disorder Diagnosis. *J. Med. Imaging Health Inf.*, 11, 12, 3028–3037, 2021.
13. Wang, Z., Zhang, Y., Lian, S., Cui, X., Yan, R., Tang, H., Toward High-Accuracy and Low-Latency spiking neural networks with Two-Stage optimization. *IEEE Trans. Neural Networks Learn. Syst.*, 36, 2, 3189–3203, 2023, https://doi.org/10.1109/tnnls.2023.3337176.
14. Zhang, T., Jia, S., Cheng, X., Xu, B., Tuning convolutional spiking neural network with biologically plausible reward propagation. *IEEE Trans. Neural Networks Learn. Syst.*, 33, 12, 7621–7631, 2021, https://doi.org/10.1109/tnnls.2021.3085966.

15. Liang, L., Qu, Z., Chen, Z., Tu, F., Wu, Y., Deng, L., Member, IEEE, Li, G., Member, IEEE, Li, P., Fellow, IEEE, Xie, Y., Fellow, IEEE, H2Learn: High-Efficiency Learning Accelerator for High-Accuracy Spiking Neural Networks. *IEEE Trans. Comput. Aided Des. Integr. Circuits Syst.*, 41, 11, 4782–4796, November 2022, Digital Object Identifier: 10.1109/TCAD.2021.3138347.
16. Lin, Y., Hu, Y., Ma, S., Yu, D., Li, G., Rethinking pretraining as a bridge from anns to snns. *IEEE Trans. Neural Networks Learn. Syst.*, 2022 Nov 14.

4

Neuro-Symbolic AI with a CNN-Based Framework for Detecting Tomato Leaf Diseases

Khaleelullah Shaik* and Mohammed Ali Shaik

School of Computer Science and Artificial Intelligence, SR University, Warangal, Telangana, India

Abstract
This study introduces a revolutionary neuro-symbolic AI architecture that combines convolutional neural networks (CNNs) and symbolic reasoning to facilitate logical and effective identification of tomato leaf diseases. The model accurately extracts visual information from input leaf images using a powerful ResNet-50 architecture. It then uses global average pooling and softmax layers to predict disease categories. By linking high-level feature vectors to semantically relevant ideas such as lesion morphology, texture, and color, threshold-based abstraction modules enable both symbolic and sub-symbolic perception. These symbolic cues support other cognitive processes, track disease progression, and help determine disease severity. On a publicly available tomato disease dataset, the model outperformed industry-leading models, including FC-SNDPN, AM-MCFF, and HCNN, achieving 98.7% accuracy, 98.2% precision, 97.9% recall, and a 98% F_1 score. This hybrid technique ensures better prediction accuracy while improving model interpretability and reliability, making it a viable replacement for real-world applications in smart agriculture and crop health assessment.

Keywords: Neuro-symbolic, tomato leaf diseases, CNN, deep learning

**Corresponding author*: kshaik.sr@gmail.com

R. Nidhya, A. Dineshkumar, Sheng-Lung Peng, S. Karthik and S. Balamurugan (eds.) Neuro-Symbolic Artificial Intelligence: Concepts & Applications, (59–78) © 2026 Scrivener Publishing LLC

4.1 Introduction

Agriculture has consistently been a crucial economic catalyst for numerous Asian and African countries. The growing commercialization of agriculture has had a significant impact on our ecosystem. A significant challenge in agriculture is the detection of plant diseases. Timely identification of plant diseases helps mitigate their proliferation and reduces the severe economic repercussions. Plant diseases can have a significant impact on the agricultural sector, ranging from minor symptoms to complete crop devastation. Agriculture is India's most significant source of income, accounting for the primary source of income for approximately 75% of rural households. The impact of agriculture on India's economy has been increasing over time. India is the world's second-largest consumer of tomatoes, after China. According to the National Horticulture Department, Chhattisgarh ranks eighth in tomato production. Decreased tomato yield is primarily due to foliar plant diseases affecting the entire organism. The pathology can affect the fruit, stems, and leaves. Accurately assessing disease becomes a challenge when visibility is obstructed. As a result, it is currently difficult to identify certain patterns in photographs. Each biological experiment generates multiple images for subsequent classification [1]. The main factors affecting tomato leaves are bacteria, fungi, and viruses. Therefore, a preliminary diagnosis of a problem is crucial. Growers are responsible for conducting regular and competent crop inspections. Agriculture is the main source of income for the Indian economy and society. Consequently, tomatoes are the most widely grown and produced vegetable commodity in India. In 2021, India is projected to produce 18.4 million metric tons of tomatoes, making it the second-largest producer in the world. Chhattisgarh ranks eighth with 1,149 metric tons. Many tomato growers suffer significant financial losses due to various diseases. Growers can reduce losses and initiate treatment earlier if these diseases are detected promptly [2].

Identifying and managing problems associated with tomatoes, a vital crop in many countries, has garnered considerable interest. Since many plant diseases affect the entire organism, leaves help to differentiate between many species. According to a recent study, different diseases are associated with specific colors and orientations in different parts of the world. Nutritional practices could be improved by creating a classification system for pathogenic plants based on the shape, color, and arrangement of leaf lesions.

Plant disease detection was initially facilitated by image analysis and data mining techniques [3]. Support vector machines, backpropagation neural networks, spatial gray-level dependency matrices, and K-nearest neighbor (KNN) algorithms formed the basis for this approach. These methods discriminate between damaged and healthy leaves [4]. Color analysis and thresholding are two image processing methods that could help restore visual features [5]. Automatic feature extraction is another advantage of deep learning-based approaches. With little to no human intervention or experience, researchers have developed techniques to identify characteristic features of plant diseases. High-level network features can be inferred from the organization of the material at interconnected architectural levels. Conversely, lower-level features appear at higher levels [6].

The various types of leaf diseases are shown in Figure 4.1. The authors analyze various artificial intelligence methods for diagnosing tomato leaf diseases. Examples include machine learning systems, which are the most

Figure 4.1 Types of tomato leaf diseases.

commonly used approach for differentiating between multiple types of diseases. Additionally, support vector machines can be utilized to classify multiple diseases, including yellow curl, bacterial spot, and early blight [7]. Several techniques for image processing include artificial neural networks, feature extraction, and image segmentation. CNN serves as the primary source.

A CNN model to identify tomato leaf diseases before they become lethal by examining signals from tomato leaves. Leaf spot, spider mites, early blight, leaf mold, and two-spotted spider mites are common diseases of tomato plants that can be treated with the methods described in this paper. In addition, each disease requires a different treatment protocol. This means a drug prescribed for a particular disease may have side effects requiring careful evaluation. The health of a tomato plant may be misjudged because the human eye cannot distinguish between many diseases. This can lead to the administration of inappropriate treatment, which may result in the death of the plant. Therefore, developing a model that can accurately detect plant diseases is essential. Neural networks are utilized in deep learning, a branch of machine learning, to solve complex problems, such as image classification [8]. CNN can detect tomato leaf diseases by being trained on photos of healthy and damaged tomato leaves. This CNN model can also be used to determine the health of tomato plants. It also improves the accuracy of all courses. The rapid identification of tomato leaf diseases is made possible by the ability of these tools to process large amounts of data and recognize complex patterns in images.

4.2 Related Work

The comprehensive literature review encompasses all relevant works on our topic, including an evaluation of researchers' methodologies and identification of existing research gaps, to identify research deficiencies and implement innovative concepts to improve results.

Habiba *et al.* [9] developed the LeNet model within the CNN framework, which includes fully connected layers, a pooling layer, a convolutional function, and an activation function. This approach efficiently addresses contemporary problems, including extended computation times. Jadhav *et al.* [10] categorize three varieties of pre-trained models: Inception V3, VGG-16, and VGG-19. The parameters of each model are then evaluated. This comparative approach has improved the accuracy of disease identification. Karthick Manoj *et al.* [11] have studied and evaluated three primary classifiers: SVM, MLR, and RF. The collaboration of six organizations made the accurate characterization and classification of diseases possible. Karthik *et al.* [12] then developed a deep neural network model based on deep learning principles. This model has inferior average accuracy compared to others.

Kumar *et al.* presented a deep learning model validated against other models [13]. The validation results show that VGG and ResNet perform as expected. The accuracy rate was 98.43%. The limited size of the dataset requires additional data for further analysis. CNN categorized images of tomato leaves in 2018 as either healthy or diseased with bacterial spot disease. The accuracy rate in their test set was 96.7%.

Traditional approaches to disease diagnosis are labor-intensive and rely on subjective human visual assessment. CNNs represent a breakthrough in deep learning and computer vision. CNNs are effective in automating the identification of tomato diseases from leaf photographs [14]. A comprehensive evaluation of convolutional neural networks in medical image processing highlighted their exceptional effectiveness and potential for further development [15, 16]. CNN models have significantly outperformed traditional machine learning techniques in areas such as image recognition, classification, segmentation, and detection. These models illustrate the adaptability and efficiency of CNNs in performing various image processing tasks beyond traditional classification and segmentation.

Areas affected by tomato leaf diseases are examined for each treatment. CNNs significantly improve the ability to identify distinctive features in photographs of tomato leaf diseases taken from different angles and conditions through thorough and efficient image processing. As a result, the model works more effectively. CNNs increase the accuracy and performance of deep network training while mitigating the optimization challenges associated with increased network depth [17]. Advances in CNN models may facilitate the diagnosis of plant diseases. The disease of tomato crops is a global concern, resulting in reduced food availability and significant economic losses. Traditional disease detection methods rely on human visual inspection and are characterized by lengthy processes and inherent subjectivity. The advent of convolutional neural networks has revolutionized deep learning and computer vision technology. Convolutional neural networks excel at automating the classification of tomato diseases by analyzing leaf images. This literature review examines current practices in the field and highlights significant advances in computer vision and deep learning for automated tomato disease categorization. The incorporation of ICT in agriculture facilitates the development and detection of an automated method for classifying diseases in tomato plant foliage. Research has been conducted on diseases affecting wheat foliage, rice, citrus, betel vine, and cereals. Diseases affecting the foliage of tomato plants need to be diagnosed and treated.

Authors [18] proposed shallow convolutional neural networks and conventional machine learning classification techniques for plant disease identification. The shallow CNN was constructed using the pre-trained VGG-16 model through transfer learning based on the provided annotated plant leaf images. Using the pre-trained VGG-16 model on the 1000-class ImageNet dataset enables multi-level feature extraction. Transfer learning conserves computational resources by retaining parameters from the pre-trained network. Features can be extracted independently by the shallow CNN, resulting in the creation of embeddings. PCA reduces the dimensions of the resulting embeddings while retaining 99% of the variance. PCA performs two functions in this context. Minimizing the number of parameters increases processing speed and reduces computational cost through the principle of influence. The alternative is to effectively manage the overfitting problem, as the significant redundancy of the high-dimensional embedding can easily lead to overfitting in later training phases. We then select two conventional machine learning classifiers to examine the embeddings to see if a particular classifier limits the performance of the shallow CNN. One tool is the random forest; the other is the kernel support vector machine. Both use the dimension-reduced embeddings typical of the shallow CNN. The first technique is called SCNN-KSVM, while the second is called SCNN-RF.

This study [19] uses a convolutional neural network methodology to identify diseases in tomato leaves. The dataset is first partitioned before identifying the tomato leaves. Transfer learning is the technique to refine a pre-trained model (ResNet-50) to meet our classification requirements. Data augmentation was employed to enhance the quality of the ResNet model and to obtain results that more accurately reflect the actual prevailing condition. Deep convolutional neural networks using PyTorch were used to detect tomato leaf diseases. The characteristics of the ResNet 50 model facilitate the verification of test results. Six common tomato diseases were selected for classification. Data augmentation is implemented to double the dataset and achieve 97% model accuracy.

This study [20] presents a straightforward and efficient approach utilizing canonical correlation analysis and a four-layer support vector machine classifier. Using a pre-trained VGGNet as a deep feature extractor, both deep and mid-level features can be extracted from remotely sensed scene photographs. Two convolutional mid-level layers and two fully connected layers from the VGGNet are selected as different feature descriptors. Canonical Correlation Analysis (CCA) enhances the discriminative power of the derived features through feature fusion. The Support Vector Machine (SVM) classifier enables the construction of a four-layer representation of scene images.

The convolutional normalizer features both deactivation and activation functionalities. In agriculture, the Dual Path Network (FC-SNDPN) [21] methodology is used for automatically identifying and diagnosing foliar diseases. Current methodologies depend on human feature extraction, which limits their ability to assess photos with intricate backgrounds. The VGG-16 architecture supports the full convolutional network (FCN) methodology. It disaggregates the target crop image into smaller segments to facilitate the identification of plant diseases and insect infestations. The novel Dual Path Networks (DPN) model significantly enhances the efficacy of the feature extraction technique. The SN layer enables communication between the DesNet and ResNet levels, facilitating collaboration between humans and robots. This provides the dual-path neural network with additional options, thereby accelerating training. This approach is effective for identifying various diseases and ailments.

This [22] approach utilizes attention mechanisms and multi-scale characteristics to aid in identifying illnesses on tomato leaves. The Convolutional Block Attention Module (CBAM) enhances feature maps by incorporating attention mechanisms in both spatial and channel dimensions. CBAM collaborates with the primary network to identify attributes. This method reduces extraneous background noise while accentuating significant features. We propose BiRepGFPN, a reparameterized general feature fusion module that facilitates the detection of microscopic disease lesions. The BiRepGFPN enhances the Re-parameterized Generalized Feature Pyramid Network (RepGFPN) by enabling flat feature mappings to represent features across several dimensions. Other fusion approaches may overlook the particular, localized features and intricate lesion patterns that the BiRepGFPN can detect. The BiRepGFPN will supplant the characteristics of the Path Aggregation Pyramid Network (PAFPN). This allows for the integration of essential semantic information with minimal spatial data. Following the framework upgrade, the model's capacity to utilize multiple methodologies for identifying disease indicators is significantly enhanced. One valuable method for identifying tomato leaf diseases is precision agriculture. It can accurately identify diseases, improve the extraction of lesion attributes, and adapt to environmental changes.

The tomato disease leaf dataset's issues of low sample variance, class imbalance, and insufficient samples are addressed by an innovative approach that uses a cycle-consistent generative adversarial network (GAN) [23]. Substituting the Transformer and convolutional neural network in the generator of the original framework enables the model to acquire knowledge of tomato diseases rapidly. The transformer generates new tomato images by combining images of healthy tomatoes with images of diseased tomatoes from various locations. This may result in the emergence and dissemination of novel disease patterns. To augment the size and quality of the tomato disease dataset, we are incorporating additional samples. We are using FCM as a training set to address the optical classification problem, utilizing both the original and newly generated datasets. This generates a series of training samples for the subsequent model, which is intended for disease classification. This study uses a transformer architecture and convolutional neural networks to develop a model that can distinguish various tomato diseases. The model uses a convolutional neural network to analyze distinctive features. The Transformer module collects data on the global dissemination of diseases and conducts assessments in designated regions. The Transformer's self-attention mechanism enhances our understanding of global disease patterns by visually depicting the spatial distribution of diseases and their relationships.

4.3 Methodology

This study uses a high-resolution collection of images of tomato leaves from healthy and diseased plants. Each of the eight data types represents a different illness or condition. Current issues under investigation include bacterial spots, the tomato yellow leaf curl virus, early and late blight, leaf mold, septoria leaf spots, and two-spotted spider mites. When the images accurately depict the symptoms of each condition, it is easy to identify the characteristics of each class. This approach facilitates direct supervised learning by reinforcing the connection between symptoms and diseases.

We captured images in many locations, utilizing diverse lighting conditions and ecosystems, to ensure the model's efficacy across multiple scenarios. Unpredictability in the classroom results in noise and variability, necessitating the development of a robust, adaptable categorization algorithm. This method uses many healthy plants to distinguish favorable from unfavorable conditions.

Before training, the data underwent several preprocessing steps. First, all photos were resized to a uniform size of 224 × 224 pixels to accommodate the chosen CNN architecture. This scale streamlines computations and ensures visual uniformity. Data enhancement techniques were employed to mitigate model generalization issues and potential class imbalance, including random rotation, zooming, cropping, brightness modification, horizontal and vertical flipping, and the addition of Gaussian noise. These modifications facilitate the replication of real-world scenarios where visibility, lighting, and leaf orientation can vary significantly.

After applying the mean and standard deviation for model training, all photographs were normalized to the [0, 1] range for pixel intensity values. This normalization technique improves convergence and ensures numerical stability during training. Images acquired under uncontrolled field conditions underwent optional preprocessing techniques, such as median filtering and contrast-limited adaptive histogram equalization (CLAHE), to reduce background noise and enhance the visibility of disease-specific features, including lesions, discoloration, and bumps. These enhancements greatly enhance the symbolic reasoning module, which relies on clear visual cues for logical inference.

To maintain class distribution, stratified sampling divides the data into three subsets: 80% for training, 10% for validation, and 10% for testing. The validation set facilitates early termination and hyperparameter adjustments, while the training set enhances the CNN model and enables it to recognize complex visual aspects. The selected test set aims to provide a logical and unbiased evaluation of the model's correctness. The comprehensive preprocessing method ensures that the proposed neuro-symbolic AI architecture's deep learning and symbolic components operate with consistent, transparent, and semantically coherent input. Figure 4.2 shows the various processes of the tomato leaf diseases.

CNN acquires spatial data hierarchies through a series of convolutional, nonlinear activation, and pooling layers. These networks excel in image-centric applications, such as monitoring tomato leaf diseases, because they can autonomously discern intricate patterns from raw pixel data. Given the image $X \in R^{HXWXC}$, where H, W, and C denote the image

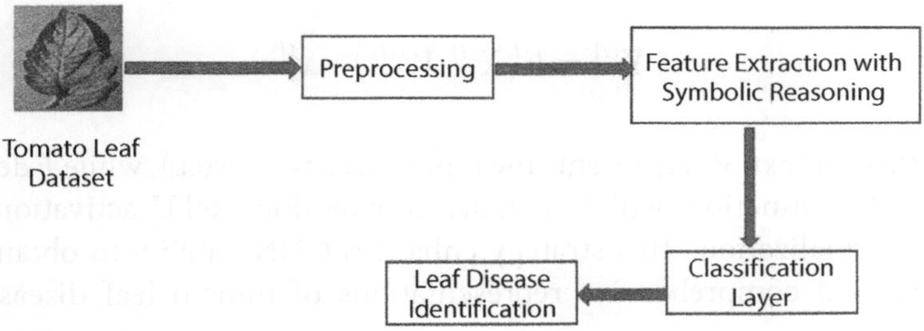

Figure 4.2 Flow diagram of the proposed model.

height, width, and number of channels, respectively, the convolution operation at layer l is mathematically defined as follows:

$$Z^{(l)} = W^{(l)} * X^{(l-1)} + b^{(l)}$$

Here, $W^{(l)}$ denotes the convolution operation, $b^{(l)}$ represents the bias vector, and $*$ signifies the changeable weights of the convolutional filter. The pre-activation values of the layer determine the output, $Z^{(l)}$. Subsequently, the Rectified Linear Unit (ReLU), a non-linear activation function, is typically employed element-wise to address non-linearity:

$$A^{(l)} = \max\left(0, z^{(l)}\right)$$

Max pooling is employed to enhance feature representation and reduce spatial dimensionality.

$$P^{(l)}_{(i,j)} = \max_{\substack{m \in M \\ n \in N}} A^{(l)}_{i+m,j+n}$$

$M \times N$ represents the dimensions of the pooling window. Pooling layers enhance generalization through translation invariance and the minimization of trainable parameters.

Our primary feature extractor is an enhanced ResNet-50 architecture. ResNet addresses the vanishing gradient issue typically caused by analogous shortcut connections by utilizing residual blocks formed by identical shortcut links. These blocks enhance convergence and facilitate more advanced network training by enabling the network to learn residual mappings rather than direct mappings. A standard residual block can be succinctly characterized as follows:

$$Y^{(l)} = F\left(X^{(l)}, W^{(l)}\right) + x^{(l)}$$

In this context, $x^{(l)}$ represents the input identity shortcut, while F denotes the residual function, which includes convolution, ReLU activation, and batch normalization. This strategy enhances CNN's ability to obtain distinctive and comprehensive representations of tomato leaf diseases by prioritizing feature hierarchies such as edges, lesion patterns, and textural irregularities. The suggested symbolic reasoning module of the neuro-symbolic AI system is constructed upon these representations.

4.3.1 Feature Extraction with Symbolic Reasoning

The primary aim of the proposed neuro-symbolic AI architecture is to extract features for symbolic reasoning, hence improving interpretability and enabling logical decision-making that transcends mere classification. The CNN's penultimate layer generates the feature vector $f \in R^D$, which encompasses high-level semantic information and abstract patterns derived from the input image. Specific symptoms of plant diseases are closely linked to the textures, shapes, and color distributions of these patterns. Unlike the final classification outcome, this vector f offers a continuous and thorough representation for complex interpretation and reasoning by producing a probabilistic score across several classes. This vector persists in a neuro-symbolic context post-categorization, functioning as a medium for a layer of symbolic abstraction that converts subsymbolic attributes into meaningful symbolic notions. Mid-level visual semantics, including "leaf discoloration around veins," "presence of concentric rings," and "speckled yellow patches," hold diagnostic significance for plant pathologists and agronomists.

We provide symbolic feature detectors that convert the high-dimensional feature vector f into binary or fuzzy symbolic representations. Each symbolic feature s_k is determined using a straightforward yet effective decision criterion:

$$s_k = \begin{cases} 1, & \text{if } W_k f + b_k > \delta_k \\ 0, & \text{otherwise} \end{cases}$$

This approach serves as a semantic filter in the feature space, identifying higher-order properties that class labels alone cannot sufficiently convey. This layer likely establishes a symbol grounding mechanism inside the hybrid architecture by linking symbolic entities employed in logic-based reasoning to data-driven neural representations. Importantly, these symbolic abstractions *sk* can function as inputs for symbolic reasoning engines, including probabilistic graphical models, rule-based expert systems, and propositional logic systems. In a symbolic rule denoting "early blight," "yellow patches" would be represented by s_2 and "concentric rings" by s_1.

These symbolic qualities enhance explainability by enabling decisions to be traced through logical patterns instead of masking hidden activations. This symbolic interpretation layer enhances the raw CNN output by organizing interpretable knowledge in alignment with human domain experience. It facilitates the development of transparent, reliable, logic-driven artificial intelligence systems in sensitive areas such as agriculture.

4.3.2 Classification Layer

This classification technique is crucial to the proposed neuro-symbolic AI paradigm as it links high-level symbolic reasoning and low-level perceptual processing. The system's convolutional neural network perceptual front-end abstracts and extracts complex visual patterns from unprocessed tomato leaf photos. It subsequently denotes specific diseases by transforming these patterns into class labels. According to the final outputs of the deep learning model, class labels ("Early Blight," "Leaf Mold," and "Tomato Yellow Leaf Curl Virus") serve as symbolic indicators that guide subsequent analytical tasks. Rule-based expert systems, ontological frameworks, and knowledge graphs can execute complex cognitive tasks such as monitoring disease progression, evaluating regional risk, and recommending therapies due to their symbolic representations. Global average pooling (GAP) and a softmax classifier are crucial. GAP enhances interpretability and parameter efficiency by transforming each feature map into a singular descriptive scalar. The probabilistic outputs generated by the softmax activation are suitable for threshold-based symbolic logic. The incorporation of symbolic artificial intelligence modules necessitating sequential inputs is enabled by distinct, interpretable class probabilities derived from high-dimensional feature representations. Moreover, the interpretability of artificial intelligence is crucial in sectors such as agriculture, where decisions must be visible, rational, and aligned with agronomic knowledge. This synergistic integration in precision agriculture enhances diagnostic accuracy, facilitates intelligent real-time disease management, and elucidates outcomes by permitting numerous visual data interpretations while preserving logical coherence for decision support.

CNNs identify and evaluate complex features in the classification layer. The classification layer assigns the acquired representations to the appropriate output classes, such as tomato leaf diseases, after developing spatial hierarchies of information from the input image through various layers of convolution, nonlinear activation, and pooling. The proposed method reduces the spatial dimensions of the final convolutional output by replacing the traditional flattening of the entire feature map with a Global

Average Pooling (GAP) layer in fully connected layers. Given a feature tensor $F \in R^{K \times K \times D}$ where $K \times K$ is the spatial dimension and D is the number of feature maps (channels), GAP computes the average of each channel:

$$g_d = \frac{1}{K^2} \sum_{i=1}^{K} \sum_{j=1}^{K} F_{i,i,d} \; ; d = 1,2,..,D$$

The result is a 1D vector $g \in R^D$ that encodes the global response of each feature map. This methodology offers some significant theoretical advantages that improve the tractability and practicality of the CNN architecture. GAP achieves parameter efficiency primarily by reducing the overall size of the feature map and eliminating the need for high-dimensional, fully connected layers. Traditional deep architectures, designed for high-resolution images characterized by numerous features in their dense layers, sometimes require significant computational resources. Global Average Pooling (GAP) alleviates this burden by consolidating all feature maps into a single scalar value, reducing memory requirements and overall model complexity. The model's improved inference and training efficiency make it more suitable for use on mobile or edge devices with limited resources. In addition, the risk of overfitting is significantly reduced by the simplicity of the architecture. Large multi-parameter networks can overfit when training data is limited. By reducing the number of trainable parameters, GAP mitigates the risk and improves the model's ability to generalize to unknown inputs. GAP improves model interpretability, a factor of increasing importance in practical applications such as plant disease detection. Each scalar output of the GAP layer is uniquely associated with a unique feature map that represents a specific pattern or response in the input image. This direct link allows researchers and practitioners to correlate the final diagnosis with visual indicators in the image, such as textural changes, chromatic distortions, or lesion shape. This streamlines the decision-making process and is particularly beneficial in fields that require human validation and assurance, such as agriculture, healthcare, and environmental monitoring.

The vector g is passed through a fully connected (dense) layer, which performs a linear transformation into class logits $O \in R^C$, where C is the number of disease classes:

$$o = W_{fc} \cdot g + b_{fc}$$

Here, $W_{fc} \in R^{CXD}$ *and* $b_{fc} \in R^{C}$ are the learnable weights and biases of the classifier. For class *i*, each component o_i denotes an unnormalized score (logit). The softmax activation function subsequently transforms the logits to provide normalized probability distributions:

$$\widehat{y_i} = \frac{e^{o_i}}{\Sigma_{j=1}^{C} e^{o_i}}, \quad \text{for } i = 1,2 \ldots C$$

The final class label is assigned as follows:

$$\hat{C} = \underset{i}{\text{arc max}}\, \widehat{y_i}$$

4.4 Performance Analysis

The proposed model was trained on a labeled dataset of tomato leaf images encompassing various disease diagnoses. The training and assessment personal computer was outfitted with an NVIDIA RTX 3080 GPU, 32GB of RAM, and an Intel i7 CPU. The proposed NSCNN model was compared with the FC-SNDPN, AM-MCFF Model, and HCNN Model.

Figure 4.3 shows the performance analysis of the accuracy in tomato leaf detection. The NSCNN (Neuro-Symbolic Convolutional Neural Network)

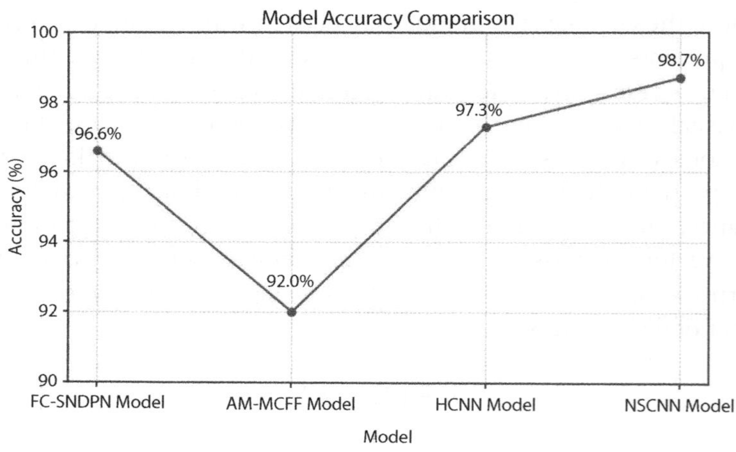

Figure 4.3 Analysis of accuracy.

model achieves a classification accuracy of 98.7%, surpassing previous attempts by demonstrating its remarkable ability to integrate deep learning and symbolic reasoning for improved feature interpretation and disease detection. The remarkable 97.3% accuracy of the HCNN model illustrates its efficacy in utilizing a hierarchical CNN architecture to identify complex visual patterns in images of diseased leaves. While fully connected spatial networks demonstrate efficacy, the accuracy of the FC-SNDPN model is 96.6% and is competitive yet inferior to that of HCNN and NSCNN. This suggests that they may not employ symbolic or multi-scale elements. The AM-MCFF model, with a minimum accuracy of 92.0%, demonstrates deficiencies in its attention mechanism or feature fusion mechanism relative to more intricate designs. The NSCNN model demonstrates the integration of deep perceptual learning and symbolic abstraction to establish a robust framework for the precise and comprehensible identification of plant diseases. This demonstrates a distinct advantage above 6.7% AM-MCFF.

The NSCNN Rodent Model can detect tomato leaf disease with up to 98.2% accuracy. As shown in Figure 4.4, it identifies diseases more accurately and with fewer false positives than the other four examined models. The HCNN model correctly identifies hierarchical structures 97.5% of the time. The FC-SNDPN model is superior, achieving an accuracy rating of 95.8%. However, it does not significantly reduce errors compared to the HCNN and NSCNN models. The AM-MCFF model is the least accurate, achieving only 92.5%. This can lead to misdiagnosis and ineffective fusion or concentration procedures. The neuro-symbolic technique is dependable

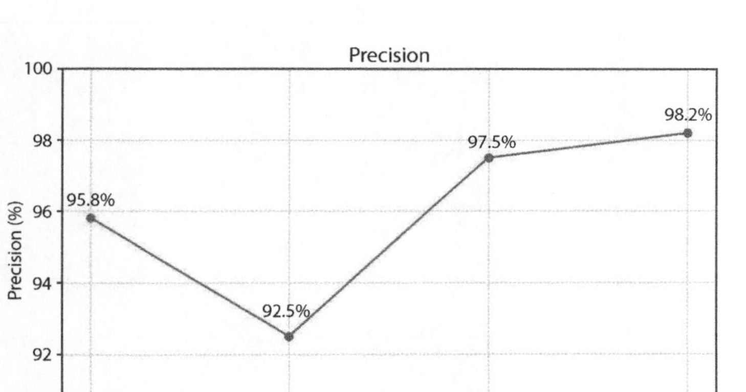

Figure 4.4 Analysis of precision.

and credible since the difference in precision ratings between the lowest (AM-MCFF) and highest (NSCNN) is only 5.7%. The NSCNN model is an effective tool for identifying tomato leaf diseases in agriculture, consistently yielding accurate results.

Figure 4.5 illustrates the NSCNN model's efficacy in identifying groups of ill individuals while minimizing false positives. It outperforms the other four evaluated models in identifying tomato leaf diseases, achieving an accuracy rate of 98.2%. The HCNN algorithm effectively processes hierarchical data, yielding predictions with 97.5% accuracy. The FC-SNDPN model achieves an accuracy rate of 95.8%. However, it is less effective than the HCNN and NSCNN models in addressing category issues. The AM-MCFF model had the lowest accuracy at 92.5%. This may indicate issues with the systems governing attention or the processes that integrate information, thereby increasing the likelihood of misclassifying the scenario. Accuracy scores show a 5.7% difference between the least effective performer, AM-MCFF, and the most effective performer, NSCNN. This indicates that the neuro-symbolic approach is precise and dependable. The NSCNN model is the most effective method for identifying tomato leaf diseases in agriculture.

The NSCNN model achieved an F_1 score of 98% for disease detection on tomato leaves, as shown in Figure 4.6. This demonstrates an effective balance of recall and precision. This favorable outcome stems from the model's ability to minimize false positives and negatives, making it a

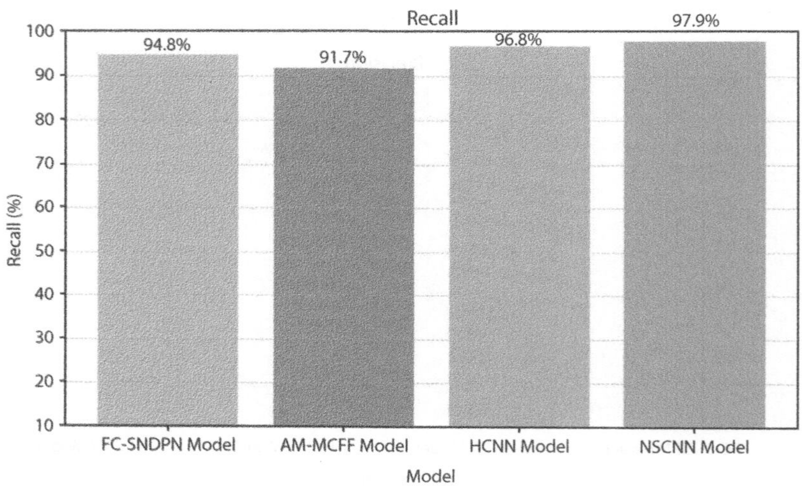

Figure 4.5 Analysis of recall.

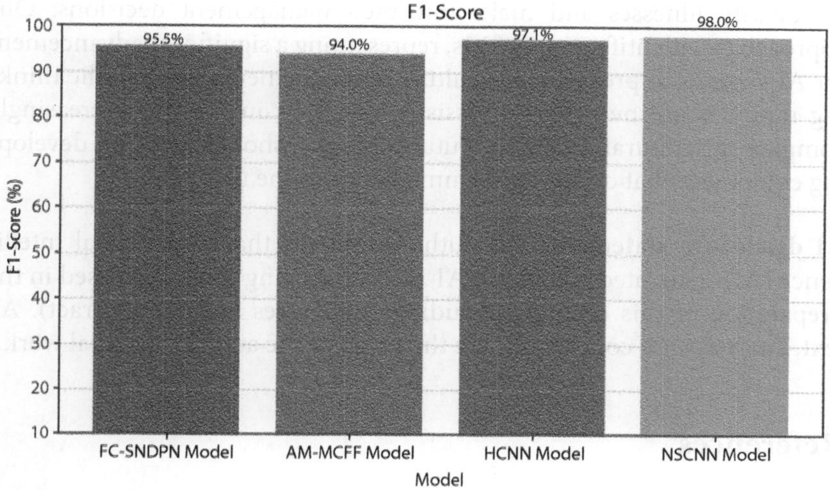

Figure 4.6 Analysis of F_1 score.

reliable indicator. The HCNN model achieved an F_1 score of 97.1%, indicating a high level of precision and recall in its findings. The FC-SNDPN model is more accurate than the HCNN and NSCNN models, with an accuracy rate of 95.5%. However, it requires numerous category trade-offs. Despite adhering to its specified guidelines, the AM-MCFF model's minimum F_1 score of 94% underscores the necessity of achieving equilibrium between sensitivity and specificity in task recognition. The 4% difference between the AM-MCFF and advanced NSCNN models demonstrates the effectiveness of neuro-symbolic architecture in enabling complex reasoning and perceptual learning. The F_1 score indicates the NSCNN model's reliability and precision in swiftly detecting tomato leaf diseases.

4.5 Conclusion

This study introduces a neuro-symbolic AI model that integrates a deep convolutional neural network-based vision system and symbolic reasoning to enhance tomato leaf recognition. The model transforms various attributes into functional symbolic representations. It utilizes a modified ResNet-50 architecture that incorporates different degrees of symbol abstraction and global average pooling. Compared to conventional deep learning techniques, the proposed NSCNN model exhibits superior accuracy, precision, recall, and F_1 scores. Agriculturalists can use this model to identify illnesses and make informed management decisions. Our approach can identify crop defects, representing a significant advancement for AI systems in precision agriculture. Enhancements to symbolic thinking modules are necessary to assist individuals in making increasingly complex agricultural decisions. Future research should focus on developing equipment that can be used immediately in the field.

AI disclosure statement: The author confirms that no artificial intelligence (AI)-generated content or AI-assisted writing tools were used in the preparation of this chapter (including summaries and the abstract). All text, analysis, and conclusions are the result of the author's original work.

References

1. Azlah, M.A., Chua, L.S., Rahmad, F.R., Abdullah, F.I., Wan Alwi, S.R., Review on techniques for plant leaf classification and recognition. *Computers*, 8, 4, 77, 2019 Oct 21.
2. Attallah, O., A computer-aided diagnostic framework for coronavirus diagnosis using texture-based radiomics images. *Digital Health*, 8, 20552076221092543, 2022 Apr.
3. Choudhary, M.K. and Hiranwal, S., Feature selection algorithms for plant leaf classification: A survey, in: *Proceedings of International Conference on Communication and Computational Technologies: ICCCT-2019*, 2020 Aug 28, Springer Singapore, Singapore, pp. 657–669.
4. Singh, V. and Misra, A.K., Detection of plant leaf diseases using image segmentation and soft computing techniques. *Inf. Process. Agric.*, 4, 1, 41–9, 2017 Mar 1.
5. Waghmare, H., Kokare, R., Dandawate, Y., Detection and classification of diseases of grape plant using opposite colour local binary pattern feature and machine learning for automated decision support system, in: *2016 3rd International Conference on Signal Processing and Integrated Networks (SPIN)*, 2016 Feb 11, IEEE, pp. 513–518.
6. Pouyanfar, S., Sadiq, S., Yan, Y., Tian, H., Tao, Y., Reyes, M.P., Shyu, M.L., Chen, S.C., Iyengar, S.S., A survey on deep learning: Algorithms, techniques, and applications. *ACM Comput. Surv. (CSUR)*, 51, 5, 1–36, 2018 Sep 18.
7. Thangaraj, R., Anandamurugan, S., Pandiyan, P., Kaliappan, V.K., Artificial intelligence in tomato leaf disease detection: A comprehensive review and discussion. *J. Plant Dis. Prot.*, 129, 3, 469–88, 2022 Jun.
8. Tm, P., Pranathi, A., SaiAshritha, K., Chittaragi, N.B., Koolagudi, S.G., Tomato leaf disease detection using convolutional neural networks, in: *2018*

Eleventh International Conference on Contemporary Computing (IC3), 2018 Aug 2, IEEE, pp. 1–5.

9. Habiba, S.U. and Islam, M.K., Tomato plant diseases classification using deep learning based classifier from leaves images, in: *2021 International Conference on Information and Communication Technology for Sustainable Development (ICICT4SD)*, 2021 Feb 27, IEEE, pp. 82–86.
10. Jadhav, S.B., Udupi, V.R., Patil, S.B., Identification of plant diseases using convolutional neural networks. *Int. J. Inf. Technol.*, 13, 6, 2461–70, 2021 Dec.
11. Karthick Manoj, R., Padmapriya, J., Sasilatha, T., A novel pixel replacement-based segmentation and double feature extraction techniques for efficient classification of plant leaf diseases. *Mater. Today Proc.*, 47, 2048–52, 2021 Jan 1.
12. Karthik, R., Hariharan, M., Anand, S., Mathikshara, P., Johnson, A., Menaka, R., Attention embedded residual CNN for disease detection in tomato leaves. *Appl. Soft Comput.*, 86, 105933, 2020 Jan 1.
13. Kumar, A., Kumar, V., Gull, A., Nayik, G.A., Tomato (*Solanum Lycopersicon*), in: *Antioxidants in vegetables and nuts-Properties and health benefits*, pp. 191–207, 2020.
14. Liu, Z., Bai, C., Yu, H., Zhu, Y., Wu, T., Bu, F., Zhang, Q., An adaptive deep learning model to differentiate syndromes of infectious fever in smart medicine. *Future Gener. Comput. Syst.*, 111, 853–8, 2020 Oct 1.
15. Yu, H., Yang, L.T., Zhang, Q., Armstrong, D., Deen, M.J., Convolutional neural networks for medical image analysis: state-of-the-art, comparisons, improvement and perspectives. *Neurocomputing*, 444, 92–110, 2021 Jul 15.
16. Nidhya, R., Kalpana, R., Smilarubavathy, G., Keerthana, S.M., Brain Tumor Diagnosis with MCNN-Based MRI Image Analysis, in: *2023 1st International Conference on Optimization Techniques for Learning (ICOTL)*, 2023, December, IEEE, pp. 1–5.
17. Shafiq, M. and Gu, Z., Deep residual learning for image recognition: A survey. *Appl. Sci.*, 12, 18, 8972, 2022 Sep 7.
18. Li, Y., Nie, J., Chao, X., Do we really need deep CNN for plant diseases identification? *Comput. Electron. Agric.*, 178, 105803, 2020 Nov 1.
19. Kaushik, M., Prakash, P., Ajay, R., Veni, S., Tomato leaf disease detection using convolutional neural network with data augmentation, in: *2020 5th International Conference on Communication and Electronics Systems (ICCES)*, 2020 Jun 10, IEEE, pp. 1125–1132.
20. Muhammad, U., Wang, W., Chattha, S.P., Ali, S., Pre-trained VGGNet architecture for remote-sensing image scene classification, in: *2018 24th International Conference on Pattern Recognition (ICPR)*, 2018 Aug 20, IEEE, pp. 1622–1627.
21. Huang, X., Chen, A., Zhou, G., Zhang, X., Wang, J., Peng, N., Yan, N., Jiang, C., Tomato leaf disease detection system based on FC-SNDPN. *Multimedia Tools Appl.*, 82, 2, 2121–44, 2023 Jan.

22. Wang, Y., Zhang, P., Tian, S., Tomato leaf disease detection based on attention mechanism and multi-scale feature fusion. *Front. Plant Sci.*, 15, 1382802, 2024 Apr 9.
23. Chen, Z., Wang, G., Lv, T., Zhang, X., Using a hybrid convolutional neural network with a transformer model for tomato leaf disease detection. *Agronomy*, 14, 4, 673, 2024 Mar 26.

5

Early Detection of Breast Cancer Using Multi-Modal Deep Learning Framework

Salma Mohammad* **and Mohammed Ali Shaik**

School of CS &AI, SR University, Warangal, Telangana, India

Abstract

Breast cancer is one of the most prevalent and deadly diseases affecting women worldwide. A prompt and accurate diagnosis is essential for reducing mortality and improving patient outcomes. Traditional diagnostic approaches often rely on a single data source, which can result in modality-specific constraints that frequently diminish diagnostic accuracy. In this research, we provide MMDL, a new approach to breast cancer detection. Combining clinical data with mammography images and histological sections is the goal of this approach. To place clinical data in context and extract spatial information from imaging modalities, the suggested method employs transformer-based encoders and convolutional neural networks (CNNs). The diagnostic patterns can be better understood by merging all of these representations into one latent space. When tested on the DDSM and BreaKHis benchmark datasets, the MMDL model achieved better results than the top unimodal approaches in terms of F_1 score, recall, accuracy, and precision. In order to improve early breast cancer screening, the results indicate that multi-modal learning, which helps doctors recognize complicated morphological and clinical data, may be useful.

Keywords: Multi-modal network, deep learning, CNN, breast cancer

**Corresponding author*: 2403C50284@sru.edu.in

R. Nidhya, A. Dineshkumar, Sheng-Lung Peng, S. Karthik and S. Balamurugan (eds.) Neuro-Symbolic Artificial Intelligence: Concepts & Applications, (79–100) © 2026 Scrivener Publishing LLC

5.1 Introduction

Breast cancer is the most common and deadly kind of cancer among women. The World Health Organization (WHO) projects that by 2022, breast cancer would result in the deaths of over 685,000 women. Precise diagnosis and prompt identification are essential to enhance therapy accessibility and improve survival rates. Distinguishing benign from malignant tumors is challenging due to the intricacies of breast cancer, including changes in tissue architecture and the limitations of single-modality diagnostic methods [1]. This complexity has not been sufficiently resolved by enhanced diagnostic imaging and pathology, notwithstanding recent progress.

Medical practitioners employ a variety of diagnostic techniques, including mammography, ultrasonography, clinical examination, and histomorphology, to identify breast cancer [2]. The mammogram, one of the most popular cancer screening procedures, looks for indications of the disease using non-invasive imaging. However, thick breast tissue or small tumors may reduce their efficacy and cause unexpected side effects [3]. Histological testing, which examines tissue samples under a microscope, is the only way to make a conclusive diagnosis of cancer. The challenges of histomorphology study are exacerbated by surgical intervention, high levels of physical activity, and interobserver variability. Age, hormone imbalances, genetic predisposition, and a personal or family history of the disease can all raise a person's risk of getting cancer [4]. Although it is known that this is not an exhaustive list, this research has discovered that relying solely on these tactics has produced positive outcomes [5].

Deep learning can assist in cancer diagnosis, classification, and segmentation when used in medical image processing [6]. Convolutional neural networks (CNNs) excel at extracting spatial information from high-dimensional visual data. These are slides utilized for mammography and histology. Existing procedures are insufficient as each patient possesses distinct therapeutic requirements [7–9]. Although algorithms integrating contextual, imaging, and clinical data are designed to enhance diagnostic accuracy, they often underperform.

In this research, just the MMDL system is examined. When mammography, histological slides, and a wealth of clinical data are combined, the accuracy of breast cancer screening is significantly increased. Multimodal data fusion seeks to reduce false positives and increase classification accuracy by generating unique and comprehensive feature representations. Each modality has its own subnetwork of deep neurons which uses transformer-based encoders for clinical tabular data and convolutional neural networks for visual modalities. Using methods like residual merging, fusion, and attention-based concatenation, data from many modalities can be standardized and combined to produce a consistent latent space. Fully integrated layers increase both cancer classification and image quality.

5.2 Related Work

Authors [10] present a deep learning approach for classifying H&E-stained breast tissue images provided for the BACH challenge. The photos are categorized into four categories: normal tissue, benign lesion, *in situ* cancer, and invasive malignancy. Patches exhibiting low nuclear concentrations or non-epithelial areas are eliminated based on nuclear density. This method enables the exclusion of uninformative regions of photographs, as the epithelium is the site where visual indicators of cancer are most prominent, in contrast to random or grid sampling. Each area in an image exhibiting elevated nuclear density is classified into one of the four previously specified categories. The predominant votes from the nuclear classifications partially influence the image's overall classification. This article [11] presents a deep learning methodology for classifying breast cancer into multiple categories using a convolutional neural network model. In addition to diagnosing malignancy, the proposed approach aims to predict specific breast cancer subtypes, such as fibroadenoma and lobular carcinoma. Experiments using histopathology images from the BreakHis dataset showed that the DenseNet CNN model outperformed existing methods in multi-class breast cancer classification with 95.4% accuracy.

This research [12] employs a neural network and the Wisconsin Breast Cancer Database to demonstrate a deep learning approach for breast cancer diagnosis. Deep learning methodologies are widely used in modern computer vision, image processing, natural language processing, and medical diagnostics applications. This study demonstrates that utilizing deep learning technology with the Wisconsin Breast Cancer Database substantially improves breast cancer diagnosis accuracy, achieving a rate of 99.67%. The study has three components. First, the dataset was partitioned into training and testing subsets. Second, graphical representations were employed for data visualization. Third, the dataset was amalgamated, and preprocessing techniques were applied to enhance and normalize the data. Eleven preprocessed features were used in this study to identify breast cancer. We generated a scaled dataset using various preprocessing techniques, including label encoding, normalization, and standard scaling, before training the model and achieving the desired accuracy. This study evaluates deep learning algorithms against alternative methodologies to demonstrate the superiority of our proposed system.

The CNN Improvements for Breast Cancer Classification (CNNI-BCC) [13] model employs a trained deep learning neural network to distinguish breast cancer subtypes for diagnostic purposes. However, the preparation and imaging procedures require substantial processing power. This paper introduces a deep learning model that can identify breast cancer in digital mammograms of varying density. Three feature selection techniques were evaluated: low-variance feature removal, univariate feature selection, and recursive feature elimination. The authors [14] present a unique computer-aided diagnostic method for diagnosing breast cancer applicable in both binary and multi-class settings. It integrates deep neural networks (ResNet-18 [15], ShuffleNet [16], and Inception-V3 [17]) with transfer learning, utilizing the publicly available BreakHis dataset.

The goal of this study [18] is to develop and evaluate a deep learning model, called BCCNN, for identifying and classifying breast cancer into eight distinct categories. Generative adversarial network approaches were employed to enhance magnetic resonance imaging images in the Kaggle dataset at magnifications of 40×, 100×, 200×, and 400×. The BCCNN model was evaluated against five pretrained ImageNet models: Xception, Inception V3, VGG16, MobileNet, and ResNet50. The assessment criteria included accuracy, precision, recall, and the F_1 score. The results indicate that image resolution at 400× magnification has improved markedly, enhancing classification performance. Preprocessing approaches highlight the importance of data quality by refining and balancing the data, thereby improving model accuracy. Overall, the results suggest that the proposed BCCNN method can facilitate multi-class breast cancer diagnosis.

Authors [19] introduce the fundamental principles of a deep learning model-based approach to predicting breast cancer risk. The proposed method uses the InceptionResNetV2 deep learning architecture with transfer learning. Our experimental study on a breast cancer dataset yielded exceptional model performance, achieving a 91% accuracy rate. Our strategy for improving breast cancer risk assessment scores using risk indicators outperforms current techniques. Warning signals improve the precision of deep learning systems. This document lists the variables associated with breast cancer risk and provides details about the characteristics, limitations, and appropriate uses of each risk assessment approach. It also addresses the increasing influence of deep learning on risk assessment.

This study [20] combines two modern deep learning methodologies, YOLO and U-Net, to improve the design of deep convolutional neural networks. The primary objective of mammography is to detect abnormalities in the breast. Several key performance metrics were employed to evaluate the method's effectiveness. The accuracy metrics, F_1 score, ROC curve, and R-squared error were computed using the publicly accessible MIAS dataset. The model outperformed its rivals with a 98.6% AUC and a 93.0% detection accuracy. With a 97% R-squared value, the model's exceptional localization ability was evident. The results suggest that deep learning could improve the efficiency and accuracy of breast cancer screening. Our proposed methods could be used to enhance breast lesion self-identification and classification. The need for pathologists is steadily declining, even if breast cancer screening has become more accurate and efficient. Improved detection and treatment of breast cancer could improve health outcomes.

5.3 Methodology

5.3.1 Data Acquisition and Preprocessing

Digital Database for Screening Mammography (DDSM): Mammography is a widely accepted and utilized diagnostic modality within the field of DDSM. The package under consideration includes a series of diagnostic digital mammograms, accompanied by the relevant pathology report. Rare alterations in breast density have been known to be indicative of a benign or malignant tumor. It is reasonable to hypothesize that this version will likely exacerbate diagnostic problems. In image-based classification systems, the type and position of lesions yield essential information. The DDSM database contains 2,620 scanned mammography studies. This viewpoint asserts that "pathology" includes the full spectrum of human emotions, ranging from pleasure to sorrow.

BreaKHis Dataset: A total of 7,909 images of biopsy specimens that have undergone histological examination are currently available in the BreaKHis database. A meticulous examination of the images provided by the 82 patients revealed no instances of abnormality. To facilitate the examination of the tumors, a range of magnifications from 40× to 400× was utilized. The tumor's malignant potential was assessed by means of a battery of tests. The application's vast visual cellular structure data facilitates rapid discrimination among distinct cancer kinds. It is imperative to examine the model from multiple angles prior to any modifications.

5.3.2 Preprocessing

The clinical data, breast cancer imaging, and tissue samples evaluated histologically are all part of the medical records that meet specified standards. A multitude of obstacles exist that hinder the utilization of diverse modalities for breast cancer screening, including intermodal interference, data shortage, and data excess. In order to enhance the data's suitability for deep learning systems, a process of compression and normalization was employed.

A broad array of resolutions and formats exists for medical imaging. A structured deep learning system necessitates the modification of pixels' size and intensity distribution prior to their utilization.

The initial image represents the following:

$$I \in R^{HXWXC}$$

Here, H is the height, W is the width, and C is the number of channels. Pixel-wise normalization is as follows:

$$I_{norm} = \frac{I(x,y) - \mu}{\sigma}$$

The variable σ denotes the variability of the dataset, while the constant μ signifies the average pixel intensity. Min-max normalization is a widely used technique that ensures mammography intensity data falls within the range of [0,1] as follows.

$$I_{norm} = \frac{I(x,y) - I_{min}}{I_{max} - I_{min}}$$

Mammograms may exhibit inadequate contrast due to the examination of sensitive tissue. Histogram equalization allocates intensity levels more equitably, thereby enhancing contrast.

Let the image intensity histogram be $p(i)$, representing the probability of pixel value $i \in [0, L-1]$, where L is the total number of gray levels. The cumulative distribution function (CDF) is the following:

$$CDF(i) = \sum_{j=0}^{i} p(j)$$

The transformation applied is the following:

$$T(i) = L - 1.CDF(i)$$

High-frequency noise is often introduced during the acquisition of medical images. Denoising preserves essential structures while enhancing the clarity of features. The Gaussian filter is used to remove the noise in the images.

$$G(x, y) = \frac{1}{2\pi\sigma^2} \exp\left(-\frac{x^2 + y^2}{2\sigma^2}\right)$$

This thorough preparation strategy aims to synchronize and harmonize multi-modal breast cancer data in tabular and visual representations. Mathematical theories ensure consistent, semantically coherent input; minimal noise and regulated feature distributions for models. These initiatives significantly enhance training stability and model generalization, both of which are essential for accurate breast cancer diagnosis.

5.3.3 Mammogram Subnetwork

A subnetwork was developed to extract morphological and geographical information from mammography images. Understanding masses, calcifications, and structural irregularities is essential for early breast cancer detection. This subnetwork is a crucial component of the Multi-Modal Deep Learning (MMDL) system, focusing solely on visual patterns in radiological breast images shown in Figure 5.1.

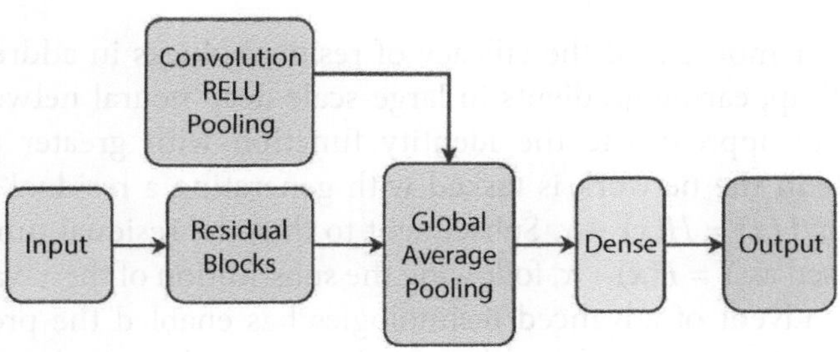

Figure 5.1 Proposed mammogram subnetwork.

The input to the mammography subnetwork is a preprocessed gray-scale or RGB image with dimensions 224×224×3, where 3 denotes the color channels. To stabilize training and enhance convergence, the image, denoted as $I \in R^{224}\times^{24}\times^{3}$, is normalized to the interval [0, 1].

The first stage of the network applies multiple convolutional layers to detect local spatial patterns.

$$F_l^k = \sigma(W_l^k * F_{l-1} + b_l^k)$$

where

- F_l^k is the k-th feature map at layer l,
- W_l^k is the convolution kernel for feature k,
- b_l^k is the bias term, and
- σ is the non-linear activation function (ReLU).

Batch normalization (BN) improves training stability by standardizing the input to each layer to have a variance of 1 and a mean of 0. BN adjusts the magnitude and displacement of the normalized output using learnable parameters (γ and β). The equation in question is ReLU(x) = max(0, x), which includes non-linearity into the activation function of a rectified linear unit. Batch normalization improves model performance, speeds up convergence, and resolves the disappearing gradient issue when combined with ReLU.

$$BN(x) = \gamma . \frac{x - \mu}{\sqrt{\sigma^2 + \epsilon}} + \beta$$
$$ReLU(x) = \max(0, x)$$

ResNet demonstrated the efficacy of residual blocks in addressing the issue of disappearing gradients in large-scale deep neural network plans. In order to approximate the identity function with greater precision, each node in the network is tasked with generating a residual mapping, denoted as $F(x) = H(x) - x$. Subsequent to this, the residual function can be expressed as $Y = F(x) + x$, following the substitution of the x-values with $F(x)$. The advent of advanced technologies has enabled the propagation of gradients to more profound layers within neural networks, a feat that was previously unattainable. Convolutional layers, batch normalization, and ReLU activation functions are the defining features of residual blocks.

This approach facilitates the expeditious and comprehensive training of networks.

$$y = F(x, W_i) + x$$

Feature down-sampling and feature pooling are the two main elements of convolutional neural network (CNN) methodologies. These methods reduce the spatial dimensions of feature maps while preserving a significant amount of data. Down-sampling can speed up processing and reduce the likelihood of overfitting by decreasing the number of variables. During feature extraction, it is a standard procedure to optimize each attribute within a given domain. This facilitates identifying the most important quality. This approach typically uses two-by-two and three-by-three grid configurations. For every integer m and n, max pooling identifies the maximum element in the array $I[m, n]$ using a stride of s and a kernel size of k. The output coordinate of the receiving field is denoted as $R(i, j)$. The formal definition of this concept is $F\_(m, n)$. Our method decreases the dimensions of the feature map while preserving its translation-invariant properties. Strided convolution is used for down-sampling instead of pooling when the convolutional kernel's stride exceeds 1. The model skillfully converts complex visual inputs into advanced semantic data in several ways.

$$MaxPool(I) = \max_{(m,n)\varepsilon R} I[m,n]$$

Later in the network, Global Average Pooling (GAP) is applied:

$$GAP(F) = \frac{1}{HXW} \sum_{i=1}^{H} \sum_{j=1}^{W} F_{i,j}$$

The Global Average Pooling (GAP) layer reduces the spatial dimensions of feature maps to a single vector by calculating the mean of each channel. This process generates a one-dimensional feature vector that accurately and succinctly characterizes the given data. Denoted by the symbol x, this vector comprises high-level features obtained using pooling algorithms, residual blocks, and multiple convolutional layers. We employ one or more fully connected layers to convert the GAP output into a more expressive and task-specific representation. The equation $z = \varphi(Wx + b)$, where W represents a trainable weight matrix and b denotes a bias vector, illustrates that the layers execute a linear transformation similar to that of a rectified linear unit. The network can identify intricate patterns that cannot be linearly separated due to the non-linearity of the activation function.

The feature embedding vector z, which belongs to the set R, captures the abstract semantic data from the mammogram, including shapes or lesion contours that are indicative of malignancy. Unlike the limited patterns of convolutional layers, this embedding integrates and examines the global context and interrelationships across the entire image. These deep layers condense intricate, high-order features into a comprehensible representation, acting as a conduit between the final classifier and the raw visual input. This embedding is essential in multi-modal systems because it must integrate with resources from other modalities, such as clinical data or histology images. Ensuring the integrated representation is both discriminative and complementary across modalities during model design and training enhances the model's diagnostic effectiveness.

The feature vector is flattened and passed through fully connected (dense) layers as follows:

$$z = \varphi(Wx + b)$$

5.3.4 Fusion Mechanism

Fusion techniques are essential for developing a coherent multi-modal deep learning model capable of reasoning across modalities. These techniques facilitate the integration of data from diverse sources, including structured clinical records, histology slides, and mammography pictures. Fusion uses complementary data from each modality to improve diagnostic accuracy, robustness, and generalizability. For example, histology provides cellular-level evidence, clinical data reveal patient-specific risk factors, and mammography detects structural abnormalities in breast cancer diagnoses. Since multi-modal systems encompass non-redundant and synergistic information, integrating several modalities is a critical design consideration.

$$Z_{fusion} = [\widehat{Z_m} \| \widehat{Z_h} \| \widehat{Z_c}]$$

The fusion procedure is based on the mathematical technique of combining feature vectors acquired independently by modality-specific subnetworks. This is feasible at multiple levels of abstraction. After low-level extraction, early fusion quickly concatenates or integrates features to generate a unified representation, which is then input into a common processing layer. The feature vectors of each modality should be denoted by $\widehat{z_m}$, $\widehat{z_h}$, and $\widehat{z_c}$. Classifying the composite characteristic is easier with supplementary processing *via* additional dense layers. While early fusion is user-friendly, it may fail to accurately represent intermodality interdependence and exhibit scale differences if not properly calibrated.

Advanced methodologies include tensor fusion, intermediate fusion techniques, attention-based approaches, and bilinear pooling. The prolonged duration of modality-specific subnetworks allows these techniques to provide greater abstraction prior to feature integration. Bilinear fusion produces a comprehensive interaction matrix by consolidating pairwise multiplicative interactions between modalities *via* an outer product operation. Tensor fusion extends this concept to a high-dimensional space, including unimodal, bimodal, and trimodal interactions. However, these methods can be computationally intensive, particularly when the embedding of each modality is complex. Compact pooling techniques, such as Multimodal Compact Bilinear (MCB) pooling, effectively reproduce high-rank interactions while maintaining practicality, expressiveness, and relevance.

Contemporary designs have achieved success through adaptive fusion techniques, such as gated or attention-based fusion, especially when addressing uncertainty and unpredictability in real-world data. Attention-based fusion facilitates contextual relevance, which enables the dynamic evaluation of the significance of each modality. The model prioritizes the most pertinent attributes for the predictive task based on the inputs provided. Gated fusion methodologies can efficiently reduce noise and enhance robustness due to their analogous soft gates that modulate the influence of each modality based on relevance. These dynamic approaches are especially beneficial in medical settings, where acquisition artifacts or inadequate patient data can limit or obstruct some modalities. Fusion techniques enable models to perform intricate reasoning across multiple input sources by consolidating various modality features into a coherent representation that encompasses both complementary and shared information.

5.3.5 Classification Model

In a binary classification problem, converting the integrated feature representation into an appropriate diagnostic output for distinguishing between benign and malignant requires a multi-modal deep learning architecture. The fusion procedure generates a singular feature vector z by utilizing abstracted clinical, histological, and mammographic data. A classification head with one or more fully connected layers uses this vector as input. These layers learn non-linear decision boundaries in the latent feature space, effectively differentiating between the diagnostic classes.

A non-linear activation function follows the affine translation of each dense layer to introduce non-linearity and increase the model's expressiveness.

$$h = \varphi(W_1 Z_{fusion} + b_1)$$

where W_1 and b_1 are the learnable weights and biases and $\varphi(\cdot)$ is a non-linear activation function such as ReLU or GELU. This hidden representation hhh is then passed through another fully connected layer followed by a sigmoid or softmax function to obtain the final probability score for each class:

$$\hat{y} = Softmax(W_2 h + b_2)$$

In the case of binary classification, the softmax reduces to a sigmoid function, outputting a scalar $\hat{y} \in [0,1]$ indicating the probability of malignancy.

The model utilizes a supervised learning strategy to minimize the cross-entropy loss between the predicted probabilities $\hat{y}$ and the actual labels y. This loss function enhances decision boundaries during back-propagation by encouraging the network to assign greater probabilities to relevant classes. The general classification head not only diagnoses but also synthesizes the multi-modal feature embeddings into a semantically coherent decision space that represents the intricate interactions among morphological, cellular, and clinical markers of breast cancer. Regularization methods such as batch normalization and dropout can be utilized in the dense layers to enhance training stability and mitigate overfitting.

5.4 Results and Discussion

During the implementation of the program on our computer, several issues were identified. The graphics processing unit (GPU) performance was augmented by employing a GeForce GTX 1050 with 8 GB of VRAM. The model's advanced processing capabilities enabled expeditious and effective alterations. The efficacy of our plan hinged upon our strict compliance with all applicable rules and regulations. The F_1 score encompasses a variety of evaluation metrics, including recall, accuracy, and precision.

Achieving exact precision is imperative when evaluating a model's performance on classification tasks. A pivotal metric for evaluating the precision of a model is the proportion of the dataset that was correctly predicted. Predictions within this domain are accurate. Results that are considered truly negative are designated as true negatives (TNs), while results that are truly positive are referred to as true positives (TPs). A classification error occurs when an object is incorrectly classified as positive (False Positive, Fp) or negative (False Negative, Fn).

$$\text{Accuracy} = \frac{Tp + Tn}{Tp + Fp + Fn + Tn}$$

The efficacy of the model can be assessed by comparing the expected and actual positive outcomes. The accuracy score is a metric used to evaluate the model's proficiency in identifying and classifying tumors.

$$\text{Precision} = \frac{Tp}{Tp + Fp}$$

The recall is a measure of a model's capacity to identify positive examples. The tumor prevalence was found to be significantly higher in the model. It is possible to ascertain the precise location of each tumor based on the information available.

$$\text{Recall} = \frac{Tp}{Tp + Fn}$$

The precision and recall metrics for a model are aggregated to calculate the F_1 score. F_1 scores serve to evaluate both recall and precision. The evaluation of models with varying precision-recall characteristics can facilitate a more profound comprehension of the intricacies inherent in the accuracy-recall trade-off.

$$F1 = \frac{Precision * Recall}{Precision + Recall}$$

5.4.1 Training and Testing Validation

The proposed model was evaluated using the BreaKHis dataset following its training on the DDSM dataset. A total of 20% of the images will be allocated for testing purposes, while a mere 8% will be utilized for training. The performance metrics for the DDSM dataset are displayed in Table 5.1. As illustrated in Table 5.2, the results of the training and testing phases for the BreaKHis dataset are presented.

As illustrated in Figure 5.2, the model demonstrates a high degree of efficacy in identifying cases of breast cancer when evaluated using the DDSM mammography dataset. The experimental results yielded an F_1 score of 99.5%, a retrieval rate of 99.8%, and an accuracy of 99.85%, employing the aforementioned set of training data. The model's capacity to differentiate between benign and malignant patterns has shown marked enhancement. The model displays remarkable predictive accuracy, even when operating with a considerably reduced training dataset. According to the most recent data, the accuracy, precision, and recall rates have

Table 5.1 Training and testing performance of DDSM dataset.

Metrics	Training data (%)	Testing data (%)
Accuracy	99.65	94.3
Precision	99.5	95.1
Recall	99.8	95
F_1 Score	99.5	94

Table 5.2 Training and testing performance of BreaKHis dataset.

Metrics	Training data (%)	Testing data (%)
Accuracy	99.55	94
Precision	99.4	95
Recall	99.72	95.2
F_1 Score	99.3	93.5

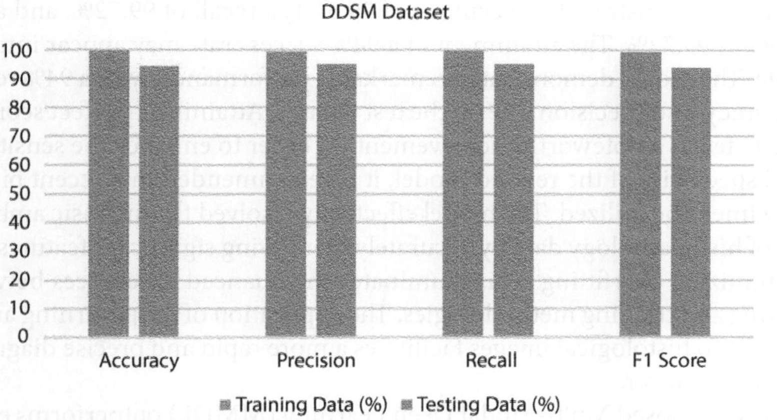

Figure 5.2 Training and testing performance of DDSM dataset.

reached 95%. The findings indicate that the F_1 score attained a remarkable 94%. When provided with data from both the training and test sets, the model demonstrated unexpectedly high performance on diagnostic tests. The multi-modal architecture of the mammography subnetwork has been shown to facilitate early breast cancer detection by enhancing preprocessing, training, and planning.

As illustrated in Figure 5.3, the model's analysis of intricate histological images from the BreaKHis dataset for breast cancer detection is demonstrated. The model differentiates between small, benign tumors and large, malignant tumors by analyzing intricate cellular patterns. The training

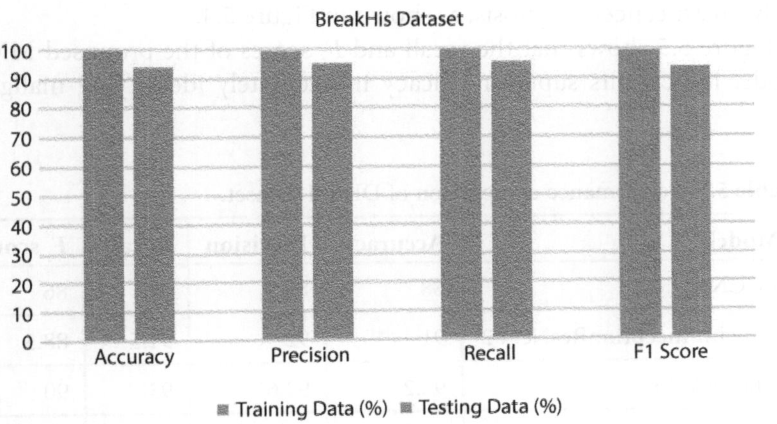

Figure 5.3 Training and testing performance of BreaKHis dataset.

dataset demonstrated an accuracy of 99.55%, a recall of 99.72%, and an F_1 score of 99.72%. The attainment of a 94% success rate may appear implausible. The model demonstrated remarkable performance, with a 94% recall, accuracy, and precision rate on the test dataset. Attaining a perfect score on the F_1 test is a noteworthy achievement. In order to enhance the sensitivity and specificity of the revised model, it is recommended that recent biopsy specimens be utilized. The model effectively resolved the intrinsic ambiguity of histopathology data by accurately identifying significant features and minimizing overfitting. This illuminates the nuanced differences between testing and training methodologies. The application of deep learning architecture to histological images facilitates a more rapid and precise diagnosis of breast cancer.

The proposed Multi-Modal Deep Learning (MMDL) outperforms existing models on the DDSM dataset, shown in Table 5.3. The BCCNN model uses convolutional architectures to achieve an 88% accuracy rate and an 89.5% precision rate in breast cancer diagnosis. Using advanced pretrained architectures for improved feature extraction, the InceptionResNetV2 model with transfer learning achieves 91% accuracy and 92% precision, significantly improving performance. Integrating Yolo and Unet demonstrates the advantages of combining object detection and segmentation for lesion localization, improving detection accuracy to 93.6% and precision to 92.2%. The MMDL model achieves a precision of 95.1% and an accuracy of 94.3%. It surpasses all previous methods due to its ability to learn from multiple modalities, including histology, clinical data, and mammograms. An integrated model could provide more precise and reliable estimations while identifying a wide array of diagnostic signals. Enhanced measurements demonstrate how multi-modal fusion can improve the precision of early breast cancer diagnosis, as shown in Figure 5.4.

Figure 5.5 shows that the recall and F_1 scores of the proposed MMDL model indicate its superior efficacy in accurately identifying malignant

Table 5.3 Performance comparison of DDSM dataset.

Models	**Accuracy**	**Precision**	**Recall**	**F_1 score**
BCCNN	88	89.5	89	86
TL with InceptionResNetV2	91	92	91.5	88.5
Unet + Yolo	92.2	93.6	93	90
MMDL	94.3	95.1	96	94

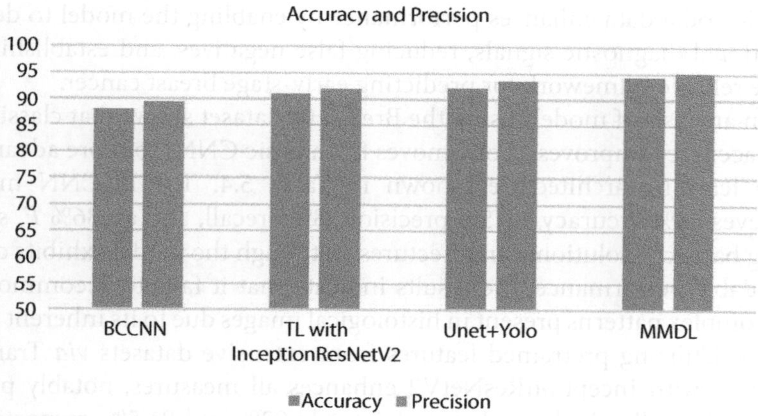

Figure 5.4 Performance of accuracy and precision in the DDSM dataset.

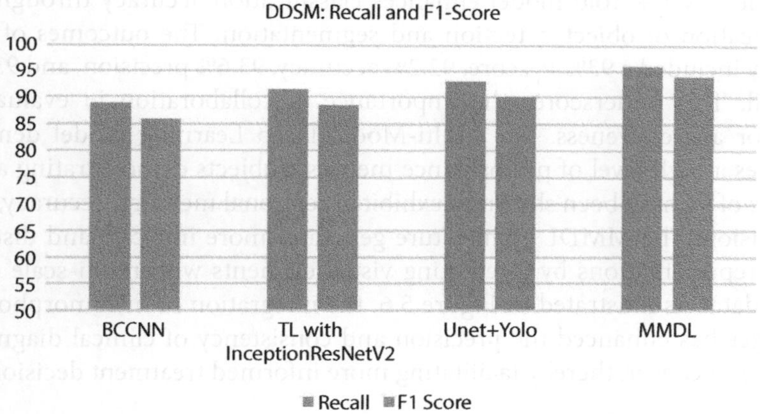

Figure 5.5 Performance of recall and F_1 Score in the DDSM dataset.

events compared to existing models using the DDSM dataset. Although the BCCNN model has adequate sensitivity, with an F_1 score of 86% and a recall of 89%, it does not achieve the ideal balance between accuracy and recall. ResNet V2's transfer learning capability is significantly improved by deep feature representations, resulting in a recall of 91.5% and an F_1 score of 88.5%. The Unet+Yolo framework achieved an F_1 score of 90% and a recall of 93% with enhanced detection techniques, improving tumor recognition and classification capabilities. The MMDL model has an exceptional ability to identify true positives, achieving an F_1 score of 94% and a maximum recall of 96%, while maintaining excellent overall classification quality.

Multi-modal data enhances performance by enabling the model to detect additional diagnostic signals, reducing false negatives, and establishing a more reliable framework for predicting early-stage breast cancer.

An analysis of models using the BreaKHis dataset shows that classification accuracy improves as one moves from basic CNNs to more advanced deep learning architectures shown in Table 5.4. The BCCNN model achieves 88% accuracy, 89.5% precision, 89% recall, and an 86% F_1 score using basic convolutional architectures. Although the model exhibits commendable performance, the results indicate that it fails to accommodate the complex patterns present in histological images due to its inherent simplicity. Utilizing pretrained features from extensive datasets *via* Transfer learning with InceptionResNetV2 enhances all measures, notably precision and recall, which reach approximately 92% and 91.5%, respectively. The F_1 score of 88.5% for minor morphological characteristics suggests the need for further efforts to balance sensitivity and accuracy.

The UNet + Yolo model enhances classification accuracy through the application of object detection and segmentation. The outcomes of this study included a 93% F_1 score, 92.2% accuracy, 93.6% precision, and 93.6% recall. This underscores the importance of collaboration in evaluating tumor aggressiveness. The Multi-Modal Deep Learning model demonstrates a high level of performance metrics. Subjects demonstrating an F_1 score of 94 have been shown to exhibit exceptional memory, accuracy, and precision. The MMDL architecture generates more intricate and distinctive representations by integrating visual elements with multi-scale clinical data. As illustrated in Figure 5.6, the integration of histomorphology images has enhanced the precision and consistency of clinical diagnoses of breast cancer, thereby facilitating more informed treatment decisions.

Table 5.4 Performance comparison of BreaKHis dataset.

Models	**Accuracy**	**Precision**	**Recall**	F_1 **score**
BCCNN	88	89.5	89	86
TL with InceptionResNetV2	91	92	91.5	88.5
Unet + Yolo	92.2	93.6	93	90
MMDL	94.3	95.1	96	94

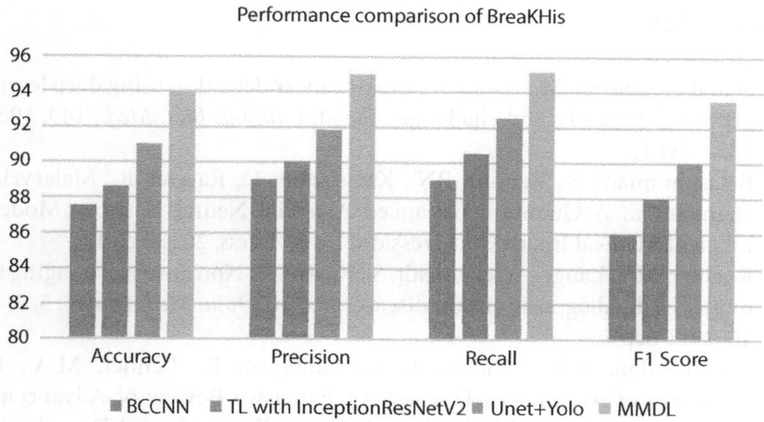

Figure 5.6 Performance comparison of BreaKHis dataset.

5.5 Conclusion

A multi-modal deep learning architecture that facilitates early, accurate, and scalable breast cancer diagnosis is presented in this proposed approach. Histopathological analysis, standardized clinical data, and mammography serve as the foundation for this proposal. It has been demonstrated that, for all evaluated variables, the incorporation of extra information from various modalities improves classification accuracy in comparison to unimodal baselines. Transformer encoders and convolutional neural networks enhance the system's comprehension of tumor features by identifying both low-level spatial patterns and high-level semantic links. Through the integration of many data representations into a single diagnostic model, the fusion technique improves forecast accuracy and reliability. Numerous investigations have confirmed its safety and efficacy. The efficacy of the method will be confirmed by further research using attention-based fusion, combining genetic information, and comprehensive multi-institutional clinical evaluations.

AI disclosure statement: The author confirms that no artificial intelligence (AI)-generated content or AI-assisted writing tools were used in the preparation of this chapter (including summaries and the abstract). All text, analysis, and conclusions are the result of the author's original work.

References

1. Dar, R.A., Rasool, M., Assad, A., Breast cancer detection using deep learning: Datasets, methods, and challenges ahead. *Comput. Biol. Med.*, 149, 106073, 2022 Oct 1.
2. Balasubramani, S., Renjith, P.N., Kavisankar, L., Rajavel, R., Malarvel, M., Shankar, A., A Quantum-Enhanced Artificial Neural Network Model for Efficient Medical Image Compression. *IEEE Access*, 2025 Feb 17.
3. Koehler, M.J., Lange-Asschenfeldt, S., Kaatz, M., Non-invasive imaging techniques in the diagnosis of skin diseases. *Expert Opin. Med. Diagn.*, 5, 5, 425–40, 2011 Sep 1.
4. Neelakandan, R.P., Kandasamy, R., Subbiyan, B., Bennet, M.A., Early Detection of Alzheimer's Disease: An Extensive Review of Advancements in Machine Learning Mechanisms Using an Ensemble and Deep Learning Technique. *Eng. Proc.*, 59, 1, 10, 2023 Dec 11.
5. Priyanka, K.S., A review paper on breast cancer detection using deep learning. *IOP Conf. Ser.: Mater. Sci. Eng.*, 1022, 1, 012071, 2021, IOP Publishing.
6. Zhu, Z., Wang, S.H., Zhang, Y.D., A survey of convolutional neural network in breast cancer. *Comput. Model. Eng. Sci.: CMES*, 136, 3, 2127, 2023 Mar 9.
7. Beeravolu, A.R., Azam, S., Jonkman, M., Shanmugam, B., Kannoorpatti, K., Anwar, A., Preprocessing of breast cancer images to create datasets for deep-CNN. *IEEE Access*, 9, 33438–63, 2021 Feb 11.
8. Chandran, V., Nidhya, R., Kumar, A.D., Thamaraiselvi, K., Retinal and cancer cell image segmentation for predicting the diseased images, in: *2014 International Conference on Green Computing Communication and Electrical Engineering (ICGCCEE)*, 2014, March, IEEE, pp. 1–6.
9. B. B K, K. K, Smilarubavathy, G., Early Detection of Pancreatic Cancer using Machine Learning Algorithm. *2024 5th International Conference on Mobile Computing and Sustainable Informatics (ICMCSI)*, Lalitpur, Nepal, pp. 202–205, 2024, doi: 10.1109/ICMCSI61536.2024.00036.
10. Golatkar, A., Anand, D., Sethi, A., Classification of breast cancer histology using deep learning, in: *Image Analysis and Recognition: 15th International Conference, ICIAR 2018, Póvoa de Varzim, Portugal, June 27–29, 2018, Proceedings 15*, Springer International Publishing, pp. 837–844, 2018.
11. Nawaz, M., Sewissy, A.A., Soliman, T.H., Multi-class breast cancer classification using deep learning convolutional neural network. *Int. J. Adv. Comput. Sci. Appl.*, 9, 6, 316–32, 2018 Jun 1.
12. Khuriwal, N. and Mishra, N., Breast cancer diagnosis using deep learning algorithm, in: *2018 International Conference on Advances in Computing, Communication Control and Networking (ICACCCN)*, 2018 Oct 12, IEEE, pp. 98–103.
13. Khalid, A., Mehmood, A., Alabrah, A., Alkhamees, B.F., Amin, F., AlSalman, H., Choi, G.S., Breast cancer detection and prevention using machine learning. *Diagnostics*, 13, 19, 3113, 2023 Oct 2.

14. Abhisheka, B., Biswas, S.K., Purkayastha, B., A comprehensive review on breast cancer detection, classification and segmentation using deep learning. *Arch. Comput. Methods Eng.*, 30, 8, 5023–52, 2023 Nov.
15. Bukhari, S.U., Syed, A., Khalid, S.S., Shah, S.S., The histological diagnosis of breast cancer by employing scale invariant ResNet 18 with spatial supervised technique, in: *Proceedings of the 14th IEEE/ACM International Conference on Utility and Cloud Computing Companion*, 2021 Dec 6, pp. 1–6.
16. Zhang, T., Pan, L., Yang, Q., Yang, G., Han, N., Qiao, S., TumorDet: A Breast Tumor Detection Model Based on Transfer Learning and ShuffleNet. *Curr. Bioinf.*, 19, 2, 119–28, 2024 Feb 1.
17. Al Husaini, M.A., Habaebi, M.H., Gunawan, T.S., Islam, M.R., Elsheikh, E.A., Suliman, F.M., Thermal-based early breast cancer detection using inception V3, inception V4 and modified inception MV4. *Neural Comput. Appl.*, 34, 1, 333–48, 2022 Jan.
18. Abunasser, B.S., Al-Hiealy, M.R., Zaqout, I.S., Abu-Naser, S.S., Convolution neural network for breast cancer detection and classification using deep learning. *Asian Pac. J. Cancer Prev.: APJCP*, 24, 2, 531, 2023.
19. Humayun, M., Khalil, M.I., Almuayqil, S.N., Jhanjhi, N.Z., Framework for detecting breast cancer risk presence using deep learning. *Electronics*, 12, 2, 403, 2023 Jan 12.
20. Rahman, M.M., Jahangir, M.Z., Rahman, A., Akter, M., Nasim, M.A., Gupta, K.D., George, R., Breast cancer detection and localizing the mass area using deep learning. *Big Data Cogn. Comput.*, 8, 7, 80, 2024 Jul 16.

6

Neuro-Symbolic Transfer Learning Model with Logic-Based Intrusion Detection System in IoT

Deepak V.[1], S. John Justin Thangaraj[2], Yogaraja C. A.[3]* and Iswariya S.[4]

[1]Department of Computer Science and Engineering, Koneru Lakshmaiah Education Foundation, Vaddeswaram, AP, India
[2]Saveetha School of Engineering, Saveetha Institute of Medical and Technical Sciences (SIMATS), Chennai, India
[3]Department of Information Technology, School of Computer Science Engineering and Information Systems, Vellore Institute of Technology, Vellore, India
[4]Department of Electronics and Communication Engineering, Koneru Lakshmaiah Education Foundation, Vaddeswaram, AP, India

Abstract

The growth of Internet of Things (IoT) networks, characterized by their diversity, dispersion, and limited resources, has raised significant security concerns. Standard intrusion detection systems (IDS) may have difficulty recognizing complex and evolving attack patterns in these scenarios. This study presents an innovative neuro-symbolic transfer learning model, integrated with a logic-based intrusion identification algorithm, to enhance risk identification in IoT systems. This strategy reduces the need for extensive labeled datasets by using bidirectional long short-term memory (BiLSTM) to effectively extract temporal features from network traffic and by using transfer learning to disseminate information across analogous domains. Incorporating symbolic logic concepts into the brain model creates a neuro-symbolic hybrid that combines rule-based irregularities with statistical patterns. This improves cognitive reasoning abilities and interpretive clarity. An analytical IDS categorizes data by threat to facilitate retrieval. The proposed approach improves the F_1 score, as well as precision, recall, and accuracy, across many attack vectors, including denial-of-service (DoS), man-in-the-middle (MITM), deception, reconnaissance, and data exfiltration. This approach is based

**Corresponding author*: yogaraja.ca@vit.ac.in

R. Nidhya, A. Dineshkumar, Sheng-Lung Peng, S. Karthik and S. Balamurugan (eds.) Neuro-Symbolic Artificial Intelligence: Concepts & Applications, (101–120) © 2026 Scrivener Publishing LLC

on a thorough analysis of existing IoT data. Real-time IoT systems integrate neuro-symbolic thinking with transfer learning to improve the scalability, adaptability, and accessibility of devices. Ultimately, this will yield more accurate detection.

Keywords: IoT security, IDS, attacks, LSTM, neuro-symbolic, transfer learning

6.1 Introduction

The Internet of Things (IoT) is transforming the way we use technology by connecting billions of smart devices online. It enables users to share information across various fields, including industrial control systems, smart homes, healthcare, and transportation. Although technology has increased our productivity and intellect, it has also made us more vulnerable to cyberattacks. Various attack vectors, such as denial-of-service (DoS) attacks, man-in-the-middle (MITM) attacks, spoofing, reconnaissance, and data exfiltration, can compromise IoT devices. This is due to dispersion, resource scarcity, and inadequate management. Developing effective intrusion detection systems (IDS) to protect IoT devices is a critical focus of contemporary science and technology [1].

However, signature- and anomaly-based intrusion detection systems are inadequate for Internet of Things environments because they cannot comprehend complex behaviors, scale appropriately, or adapt to novel attack patterns. IoT networks collect an extensive array of data; some of which may not require full comprehension in every context. Therefore, it is essential to develop IDS models that can adapt to novel attack strategies and perform well in various settings. In machine learning [2] and deep learning [3], long short-term memory (LSTM) networks, a category of recurrent neural networks, have demonstrated significant potential for identifying patterns in temporal network traffic [4]. However, the lack of transparency and reliance on data in *k*-nearest neighbor and neural-based algorithms may make them difficult to use in practical situations. This complicates the assessment of their reliability in critical systems.

After these constraints were removed, neuro-symbolic systems received significant scientific attention [5]. These systems integrate symbolic logic with brain architecture. These models aim to combine the data-learning capabilities of neural networks with the logical precision and wide range of applications of symbolic methods. In deep learning systems, rule-based reasoning is more effective for information retrieval and object recognition [6].

This holds equal significance in the Internet of Things, where security is paramount. This approach uses pre-existing data from various IoT environments *via* transfer learning. However, this approach requires prolonged retraining durations and annotated datasets.

This research introduces two innovations: a logic-based intrusion detection system for IoT device networks and a novel neuro-symbolic transfer learning framework. The system uses a bidirectional long short-term memory (BiLSTM) architecture to rapidly extract temporal information from IoT-generated traffic data. Integrating historical and predictive data effectively allows for the identification of intricate, bidirectional traffic patterns. Transfer learning improves IoT performance by altering the representation of qualities across multiple locations. The logically grounded inference layer of the BiLSTM model improves object recognition. This layer analyzes semantic and contextual patterns in data to identify issues and distinguish between different types of intrusions. It accomplishes this by employing a set of widely recognized symbols. Symbolic logic improves system robustness and comprehensibility by offering rational arguments and warnings about identified risks. Integrating neural probabilities with logic-based confidence ratings establishes a novel cognitive strategy that enhances the accuracy and adaptability of existing methods.

To gain a comprehensive understanding of the proposed strategy, we analyze IoT data from various hazardous areas. We evaluate the system's performance using additional metrics, such as precision, accuracy, recall, and F_1 score. The neuro-symbolic transfer learning system has two primary advantages. First, it can address a broader spectrum of attacks, including complex ones such as deception and data exfiltration. Second, the logic-based component of IoT security monitoring streamlines the solution and reduces false positives, addressing two critical issues. This article outlines the development of a basic intrusion detection system that can be further enhanced. It employs deep learning, transfer learning, and symbolic logic. Enhancing the sophistication and reliability of cybersecurity solutions for future IoT implementations can address several critical issues in IoT security. This can be achieved by improving the adaptability, precision, and clarity of their defect detection capabilities.

The rest of the paper is as follows: Section 6.2 discusses the various IDS detection models, Section 6.3 describes the Neuro-Symbolic Transfer Learning and BiLSTM Model, and the results and discussion are discussed in Section 6.4. Finally, Section 6.5 concludes the overview of the paper and future work.

6.2 Literature Review

A convolutional neural network and long short-term memory network model [7] is used to efficiently extract entropy and compute compression on unencrypted, real-time HTTP data, utilizing normalized Unicode letter encoding for spatial feature learning. To demonstrate the model's effectiveness, we conducted numerous tests on two publicly accessible datasets: CSIC-2010 and CICIDS2017. AI-IDS distinguishes between benign data and sophisticated attacks, including concealed or encoded threats and anomalous patterns, by classifying payloads as true or false positives. Inspired by previous successes, this scalable and adaptable system was constructed with Docker images that segregate user-defined functions into independent images. Furthermore, it facilitates the formulation of Snort rules for signature-based intrusion detection systems. Through continuous training, the computer can accurately forecast malicious activities and precisely evaluate upcoming internet threats.

A novel generalized performance measure [8] has been developed to evaluate and compare the effectiveness of AI-driven supervised classifiers. A variety of tests and performance metrics were employed to obtain this measurement. Utilizing a segment of the KDD Cup 1999 benchmark data for training and testing objectives facilitated the assessment of diverse classifier performances. The KDD dataset comprises calculated metrics, network traffic logs, supplementary components, and other items collected from various sources. This study examines the efficacy of supervised AI classifiers using several performance criteria. Based on the study's authentic findings, the Tagged Tree-J48 classifier is the most reliable and beneficial. Neural networks, in conjunction with MLP, Bagged Tree-J48, and Naïve Bayes, demonstrate robust performance in R2L attack classification. Bagged Tree-J48 and JRip are both proficient at detecting user-to-root (U2R) intrusions, denial of service (DoS) attacks, and queries. The results suggest which classifiers are necessary for detecting intrusions within a large group. Through meticulous analysis of empirical data, it may be possible to determine which classifiers are most appropriate for specific attack types. This study emphasizes relevant research trajectories and demonstrates the application of AI-based classifiers for intrusion detection.

The research presents [9] a dynamic model for an intelligent intrusion detection system that uses a particular type of artificial intelligence. This approach uses fuzzy logic, neural networks, and network profiling to extract data directly from networks. The three primary types of hybrid threat detection are host-based, usage-based, and anomaly-based.

Fuzzy logic facilitates the formulation of if-then statements that distinctly delineate security issues. Neural networks and self-organizing maps are employed to assess host vulnerabilities. Identifying these vulnerabilities will allow for the future diversion of traffic from its original source. Both methodologies are necessary for obtaining information regarding system audits and network traffic.

This work [10] examines the innovative application of ensembles in machine learning for intrusion detection. The CICIDS-2017 dataset features were developed to improve classification accuracy and reduce false positives. The intrusion detection system employed in this work utilizes machine learning techniques, including support vector machines, random forests, and decision trees. After training, the ensemble technique's voting classifier achieved an accuracy rate of 96.25%. The LIME approach improves the reliability and comprehensibility of black-box intrusion detection systems within Explainable AI. Test results show that XAI-LIME outperforms other methods when generating responses and explanations.

Peddabachigari *et al.* [11] proposed methods for using hybrid intelligent systems to detect intrusions. They used the KDD Cup 99 intrusion dataset to evaluate the effectiveness of new intrusion detection algorithms. The researchers examined temporal correlation and sparse maximum likelihood estimation. Subsequently, they devised an ensemble methodology that integrates a support vector machine with a decision tree. This approach uses commonly employed classifiers, such as decision trees and support vector machines. The DT algorithm outperformed Probe, U2R, and R2L in all aspects. The hybrid DT-SVM algorithm either outperforms or matches the performance of the conventional SVM technique. The ensemble method was effective for both the R2L and Probe categories. The Probe class achieved complete accuracy with the ensemble method. Consequently, other classes can achieve complete accuracy when utilized with the appropriate base classifier. The optimal approach is to develop a hierarchical, intelligent intrusion detection system that effectively integrates advanced, individual base classifiers with ensemble methodologies.

Li *et al.* [12] proposed the ditto design to enhance the durability and fairness of federated learning systems. A statistical study indicates that attack resistance involves resource competition within heterogeneous networks, which are distinguished by uniform device performance. To mitigate these constraints, we propose a scalable solution that utilizes the Ditto framework. To determine whether the Ditto framework could offer robustness and fairness, we conducted a theoretical analysis of a set of linear problems. The study provided statistical data indicating that Ditto outperforms novel customization strategies in producing models that are more accurate, robust, and equitable than conventional baselines.

Mohseni *et al.* [13] evaluated the feasibility of incorporating machine learning safety into outdoor applications and activities, as well as the associated constraints. First, we assess the reliability of machine learning algorithms based on established safety standards and discuss their limitations in unregulated open environments. The concluding category of methodologies is run-time error detection. Three solutions facilitated the attainment of ML dependability objectives: augmented run-time error detection, a more secure design, and greater model performance and resilience. The objective of machine learning safety research is to mitigate the long-term hazards associated with these technologies. Relevant scenarios include those in which general machine learning skills surpass safety restrictions or where safety concerns are anticipated to become more complex over the coming decade.

The Feature Attention-based Extended Convolutional Capsule Network (FA-ECCN) model [14] predicts normal, drowsy, distracted, fatigued, aggressive, and impaired driving behaviors using feature attention. The binary fire hawks-based optimized link state routing protocol manages traffic based on predetermined trust levels. Binary fire hawks optimization evaluates node and connection stability to determine the optimal routing strategy. Ultimately, the security of vehicle *ad hoc* network data storage has improved due to developments in blockchain storage. Delegated practical Byzantine fault tolerance enables the validation process. The proposed approach utilizes trust-based routing and blockchain technology to securely transmit data to neighboring vehicles, enabling accurate predictions of driver behavior.

This study [15] presents a combined IP traceback methodology that reduces overhead. Using the 16-bit ID field in the packet header makes it easier to designate packets more precisely, and the hash table helps with packet logging. Path reconstruction begins at the original source border router using the packet's mark value. Unlike analogous strategies, the proposed methodology has undergone empirical validation. Many studies on network intrusion detection systems (NIDS) have been conducted to mitigate these risks. Of all the models designed to enhance NIDS efficacy, those that use artificial intelligence-based anomaly detection represent the most effective technology utilized in NIDS. However, artificial intelligence algorithms cannot identify network vulnerabilities or comprehend hostile activity without balanced data [16]. This study introduces an innovative, AI-based NIDS designed to address data imbalance issues and improve the efficacy of prior systems. To address the aforementioned issue, we used an advanced generative model capable of producing reliable synthetic data for moderate assault flow. Our focus was on deep learning models, utilizing autoencoders and generative adversarial networks, with an emphasis on reconstruction error assessed through a Wasserstein distance metric.

This article introduces a deep neural network [17] for real-time network intrusion detection. It also provides an evaluation of popular machine learning models and an advanced preprocessing technique. Preprocessing includes univariate analysis, feature selection, outlier management, data standardization, and principal component analysis (PCA)-based dimensionality reduction. The dataset was partitioned into training and testing sets at an 80:20 ratio. ET outperforms the three conventional models (GB, DT, and ET) in terms of accuracy, precision, recall, F_1 score, and kappa.

This article [18] presents Deep-IDS, an innovative application of deep learning in intrusion detection systems (IDSs). It uses a 64-unit Long Short-Term Memory (LSTM) [19] network to analyze the CIC-IDS2017 dataset. The optimal architecture of Deep-IDS renders it a model framework for establishing edge servers. Deep-IDS protects against denial-of-service, replay, brute-force, and man-in-the-middle attacks between Internet of Things (IoT) nodes and the Internet. This study examines the trade-off between the false alarm rate (FAR) and the detection rate (DR) to improve Deep-IDS's efficacy in real-time applications.

6.3 Neuro-Symbolic Transfer Learning + BiLSTM Model

The Neuro-Symbolic Transfer Learning (NSTL) model uses a logic-driven intrusion detection technique to address critical security, scalability, and understanding challenges in Internet of Things (IoT) networks. Traditional intrusion detection systems are ineffective in IoT settings due to their inability to manage emerging threats effectively, reach definitive findings, or generalize. Using deep neural networks for observation and symbolic logic for clarification helps us overcome these issues. Deep learning models that use transfer learning can identify intricate patterns in network traffic data. This is the most important section. A neurosymbolic reasoning module uses reasoning to facilitate decision-making. This hybrid approach improves the transparency and reliability of automated security systems by providing security analysts with the rationale behind each action. However, this exacerbates both novel and existing dangers.

The system incorporates neuro-symbolic cognition and uses logical reasoning to categorize and identify hazards. It processes data and uses transfer learning to attain cognitive attributes. First, unprocessed IoT traffic data is acquired from various sensors and peripheral devices. The disorderly and unstable nature of this data makes it distinctive. A crucial phase in preparing data for neural computing is integrating all components and ensuring their functionality. An IoT dataset from the industry enhances a transfer learning framework that is often trained as a recurrent or deep convolutional neural network. The neuro-symbolic layer of the brain uses first-order logic to generate outputs. This allows for the use of both rule-based and data-driven reasoning, which are two distinct methodologies for conveying information. A logic-based intrusion detection system (IDS) uses an inference engine and domain-specific rules to determine if a pattern is normal behavior or a potential incursion.

6.3.1 IoT Data Preprocessing

The efficacy of IoT data preprocessing is crucial for feature extraction and optimizing model performance. IoT traffic data encompasses a wide range of numerical and categorical information, typically generated by a combination of sensors, actuators, and communication protocols. However, this information may be disordered, insufficient, or susceptible to device variability. Our preprocessing methodology begins with cleansing and normalizing the data to address these issues. We apply mean imputation to numerical characteristics and mode imputation to missing values in categorical variables. Device identifiers and timestamps are examples of superfluous or nonessential data that can be eliminated or combined with vital, session-specific information. Outlier detection, a statistical method, is employed to prevent innocuous yet anomalous data from distorting the training process. This method uses z-score analysis and the interquartile range. Min-max scaling and z-score standardization are two normalization techniques that ensure attributes remain within a continuous range. These strategies reduce the generation of high-magnitude variables and facilitate neuronal convergence.

After purification, the attributes are altered and encoded to standardize the format of the dataset for neural and symbolic processing. One-hot encoding combined with label encoding can represent categorical attributes, such as protocol type, service type, and indicator status, depending on the attribute's cardinality and relevance. Transforming temporal data into numerical or periodic formats can identify session-level behaviors and timing anomalies. Two methodologies for selecting features that identify the most critical elements for intrusion detection are recursive feature elimination (RFE) and information gain ranking. The final feature vector serves as a representation of symbolic logic and an input for deep neural networks. Discrete identities and protocol types are transformed into logical predicates for rule-based inference. Meanwhile, packet size and connection duration serve as valuable inputs for neural embeddings. This preprocessing method allows the model to identify statistical patterns and logical relationships, creating a solid basis for the subsequent hybrid neuro-symbolic learning framework.

6.3.2 Transfer Learning-Based Feature Extractor

The Neuro-Symbolic Transfer Learning model primarily uses a Bidirectional Long Short-Term Memory (BiLSTM) network to discern temporal connections and contextual associations in Internet of Things (IoT) network data. Temporal trends demonstrate that IoT communication can be cooperative or adversarial. Conventional feedforward methods are unable to address these dependencies. Despite the constraints posed by a limited quantity of labeled IoT datasets, the model can comprehend the historical and prospective configurations of each input sequence within a transfer learning framework utilizing BiLSTM.

The input sequence is denoted as follows:

$$X = \{x_1, x_2, \ldots x_T\} \quad , x_t \in R^d$$

where T represents the sequence length (e.g., a temporal window of packets) and d denotes the dimensionality of the feature vector at each timestep (e.g., packet metadata). In the IoT domain, a pre-trained BiLSTM model built initially on a substantial cybersecurity dataset is enhanced through domain-adaptive training.

6.3.3 BiLSTM Feature Extraction

The BiLSTM network is distinctive among recurrent neural networks as it integrates both forward and backward dependencies. It effectively identifies temporal trends when presented with sequential data. IoT-based intrusion detection utilizes sequential network traffic data, leveraging contextual information and packet sequencing to identify anomalous activities. A bi-LSTM assesses the complete context of each data unit by employing both past-to-future (forward LSTM) and future-to-past (backward LSTM) methodologies.

The forward LSTM computes hidden states as follows:

$$\overrightarrow{h_t} \text{ from } t = 1 \text{ to } T$$

The backward LSTM computes hidden states as follows:

$$\overleftarrow{h_t} \text{from } t = T \text{ to } 1$$

The hidden state at time t is the concatenation:

$$h_t = [\overrightarrow{h_t}, \overleftarrow{h_t}] \in R^{2h}$$

Integrating the sequence's forward and backward hidden states provides a comprehensive examination of its temporal phases. Both methodologies are essential for identifying concealed or context-dependent cyberattacks on Internet of Things (IoT) devices. The model can identify correlations and provide recommendations based on anticipated and prior sequence elements. Bidirectional LSTMs outperform unidirectional LSTMs in the assessment of intricate temporal patterns and the representation of variations in Internet of Things connections. Unidirectional LSTMs can only detect one-way associations. The outputs of the BiLSTM layer are often combined with a fixed-length vector embedding to preserve essential sequence information. These embeddings generate strong feature representations that can be rapidly categorized or converted into symbolic inputs for logic-based intrusion detection systems. This concept improves intrusion detection precision by applying sequence modeling techniques and a comprehensive understanding of temporal dynamics. Bi-LSTMs are widely used for feature extraction.

Each LSTM cell updates its hidden state using the standard gating mechanisms:

$$f_t = \sigma(W_f x_t + U_f h_{t-1} + b_f)$$
$$i_t = \sigma(W_i x_t + U_i h_{t-1} + b_i)$$
$$i_o = \sigma(W_o x_t + U_o h_{t-1} + b_o)$$
$$\widetilde{c_t} = tanh(W_c x_t + U_c h_{t-1} + b_c)$$
$$c_t = f_t \odot c_{t-1} + i_t \odot \widetilde{c_t}$$
$$h_t = o_t \odot tanht(c_t)$$

where

- σ is the sigmoid activation.
- $\odot$ denotes element-wise multiplication
- W∗,U∗, and b∗ are the trainable parameters.

The final sequence embedding z∈R^{2h} is obtained by pooling over the time dimension:

$$z = Pooling\{h_1, h_2 \ldots h_T\}$$

6.3.4 Transfer Learning and Domain Adaptation

Let the source domain be $D_s = \{X_i^S, y_i^S\}$ and the target IoT domain $D_T = \{X_i^T, y_i^T\}$. The BiLSTM model is pre-trained on D_s, then fine-tuned on D_T. To mitigate distribution mismatch, we introduce Maximum Mean Discrepancy (MMD) as a regularization loss:

$$MMD^2(D_s, D_T) = \left\| \frac{1}{N_s} \Sigma_{i=1}^{N_s} \varphi(z_i^s) - \frac{1}{N_T} \Sigma_{i=1}^{N_T} \varphi(z_j^T) \right\|_H^2$$

where

- φ(z) maps the embedding into a Reproducing Kernel Hilbert Space

- H is the kernel space
- N_s and N_T are the sample sizes.

The total training objective is a weighted combination of cross-entropy classification loss and domain adaptation loss:

$$L_{Total} = L_{CE} + \lambda . L_{MMD}$$

$$L_{CE} = -\frac{1}{N_T}\sum_{j=1}^{N_T}\sum_{c=1}^{C} y_{j,c}^{T} \log(\hat{y}_{j,c}^{T})$$

$\hat{y}_{j,c}^{T}$ is the predicted probability for class c and λ is a trade-off parameter.

6.3.5 Neuro-Symbolic Integration

In artificial intelligence, neuro-symbolic integration refers to the combination of two distinct yet complementary paradigms: neuro-symbolic learning and symbolic reasoning. When creating the proposed architecture, these features must be considered to provide reliable, broadly applicable, and comprehensible intrusion detection for Internet of Things environments. Although conventional neural networks, particularly those using BiLSTM, can extract intricate statistical patterns and representations from raw data, they often operate as "black boxes," lacking transparency and interpretability. Symbolic reasoning systems based on precise logical concepts and ontologies that facilitate clear decision-making and rule enforcement face challenges when processing high-dimensional, noisy, or unstructured data. Integrating logical systems for explanation, consistency, and abstraction within neuro-symbolic architecture alongside neural networks for feature extraction yields favorable results.

A symbolic mapping function alters the elevated latent representations in a manner analogous to grouping, vector quantization, or tokenization. Feature extractors are synthesized into symbolic representations *via* transfer learning with BiLSTM. "Malformed payload" and "high-frequency packet transfer" refer to logical events. A compilation of first-order logic (FOL) rules, also known as propositional rules, is associated with symbolic inputs based on the system state, providing either intrusive or benign circumstances. The symbolic inference engine uses the framework's principles to derive logical conclusions.

$$IF\ s_1 \wedge s_2 \wedge \ldots \wedge s_n \Rightarrow Intrusion(type)$$

where $S_i \in \Sigma$ are the symbolic predicates derived from the neural features. For instance, the rule engine can infer a possible DoS attack if symbolic tokens indicate erratic port scanning and quick payload modification. To integrate neural confidence with symbolic reasoning, a confidence fusion function F is introduced, which combines the neural prediction probability $P_{NN}(y|x)$ and the symbolic rule score $R(y|s)$ into a unified decision score:

$$P_{final}(y|x) = \alpha.P_{NN}(y|x) + (1-\alpha).R(y|s)$$

Here, $\alpha \in [0,1]$ is a tunable parameter balancing the neural network's probabilistic confidence and the symbolic rule-based logic. $R(y|s)$ can be computed *via* rule matching or probabilistic soft logic (PSL), where each rule contributes to a cumulative confidence score.

Algorithm 6.1: Logic-Based Intrusion Detection Algorithm

Input:
Neural feature vector $z \in R^d$
Symbolic mapping function $\psi: R^d \rightarrow \Sigma$
Rule base $R=\{r_1, r_2, \ldots, r_n\}$
Neural prediction $P_{NN}(t)$ for each attack class $t \in Y$
Fusion parameter $\alpha \in [0,1]$
Output
Final predicted class label $\hat{y} \in Y$
Begin()
$\Sigma = \psi = \{s_1, s_2, \ldots s_k\}$
For each attack class $t \in Y, set\ P_{logic}(t) \leftarrow 0$
for each rule $r_i \in R$:
    if all predicates in rule $r_i \subseteq \Sigma$
    $\mu(r_i) \leftarrow \min\,(\mu(rs_i))$
    $P_{logic}(t) \leftarrow max\left(P_{logic}(t), \mu(r_i)\right)$
for each $t \in Y$
    $P_{final}(y|x) = \alpha.P_{NN}(y|x) + (1-\alpha).R(y|s)$
$\hat{y} = argmax_{t \in y} P_{final}(t)$

The Logic-Based Intrusion Detection Algorithm (LBIDA) is a neuro-symbolic framework component that uses symbolic reasoning. It examines the symbolic attributes of Internet of Things (IoT) data using formal logic to identify security vulnerabilities. It enhances the logical coherence, transparency, and comprehensibility of intrusion detection systems. It transcends basic statistical correlations, enabling individuals to make decisions based on established criteria. LBIDA is typically elucidated through propositional or first-order reasoning. The following findings were derived from an analysis of common attack tactics, traffic patterns, and protocol vulnerabilities in IoT systems. These criteria are easily fulfilled.

The LB-IDA uses deep learning architectures, such as BiLSTM, to convert neural feature vectors into symbolic predicates. The High_Traffic, Port_Scan, Payload_Anomaly, and Repeated_Access indicators all signify that a significant event is occurring. Symbolic mapping is the ability to associate abstract, high-level, logically assessed concepts with tangible, physical entities. The inference engine analyzes a series of logical assertions demonstrating how combinations of these predicates signify a specific threat. The primary caution is that "High traffic and malformed packets indicate a denial-of-service attack." These regulations allow the system to quickly identify patterns, making neural model confidence scores unnecessary.

LB-IDA provides confidence ratings for partial rule matching to help people understand complex or interconnected tasks. It uses fuzzy logic, probabilistic soft logic, and other soft logic concepts. These enable the system to function well despite prevalent challenges in Internet of Things environments, such as ambient noise, misinterpretations, and insufficient data. We combine individual data with our existing dataset using logic-based system outputs and neural network predictions. This approach yields the ultimate forecast by integrating neural probabilities with logical concept assessments. The logical component must explain the rationale behind the conclusions. Hence, cybersecurity frameworks are reliable and responsible.

The Logic-Based Intrusion Detection Algorithm uses symbolic intelligence for intrusion detection. By adhering to specific protocols, the system can identify vulnerabilities, respond to recognized attack patterns, and produce understandable results. The algorithm's ability to effectively manage the complex, dynamic, and limited resources of Internet of Things networks makes it a vital part of the hybrid neuro-symbolic architecture.

6.4 Results and Discussion

We evaluated the logic-based intrusion detection technique (LB-IDA) and the neuro-symbolic transfer learning model using publicly accessible IoT network traffic data. The primary dataset was UNSW-NB15, an extensive compilation of annotated traffic data. The most prevalent techniques employed to compromise real-world IoT devices include denial-of-service, distributed denial-of-service, man-in-the-middle attacks, spoofing, reconnaissance, and data exfiltration.

The raw network traffic data underwent preprocessing with standardization techniques, including data purification, label encoding, min-max or z-score scaling, and symbolic prediction extraction. Time-series data, including connection time, packet intervals, byte ratios, and flag statuses, was structured into sequences to facilitate integration into the BiLSTM model. The BiLSTM consists of both forward and backward LSTM layers with 128 hidden units. Using a deep layer and dropout regularization of 0.3 significantly reduced overfitting. Using cross-entropy with a learning rate of 0.001 simplifies the Adam optimizer and categorizes the loss function. The symbolic representation of the BiLSTM feature embeddings was constructed using discretization and threshold-based logical mappings. The rule engine used propositional logic and soft-matching techniques to identify complex attack fingerprints within symbolic patterns.

All experiments were conducted on a workstation with an Intel Core i7 CPU, an NVIDIA RTX 3080 GPU, and 32 GB of RAM. The workstation had Python 3.9 installed, along with TensorFlow and Keras. The training and testing datasets were divided in an 80:20 ratio to maintain class distribution during the assessment phases. Numerous studies pursued statistical robustness and generalizability through five-fold cross-validation. The neuro-symbolic transfer learning model's performance is measured using the accuracy, precision, recall, and F_1 score.

The Neuro-Symbolic Transfer Learning Model with Logic-Based Intrusion Detection exhibits remarkable reliability, achieving an average precision of 94.3% across all IoT attack categories in distinguishing benign traffic from genuine threats, as shown in Figure 6.1. The model achieved a maximum accuracy of 98.2% for regular traffic and showed exceptional performance against standard assaults, including Reconnaissance (94.7%) and DoS (96.4%). It effectively reduced false positives. Although Spoofing (93.5%) and MITM (92.8%) exhibit slightly diminished accuracy, the model's consistent performance demonstrates its capability to manage intricate and overlapping patterns. The 90.1% minimum accuracy for data exfiltration indicates that enhanced symbolic reasoning or feature augmentation is necessary for covert attacks. The model is appropriate for real-time IoT security applications as it enhances detection efficacy while maintaining interpretability and stability through logistic-based rules and BiLSTM feature extraction.

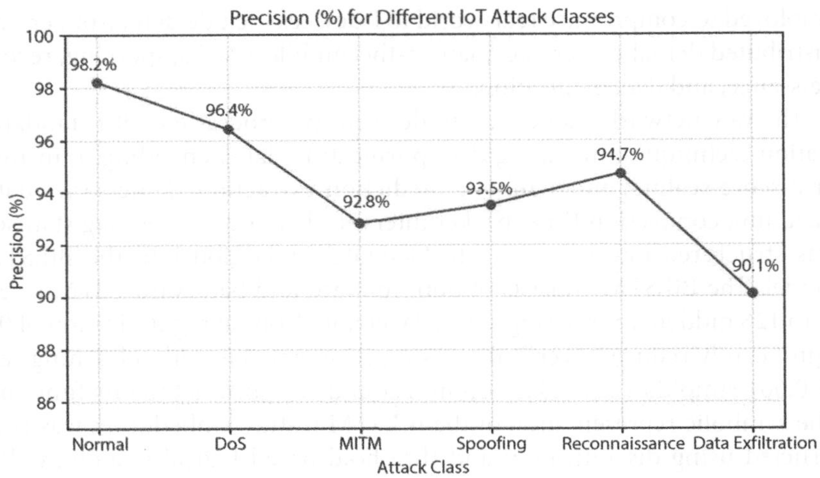

Figure 6.1 Precision of IoT attacks.

The proposed Neuro-Symbolic Transfer Learning Model boasts exceptional detection capabilities for various categories of IoT threats, as shown in Figure 6.2. It achieves an impressive 97.5% recall rate for typical traffic and demonstrates excellent accuracy in identifying legitimate activity. Reconnaissance has a memory rate of 92.1%, and denial-of-service attacks have a recall score of 95.7%, indicating the model's ability to identify

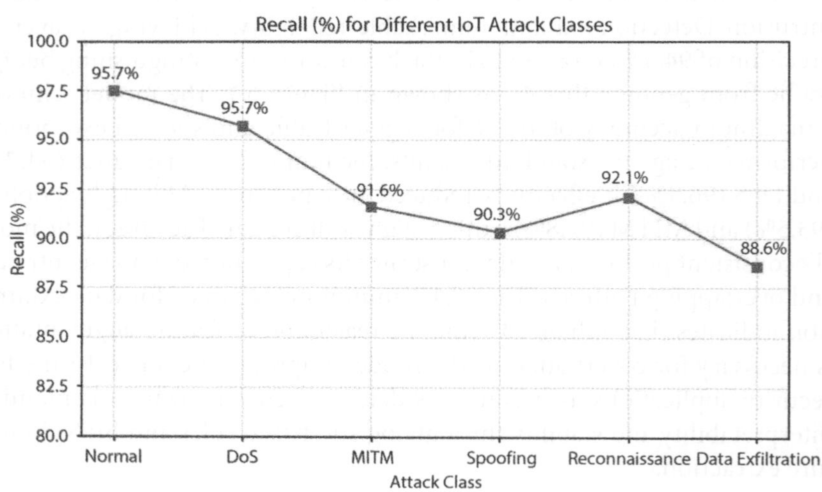

Figure 6.2 Recall of IoT attacks.

aggressive and anomalous threat behaviors. Man-in-the-middle attacks accounted for 91.6% of all attacks, followed by deception attacks at 90.3% and data exfiltration attacks at 88.6%. Oversight of these attack types is challenging due to their complex activities and interactions. Although the model achieved an average recall rate of 92%, the findings suggest that incorporating symbolic rules and improving temporal sequence learning could enhance the detection of low-signal attacks. The model's comprehensive and effective recall metrics are used in many IoT applications for real-time intrusion detection.

Figure 6.3 shows the F_1 score of the Neuro-Symbolic Transfer Learning Model, which indicates its consistently high accuracy and recall across various IoT threat levels. The model's ability to accurately recognize benign behavior while minimizing false negatives is demonstrated by its 97.8% F_1 score for standard traffic. The model's 96 percent F_1 score for denial-of-service attacks demonstrates its ability to identify prevalent, overt threats. The F_1 score for man-in-the-middle (MITM) attacks is 92.2%, while the score for reconnaissance threats is 93.4%. These scores indicate a decrease in the sensitivity and specificity of the detection method. Data exfiltration is the most detrimental attack tactic, with an F_1 score of 89.3 percent. The F_1 score for spoofing is 91.9%. This suggests that improved management is necessary for low-signal or covert attacks. Consistently high F_1 scores demonstrate that the neuro-symbolic architecture can maintain detection accuracy across various IoT threat scenarios.

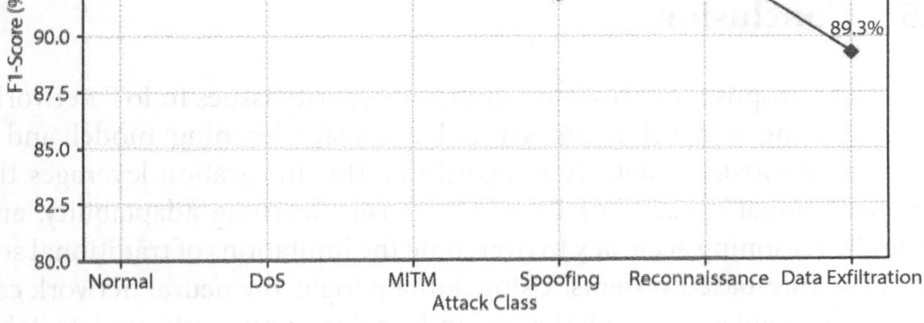

Figure 6.3 F_1 Score of IoT attacks.

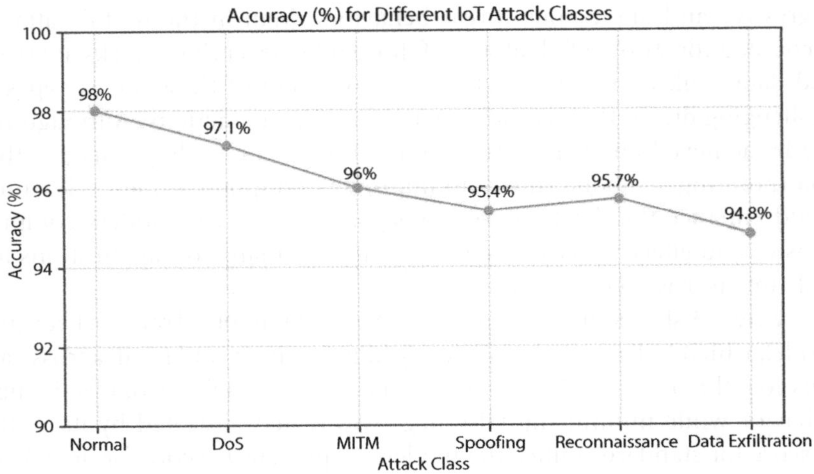

Figure 6.4 Accuracy of IoT attacks.

The classification approach guarantees exceptional detection capabilities due to its extraordinary accuracy in identifying all types of attacks, as shown in Figure 6.4. The device must identify a consistent flow with 98% accuracy to minimize false alarms. The most precise attacks are denial-of-service (DoS) attacks (97.1%), followed by reconnaissance (95.7%), data exfiltration (94.8%), deception (95.4%), and man-in-the-middle (MITM) attacks (96%). An accuracy rate of 94% suggests potential difficulties in detection due to concealed characteristics or resemblance to legitimate traffic patterns. Notably, the significantly lower accuracy in identifying data exfiltration efforts implies that this category may be more challenging to detect. The model's heightened sensitivity to many types of threats makes it ideal for comprehensive network security monitoring.

6.5 Conclusion

This study proposes addressing significant security issues in IoT networks by integrating a novel neuro-symbolic transfer learning model and a logic-based intrusion detection algorithm. This integration leverages the representational capacity of BiLSTM, transfer learning adaptability, and symbolic reasoning accuracy to overcome the limitations of traditional statistical or rule-based systems. Using domain logic, the neural network can accurately evaluate current threats and analyze previously undetectable attack methodologies. The model exhibits superior performance in key metrics, including precision, recall, accuracy, and F_1 score. It can identify various attack types, including covert incursions and data exfiltration. Its modular design enables scalability and real-time deployment across many dynamic IoT scenarios. Our efforts have significantly advanced the development of adaptable, adaptive, and interpretable security systems that are well-suited to the ever-evolving threat landscape of the IoT.

AI disclosure statement: The author acknowledges the use of AI-based tools for minor language editing or grammatical correction. However, all intellectual contributions, analyses, and conclusions presented in this chapter are entirely the author's own.

References

1. Butun, I., Österberg, P., Song, H., Security of the Internet of Things: Vulnerabilities, attacks, and countermeasures. *IEEE Commun. Surv. Tutorials*, 22, 1, 616–44, 2019 Nov 13.
2. Bout, E., Loscri, V., Gallais, A., How machine learning changes the nature of cyberattacks on IoT networks: A survey. *IEEE Commun. Surv. Tutorials*, 24, 1, 248–79, 2021 Nov 12.
3. Bala, B. and Behal, S., AI techniques for IoT-based DDoS attack detection: Taxonomies, comprehensive review and research challenges. *Comput. Sci. Rev.*, 52, 100631, 2024 May 1.
4. Saleem, A.D. and Abdulrahman, A.A., Attacks detection in Internet of Things using machine learning techniques: a review. *J. Appl. Eng. Technol. Sci.*, 6, 1, 684–703, 2024.
5. Kalutharage, C.S., Liu, X., Chrysoulas, C., Neurosymbolic learning and domain knowledge-driven explainable AI for enhanced IoT network attack detection and response. *Comput. Secur.*, 151, 104318, 2025 Apr 1.
6. Muna, R.K., Hossain, M.I., Alam, M.G., Hassan, M.M., Ianni, M., Fortino, G., Demystifying machine learning models of massive IoT attack detection with Explainable AI for sustainable and secure future smart cities. *Internet Things*, 24, 100919, 2023 Dec 1.
7. Kim, A., Park, M., Lee, D.H., AI-IDS: Application of deep learning to real-time Web intrusion detection. *IEEE Access*, 8, 70245–61, 2020 Apr 10.
8. Kumar, G. and Thakur, K., An Analysis of AI-based Supervised Classifiers for Intrusion Detection in Big Data, in: *Big Data Analytics*, pp. 26–46, CRC Press, United Kingdom, 2018.
9. Idris, N.B. and Shanmugam, B., Artificial intelligence techniques applied to intrusion detection, in: *2005 Annual IEEE India Conference-Indicon*, 2005 Dec 11, IEEE, pp. 52–55.

10. Patil, S., Varadarajan, V., Mazhar, S.M., Sahibzada, A., Ahmed, N., Sinha, O., Kumar, S., Shaw, K., Kotecha, K., Explainable artificial intelligence for intrusion detection system. *Electronics*, 11, 19, 3079, 2022 Sep 27.
11. Peddabachigari, S., Abraham, A., Grosan, C., Thomas, J., Modeling intrusion detection system using hybrid intelligent systems. *J. Network Comput. Appl.*, 30, 1, 114–32, 2007 Jan 1.
12. Li, T., Hu, S., Beirami, A., Smith, V., Ditto: Fair and robust federated learning through personalization, in: *International Conference on Machine Learning*, 2021 Jul 1, PMLR, pp. 6357–6368.
13. Mohseni, S., Wang, H., Yu, Z., Xiao, C., Wang, Z., Yadawa, J., Practical machine learning safety: A survey and primer. arXiv 2021. arXiv preprint arXiv:2106.04823.
14. Swamynathan, C., Shanmugam, R., Mohan Kumar, K.P., Subbiyan, B., Traffic Prevention and Security Enhancement in VANET Using Deep Learning with Trusted Routing Aided Blockchain Technology. *Trans. Emerging Telecommun. Technol.*, 35, 11, e70004, 2024 Nov.
15. Balraj, S., Leelasankar, K., Ayyanar, A., Yesudhas, H.R., Kumar, R., Long, H.V., Hoang Son, L., An Effective Traceback Network Attack Procedure for Source Address Verification. *Wireless Pers. Commun.*, 118, 1675–96, 2021 May.
16. Park, C., Lee, J., Kim, Y., Park, J.G., Kim, H., Hong, D., An enhanced AI-based network intrusion detection system using generative adversarial networks. *IEEE Internet Things J.*, 10, 3, 2330–45, 2022 Oct 3.
17. Vadisetty, R. and Polamarasetti, A., Enhancing Intrusion Detection Systems with Deep Learning and Machine Learning Algorithms for Real-Time Threat Classification, in: *2024 Asian Conference on Intelligent Technologies (ACOIT)*, 2024 Sep 6, IEEE, pp. 1–6.
18. Racherla, S., Sripathi, P., Faruqui, N., Kabir, M.A., Whaiduzzaman, M., Shah, S.A., Deep-IDS: A Real-Time Intrusion Detector for IoT Nodes Using Deep Learning. *IEEE Access*, 2024 May 3.
19. Pavithra, D., Parameswaran, T., Choudhry, M.D., Amrutha, S., Deepa, T., Kiruthiga, R., Application of LSTM Networks for Continuous Patient Monitoring and Anomaly Detection in Wearable Health Devices. *Indian J. Sci. Technol.*, 17, 37, 3909–3921, 2024.

7

Integrating Artificial Intelligence in Neuro-Symbolic: Challenges, Applications, and Future Directions

J. D. Dorathi Jayaseeli, D. Malathi, R. S. Ponmagal, G. Abirami, S. Nagadevi and M. Senthil Raja*

Department of Computing Technologies, School of Computing, SRM Institute Science and Technology, Kattankulathur, Chennai, India

Abstract

The objective of neuro-symbolic artificial intelligence (NSAI) is to integrate the optimal features of neural networks and symbolic systems to yield outcomes that are both pertinent and intelligible. Utilizing symbolic approaches enables us to uncover novel applications for subjects, enhance our comprehension of them, and attain significantly improved results. Neural networks excel at recognizing patterns in unstructured data. Integrating the two methodologies may yield a more resilient, efficient, and rational foundation for AI evaluation and reasoning. This paper examines NSAI comprehensively, addressing its historical background, current state, and prospective future applications. This paper encompasses all facets of NSAI, including computer vision, natural language processing, reinforcement learning, and program synthesis. Implementation constraints, scalability, potential for innovation, and data prerequisites are all meticulously analyzed. The subject addresses the current status, prospective developments, and practical implementations of multimodal reasoning systems, integrated frameworks, and interpretable models.

Keywords: AI, neuro-symbolic, deep learning, NLP

**Corresponding author*: senthilm6@srmist.edu.in

R. Nidhya, A. Dineshkumar, Sheng-Lung Peng, S. Karthik and S. Balamurugan (eds.) Neuro-Symbolic Artificial Intelligence: Concepts & Applications, (121–142) © 2026 Scrivener Publishing LLC

7.1 Introduction

Artificial intelligence has progressed markedly during the past decade across various fields, including natural language processing, robotics, healthcare, and autonomous systems. The capacity of neural networks and deep learning to analyze unstructured data positions them at the front of AI progress. Notwithstanding their accomplishments, these models may still encounter difficulties in processing and integrating structured data on a worldwide scale. Symbolic AI exhibits considerable intelligence and can emulate cognitive processes; nonetheless, it encounters difficulties in comprehending basic concepts and adapting to intricate real-world scenarios. Symbolic AI relies on principles, logic, and symbolic representations.

Researchers employ a hybrid methodology known as neuro-symbolic artificial intelligence (NSAI). The National Security Agency (NSA) has incorporated connectionist (neural) methodologies into a framework for intricate symbolic reasoning. The primary objective is to cultivate artificial intelligence (AI) that possesses the capacity for autonomous and abstract reasoning. The utilization of neuro-symbolic systems has been demonstrated to enhance learning and cognitive processes by facilitating the coordination of brain activity. These advancements contribute to enhancing the adaptability, reliability, accessibility, and versatility of AI systems [1].

Neuro-symbolic integration is well supported by both theory and practice. Discrete symbolic systems and continuous neural networks employ distinct learning algorithms, which complicates data representation, training, and design. Students must have a strong desire to learn in order to excel in symbolic logic and cognitive learning courses, which offer unique innovative pedagogical tactics, frameworks, and environments. The creation and application of neuro-symbolic models in hybrid systems are challenging due to their interpretability, scalability, and processing costs [2].

The integration of AI with neuro-symbolic systems offers numerous advantages. The transparency, analytical skills, and structured data of NSAI are beneficial for automated systems, regulatory frameworks, and healthcare diagnostics. The ability of AI to discern patterns within a symbolic knowledge base of prescription drugs would significantly enhance diagnostic accuracy and foster the confidence of healthcare providers. Autonomous vehicles and robots employ symbolic reasoning when unexpected cognitive outputs are rare [3].

The challenges associated with integrating artificial intelligence (AI) with neuro-symbolic systems are exemplified in this context. The utilization of data, ethical design concerns, technological limitations, and potential social implications are all aspects that fall within the purview of this subject. To comprehend the significance and potential of neuro-symbolic AI, it is imperative to be cognizant of the current and future advancements in this domain. Anticipating and planning for future advancements in artificial intelligence (AI) is imperative for the successful initiation of AI-related projects and the promotion of collaborative efforts.

This chapter explores the integration of neuro-symbolic systems with artificial intelligence, addressing its fundamental concepts, practical applications, and prospective enhancements. This course will encompass a wide range of theoretical and applied domains within the field of neuro-symbolic AI. The merits and drawbacks of neurobiological and metaphorical methods will be examined in this presentation. The present study investigates the following areas: security, language, robotics, and perception. In conclusion, the primary achievements and challenges in the development of intelligent, open, and helpful AI systems will be emphasized.

7.2 Neuro-Symbolic AI: An Overview

Neuro-symbolic AI is a new area of artificial intelligence that examines the interactions between neural networks, information representation frameworks, and symbolic systems. Although artificial neural networks are "opaque systems devoid of interpretability and reasoning," they can learn rapidly and react to non-traditionally structured data. Since then, symbolic AI research has advanced and become increasingly complex. By integrating them, we hope to address the shortcomings of each approach alone. Data processing, interpretation, and assessment are all enhanced by the employment of symbolic tools. Deep learning techniques are used by NSAI models to extract insights from datasets.

The layers in question convey information in accordance with a neuro-symbolic paradigm.

Neural (Sub-symbolic) Layer: The neural (sub-symbolic) layer facilitates perception, pattern recognition, and feature extraction from unstructured inputs, including text, music, and images [4].
Symbolic Layer: The symbolic layer encompasses the laws, ontologies, formal languages, and cognitive processes that dictate the representation, reasoning, and decision-making of knowledge.

Computers utilizing NSAI must acquire two essential cognitive abilities that are robust abstract reasoning and improved sensory perception, before they can rival humans in complex cognitive tasks. Neuro-symbolic systems employ convolutional neural networks (CNNs) to recognize objects in images. Symbolic logic may be advantageous when representation is difficult or the relationships between entities are ambiguous.

7.2.1 Neuro-Symbolic Properties

Interpretability: Understanding neuro-symbolic systems requires adherence to specific symbolic frameworks and patterns. Deep neural network's complex topologies enable them to generate logical patterns using symbolic features. Transparency is essential in domains like healthcare and law, where informed choices are essential. It appears that the primary objective of AI-driven solutions is to increase accountability and autonomy [5].

Generalization: A model can employ generalizable concepts and symbolic thinking to learn more. The NSAI may use trend analysis and logic to update the data at regular intervals. Retraining might not be necessary for small input changes. Systems that possess this ability are better able to adjust to shifting conditions [6].

Compositionality: "Compositive" models are a unique type of artificial intelligence framework that uses well-established principles to solve complicated problems. People use language and reasoning to understand what they don't understand. Despite their complexity, neural networks benefit from symbolic frameworks. This approach aims to make it easier for people to learn a second language.

Data Efficiency: Unlike traditional deep learning, which relies on large datasets, neuro-symbolic models can overcome this difficulty by employing rule-based inference. Learning from a limited number of labeled examples can be made more effective by using symbolic information. To improve student involvement in the classroom, one small step could be enough. This choice will determine whether present and future financial objectives are met. Effective and economical use of data can lower operating expenses and improve training results [7].

Robust Reasoning: The symbolic logic of NSAI facilitates a more profound comprehension of the brain's operations than neural networks. It is imperative to recognize the paramount importance of user safety in sectors such as cybersecurity and driverless cars, where expeditious recovery is of the essence. A logical consistency evaluation may produce unreliable results. It has been demonstrated that an increase in the level of uncertainty can enhance the performance of NSAI systems [8].

Modularity and Reusability: The incorporation of symbolic representations or sub-networks from other projects has been demonstrated to enhance the flexibility of neuro-symbolic frameworks. The transmission of data between these locations is seamless. It has been demonstrated that scalability has been enhanced, and the time required to build has been reduced to a significant extent. AI systems are manageable due to their modularity and adherence to fundamental principles of software engineering.

7.3 Evolution of Neuro-Symbolic AI

Neuro-symbolic AI combines neural networks, which have become more prominent due to advances in machine learning and deep learning, with symbolic AI, which was the main focus of early artificial intelligence research. Since the emergence of AI, many individuals have contemplated integrating these two schools of thought. This advancement has only been possible due to improved data collection methods and accelerated processing rates.

From the 1950s to the 1970s, symbolic AI, also known as "Good Old-Fashioned Artificial Intelligence" (GOFAI), dominated the field [9]. Researchers used formal logic, rules, and search methods to define knowledge. Symbolic systems can sometimes simulate speech and reasoning, as demonstrated by programs such as ELIZA [10] and SHRDLU [11]. Traditionally, intelligence was viewed as the outcome of deliberate, systematic, and rule-governed symbol manipulation. However, these systems cannot accommodate the erratic requirements of real-world input and perception.

Neural network research began in the 1950s with Frank Rosenblatt's creation of the perceptron [12]. However, Marvin Minsky and Seymour Papert's 1969 publication exposed neural networks' limitations, particularly their inability to perform XOR operations using a single-layer perceptron. This led to significant criticism. Neural networks then entered a period of stagnation known as the "AI winter."

Connectionist models that use backpropagation-trained, multi-layer neural networks experienced a resurgence in the 1980s and 1990s [13]. The simultaneous evolution of expert systems and knowledge engineering enhanced the advancement of symbolic artificial intelligence. Paul Smolensky and others introduced the sub-symbolic-symbolic distinction, a revolutionary concept in the study of combinatorial approaches. It was the first attempt to integrate neural networks, combining pattern recognition with the abstraction and logic of symbolic reasoning.

Substantial progress in deep learning was made over the 2010s, primarily due to the application of convolutional and recurrent neural networks, the expansion of extensive datasets, and the advancement of powerful GPUs. Deep learning has revolutionized numerous fields, including computer vision, speech recognition, and natural language processing. However, restricted interpretability, insufficient generalization, and erroneous reasoning have reemerged. Researchers began to regard symbolic artificial intelligence as an adjunct to deep learning rather than a substitute [14].

Our goal was to appropriately depict the current state of neuro-symbolic AI (NSAI). Symbolic frameworks that leverage the learning and observing capabilities of neural networks enabled the NSAI to build on this remarkable achievement. Logic Tensor Networks (LTNs), Neuro-Symbolic Concept Learners (NS-CL), and Deep ProbLog are three well-known systems that integrate probabilistic logic and deep learning. To solve challenging issues like knowledge-based reasoning, visual question responding, and program synthesis, combine cognitive perception with symbolic reasoning [15].

Neuro-symbolic AI techniques may help advance artificial general intelligence. These techniques will yield better and more trustworthy evidence-based outcomes [16]. Researchers studying artificial intelligence are increasingly using neuro-symbolic models as an alternative to more traditional neural networks and symbolic representations. The new edition focuses on intelligence testing grounded in cognitive processes and scientific facts. To increase the frequency of usage of neuro-symbolic approaches, researchers are putting a lot of effort into making them more scalable, flexible, and reliable [17].

7.4 Neural-Symbolic Integration

The "Neuro-Symbolic Integration" program aims to combine the cognitive advantages of symbolic systems with the learning benefits of neural networks. Participants hail from various professional fields. The goal is to develop intelligent systems that function similarly to symbolic artificial intelligence. Like neural networks, these systems will quickly collect and identify information. Furthermore, students will use their knowledge and cognitive abilities to solve problems. This hybrid methodology rectifies the deficiencies of both paradigms, empowering robots to comprehend, enhance, and rationalize their actions across diverse, complex tasks.

Neural networks excel at understanding unstructured inputs, such as text, music, and images; recognizing patterns; and modeling language. However, they generally struggle with compositional generalization, explainability, symbolic cognition, and logical reasoning. In contrast, symbolic systems are easily understood, require minimal information, and can be segmented into distinct components. However, they are ineffective in uncertain or dynamic circumstances and depend significantly on human-established conventions. Neural-symbolic systems aim to replicate human cognitive and learning mechanisms to create artificial intelligence.

7.4.1 Symbolic Neuro-Symbolic Model

As shown in Figure 7.1, the neuro-symbolic paradigm integrates the optimal characteristics of brain learning and symbolic reasoning into a cohesive framework. These two concepts are highly complementary. According to the theory, advanced cognitive processes are enhanced by a systematic understanding of symbolic concepts such as logic, rules, and ontologies. This region of the brain governs essential perceptual processes, including pattern identification, feature extraction, and learning from unstructured data. A neuro-symbolic approach was developed to overcome the drawbacks of conventional symbolic systems, namely, their lack of generalizability and transparency. This reduction in mental constraints enables the creation of complex compositional representations of symbolic concepts. The capacity of neural networks to identify objects and gather information enhances their ability to visually depict concepts such as "a red cube on a blue sphere." This suggests the potential for the application of reasoning in the context of crime scene investigation. While symbolic outputs have been demonstrated to influence cognitive learning, symbolic inputs have been shown to influence decision-making across a variety of paradigms. These models enhance data efficiency, clarity, and generalization, making them ideal for organizations requiring human intelligence and reliability. Current implementations of Deep ProbLog, Logic Tensor Networks, and Neuro-Symbolic Concept Learners demonstrate that differentiable learning and logical reasoning can be integrated into a unified framework.

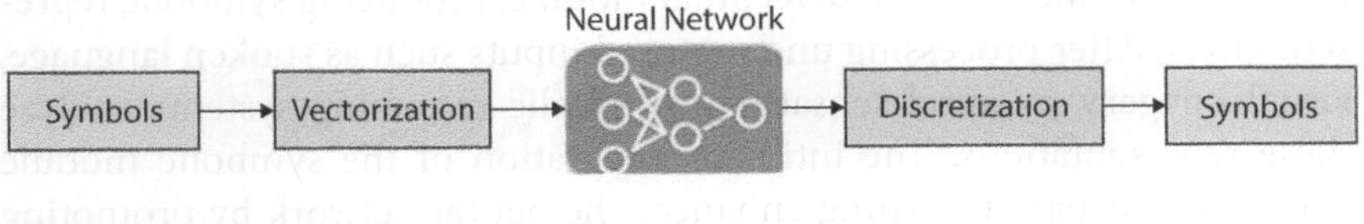

Figure 7.1 Representation of the neuro-symbolic model.

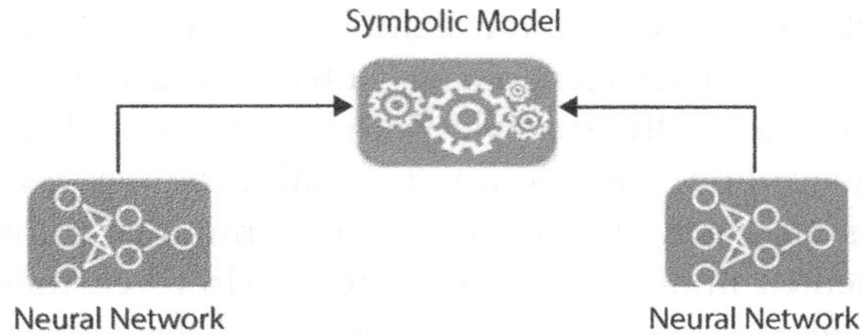

Figure 7.2 Representation of the symbolic model.

7.4.2 Symbolic Model

A symbolic model is a hybrid system comprising primarily neural modules, supplemented by symbolic problem solvers and symbols shown in Figure 7.2. Despite particular distinctions between neurobiological and symbolic elements, the fundamental cognitive process is governed by symbolic logic. According to Kautz, an example of a neural network functioning as a heuristic evaluation tool, while Monte Carlo Tree Search is the primary problem-solving method, is DeepMind's AlphaGo. A sequence-to-sequence neural architecture is combined with a symbolic stack machine to develop a neuro-symbolic model that enables recursion and sequence manipulation, thus enhancing the learning and expansion of compositional rules. This model generates its execution trace with a neural network. To delineate abstract input/output requirements, a rule-based architecture for program synthesis from unprocessed visual inputs is proposed, founded on neural perception modules. VisProg, HuggingGPT, and ViperGPT are recent examples of advancements in utilizing large language models to decompose complex tasks into smaller, more manageable assignments, each executed by a specialized, pretrained AI model [18].

7.4.3 Neural Learning + Symbolic Solver Model

Neuro-symbolic computing integrates neural learning with symbolic solvers, as shown in Figure 7.3. This allows neural networks to derive insights from unstructured data while providing systematic planning, reasoning, and decision-making capabilities. The hypothesis posits that a specific brain region functions as a perceptual module, producing symbolic representations. After processing unstructured inputs such as spoken language, visual imagery, or aural sensations, symbolic reasoning systems analyze these representations. The intimate integration of the symbolic module with gradient-based learning enhances the neural network by promoting

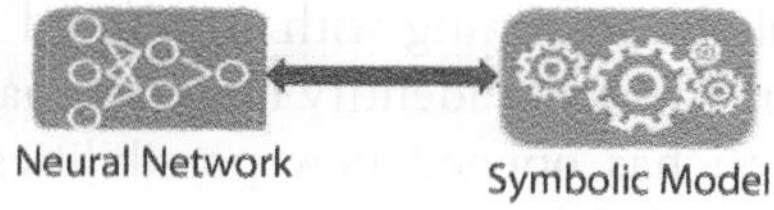

Figure 7.3 Representation of the neural learning + symbolic solver model.

logical inference, rule-based control, and the generation of feedback signals. While a symbolic reasoning module answers inquiries using predefined logic, a neural module improves the perception model by integrating visual notions with symbolic data. Many deep learning techniques for program synthesis belong to this category [19]. These methods generate rule systems or symbolic programs that fulfill advanced criteria. Recent advancements in neural-symbolic reinforcement learning integrate symbolic planning with reinforcement learning to enhance decision-making precision. In these systems, symbolic planning regulates task execution, while experience-based involvement enhances the effectiveness of symbolic strategies.

To enhance adaptability, [20] illustrates the integration of symbolic planning within the reinforcement learning paradigm. Significant achievements in this field include neural theorem provers (NTPs) [21], conditional theorem provers (CTPs) [22], NLProlog [23], Neurolog [24], Difflog [25], and DeepProbLog [89], the latter of which incorporates neural predicates into the probabilistic logic programming language ProbLog. DeepProbLog is a probabilistic fact generation tool based on neural networks that employs symbolic inference to facilitate gradient backpropagation for optimal training. These images illustrate the potential of neuro-symbolic. Integrating data-driven learning with systematic, logical reasoning in symbolic systems can produce more intelligent, interpretable, and practical artificial intelligence.

7.5 Applications of Neuro-Symbolic AI

7.5.1 Natural Language Processing

Deep learning methodologies have greatly improved large language models and transformers for natural language processing. However, these models still face challenges related to complex reasoning, compositional generalization, interpretability, and knowledge-based reasoning. Neuro-symbolic artificial intelligence overcomes these limitations by combining the strengths of symbolic reasoning with structured representations and the ability of neural networks to identify linguistic patterns in large datasets. This combination has opened new possibilities in significant and advanced NLP domains [26].

Semantic parsing aims to convert natural language into formal representations, such as SQL queries, executable scripts, and cognitive frameworks. Transformers are neuro-symbolic models that use brain encoders to translate text into intermediate representations. Solvers or symbolic interpreters then analyze or utilize these representations. This hybrid methodology improves system comprehension and precision, aligning it more closely with human needs. Symbolic backend models, such as NLProlog and NeuroLog, transform natural language inputs into logical assertions that are then used to generate responses or actions.

A fundamental challenge arises in multi-hop or reasoning-intensive question answering (QA) because the system must integrate information from multiple knowledge sources. Traditional LLM outcomes are generally imprecise or erroneous [27]. The Neuro-Symbolic Concept Learner is an example of how neuro-symbolic methods differentiate cognitive capability from verbal and visual comprehension. Unlike symbolic engines, which evaluate based on established criteria or logical structures, NS-CL uses neural networks to identify items and relationships within text. Modular tools and APIs, such as ViperGPT and VisProg, decompose language issues into symbolic operations that can be executed conditionally or sequentially.

Symbolic reasoning populates knowledge bases and extracts information to address gaps, maintain consistency, and uncover underlying connections. After using brain models to identify items and interactions, neuro-symbolic strategies use ontologies or symbolic rules to improve information extraction and address deficiencies. This enhances the quality and reliability of information systems, especially in critical sectors such as banking, healthcare, and law.

Neuro-symbolic integration improves the effectiveness of conversational AI and voice systems. Symbolic aspects govern dialogue states, user intentions, and logical constraints, while neural models generate or interpret utterances. Cognitive modules in task-oriented conversational systems operate autonomously, while symbolic planners adhere to task sequences and organizational protocols. This yields more coherent and informed communication than brain models alone [28].

Neuro-symbolic models facilitate natural language processing and comprehension of common-sense reasoning. Two frameworks that use deductive reasoning to explore hypothetical scenarios through symbolic logic and pretrained language models are neural theorem provers (NTPs) and commonsense transformers. These technologies yield readily apparent outcomes in domains requiring reliability and transparency.

7.5.2 Medical Applications

Incorporating neuro-symbolic artificial intelligence into clinical decision support systems can significantly enhance their efficacy within the medical field, thereby creating a more beneficial environment. Neuro-symbolic reasoning enhances diagnostic precision and personalization by integrating neural networks' flexibility with symbolic AI's analytical capabilities. Research shows that NSR's ability to diagnose acute abdominal discomfort accurately exemplifies its diagnostic precision. The quantum-based deep learning approach is also used to improve medical image data storage [35].

Neuro-symbolic integration is a method that merges deep learning with symbolic reasoning to yield substantial insights that enhance patient care. The principal use is the administration of electronic health records. Ultsch's Neuro-Data-Mine methodology necessitates the transformation of sub-symbolic medical data into symbolic data to evaluate extensive datasets. This work advances precision medicine by illustrating how neuro-symbolic tools can improve and optimize data processing for complex tasks such as CSF sample analysis [29].

Hatzlygeroudis and Prentzas developed hybrid formalisms to enhance the precision of medical assessments. These formal frameworks are effective for detecting inflammatory bone disease [30]. These systems possess neurological and commercial elements. Neuro-symbolic systems exhibit a markedly enhanced capacity to rapidly recognize intricate patterns and derive conclusions compared to conventional methods.

Omlin and Snyder illustrated the therapeutic potential of neuro-symbolic techniques through magnetic resonance spectroscopy [31]. The operation of inductive bias in neural networks has been extensively studied and developed in recent years. Bologna elucidates neural networks in the context of medical diagnosis with the Discretized Interpretable Multilayer Perceptron (DIMLP). Neural networks facilitate the identification of sickness biomarkers and provide individualized recommendations.

A diagnostic tool that combines rule-based, case-based, and neural network approaches was developed by Obot and Uzoka [32] to address these issues. The creation of trustworthy and understandable AI systems for healthcare has been sped up by this combinatorial approach. The explanations it gives are more comprehensive than those of conventional neural networks.

An effective clinical decision support system, neuro-symbolic AI, combines the precision of symbolic reasoning with the flexibility of neural networks to improve health outcomes. Enhancing the precision of diagnoses and customizing treatment regimens can lead to better patient care on a global scale.

7.5.3 Neuro-Symbolic AI in Robotics

Advancements in neuro-symbolic AI have enabled robots to execute intricate tasks that were previously considered inconceivable. This objective is realized through the integration of the adaptability of neural networks with the inherent reasoning capabilities of symbolic AI. This newfound comprehension has the potential to equip robots with enhanced visual acuity, improved reasoning capabilities, and the ability to navigate complex and uncertain scenarios with proficiency. Robots can evaluate the physical attributes of objects and how they interact with the environment. They can also acquire new skills from human demonstrations and convert them into symbolic representations. These applications are broad.

Coraggio *et al.* [33] developed a neuro-symbolic framework for robot self-localization in sensor-constrained environments, utilizing natural ambient elements as navigational cues. This technology integrates landmark detection and encoding, merging symbolic AI's logical reasoning with neural networks' perceptual capabilities to facilitate complex decision-making processes.

Authors [34] created an innovative active video surveillance system that integrates virtual neural sensors with BDI agents to enhance the system's intelligence and responsiveness. This integration highlights the advantages of merging neural networks' perceptual capabilities with symbolic artificial intelligence's reasoning abilities to develop a highly adaptable surveillance system capable of operating autonomously in dynamic environments.

Google Inc., ByteDance Inc., and Tsinghua University demonstrated enhanced techniques for array sorting, critical path identification, and complex challenges such as Blocks World on the neuro-symbolic Neural Logic Machine (NLM). This methodology shows how NeSy can improve robotic performance by simplifying generic concepts and achieving expected results from randomized configurations.

7.5.4 Neuro-Symbolic AI in Computer Vision

Golovko *et al.* [36] developed an intelligent decision support system that uses neuro-symbolic artificial intelligence in computer vision to improve product label quality control. The IDSS demonstrates the efficacy of neuro-symbolic techniques in real-world manufacturing by emphasizing the collaboration of deep neural networks for image localization and identification and semantic networks for advanced data processing.

Bologna and Hayashi [37] used symbolic concepts in deep, interpretable, discretized multilayer perceptrons to improve the transparency of deep learning systems. Their research highlights the importance of balancing interpretability and precision in deep learning models. This is particularly important when implementing AI in sensitive areas, such as medical diagnostics.

Grieco *et al.* [38] propose that analyzing the interplay of visual and auditory stimuli and generating pattern exemplars from "mental" imagery markedly enhances the amalgamation of language and multimedia. These results highlight the complexity of neuro-symbolic AI in integrating cognitive processes with sensory data. This provides innovative approaches for recognizing and generating patterns.

Barbosa *et al.* [39] propose that the neuro-symbolic approach is essential for classifying GPS trajectories based on their temporal and spatial patterns. Their findings suggest that combining the adaptability of neural networks with the systematic reasoning of symbolic artificial intelligence improves trajectory analysis, understanding, and processing. Khan and Curry [40] advanced multimedia event processing and emphasized the importance of neuro-symbolic AI in computer vision and related fields. Yi *et al.* [41] examined reasoning, visual perception, and language comprehension through Neural-Symbolic Visual Question Answering (VQA). Sareen *et al.* proposed heart disease prediction using ensemble learning [42].

Combining graph neural networks with symbolic reasoning improves the capacity of artificial intelligence systems to understand complex visual scenarios. This is achieved by integrating visual features and their interrelations into external knowledge bases. Future studies may focus on strengthening these connections to manage increasingly abstract visual concepts and their interactions more effectively. The Neuro-Symbolic Concept Learner architecture has markedly advanced the recording of the knowledge graph by integrating concepts with visual elements. By incorporating broader concepts and visual attributes, this paradigm will improve the accuracy and applicability of neuro-symbolic systems in computer vision.

Golovko *et al.* [36] created a decision support system to demonstrate how neuro-symbolic AI could enhance product labeling quality control. Exploring the possible applications of these technologies in innovative industrial sectors may result in diverse organizations adopting unique quality control methodologies. Bologna and Hayashi [37] assert that balancing the model's accuracy with comprehensibility enhances the interpretability of symbolic representations in deep learning models. Future research may focus on innovative methods to improve the effectiveness of deep learning models while increasing their transparency and comprehensibility.

7.5.5 Neuro-Symbolic AI in Optimization Techniques

Neuro-symbolic AI has made significant progress in computer programming and optimization. Semi-automated methods are used in programming synthesis to find solutions that fulfill a specific goal. The advancement of programs for activities such as search and classification algorithms can be expedited by utilizing neuro-symbolic AI systems, which integrate neural network architectures with symbolic reasoning, thereby resolving this difficulty. Neuro-symbolic AI software performs better when it combines symbolic reasoning with insights acquired from training neural networks on program functionality.

Bhatia *et al.* [43] developed an effective neuro-symbolic program corrector to help beginners overcome optimization challenges. This methodology uses neural networks and symbolic artificial intelligence to detect and address problems in student programming. For novice coders, feedback automation can be a significant aid. Minimal, context-sensitive modifications are implemented through the utilization of the neuro-symbolic technique, which entails a meticulous examination of the semantic ramifications inherent within the code. Consequently, all typographical and grammatical errors were rectified.

The integration of logical neural networks (LNN) and inductive logic programming (ILP) was pioneered by Sen *et al.* [44]. This approach integrates the adaptability of LNN with the inferential capabilities of ILP, resulting in the development of a neuro-symbolic ILP framework. The combination of these two factors has the potential to generate substantial and long-lasting consequences. Consequently, AI has undergone substantial advancements, particularly in the domains of optimization and programming.

Chaudhuri *et al.* [45] contend that neural networks and symbolic programming frameworks are the only means to address the issues with data-driven and rule-based systems. The absence of these elements renders the development of dependable, adaptable, and user-focused AI systems impracticable.

In their investigation, Ritchie *et al.* [46] employed neuro-symbolic models to explore the intricacies of creating, storing, and retrieving visual information. A substantial transformation in the domain of computer graphics may emerge from the evolution of algorithms that are more robust and adaptable. Balasubramanian and Reddy's neuro-symbolic program synthesis has the potential to fundamentally alter the methodology used in healthcare policy research and analysis. Subsequent analysis revealed the efficacy of the therapeutic approach. Varela's research suggests that hybrid neural networks may be more successful in achieving meta-learning objectives [47].

7.6 Challenges and Future Directions in Neuro-Symbolic AI

The integration of neural networks with symbolic reasoning, known as neuro-symbolic AI, offers both great promise and formidable challenges. In the course of the evaluation of the training approach, the following four variables were given primary consideration: scalability, interpretability, generalizability, and architectural complexity. The subsequent list of significant challenges confronts practitioners and specialists in this field.

7.6.1 Architectural Complexity and Integration Difficulty

First, constructing a coherent framework that integrates neural learning and symbolic reasoning is inherently challenging. Unlike predominantly distributed, continuous, and differentiable neural networks, symbolic systems are characterized by non-differentiability, rule-based frameworks, and discreteness. While hybrid models can unify fundamentally disparate perspectives, they may result in fragile and unstable integrations. Achieving proximity without compromising performance, learning dynamics, or modularity is problematic.

7.6.2 Differentiable Reasoning and Optimization

Gradient descent's ability to emulate the differentiability of symbolic cognitive elements for comprehensive training poses a substantial challenge to neuro-symbolic artificial intelligence. Gradient-based optimization is incompatible with many symbolic tasks, including rule execution, theorem proving, and logical reasoning. Many methodologies, such as Logic Tensor

Networks, Deep ProbLog, and differentiable logic programming, attempt to address this issue but usually sacrifice either scalability or representational expressiveness.

7.6.3 Knowledge Representation and Abstraction

Ontologies, logical principles, and programs are examples of structured symbolic information that is difficult to describe in a way that neural networks can utilize most efficiently. Encoding this information into vector spaces while preserving the necessary logical structure, compositionality, and hierarchical connections poses a significant challenge. Nevertheless, creating relevant symbolic representations from neuronal embeddings, a type of information distillation, is challenging, especially for applications that require accuracy and semantic precision.

7.6.4 Scalability and Computational Cost

Neuro-symbolic models elucidate the interplay between diverse modules of varying levels of abstraction and complex cognitive processes. Therefore, this system requires greater computational capacity than neuronal and fundamentally symbolic systems. Using logical inference or symbolic planning in reinforcement learning and Q&A systems can have significant practical implications. Examples of real-time or large-scale projects encountering significant scaling challenges include autonomous systems, industrial automation, and web-scale information retrieval.

7.6.5 Lack of Unified Benchmarks and Evaluation Metrics

There are no rules or suggestions for evaluating cognitive and reasoning capabilities in neuro-symbolic systems. Current benchmarks focus primarily on symbolic reasoning metrics (e.g., theorem coverage, logical consistency) or machine learning metrics (e.g., accuracy, F_1 score). However, these metrics are insufficient for investigating the interplay between visual perception and cognition. This requires a paradigm shift and monitoring progress in robotics, computer vision, natural language processing, program synthesis, and other fields.

7.6.6 Data and Supervision Requirements

Unlike neural models, which rely on large labeled datasets, symbolic artificial intelligence often uses well-designed rules. Neuro-symbolic artificial intelligence usually requires substantial annotated training data and organized symbolic knowledge. The complexity and unpredictability of real-world information make associating trained cognitive models with symbolic control difficult. Discrepancies between symbolic rules and training data may be difficult to reconcile.

7.6.7 Generalization and Transferability

The primary aim of neuro-symbolic artificial intelligence is to improve generalization through symbolic abstraction. However, achieving significant zero- or few-shot generalization across different activities, subjects, or locations presents practical challenges. Despite neural networks often demonstrating overfitting to training data, symbolic components may struggle to adapt to new concepts or situations. Developing models that combine symbolic information with neurobiological characteristics is difficult.

7.6.8 Explainability and Trust

Unlike brain networks, which lack interpretability, symbolic systems are inherently interpretable [48]. When both components of the hybrid model function simultaneously, it is difficult to see and understand the decision-making processes. This erodes confidence and accountability, especially in critical sectors such as autonomous vehicles, healthcare, and legal reasoning. Constructing neuro-symbolic systems with elucidation, debugging, and validation tools can be difficult.

7.6.9 Robustness to Noise and Ambiguity

Ambiguity and extraneous noise are often inherent in real-world data [49]. Symbolic thinking generally requires precise, clearly articulated inputs, yet neural networks can handle chaotic inputs. Neuro-symbolic systems must balance these conflicting requirements to prevent catastrophic failures of symbolic modules caused by incomplete or erroneous inputs from the brain module.

7.7 Conclusion

Neuro-symbolic artificial intelligence is a novel innovation that combines the beneficial features of neural and symbolic systems to overcome their limitations. This book examines the philosophical foundations, evolution, integration strategies, and numerous applications of this hybrid paradigm, emphasizing its potential. Advancing integrated hybrid structures, rapid learning algorithms, and scalable, interpretable reasoning mechanisms is one of several technological challenges that must be overcome to utilize neuro-symbolic systems effectively. Future studies must focus on disseminating knowledge in low-data contexts, constructing coherent and differentiable models, and promoting cross-modal cognitive advancement. Neuro-symbolic AI excels in transparency, interpretability, and resilience, which are increasingly demanded as artificial intelligence systems are integrated into critical sectors. The community can establish neuro-symbolic AI as a vital component of reliable, human-centric AI by promoting interdisciplinary collaboration and funding for foundational and applied research.

AI disclosure statement: The author confirms that no artificial intelligence (AI)-generated content or AI-assisted writing tools were used in the preparation of this chapter (including summaries and the abstract). All text, analysis, and conclusions are the result of the author's original work.

References

1. Thomas, C.K. and Saad, W., Neuro-symbolic artificial intelligence (AI) for intent based semantic communication, in: *GLOBECOM 2022-2022 IEEE Global Communications Conference*, 2022 Dec 4, IEEE, pp. 2698–2703.
2. Smirnov, A.V., Ponomarev, A.V., Shilov, N.G., Levashova, T.V., Collaborative Decision Support Systems Based on Neuro-Symbolic Artificial Intelligence: Problems and Generalized Conceptual Model. *Sci. Tech. Inf. Process.*, 50, 6, 635–45, 2023 Dec.
3. Hitzler, P., Ebrahimi, M., Sarker, M.K., Stepanova, D., Neuro-symbolic AI and the semantic web. *Semant. Web.*, 15, 4, 1261–3, 2024 Oct 4.
4. Calegari, R., Ciatto, G., Omicini, A., On the integration of symbolic and sub-symbolic techniques for XAI: A survey. *Intell. Artif.*, 14, 1, 7–32, 2020 Sep 17.
5. Kapanipathi, P., Abdelaziz, I., Ravishankar, S., Roukos, S., Gray, A., Astudillo, R., Chang, M., Cornelio, C., Dana, S., Fokoue, A., Garg, D., Leveraging abstract meaning representation for knowledge base question answering. *arXiv preprint arXiv:2012.01707*, 2020 Dec 3.
6. Al-Ajlan, A., The comparison between forward and backward chaining. *Int. J. Mach. Learn. Comput.*, 5, 2, 106, 2015 Apr 1.

7. Ultsch, A. and Rolf, S., The Completion of Missing Values by Neural Nets for Data Mining, in: *Classification, Automation, and New Media: Proceedings of the 24th Annual Conference of the Gesellschaft für Klassifikation eV, University of Passau, March 15—17, 2000*, Springer Berlin Heidelberg, Berlin, Heidelberg, pp. 227–234, 2002.
8. Folger, R. and Stein, C., Abduction 101: Reasoning processes to aid discovery. *Hum. Resour. Manage. Rev.*, 27, 2, 306–15, 2017 Jun 1.
9. Poltronieri, F.A. and Hänska, M., Technical images and visual art in the era of artificial intelligence: from GOFAI to GANs, in: *Proceedings of the 9th International Conference on Digital and Interactive Arts*, 2019 Oct 23, pp. 1–8.
10. Shum, H.Y., He, X.D., Li, D., From Eliza to XiaoIce: challenges and opportunities with social chatbots. *Front. Inf. Technol. Electron. Eng.*, 19, 10–26, 2018 Jan.
11. Ontanon, S., Shrdlu: A game prototype inspired by winograd's natural language understanding work, in: *Proceedings of the AAAI Conference on Artificial Intelligence and Interactive Digital Entertainment*, 2018 Sep 25, vol. 14, No. 1, pp. 268–270.
12. Abiodun, O.I., Jantan, A., Omolara, A.E., Dada, K.V., Mohamed, N.A., Arshad, H., State-of-the-art in artificial neural network applications: A survey. *Heliyon*, 4, 11, 2018 Nov 1.
13. Rana, A., Rawat, A.S., Bijalwan, A., Bahuguna, H., Application of multi layer (perceptron) artificial neural network in the diagnosis system: A systematic review, in: *2018 International Conference on Research in Intelligent and Computing in Engineering (RICE)*, 2018 Aug 22, IEEE, pp. 1–6.
14. Dong, S., Wang, P., Abbas, K., A survey on deep learning and its applications. *Comput. Sci. Rev.*, 40, 100379, 2021 May 1.
15. Lu, Z., Afridi, I., Kang, H.J., Ruchkin, I., Zheng, X., Surveying neuro-symbolic approaches for reliable artificial intelligence of things. *J. Reliab. Intell. Environ.*, 10, 3, 257–79, 2024 Sep.
16. Goertzel, B., Artificial general intelligence: concept, state of the art, and future prospects. *J. Artif. Gen. Intell.*, 5, 1, 1, 2014.
17. Brown, T., Mann, B., Ryder, N., Subbiah, M., Kaplan, J.D., Dhariwal, P., Neelakantan, A., Shyam, P., Sastry, G., Askell, A., Agarwal, S., Language models are few-shot learners. *Adv. Neural Inf. Process. Syst.*, 33, 1877–901, 2020.
18. Weng, J., Symbolic models and emergent models: A review. *IEEE Trans. Auton. Ment. Dev.*, 4, 1, 29–53, 2011 Jun 9.
19. Mou, L., Lu, Z., Li, H., Jin, Z., Coupling distributed and symbolic execution for natural language queries, in: *International Conference on Machine Learning*, 2017 Jul 17, PMLR, pp. 2518–2526.
20. Yang, F., Lyu, D., Liu, B., Gustafson, S., Peorl: Integrating symbolic planning and hierarchical reinforcement learning for robust decision-making. *arXiv preprint arXiv:1804.07779*, 2018 Apr 20.

21. Rocktäschel, T. and Riedel, S., End-to-end differentiable proving. *Adv. Neural Inf. Process. Syst.*, 30, 2017.
22. Minervini, P., Riedel, S., Stenetorp, P., Grefenstette, E., Rocktäschel, T., Learning reasoning strategies in end-to-end differentiable proving, in: *International Conference on Machine Learning*, 2020 Nov 21, PMLR, pp. 6938–6949.
23. Weber, L., Minervini, P., Münchmeyer, J., Leser, U., Rocktäschel, T., Nlprolog: Reasoning with weak unification for question answering in natural language. *arXiv preprint arXiv:1906.06187*, 2019 Jun 14.
24. Tsamoura, E., Hospedales, T., Michael, L., Neural-symbolic integration: A compositional perspective. *Proc. AAAI Conf. Artif. Intell.*, 35, 6, 5051–5060, 2021 May 18.
25. Si, X., Raghothaman, M., Heo, K., Naik, M., Synthesizing datalog programs using numerical relaxation. arXiv preprint arXiv:1906.00163, 2019 Jun 1.
26. Keber, M., Grubišić, I., Barešić, A., Jović, A., A review on neuro-symbolic AI improvements to natural language processing, in: *2024 47th MIPRO ICT and Electronics Convention (MIPRO)*, 2024 May 20, IEEE, pp. 66–72.
27. Pennington, J., Socher, R., Manning, C.D., Glove: Global vectors for word representation, in: *Proceedings of the 2014 Conference on Empirical Methods in Natural Language Processing (EMNLP)*, 2014 Oct, pp. 1532–1543.
28. Dai, H., Tian, Y., Dai, B., Skiena, S., Song, L., Syntax-directed variational autoencoder for structured data. arXiv preprint arXiv:1802.08786, 2018 Feb 24.
29. Balasubramani, S., Renjith, P.N., Ramesh, K., George, A.H., George, A.S., Shahul, A., A detailed analysis of many different artificial intelligence-based healthcare systems, in: *Handbook of Research on Thrust Technologies' Effect on Image Processing*, pp. 56–72, IGI Global, USA, 2023.
30. Hatzilygeroudis, I. and Prentzas, J., Neurules: improving the performance of symbolic rules. *Int. J. Artif. Intell. Tools*, 9, 01, 113–30, 2000 Mar.
31. Omlin, C.W. and Snyders, S., Inductive bias strength in knowledge-based neural networks: application to magnetic resonance spectroscopy of breast tissues. *Artif. Intell. Med.*, 28, 2, 121–40, 2003 Jun 1.
32. Obot, O.U. and Uzoka, F.M., A framework for application of neuro-case-rule base hybridization in medical diagnosis. *Appl. Soft Comput.*, 9, 1, 245–53, 2009 Jan 1.
33. Coraggio, P., De Gregorio, M., Forastiere, M., Robot navigation based on neurosymbolic reasoning over landmarks. *Int. J. Pattern Recognit Artif Intell.*, 22, 05, 1001–14, 2008 Aug.
34. De Gregorio, M., An intelligent active video surveillance system based on the integration of virtual neural sensors and BDI agents. *IEICE Trans. Inf. Syst.*, 91, 7, 1914–21, 2008 Jul 1.
35. Balasubramani, S., Renjith, P.N., Kavisankar, L., Rajavel, R., Malarvel, M., Shankar, A., A Quantum-Enhanced Artificial Neural Network Model for Efficient Medical Image Compression. *IEEE Access*, 2025 Feb 17.

36. Golovko, V., Kroshchanka, A., Kovalev, M., Taberko, V., Ivaniuk, D., Neuro-symbolic artificial intelligence: application for control the quality of product labeling, in: *International Conference on Open Semantic Technologies for Intelligent Systems*, 2020 Feb 19, Springer International Publishing, Cham, pp. 81–101.
37. Bologna, G. and Hayashi, Y., Characterization of symbolic rules embedded in deep DIMLP networks: A challenge to transparency of deep learning. *J. Artif. Intell. Soft Comput. Res.*, 7, 4, 265–86, 2017.
38. Grieco, B.P., Lima, P.M., De Gregorio, M., França, F.M., Producing pattern examples from "mental" images. *Neurocomputing*, 73, 7-9, 1057–64, 2010 Mar 1.
39. Barbosa, R., Cardoso, D.O., Carvalho, D., Franca, F.M., Weightless neuro-symbolic GPS trajectory classification. *Neurocomputing*, 298, 100–8, 2018 Jul 12.
40. Khan, M.J. and Curry, E., Neuro-symbolic Visual Reasoning for Multimedia Event Processing: Overview, Prospects and Challenges, in: *CIKM (Workshops)*, 2020.
41. Yi, K., Wu, J., Gan, C., Torralba, A., Kohli, P., Tenenbaum, J., Neural-symbolic vqa: Disentangling reasoning from vision and language understanding. *Adv. Neural Inf. Process. Syst.*, 31, 2018.
42. Sareen, S., Prakhar, Kavisankar, L., Heart health status detection using ensemble learning with hyperparameter optimization. *AIP Conf. Proc.*, 3075, 1, 020189, 2024 Jul 29.
43. Bhatia, S., Kohli, P., Singh, R., Neuro-symbolic program corrector for introductory programming assignments, in: *Proceedings of the 40th International Conference on Software Engineering*, 2018 May 27, pp. 60–70.
44. Sen, P., de Carvalho, B.W., Riegel, R., Gray, A., Neuro-symbolic inductive logic programming with logical neural networks. *Proc. AAAI Conf. Artif. Intell.*, 36, 8, 8212–8219, 2022 Jun 28.
45. Chaudhuri, S., Ellis, K., Polozov, O., Singh, R., Solar-Lezama, A., Yue, Y., Neurosymbolic programming. *Found. Trends® Program. Lang.*, 7, 3, 158–243, 2021 Dec 8.
46. Ritchie, D., Guerrero, P., Jones, R.K., Mitra, N.J., Schulz, A., Willis, K.D., Wu, J., Neurosymbolic models for computer graphics. *Comput. Graphics Forum*, 42, 2, 545–568, 2023 May.
47. Varela, F.A., *The effects of hybrid neural networks on meta-learning objectives*, University of Washington, 2022.
48. Mythili, S., Nidhya, R., Kumar, R.A., AI-driven security framework for enhanced threat detection in mobile satellite networks. *ICTACT J. Commun. Technol.*, 16, 1, 2025.
49. Smilarubavathy, G. and Ka, M.A., Empowering Product Purchase Decisions through AI-Driven Review Analysis and Summarization, in: *2024 International Conference on Inventive Computation Technologies (ICICT)*, 2024, April, IEEE, pp. 155–162.

Part 2

NEURO-SYMBOLIC AI: APPLICATIONS

8

A Rule-Based Decision Framework for Accident Prevention in Intelligent Transport Systems

D. Pavithra[1]*, T. Deepa[2], Shaik Naseema[3], R. Nidhya[4], G. Smilarubavathy[5] and C. Kumar[6]

[1]*Department of IT, Dr. N. G. P. Institute of Technology, Tamilnadu, India*
[2]*Department of CSE, PSNA College of Engineering and Technology, Tamilnadu, India*
[3]*Department of CSE, Annamacharya University, Andhra Pradesh, India*
[4]*Dept. of Computer Science & Engineering, Madanapalle Institute of Technology & Science (MITS) Deemed to be University, Madanapalle, Andhra Pradesh, India*
[5]*Department of CSE, St. Joseph's Institute of Technology, Tamilnadu, India*
[6]*Department of ECE, MITS Deemed to be University, Madanapalle, Andhra Pradesh, India*

Abstract

Intelligent transportation systems (ITS) are essential to diminish traffic deaths and enhance road safety. The growing number of vehicles on the road makes driving more complicated. This study uses an innovative rule-based methodology to investigate critical determinants of collision likelihood, such as speed, lane shifts, vehicle spacing, traffic congestion, weather conditions, and erratic driving. The proposed system's elements enhance data acquisition, purification, and normalization, allowing for instantaneous decision-making according to established criteria. Experts developed a rule-based inference engine that analyzes standardized data for potential dangers. By swiftly notifying the driver and surrounding motorists of a potential collision, the device can reduce the likelihood of an accident. This technology accurately replicates traffic by identifying near-misses, reducing accident occurrences, and quickly adapting to changing road conditions. Incidents and near-misses are significantly rarer during peak hours. As the system advances, an increasing number of individuals will be able to utilize it. The rule-based method is an excellent choice for real-time intelligent transportation system applications due to its simplicity, cost-effectiveness, and user-friendliness.

**Corresponding author*: Pavimba07@gmail.com

R. Nidhya, A. Dineshkumar, Sheng-Lung Peng, S. Karthik and S. Balamurugan (eds.) Neuro-Symbolic Artificial Intelligence: Concepts & Applications, (145–166) © 2026 Scrivener Publishing LLC

***Keywords*:** Intelligent transportation system, IoV, accident prevention, rule-based model

8.1 Introduction

The increased number of vehicles in urban areas has led to greater road dangers, worsened traffic congestion, and, most notably, an increase in accidents. According to the World Health Organization (WHO), one person dies in a car accident every day, and millions more are injured or disabled [1]. These concerning statistics underscore the need for proactive, flexible, and innovative strategies to reduce the incidence of accidents across all modes of transportation. Given the current state of traffic, traditional accident prevention strategies, which primarily rely on reactive measures such as emergency braking and accident data analysis, are insufficient [2]. To reduce errors, firms are developing advanced, real-time predictive systems.

Intelligent transportation systems (ITS) have the ability to transform outdated roadways into intelligent, adaptive ecosystems [3]. ITS enhances transportation safety, efficiency, and environmental sustainability by utilizing sensors, real-time data processing, traffic management systems, and vehicle-to-vehicle communication. The primary goal is to prevent collisions by quickly recognizing hazardous driving conditions and implementing necessary safety protocols. This proactive strategy aims to reduce accident-related expenses, improve traffic flow, and lower fatalities and injuries.

For intelligent mobility solutions to operate, vehicles must be connected to centralized infrastructure and systems that perpetually transmit and receive data [4]. The Internet of Vehicles (IoV) enhances traffic safety by facilitating communication among vehicles *via* a network of terminals that monitor variables such as weather conditions, vehicle location, driving habits, and lane changes [5]. Drivers must exercise heightened caution when navigating sudden turns or stopping in close proximity to other vehicles. Solid judgment is fundamental to the decision-making algorithms of Intelligent Transportation Systems (ITS) and the Internet of Vehicles (IoV). Nonetheless, their intricacy and design make them more effective at preventing accidents [6].

Researchers are examining the predictive capabilities of machine learning and deep learning in disaster situations [7, 8]. These systems are highly advanced and require substantial training data. They are also excessively costly for real-time vehicles with constrained capabilities. Rule-based systems provide unequivocal, rapid, uniform, and comprehensible outcomes.

These systems use conditional criteria to identify and prevent negative outcomes. Several factors contribute to this, including vehicle speed, lane changes, inter-vehicle distance, traffic congestion, adverse weather conditions, and erratic driving behaviors [9–11]. Through data pattern analysis, these systems develop intricate algorithms, allowing users to obtain accurate and prompt responses.

This research advocates establishing a comprehensive, rule-based framework to improve the safety of intelligent transportation networks and heavy vehicles. The system ensures continuous connectivity between vehicles and roadside sensors. It enables the swift evaluation of incidents and the immediate dissemination of messages. The proposed system includes real-time notifications, rule-based deductions, data gathering, data purification, and consistency testing. By reducing the number of mandated procedures, each component aims to streamline the process of recognizing and addressing emergencies. This highly adaptable concept is applicable to both centralized and decentralized transportation and communication systems.

The system's primary advantage is its ability to swiftly and effortlessly identify threats without requiring complex learning models. The program's main challenges are aggressive driving in adverse weather conditions, frequent lane changes in congested areas, and inadequate vehicle spacing. Researchers routinely analyze driving behaviors to assess accident probabilities and improve road safety. The system uses a logical inference engine to evaluate behaviors, detect hazards, and alert the appropriate traffic control systems or vehicles.

Our model improves the safety and efficiency of intelligent transportation systems by reducing incidents that cause traffic congestion and enhancing traffic flow. This method minimizes accidents and near misses by analyzing data and developing scenarios. It is the optimal selection for IoV systems that must handle substantial traffic volumes because it excels on highways and in urban environments.

8.2 Related Work

Extended Support Vector Data Description (E-SVDD) [12] is an analytical method designed to evaluate and manage dynamic clusters within an automotive collision avoidance system. It enables more precise forecasting of macroscopic and microscopic processes. The E-SVDD technique and system modeling revealed that the time-to-collision concept is crucial for establishing the pertinent generalized theoretical framework. A groundbreaking method was devised to develop collision avoidance control logic and generate real-time predictions of macrosystem and microsystem behavior. The method is efficient. This model compared the suggested collision avoidance system to the standard approach using actual driving data and a computer simulation. The proposed control logic demonstrated greater success and efficiency.

Autonomous vehicles use trajectory planning and tracking technologies to maintain their route. For path planning, a three-dimensional virtual hazardous potential field is generated by integrating the trigonometric functions of the roadway with the exponential functions of obstacles [13]. The way a vehicle interacts with its surroundings determines the optimal strategy for avoiding collisions. To oversee the intended trajectory for collision-avoidance maneuvers, the path-tracking controller first converts the tracking task into a multiconstrained model predictive control problem. Then, it computes the front steering angle to prevent a collision with an oncoming vehicle. Simulink and CarSim facilitate simulations in environments with changing boundaries. Despite the remarkable mobility and dynamic tracking skills of the MMPC-based path-tracking controller, simulation findings indicate that the proposed path-planning method performs effectively under diverse driving conditions.

This research presents a Road Accident Prevention (RAP) technique [14] that uses a vehicular backbone network (VBN) architecture to improve highway safety for vehicular *ad hoc* networks. The RAP program aims to reduce highway traffic accidents, thereby decreasing injuries and fatalities. Upon identifying a potential emergency, the RAP program begins a four-phase preventive campaign. A VBN framework facilitates message dissemination. The RSU produces a Prediction Report (PR) using real-time vehicle and traffic data. An Emergency Warning Message (EWM) is dispatched in response to anomalous PRs and transmitted to vehicles exhibiting elevated Risk Factors (RF) within High-Risk Zones (HRZ), regardless of their proximity to the RSU's direct communication range. The VBN architecture improves system scalability and range by efficiently transmitting EWMs beyond RSU coverage. Simulation results show that RAP decreases end-to-end delay by 14.38% and improves warning distribution efficiency by 19% at a vehicle density of 160. Furthermore, the VBN architecture diminishes the quantity of necessary RSUs, thereby reducing infrastructure costs. The method's practical applicability in intelligent transportation systems is demonstrated by its favorable outcomes in four-lane highway environments.

Vehicular accidents are more likely to occur in situations where traffic is moving slowly and unexpectedly, particularly on highways and major roads. The use of stationary traffic sensors on highways is decreasing [15], especially in rural areas. This study introduces an innovative method for traffic surveillance and alert notifications using an Internet of Things (IoT) cloud framework. OpenStreetMap displays real-time traffic conditions by aggregating geolocation and velocity data from a GSM/GPRS/GPS TK103 tracker installed in vehicles. An OpenGTS server acquires and archives this data in an SQL database. A GeoJSON parsing microservice processes incoming unstructured geolocation data before saving it in a distributed MongoDB database. An additional microservice monitors changes in the locations of vehicles within a specific area and notifies mobile applications of unexpected traffic conditions.

This decision support system is to develop techniques that effectively reduce the frequency and severity of road accidents [16]. Recent studies have demonstrated that in-car decision support systems significantly enhance driving behavior and decrease the likelihood of collisions. A comprehensive in-vehicle Decision Support System (DSS) has been developed that alerts drivers to collision clusters using a statewide historical accident dataset comprising over 266,000 incidents. Here, it presents the design and field evaluation of an in-vehicle decision assistance system integrating alerts and location data. During a four-week statewide field test, 57 experienced drivers collected vehicle data over 170,000 kilometers using a connected car prototype system. Ultimately, we demonstrate how temporal in-vehicle alerts about accident-prone areas can significantly improve driver behavior. Additionally, we present initial evidence suggesting that an individual's predisposition has a substantial impact on the effectiveness of in-vehicle decision support systems.

The proposed method anticipates crashes and guides compliant drivers toward nearby vehicles with irregularities by accurately recognizing rogue drivers through VANET communication. The suggested model comprises three distinct parameters, each with sub-parameters utilized in the goal function. Each objective function is statistically validated to accurately identify sources of anomalies [17].

Driver awareness and comprehension are crucial for reducing car accidents. Authors [18] developed an algorithm that mitigates head-on, T-bone, and rear-end collisions, as well as pedestrian errors. Our dynamic, real-time approach utilizes a deep learning image classification framework to prevent rear-end and proximate collisions. The processing unit is a Raspberry Pi 4 Model B with 8 GB of RAM that operates Python 3 with the OpenCV software. A deep learning architecture performs position tracking, distance measurement, and object detection in real time across various ambient conditions without the need for sensors. The Raspberry Pi NoIR Camera Module V2 provides the MobileNet DLA with real-time frames for Single Shot Multibox Detection. This technology can precisely calculate the distance between vehicles and other objects every 0.09 seconds (11 fps) and generate warning signals as needed using real-time positional data. Multivariate analysis and repeated measures ANOVA assess output data instantaneously. The Multimodal Early Accident Alarming System significantly assists inattentive drivers.

This study [19] presents a prototype that uses a Raspberry Pi, a Pi camera, and sensors to monitor a driver's eye movements, identify hazardous substances, detect yawning, and evaluate alcohol consumption. The goal is to enhance driving safety and prevent accidents. Integrating Internet of Things and machine learning technologies into vehicles enables rapid emergency responses by transmitting driving patterns and driver behavior to the cloud. A sound system that alerts motorists to potential distractions can save lives. Machine learning and cloud services evaluate and store data to identify fatigued drivers. The device's efficacy and utility have been validated through experimental testing.

This study [20] examines logistic regression, decision trees, random forests, deep neural networks, support vector machines, K-nearest neighbors, naïve Bayes, empirical Bayes, geospatial analysis, and the UIMA, NSGA-II, and MOPS algorithms. The paper addresses contemporary concerns, safety protocols, and potential solutions to mitigate traffic and accidents on roadways. Temporal data, advanced optimization algorithms, machine learning, and GIS-based spatial statistical methods are used to create accurate predictive models that identify accident hotspots, reduce traffic congestion, improve safety, and lower the frequency of incidents. Accident prediction systems require spatial information to mitigate urban traffic congestion. Spatial analysis improves road safety planning by identifying high-risk areas, assessing interventions, and allocating funds to support road safety initiatives and decision-making in resource-constrained environments. Therefore, machine learning, spatial analytical methods, sophisticated optimization algorithms, improvements in traffic flow management, and enhancements to these attributes must be incorporated into road safety research and transportation planning.

The proposed driver decision support system (DDSS) [21] categorizes individuals as proficient or poor drivers to predict driving behavior. Integrated with ITS, the DSS can detect anomalous vehicle behavior and alert other vehicles to decelerate or change lanes to prevent crashes. The K-means clustering algorithm categorizes drivers according to their driving behavior to facilitate predictive analysis. For evaluation, we employ Naïve Bayes, decision trees, K-nearest neighbors, support vector machines, and logistic regression. ITS systems have been enhanced, resulting in reduced accident rates due to the integration of DDSS connectivity. By studying and assessing drivers' performance, we can implement legislation that discourages accidents and promotes safe driving behaviors. This research improves the transportation system by reducing accidents caused by negligent driving. The suggested DDSS could enhance road safety and reduce accident rates. It uses an innovative method to predict and control driver's behavior. Our findings suggest that the driver's behavior prediction method is reliable and beneficial.

This study [22] presents an effective method for using facial expression recognition technology to determine if a driver is distressed. This model uses the VGG-16 model and transfer learning to evaluate stress levels in drivers. This approach reduces the amount of training data required while enhancing task adaptability by utilizing data from the pretrained model. We use a collection of images of contented and dissatisfied drivers to evaluate and train the proposed model. The proposed method analyzes drivers' facial expressions to detect behaviors atypical of grieving. Upon detecting indications of unhappiness, the technology relinquishes control from the driver to the vehicle's autonomous systems. The objective of this automated system is to reduce accidents caused by drunk driving.

8.3 Rule-Based Accident Prevention System

8.3.1 Data Acquisition Module

The Data Acquisition Module powers the Rule-Based Framework for Disaster Prevention and Mitigation. It continuously gathers real-time data from sensors, subsystems, and external sources to provide a comprehensive overview of vehicle dynamics and the surrounding environment. The module's primary objective is to improve the accuracy, usefulness, and comprehensiveness of data collection in various contexts. This allows for decision-making based on established rules and more precise estimates.

The vehicle's speed is monitored by OBD-II, GPS devices, and wheel speed sensors. These facilitate the computation of acceleration and deceleration rates. Front and rear cameras, steering angle sensors, and inertial measurement units (IMUs) can identify lane changes in a vehicle. The vehicle's biological sensors and cameras can detect unusual behaviors, such as a driver suddenly speeding up or slowing down, or showing signs of fatigue. Vehicle-to-vehicle and vehicle-to-infrastructure communication systems use traffic flow data, vehicle density, and additional dangers to assess traffic conditions. Thermometers, rain gauges, and visibility sensors enable meteorological data collection. Integrating meteorological API data from multiple sources can improve understanding.

The module improves measurement precision and reliability by integrating data from multiple redundant sensors. Each data stream is time-stamped using GPS or vehicle clock synchronization to ensure optimal temporal alignment. Furthermore, local preprocessing of significant events, data buffering, and edge processing mitigate the latency associated with central processing. The system's modular, expandable design makes it suitable for various vehicle types and weather conditions.

8.3.2 Normalization Process

Vehicle Speed

Vehicle speed is a crucial factor in accident prevention because it directly affects mobility, stopping distance, and the intensity of impact. To provide a uniform interpretation across various traffic scenarios, vehicle speed is standardized to match the recommended or permitted speed limit of the section of road in use.

$$V_n = {}^{V_c}\!/_{V_T}$$

where

V_n is the normalized speed,
V_c is the current speed, and
V_T is the threshold speed.

During the normalization process, the actual vehicle speed is scaled to match the maximum allowable speed using the min-max normalization approach. As a result, a number between 0 and 1 is produced. The car is accelerating if the number is greater than 1, and it is approaching or at the speed limit if the number is around 1. For example, a car traveling at 90 km/h in a 120-km/h zone may often reach 0.75, typically considered a reasonably safe speed. The system may flag normalized values above a certain threshold, such as 0.85 or 0.90, as dangerous, especially when adverse circumstances, like inclement weather or heavy traffic, are present. This normalization helps the rule-based engine continuously adapt its inference logic to the contextual speed environment. It also helps assess overspeeding in absolute terms and what is considered safe from both legal and cultural standpoints. Furthermore, the system can adapt to a range of route types, including urban, suburban, and interstate, by tailoring safety criteria to local limits rather than rigid international standards. Speed normalization is a crucial component in enhancing the overall dependability of the accident prevention system and the accuracy of real-time decisions.

Lane Changes

Although a driver who frequently changes lanes may demonstrate proficiency and resolve, they may also exhibit aggressive or hazardous behavior. The proposed approach allows for a consistent analysis of traffic patterns under various conditions and on different routes by permitting frequent lane changes. By evaluating the frequency of lane changes over a specified distance or time interval — such as 5 kilometers — against a predetermined upper limit that signifies the maximum safe driving speed, one can determine whether a condition is standard. The maximum lane change rate is monitored every minute. The normal setting for this is five changes per minute. This threshold can be objectively established using historical data or traffic safety regulations. The normalized lane change value is the following:

$$L_n = {}^{L_{nc}}\!/_{L_T}$$

where

L_n is the normalized lane change,
L_{nc} is the number of lane change, and
L_T is the lane change threshold.

An increase in the frequency of lane changes signals more aggressive or erratic driving behavior, with potential outcomes ranging from 0 to 1. An automobile that changes lanes 3 times per minute, when the maximum allowed frequency is 5, would receive a normalized score of 0.6, indicating notably aggressive behavior. Frequent lane changes reduce the reaction time of adjacent vehicles in congested or high-speed traffic, thereby increasing the risk of side collisions and near misses. Incorporating this normalized data may assist the rule-based methodology in identifying anomalous lane-switching behavior and refining the risk assessment. This is particularly significant when considering additional factors such as proximity, high speeds, or poor visibility. Managing the frequency of lane changes helps anticipate hazardous behavior, ascertain driving intent, and implement early accident avoidance measures.

Inter-Vehicle Distance

The inter-vehicle gap, defined as the distance between a vehicle and the one in front of it, is crucial for mitigating rear-end collisions. The proposed system automatically adjusts the following distance according to the vehicle's current speed using the "two-second rule" or a similar, speed-dependent safety distance method. The normalized inter-vehicle distance, defined as the difference between the required safe distance (D_s) and the actual measured distance (D_A), which increases with velocity, must be understood to ensure adequate response time and braking distance.

$$D_n = {}^{D_A}\!/_{D_s}$$

where

D_n is the normalized distance,
D_A is the actual distance, and
D_s is the safe distance.

The normalization results in a value of 0 when the actual distance exceeds the safe threshold. This indicates a low-risk situation. As the vehicle approaches the one ahead, the data indicates a high-risk situation. They inhabit the vicinity. An actual distance of 20 meters produces a normalized value of 0.43 in relation to a safe distance of 35 meters at 90 km/h, indicating a potentially dangerous condition. A score approaching 1 indicates sluggish growth and a higher risk of collision if a vehicle stops suddenly behind another. The device can identify tailgating in real time by standardizing the distance between vehicles and triggering alarms or corrective actions, such as driver notifications or adaptive cruise control. This technology enables the rule-based system to continuously evaluate vehicle spacing and maintain appropriate driving distances in various conditions and at different speeds in both urban and highway environments.

Weather Conditions

An accident prevention system must accurately reflect the significant impact of weather on road safety, vehicle dynamics, and driver behavior. To fully integrate meteorological data into the rule-based model, qualitative weather descriptors are converted into a quantitative hazard score and normalized on a scale of 0 to 1. Driving conditions deteriorate as values increase. Various meteorological factors significantly influence road traction, visibility, and driver perception. Factors like clear weather, light precipitation, fog, snowfall, severe storms, and overcast conditions all have an impact.

Table 8.1 Normalized value based on weather conditions.

Weather condition	Score	Normalized value
Clear	0	0.0
Cloudy	1	0.2
Rainy	2	0.4
Foggy	3	0.6
Snowy	4	0.8
Storm/Extreme	5	1.0

Light rain or fog receives a score ranging from 0.4 to 0.6, while clear weather receives a score of 0. Table 8.1 assigns 1 point to adverse weather conditions, such as fog or snowstorms. This normalization allows the computer to consider weather risk alongside other contributing factors. This significantly enhances its ability to draw conclusions. The rule engine is more sensitive to changes in lane, speed, and deceleration when the snow-normalized meteorological parameter is set to 0.8. This improves the system's responsiveness in dangerous situations. This technology integrates real-time data from external sources, such as meteorological application programming interfaces (APIs), with internal sensor data, including visibility and precipitation. This enables the system to adapt to environmental changes. Transforming complex, standardized meteorological data into a hazard score improves road safety evaluations. It improves predictive accuracy and reduces the likelihood of adverse outcomes in inclement weather.

Traffic Density

Traffic density is a crucial contextual factor in accident prediction because it directly affects mobility space, reaction time, and the likelihood of collisions involving multiple vehicles. The optimal method for assessing traffic density is to calculate the number of vehicles per kilometer of roadway. This can be achieved using a congestion index that utilizes V2V or V2I communications. A rating ranging from 0 to 1 is established based on the initial count; 0 signifies unobstructed flow, while 1 indicates severe congestion, as shown in Table 8.2. Vehicle densities of 70 or more per kilometer may reach 0.8 or higher, indicating significant congestion and restricted mobility. The standard is 0.3, or 30 cars per kilometer. This normalization

Table 8.2 Normalized value based on traffic level.

Traffic level	Vehicles/km	Normalized value
Low	<30	0.2
Moderate	30–70	0.5
High	>70	0.8–1.0

allows the system to adapt to changing traffic conditions in urban, suburban, and interstate environments by maintaining consistent decision criteria. The rule engine exhibits heightened caution when vehicle proximity increases alongside rising normalized traffic density values, resulting in reduced speed limits and stricter lane change regulations. Refining the density measure to account for unpredictable traffic flow, including stop-and-go patterns, can significantly enhance the efficacy of risk assessment and modeling. This method improves the accident avoidance system's situational awareness and responsiveness by converting real-time traffic data into a customized warning signal, allowing vehicles to respond to current traffic congestion.

Abnormal Driver Behavior

Substandard driving behaviors have a significant impact on road safety, making early accident prevention essential. Driver monitoring systems (DMS), in-vehicle sensors, and behavioral analytics algorithms help identify and assess atypical driving behaviors. These behaviors include fatigue, distraction, abrupt acceleration or deceleration, and intentional or unintentional lane changes. These behavioral indicators significantly impact driving safety. Several signals are combined to create a composite behavioral risk score. Then, the entire score is standardized to a range of 0 to 1, where 0 denotes typical safe driving and 1 denotes atypical or hazardous driving. The mean score for aggressive and distracted driving is 0.7. For a prudent driver, the distraction and rapid deceleration values are 0.4 and 0.3, respectively. Driving conduct exceeding the 0.6 level is considered high risk, as shown in Table 8.3. This continuous scoring method enables the platform to illustrate changes in driver condition and behavior dynamically. This facilitates prompt responses, such as issuing visual or auditory alerts or executing partially autonomous corrective measures. The technology improves decision-making accuracy by identifying and evaluating behavioral patterns to distinguish between occasional errors and consistent misconduct. Integrating this normalized behavioral score into a

Table 8.3 Normalized value based on driver behavior.

Behavior type	Detected	Weight	Contribution
Distraction	Yes	0.4	0.4
Drowsiness	No	0.3	0.0
Aggressive Braking	Yes	0.3	0.3

rule-based framework that assesses driver-related dangers, vehicle factors, and environmental factors improves understanding of accident frequency. It increases the likelihood of proactive accident prevention.

8.3.3 Rule-Based Inference Engine

The rule-based inference engine executes most of the decisions in the suggested accident prevention system. Various input data, including vehicle velocity, lane change incidence, inter-vehicle spacing, traffic density, meteorological conditions, and atypical driver behavior, are systematically assessed. The engine then uses established safety standards to evaluate risk and implement the necessary remedial measures.

Algorithm 8.1 Rule-Based Inference Engine for Accident Avoidance.

Input:
V_n ← Normalized Vehicle Speed
L_n ← Normalized Lane Change Frequency
Dn ← Normalized Inter-Vehicle Distance
W_n ← Normalized Weather Condition
T_n ← Normalized Traffic Density
DB_n ← Normalized Abnormal Driver Behavior
Output:
Risk_Level ∈ {Low, Moderate, High, Critical}
Action ∈ {No_Action, Alert_Driver, Reduce_Speed, Activate_Assist}
Begin:
Initialize Risk_Score ← 0
Define Risk_Weights for each parameter:
  Wv ← 0.2// weight for speed
  Wl ← 0.15 // weight for lane change
  Wd ← 0.2// weight for distance
  Ww ← 0.15 // weight for weather

```
  Wt ← 0.1  // weight for traffic
  Wb ← 0.2  // weight for behavior
Compute weighted Risk_Score:
  Risk_Score ← (V_n × Wv) + (L_n × Wl) + (D_n × Wd) + (W_n × Ww) + (T_n ×
  Wt) + (DB_n × Wb)
Evaluate Risk_Level based on Risk_Score:
  If Risk_Score < 0.3:
    Risk_Level ← Low
    Action ← No_Action
  Else if Risk_Score ≥ 0.3 and Risk_Score < 0.5:
    Risk_Level ← Moderate
    Action ← Alert_Driver
  Else if Risk_Score ≥ 0.5 and Risk_Score < 0.7:
    Risk_Level ← High
    Action ← Reduce_Speed
  Else:
    Risk_Level ← Critical
    Action ← Activate_Assist

Output Risk_Level and corresponding Action

End
```

First, the relative intensity or deviation of each input value from a safe condition is normalized to a [0, 1] scale. These values are then evaluated using a framework of expert-defined if-then criteria based on empirical data, risk models, and road safety rules. These limitations significantly enhance the likelihood of accidents by addressing both individual threshold violations, such as speeding in fog, and composite behaviors, including excessive speeding in crowded traffic with insufficient following distance. After assessing the situation, the inference engine uses forward chaining to orchestrate warning or intervention strategies and provide a suitable risk response (low, moderate, high, or critical). The interpretability and real-time responsiveness of this logical reasoning framework make it ideal for onboard car safety systems.

This technique assigns a weight to each component according to its relevance to road safety because driving irregularities and vehicle spacing significantly impact accident probability. Weighted data is then aggregated to yield a composite risk score. This score reflects the current state of vehicular safety. Risk can be classified into one of four categories: low, moderate, high, or critical. The optimal choice is determined by the risk score. Each category influences the system's operation differently, depending on the circumstances. Although it may not be used in secure conditions, it can emit an alarm, autonomously stop the vehicle, or activate advanced driver-assistance features in dangerous situations. The system uses several concepts defined by experts, including alerting users to dangerous weather conditions that may pose risks when traveling at high speeds or changing lanes frequently. Rule-based reasoning combined with a weighted risk assessment ensures reliability, efficiency, and a rapid response. The system continuously adjusts safety elements according to driving behavior, thereby reducing the likelihood of accidents.

8.3.4 Real-Time Decision and Alert Generation

The proposed rule-based accident avoidance system mitigates expected road risks by facilitating swift and efficient safety interventions through real-time decision-making and alarm generation. The Rule-Based Inference Engine generates a risk score, enabling the system to respond promptly based on one of four predefined risk categories: Low, Moderate, High, or Critical. The responders recommended passive and aggressive safety measures. Currently, no legislation exists to mitigate the likelihood of modest, low-risk driving distractions. Subtle visual or auditory signals of moderate risk progressively notify the driver of challenges, such as slight weather fluctuations, increased traffic, or reduced speed. When the risk level exceeds high, the framework uses more assertive feedback methods, such as vibrating steering wheels, dashboard light notifications, and auditory alerts that instruct the driver to take specific actions, such as decelerating or increasing the following distance. Lane centering, automated deceleration, and emergency braking are semi-autonomous features that enhance Advanced Driver-Assistance Systems (ADAS) by improving reaction precision and reducing human response times in high-speed, low-visibility, and unexpected driving conditions.

To maintain continuous situational awareness, the real-time decision and alert module utilizes a monitoring loop with high refresh rates to collect data from external sources, including onboard sensors, vehicle control units, and traffic APIs. This technique fosters contextual thinking. For example, maintaining a specific speed on a dry roadway may be prudent, but this could become perilous in torrential rain. The system autonomously modifies its warning thresholds and response strategies based on recognized behavioral and environmental variables. The alert system limits the number of signals presented to the driver at one time to ensure that only the most critical warnings are shown. Augmenting warning sensitivity and diminishing false alarms based on prior driver enhancements would provide the module with enhanced user autonomy. Technological developments enable real-time risk assessment and decision-making, which significantly reduce traffic accidents and foster proactive safety and confident driving.

8.4 Simulation Results

Several simulation tools are utilized to manage the VANET routing systems. This system implements Simulation of Urban Mobility (SUMO) and Network Simulator-3 (NS-3). SUMO, a widely used open-source traffic simulation software, is employed to analyze and assess vehicular behavior in urban environments. SUMO, a multifaceted tool, facilitates the alteration of road networks, vehicle classifications, traffic flow dynamics, and various simulation components. SUMO can simulate extended urban mobility scenarios, encompassing traffic light operations, road traffic flow, and individual vehicle movements. It can assimilate real-world road networks in various formats, including OpenStreetMap data, and provide authentic traffic scenarios based on actual traffic patterns. SUMO can produce a trace file that includes vehicle movement data within the simulation scenario shown in Figure 8.1.

Figure 8.2 shows how effective the proposed Rule-Based Accident Avoidance Framework is at reducing incident frequency at different

Figure 8.1 SUMO simulation map.

traffic volumes. The data clearly demonstrate a consistent and measurable improvement in safety performance. In a simulation with 50 vehicles, the number of incidents decreased from 8 without the system to 5 with the proposed technique, a 37.5% reduction. The number of accidents decreased from 14 to 8, indicating a 42.8% reduction per 100 vehicles despite the overall increase in vehicle count. Despite the system's increasing complexity, the framework remains effective with 200 cars, as evidenced by a 45% decrease in accidents, from 20 to 11. At the highest evaluated density, accident rates decreased by 37.5% for 300 vehicles (from 24 to 15), by 33.3% for 400 vehicles (from 27 to 18), and by 30% for 500 vehicles (from 30 to 21). These results suggest that increased density has advantages. Although the proportion of high-vehicle incidents decreases due to increased traffic complexity, the data indicate that the system consistently enhances safety. The rule-based approach is particularly effective at implementing rapid, proactive, and comprehensible safety measures in urban and highway environments. The consistent reduction in accidents despite fluctuating traffic volumes illustrates the strategy's adaptability and effectiveness.

The system's effectiveness in identifying near-miss incidents across various traffic circumstances can be determined by examining the graph's numerical patterns. Figure 8.3 shows that out of six near-miss incidents observed during 50 vehicle inspections, the system accurately detected three, resulting in a 50% detection rate. With 100 vehicles, incidents and detections increased to eight and four, respectively, though the relative

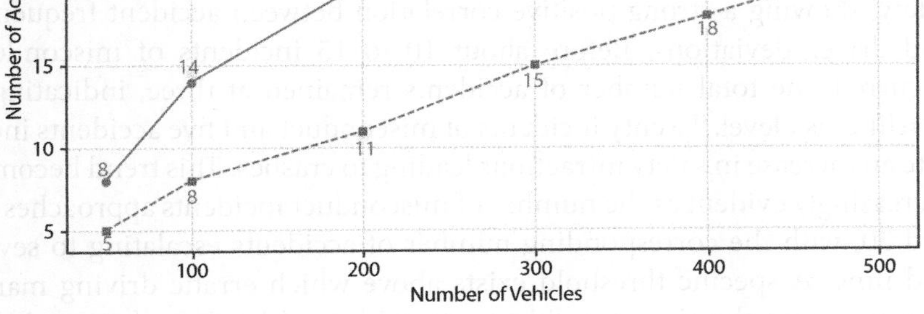

Figure 8.2 Number of accidents vs vehicles.

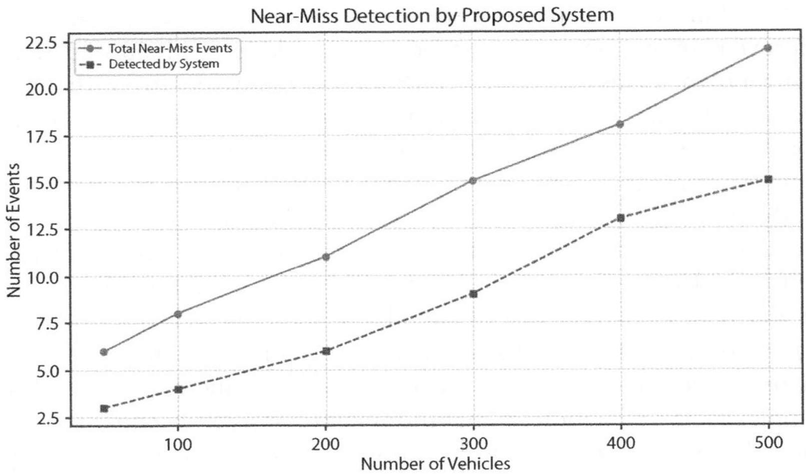

Figure 8.3 Near-miss detection.

efficiency remained the same. The algorithms identified six out of 11 instances where the number of vehicles neared 200, yielding a detection rate of over 54.5%. This pattern continued beyond 400 vehicles, increasing to 13 out of 18 (72.2%) following nine detections from 15 near-miss incidents (60%). Among a maximum of 500 vehicles, the system detected 15 out of 22 near-miss incidents, yielding a detection rate of 68.2%. These results unequivocally indicate a correlation between the frequency of near-miss crashes and increased vehicle interactions, which subsequently lead to greater traffic congestion. The proposed method improves the detection coverage of absolute and percentage data, making it suitable for increasing complexity. The consistent increase in detection levels and accuracy evidences the system's reliability and responsiveness to changing traffic conditions.

Figure 8.4 illustrates the significant impact of driver deviations on road safety, showing a strong positive correlation between accident frequency and driver deviations. Before about 10 to 15 incidents of misconduct occurred, the total number of accidents remained at three, indicating a baseline risk level. Twenty incidents of misconduct and five accidents indicate an increase in safety infractions leading to crashes. This trend becomes increasingly evident as the number of misconduct incidents approaches 25 and 30, with the corresponding number of accidents escalating to seven and nine. A specific threshold exists above which erratic driving markedly increases the risk of accidents, as evidenced by the substantial rise

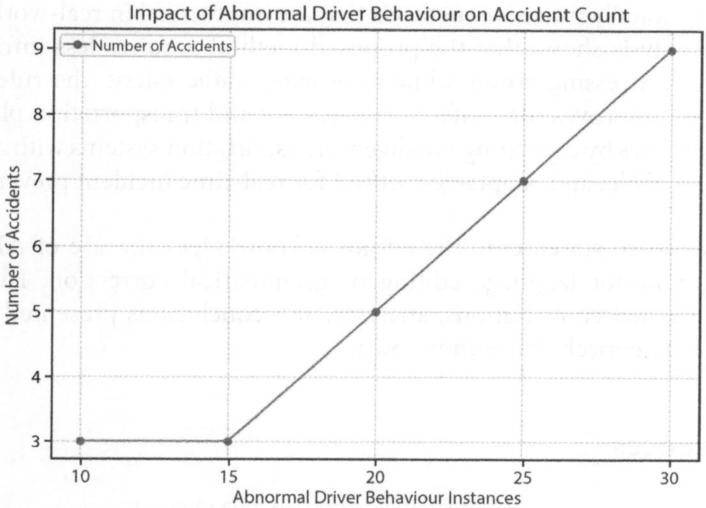

Figure 8.4 Number of accidents based on abnormal driver behavior.

in accident rates associated with 20 anomalous behaviors. These findings highlight the importance of continuous monitoring and preventive measures, as even minor instances of deviant behavior can significantly reduce the likelihood of future occurrences. The importance of driver behavior in accident prediction is emphasized, as well as the potential of autonomous interventions, real-time feedback, and alert systems to improve traffic safety.

8.5 Conclusion

The objective of the rule-based methodology discussed in this work is to help prevent accidents by assisting intelligent transportation systems prior to their occurrence. This technology can detect and assess numerous adverse conditions in real time. This method uses standardized data on velocity, lane changes, vehicle separation, driver behavior, traffic dynamics, and weather to create a coherent inference engine. It promptly alerts drivers and adjacent vehicles to potential hazards through organized conditional reasoning. The system's ability to detect near-misses improves with an increased volume of vehicles on the road, thereby reducing the incidence of accidents. This demonstrates the system's adaptability and operational capability. The framework accelerates reactions by bypassing computationally intensive methods that are impractical in real-world contexts. Analysis shows that the proposed method requires less infrastructure and processing power while improving traffic safety. The rule-based paradigm improves road safety management and transportation planning in smart cities by equipping intelligent transportation systems with a transparent, reliable, and adaptable method for real-time incident prevention.

AI disclosure statement: The author acknowledges the use of AI-based tools for minor language editing or grammatical correction. However, all intellectual contributions, analyses, and conclusions presented in this chapter are entirely the author's own.

References

1. https://www.who.int/publications/i/item/9789240086517.
2. Peelam, M.S., Gera, M., Chamola, V., Zeadally, S., A review on emergency vehicle management for intelligent transportation systems. *IEEE Trans. Intell. Transp. Syst.*, 2024 Aug 20.
3. Elassy, M., Al-Hattab, M., Takruri, M., Badawi, S., Intelligent transportation systems for sustainable smart cities. *Transp. Eng.*, 14, 100252, 2024 Apr.
4. Dui, H., Zhang, S., Liu, M., Dong, X., Bai, G., IoT-enabled real-time traffic monitoring and control management for intelligent transportation systems. *IEEE Internet Things J.*, 11, 9, 15842–54, 2024 Jan 9.
5. Ye, S., Wu, Q., Fan, P., Fan, Q., A Survey on Semantic Communications in Internet of Vehicles. *Entropy.*, 27, 4, 445, 2025 Apr 20.
6. Hamdi, W., Ksouri, C., Bulut, H., Mosbah, M., Network slicing based learning techniques for iov in 5g and beyond networks. *IEEE Commun. Surv. Tutorials*, 2024 Mar 1.
7. Joshi, M., Patel, A., Tripathy, A.K., Critical Analysis of ML-Based Service Provisioning in the Internet of Vehicles, in: *2024 4th International Conference on Artificial Intelligence and Signal Processing (AISP)*, IEEE, pp. 1–5, 2024 Oct 26.
8. Lin, Z., Cui, H., Liu, Y., Distributed Deep Learning Based on Edge Computing over Internet of Vehicles: Overview, Applications, Challenges. *IEEE Access*, 2024 Sep 5.
9. Kumar, N., Sood, S.K., Saini, M., IoV-fog-assisted framework for accident detection and classification. *ACM Trans. Embedded Comput. Syst.*, 2023.
10. Juvvalapalem, S. and Kanagaraj, V., Optimizing Lane-Change Decisions in VANETs: A Communication-Driven Approach. *Int. J. Commun. Syst.*, 38, 7, e70075, 2025 May 10.

11. Balasubramani, S. and Aravindhar, D.J., Impact of Driver Behavior in VANET Data Transmission, in: *2022 6th International Conference on Intelligent Computing and Control Systems (ICICCS)*, IEEE, pp. 759–764, 2022 May 25.
12. Yang, I.B., Na, S.G., Heo, H., Intelligent algorithm based on support vector data description for automotive collision avoidance system. *Int. J. Automot. Technol.*, 18, 1, 69–77, 2017 Feb.
13. Ji, J., Khajepour, A., Melek, W.W., Huang, Y., Path planning and tracking for vehicle collision avoidance based on model predictive control with multi-constraints. *IEEE Trans. Veh. Technol.*, 66, 2, 952–64, 2016 Apr 22.
14. Gokulakrishnan, P. and Ganeshkumar, P., Road accident prevention with instant emergency warning message dissemination in vehicular *ad-hoc* network. *PLoS One*, 10, 12, e0143383, 2015 Dec 4.
15. Celesti, A., Galletta, A., Carnevale, L., Fazio, M., Ĺay-Ekuakille, A., Villari, M., An IoT cloud system for traffic monitoring and vehicular accidents prevention based on mobile sensor data processing. *IEEE Sens. J.*, 18, 12, 4795–802, 2017 Nov 24.
16. Ryder, B., Gahr, B., Egolf, P., Dahlinger, A., Wortmann, F., Preventing traffic accidents with in-vehicle decision support systems-The impact of accident hotspot warnings on driver behaviour. *Decis. Support Syst.*, 99, 64–74, 2017 Jul 1.
17. Balasubramani, S. and Arvindhar, D.J., A predictive decision model for an efficient detection of abnormal driver behavior in intelligent transport system. *J. Manage. Inf. Decis. Sci.*, 24, 1–0, 2021.
18. Kabir, M.F. and Roy, S., Real-time vehicular accident prevention system using deep learning architecture. *Expert Syst. Appl.*, 206, 117837, 2022 Nov 15.
19. Uma, S. and Eswari, R., Accident prevention and safety assistance using IoT and machine learning. *J. Reliab. Intell. Environ.*, 8, 2, 79–103, 2022 Jun.
20. Berhanu, Y., Alemayehu, E., Schröder, D., Examining Car Accident Prediction Techniques and Road Traffic Congestion: A Comparative Analysis of Road Safety and Prevention of World Challenges in Low-Income and High-Income Countries. *J. Adv. Transp.*, 2023, 1, 6643412, 2023.
21. Balasubramani, S., Aravindhar, J., Renjith, P.N., Ramesh, K., DDSS: Driver decision support system based on the driver behaviour prediction to avoid accidents in intelligent transport system. *Int. J. Cognit. Comput. Eng.*, 5, 1–3, 2024 Jan 1.
22. Ahmed, M.H., Saeed, Y., Mehmood, A., Saeed, M., Ahmed, N., Ilyas, Q.M., Iqbal, S., Abid, N., Real-Time Driver Depression Monitoring for Accident Prevention in Smart Vehicles. *IEEE Access*, 2024 May 30.

9

A Hybrid Logic-Driven and Neural Parsing Framework for Enhanced Emotion Recognition in Natural Language Processing

R. Nidhya[1]*, V. Arun[2], T. Maragatham[3], D. J. Ashpin Pabi[1], Ajaypradeep N.[4] and Manish Kumar[5]

[1]*Dept. of Computer Science & Engineering, Madanapalle Institute of Technology & Science (MITS) Deemed to be University, Madanapalle, Andhra Pradesh, India*
[2]*School of Computing, SRM Institute of Science and Technology, Tamilnadu, India*
[3]*Department of Computer Technology-PG, Kongu Engineering College, Tamilnadu, India*
[4]*Department of AI & ML, Rajalakshmi Institute of Technology, Tamilnadu, India*
[5]*Department of CSE, Thapar Institute of Engineering & Technology, Punjab, India*

Abstract

Natural language processing (NLP) can deduce an individual's emotional state from their syntax and semantics. This proposed method presents an innovative hybrid methodology for the learning, development, and application of an emotion detection system. This approach employs a transformer architecture derived from BERT and a logic-driven neural parsing algorithm (LDNPA). Proponents assert that contextualized BERT embeddings consistently generate semantic text representations. The LDNPA is thought to interpret intricate emotional signals and incorporate them into its decision-making process. Our methodology integrates rule-based reasoning with data-driven neural computation, surpassing conventional statistical models. Consider this strategy if you are experiencing financial or emotional challenges. The findings indicate that IEMOCAP and CMU-MOSEI have both achieved significant advancements. This model's 95% F_1 score on CMU-MOSEI and 96% accuracy on IEMOCAP demonstrate its superiority over the baseline models of CNN, LSTM, and RNN. The findings indicate that integrating

**Corresponding author*: Nidhuraji88@gmail.com

R. Nidhya, A. Dineshkumar, Sheng-Lung Peng, S. Karthik and S. Balamurugan (eds.) Neuro-Symbolic Artificial Intelligence: Concepts & Applications, (167–188) © 2026 Scrivener Publishing LLC

deep learning with logic in natural language processing systems may enhance their capacity to identify and emphasize various emotions.

Keywords: Natural language processing, emotion recognition, BERT, deep learning

9.1 Introduction

The employment of "natural language" patterns is a recurrent phenomenon in the human-computer interaction paradigm. The efficacy of NLP for an individual is profoundly affected by their emotional intelligence [1]. Natural language processing has several practical applications, including chatbots, AI, psychological testing, sentiment analysis, and human-machine interactions. Human expressions are situational, imprecise, and often misread, which makes articulating emotions problematic. Verbal communication, surrounding objects, and the language used both explicitly and implicitly can all express emotions [2]. Despite their simplicity, conventional rule-based systems may struggle to achieve consistent generalizations across diverse languages and lexical patterns. Data-driven deep learning models [3], such as RNNs [4], LSTMs [5, 6], and BERT [7], may lack the capacity to elucidate or rationalize their decisions. Therefore, a hybrid system must be developed that integrates the optimal features of neural networks and symbolic logic. This methodology would combine the organization and clarity of symbolic logic with the accuracy and flexibility of neural networks.

Recent advancements in transformer-based models, particularly Bidirectional Encoder Representations from Transformers (BERT) [8], have had a significant impact on natural language processing. BERT excels at various NLP tasks, such as semantic inference, text classification, and query response. During the preparation and tokenization stages, BERT produces valuable semantic embeddings from the input text [9]. This illustrates the interrelation of different embeddings at local and global levels. Enhancing the input assumptions of the logic-driven parser augments the accuracy of parsing judgments [10].

Many studies have demonstrated the efficacy of a neural parsing model that utilizes BERT and LDNPA embeddings. LDNPA employs structural reasoning, rule-based emotional indicators, and syntactic analysis to facilitate readers' understanding of the relationships between different parts of a book. Compare and contrast the expressions "I am sad" and "I am not sad."

What are the similarities and differences between them? Both illustrate the concept's potential value. Incorporating conjunctions, negations, and exclamatory terms significantly enhances sentences [11]. Their physical and psychological attributes may influence an individual's emotional state. Logical structures and symbolic constraints have been shown to regulate complicated cognitive processes and prevent overfitting [12].

This research presents a novel approach to enhancing emotional intelligence. The LDNPA uses the logic-based linguistic framework developed by BERT. A literature review identified three primary causes of suboptimal performance in deep neural networks. These causes include emotional sensitivity, lack of awareness, and receptiveness to novel experiences. The desired outcome was realized through the implementation of the specified Uniform Resource Locator (URL). The employment of broadly accepted linguistic and emotional norms has been demonstrated to enhance cognitive and emotional efficacy. Despite their inherent ambiguity, their position remains constant. The integration of these methodologies has been demonstrated to result in the development of a precise, comprehensible, and contextually adaptive emotion recognition system. It is imperative to acknowledge the numerous advantages associated with this approach.

The advent of emotion recognition technology can be attributed, in no small part, to the systematic approach that has been employed. In the context of analyzing court documents or conducting a mental health evaluation, the assessment of emotional categorization precision is as crucial as identifying the underlying causes. Despite the prevalence of rational cognitive processes, misunderstandings and confusion do arise. The efficacy of our strategic initiatives has been demonstrated. Developing NLP systems that can understand emotions is a significant advancement.

This work examines the limitations of existing emotion identification models and proposes a hybrid approach that strikes a balance between clarity, semantic richness, and structural reasoning. The proposed methodology, which combines neural learning and symbolic logic, is a robust and reliable means of determining individuals' emotions in natural language. The subsequent sections of the paper are organized as follows: the rest of the paper is structured as follows: Section 9.2 discusses related work in emotion recognition and hybrid NLP models. Section 9.3 explains the architecture of the proposed model, including BERT-based preprocessing, logic parsing, and fusion layers. Section 9.4 presents experimental design, datasets, and results. Finally, Section 9.5 concludes with insights and future research directions.

9.2 Literature Review

The Circumplex Affect Model [13] assessed the influence of social media interactions on our emotions. The primary objective was to identify the languages used most frequently. The network's overall effectiveness can be evaluated by examining the connections among the nodes. This study examines two aspects of user behavior: forum usage and link sharing. A system identified the 200 most common emotions tweeted by Mechanical Turk users and examined them in the context of psychological study themes. Multiple psychological studies indicate that an individual's mood significantly influences the duration of their social media engagement. Attitudes also seem to influence the consistency and frequency with which information is disseminated online. The fundamental objective of this research is to ascertain the link between emotional intelligence and the CS Circumplex. This may help dispel common misconceptions about the Internet and promote the growth of our enterprise.

Researchers [14] compared three word-emotion lexicons: NRC, DepecheMood, and EmoSenticNet. They used data from social media and a Twitter library to evaluate the lexicons. The researchers developed a system that utilizes heuristics and natural language processing techniques to evaluate books like a human assessment. Comprehensive human research substantiates the notion that emotional evaluations develop over time. Despite their diligent attempts, dictionaries persist in inaccurately portraying authentic human language, as research indicates. Expressions and their constituent words enhance *F*-scores and convey emotional nuances. A multitude of false positives emerged from the robust correlation between heightened volatility and numerous emotional factors. There is significant phonological variance among languages due to idioms and expressions that convey similar concepts in different ways. Depeche Mode asserts that the NRC language effectively conveys wrath, terror, and happiness but inadequately expresses grief. Despite the use of word-emotion lexicons to predict social media engagement, research shows that language and tone continue to affect an individual's appeal. This study will examine the phenomenon of emotion recognition.

The authors [15] assert that analyzing microblog entries from Chinese internet users requires advanced sentiment analysis methodologies. Their six-dictionary strategy encompasses slang, technical language, degree modifiers, and idioms. To assess its efficacy in specific situations, we must utilize Twitter more regularly in our contacts. The use of adjectives and emotive language determines the tone of written work. The film received a wide range of critiques, from "excellent" to "atrocious." To enhance your emotional intelligence, it is essential to understand the linguistic conventions used on microblogging platforms. Network administrators may use this concept to evaluate employee satisfaction. Recent advancements in sentiment analysis allow us to better understand and anticipate human emotions. The first step in improving the efficacy of online data monitoring is standardizing the terminology used to describe different emotional states. In recent years, there has been substantial progress in graph theory.

The sophisticated Semantic-Emotion Neural Network (SENN) deep learning framework identifies emotions in text [16]. SEND uses a convolutional neural network (CNN) emotion encoder and a bidirectional long short-term memory (BiLSTM) semantic encoder to integrate verbal and nonverbal behavioral data. The comparison reveals that the CNN emphasizes language and context more than the BiLSTM does. Conversely, BiLSTM produces word meanings through emotion-specific embeddings. Integrating these two representations produces an efficient, emotion-based text categorization encoder. The model's performance is enhanced by incorporating intricate, pretrained word embeddings that correspond to Ekman's six fundamental emotions. The SENN model demonstrated remarkable performance in 11 distinct emotion datasets. The application of computational and emotional analytics holds promise in further refining these methods. A consideration of the auditory information received may result in the development of an enhanced ability to comprehend and employ emotional language. A significant area of interest among SENN members pertains to the investigation of the influence of social media and user-generated content on mental well-being.

This research [17] uses deep learning and semantic text analysis (DLSTA) to enhance computers' understanding of human emotions. The proposal uses data analysis techniques from technical sources to determine public opinion on various issues. Word embeddings are used in natural language processing to generate responses, evaluate vocabulary, and determine sentiment. DLSTA examines literary works from language and semantic standpoints to facilitate the understanding of emotions. The system encompasses data processing, fundamental emotional comprehension, and the influence of social interactions. Using the right terminology is crucial for efficient communication with robots. The DLSTA model uses deep learning to analyze and understand data. Understanding the meaning of words can help you discern an individual's emotions.

A sophisticated Image-Text Interaction Network (ITIN) [18] is used for multimodal sentiment analysis to identify connections between text and emotive imagery. The proposed approach ensures the precision of word-image pairings *via* an attention-based cross-modal alignment module. A cross-modal gating module selects features that enhance deep engagement and solve problems with misaligned region-word combinations. Integrating text and visuals enhances the capacity of sentiment analysis to predict human behavior in specific contexts. The ITIN model was most effective when using only publicly available datasets. Ablation test results indicate that the model functions within the expected parameters. However, the model's deficiencies are evident when it fails to adequately represent the interactions among the different elements of the image.

This study [19] assessed the emotional tone of 61,862 tweets regarding MPox and COVID-19 with the VADER sentiment analysis method. The subsequent methodologies were employed to categorize the tweets according to their tone: 21% of poll respondents identified as pessimistic, 39% as optimistic, and 41% as analytical. The "hashtag analysis" segment of the study systematically identifies the 50 most prominent hashtags. Pretreatment procedures such as tokenization and stopword elimination must be completed before conducting a keyword analysis to determine the top 100 terms.

This paper [20] introduces the LeBERT sentiment analysis model. It employs CNN, BERT embeddings, n-grams, and sentiment lexicons to categorize binary emotions. This method surpasses previous word embedding models by using emotion lexicons and n-grams to detect intense emotions. Using BERT for partial segment encoding generates full-text embeddings that are of reduced dimensionality and exhibit greater sparsity. Further investigation is needed to determine the effectiveness of various vector representations in specific contexts. A convolutional neural network is a deep learning model that utilizes classifiers to assess textual attributes and differentiate between high- and low-quality content [21].

AMSAER [22] facilitates the assessment of an individual's emotional state. This strategy uses words, pictures, and music simultaneously. The AMSAER system retrieves data from multiple sources using unimodal models. Enjoyment of reading increases when tactile, visual, and auditory stimuli are present. Attention training has been shown to improve the brain's ability to integrate visual, auditory, and tactile stimuli. Trimodal and bimodal correlations with model data can yield precise intermediate projections.

The Emoji Sentiment Lexicon (Emo-SL) [23] helps understand emotions expressed by Arabic Twitter users. We use machine learning and emoticons. After analyzing over 58,000 Arabic tweets containing emoticons, researchers developed Emo-SL. They categorized emoticons into 222 classifications based on the emotions they evoke, enabling individuals to distinguish between those representing joy and those denoting melancholy. Emoji data can be used with text due to its consistency and reliability.

9.3 Methodology

Our hybrid approach to emotion detection primarily involves preprocessing and tokenization modules that use the Bidirectional Encoder Representations from Transformers (BERT) architecture. BERT has demonstrated remarkable sensitivity in understanding syntactic structure and contextual semantics in various natural language processing applications. We generate structured numerical representations of unprocessed text suitable for the system's neurological and cognitive functions.

The first step in the process is tokenization, which segments the text for application to the model. BERT uses wordpiece tokenization to segment words into smaller subword units. This approach efficiently handles non-lexical sentences while preserving morphological attributes. BERT uses specific tokens at the beginning and end of each input sequence, as well as between sentence pairs [SEP]. The [CLS] token represents the entire sequence and plays two key roles in classification tasks. The [CLS] and [SEP] tokens are derived from the phrase "I am happy."

Each token is represented by one of three embeddings after tokenization: location, segment, or token. A token's inherent characteristics contribute to its identity. Segment embeddings often denote chunks of input sequences and facilitate tasks such as forecasting subsequent words using phrases A and B. The token sequence provides the model with spatial embeddings because transformers are position-invariant. The embedding of each token comprises three fundamental components.

$$E_i = T_i + S_i + P_i$$

where

E_i is the final input embedding for the ith token,

T_i is the token embedding,

S_i is the segment embedding, and

P_i is the position embedding.

The input embeddings are then sent to the transformer encoder, a multi-layer architecture comprising feed-forward neural networks and self-attention processes. This enables the model to evaluate each token simultaneously and allocate weights according to their relative importance in the sequence. Formally, the attention function accomplishes this:

$$Attention(Q,K,V) = softmax\left(\frac{QK^T}{\sqrt{d_k}}\right)V$$

The input embeddings provide the query (Q), key (K), and value (V) matrices. These matrices illustrate the dimensions of the relevant vectors in a minor way. This attentional system can identify complex word associations regardless of their position within a phrase, even when linguistic patterns and emotional tones vary significantly.

The components of each transformer block are assembled in a specific way. Before using the ReLU activation function, this layer performs two linear transformations. This layer significantly enhances contextualized representations. Optimizing training efficacy requires enhancing residual connections, gradient propagation, and layer normalization.

The transformer stack generates a series of contextual embeddings, each associated with a distinct token. In this instance, the [CLS] token is readily observable.

$$h_{[CLS]} = BERT_{final}([CLS])$$

This embedding provides a comprehensive summary of the series while fulfilling multiple functions. The brain's cognitive neuronal decision layers facilitate emotion categorization. The [CLS] vector incorporates sentiment orientation, contextual elements, linguistic subtleties, and emotional data.

The integration of a methodology with BERT's extensive multilingual capabilities resulted in a substantial enhancement in preprocessing and tokenization. The integration of intricate representations with statistical and symbolic components enables the precise differentiation of emotions.

9.3.1 Logic-Driven Neural Parsing Algorithm (LDNPA)

The Logic-Driven Neural Parsing Algorithm (LDNPA) has been demonstrated to possess the capacity to identify emotional conflicts. The four foundational elements of critical thinking, which are logic, systems, language, and semantics, can all be enhanced through education. The LDNPA utilizes syntactic structures, semantic role labeling, and logical principles to achieve outcomes, eschewing the employment of intricate deep learning models. The final objective is a design that is more user-friendly and accessible. This method utilizes a comprehensive set of linguistic components, including intensifiers, negations, and causal relationships, to facilitate precise emotional assessment. A system that merely acquires data from the real world may encounter challenges.

A foundational component of LDNPA's intricate processing architecture is language parsing. The provided sentences are interpreted through the lens of syntactic analysis. The Stanford University applications spaCy and CoreNLP facilitate the visualization of word dependency trees. This concept encompasses all nouns, verbs, objects, negations, and prepositions. Her statements indicate a state of profound psychological distress. The parser identifies "happy" as the principal adjective and "not" as the negation. These verbal signals' logical frameworks aid individuals in emotional decision-making.

Using semantic role labeling (SRL), sentences are assigned functional roles according to their structure. SRL articulates the sentiment, its origin, and its intended recipient. He experiences the adverse consequences of betrayal, feeling primarily rage. The treachery enraged him. To completely understand emotions, a computer must perceive events, ascertain their nature, comprehend their causes, and evaluate their significance within a broader framework.

LDNPA uses a rule-based engine and a carefully chosen emotion lexicon, such as SenticNet or the NRC Emotion Lexicon, after parsing and categorizing. "Elated" signifies a mood of delight and optimism. It evokes sentiments and emotions that can be readily articulated through expressive language. LDNPA clarifies this concept by offering several examples of how syntactic cues can affect natural emotions. "Not happy" exemplifies the distinction between the two feelings. Using expressions such as "extremely sorrowful" intensifies emotions. The neural prediction layer obtains the logic-based adjustment factor produced by these adaptive algorithms.

By incorporating rationally informed soft constraints into the training loss function, the LDNPA demonstrates a unique ability. The model is penalized for deviating from established language and affective logic standards through a logical consistency term (L_{logic}), in addition to the cross-entropy loss (L_{CE}). The combined loss is defined as follows:

$$L_{LDNPA} = L_{CE} + \lambda_1 . L_{logic} + \lambda_2 . L_{syntax}$$

where λ_1 and λ_2 are the tunable hyperparameters and L_{syntax} penalizes inconsistency with syntactic patterns such as misplaced modifiers or incorrect scope of negations.

LDNPA achieves an enhancement through its logic-augmented attention weighting. Unlike conventional attention mechanisms, which regard all token connections as variable parameters in models like BERT, LDNPA employs logical saliency to regulate attention levels. LDNPA, on the other hand, employs logical saliency to regulate attention levels. Incorporating a logical bias term increases the importance of emotional triggers ("thrilled" and "furious"), negators ("not" and "barely"), and causal connectors ("because" and "due to").

$$Attention_{i,j} = softmax\left(\frac{Q_i K_j^T}{\sqrt{d}_k} + \gamma . M_{logic}(i,j)\right)$$

where M_{logic} (i,j) encodes logic-based importance between token i and token j and γ controls the strength of logic modulation. This results in better focus on emotionally significant portions of the text.

LDNPA generates a comprehensive, experimentally substantiated emotional profile of the proposed drug. This profile outlines the polarity and intensity of the anticipated emotional spectrum, including happiness, fury, and grief, as well as the causes and manifestations of these emotions. After receiving the expected label, the model presents a rule trace or explanatory pathway. For example, it might say "Emotion identified: Sadness — modified by 'very' → Intensity; negated by 'not' → Polarity: Neutral." Applications requiring explainable artificial intelligence, such as instructional sentiment analysis and mental health diagnosis, benefit from the approach's transparency.

The LDNPA provides a consistent and methodical framework for evaluating emotional data with the objective of enhancing emotion detection systems. This approach has the potential to integrate deep learning capabilities and linguistic precision by integrating advanced neural networks with symbolic reasoning. In industries where precision and accuracy are paramount, the deployment of reliable, multilingual natural language processing solutions is of the essence. Collaborative efforts have been shown to enhance each of these qualities.

9.3.2 Emotion Classification Layer

The third and most critical component of the proposed hybrid model is the Emotion Classification Layer. Text can be categorized into discrete or continuous emotions using deep semantic representations, contextual encoders, and equation parsers. This layer enhances the accuracy and precision of the hybrid model without altering its fundamental properties by integrating brain activations with logic-augmented embeddings.

The categorization of emotional reactions through natural language processing poses a significant challenge due to the situational and subjective nature of such responses. To overcome these obstacles, we enhanced our classification layer with a mixed input representation. This representation combines contextualized embeddings, generated by a Transformer model such as BERT, with the optimal, rule-compliant output of the Logic-Driven Neural Parsing Algorithm (LDNPA). Combining statistical and symbolic inputs yields a vector with strong semantic roots and well-organized emotional responses.

In this case, d represents the hidden size (e.g., 768), and $h_{BERT} \in R^d$ specifies the hidden state corresponding to the particular [CLS] token from BERT's final layer. The rationally improved emotional vector produced by LDNPA is represented by $h_{LDNPA} \in R^k$. Familiarity with accepted emotional language, intensity scales, contributory factors, and denial techniques is necessary.

$$z = [h_{BERT}; h_{LDNPA}] \in R^{d+k}$$

The definition and structure of the feature space are significantly improved by the broadcast aggregated representation, z, *via* a fully connected feed-forward network (FFN). The FFN employs nonlinear activation functions in one or more of its hidden layers. The Rectified Linear Unit (ReLU) function is widely used in various domains due to its exceptional processing efficiency and versatility.

$$a_1 = ReLU(W_1 z + b_1)$$

$$a_2 = ReLU(W_2 z + b_2)$$

where W_1 and W_2 are the learnable weight matrices and b_1 and b_2 are the bias vectors. Applying the softmax function to the modified vector produces the final output layer, which is responsible for generating a probability distribution across the designated emotional categories.

$$\hat{y} = softmax(W_0 a_2 + b_0)$$

Here, $\hat{y} \in R^C$ denotes the predicted probability for each of the C emotion categories (e.g., Joy, Sadness, Anger, Fear, Surprise, Disgust, Neutral) and W_0 and b_0 are the output layer's parameters.

The training objective for the classification layer is to minimize the categorical cross-entropy loss between the predicted distribution $\hat{y}$ and the true label $y \in \{0,1\}^C$:

$$L_{CE} = -\sum_{i=1}^{C} y_i \log(\hat{y})$$

Integrating additional penalties that enhance alignment with LDNPA outputs enables us to methodically constrain the learning process and optimize the overall loss function. This composite loss function is expressed as follows:

$$L_{total} = L_{CE+} \lambda_{logic} . L_{LDNPA} + \lambda_{reg} . \|\varnothing\|^2$$

Various emotions can be expressed authentically, particularly in extended phrases or multi-turn dialogues (e.g., joy and astonishment, or grief and anger). Furthermore, we propose a multi-label classification approach. This approach enables the independent scoring of each emotional class by utilizing distinct sigmoid activations for each class in the output layer, rather than using softmax.

$$\hat{y} = \sigma(W_i^T a_2 + b_i)$$

The Emotion Classification Layer contains symbolic classification elements and aggregated attention weights. The computer recognized the predominant emotion and its characteristics. Since "fife" was more prevalent than "not joyful," further investigation was warranted. The layer's transparency may facilitate decision-making in ambiguous situations or situations requiring approvals.

Label smoothing reduces the likelihood that mood fluctuations will influence people in a dataset. It allows for greater focus on longer input sequences and reduces the likelihood that individuals will use the techniques employed in the subsequent classification layer. Using these methodologies on datasets with unforeseen or individualized emotional annotations produces superior outcomes.

The Emotion Classification Layer of our hybrid model can do more than predict labels. It enhances learning through a synthesis of logical and neurological reasoning, symbolic representations, and mathematical transformations. This layer integrates comprehensive phrase analysis with deep learning to yield accurate emotional classifications. These attributes render emotional computing models suitable for deployment in perilous circumstances.

9.4 Results and Discussion

The IEMOCAP and CMU-MOSEI multimodal emotion datasets were utilized to assess the newly developed hybrid model for emotion recognition. Table 9.1 in this dataset illustrates the evaluation of several media types, including text, images, and music, regarding their emotional influence. The IEMOCAP dataset comprises 7,380 samples, making it rather extensive. Of these, 5,162 are allocated for training, 737 for validation, and 1,481 for testing. The six primary emotional states that partners may identify are neutrality, pleasure, wrath, excitement, and passion. The CMU-MOSEI collection comprises 20,477 samples. Of these, 1,656 are designated for validation, 4,168 are allocated for testing, and 14,525 are assigned for training.

Table 9.1 Dataset description.

Label	IEMOCAP	Label	CMU-MOSEI
Angry	1103	Angry	4600
Excited	1041	Disgusted	3755
Frustrated	1849	Fear	1803
Happy	595	Happy	10752
Neutral	1708	Sad	5601
Sad	1084	Surprise	2055

This dataset presents six emotions: surprise, joy, grief, fear, anger, and contempt. Due to the availability of numerous datasets with varying features, the hybrid model can be evaluated across diverse emotional and multimodal scenarios. This ensures the model's efficacy in novel contexts and enables extensive learning.

As illustrated in Figure 9.1, the model performs well across many emotional categories in the IEMOCAP dataset. It demonstrates a robust balance between precision and recall, as indicated by its 96% F_1 score for neutral and angry emotions. The recall, accuracy, and precision rates for the neutral class are 91%, 94%, and 92.5%, respectively. Based on robust emotional indicators, the algorithm can predict an individual's level of rage with 95%, 92%, and 93% accuracy. Accuracy ratings of 93% and 91%, along with F_1 scores of 94% and 94.5%, indicate that the impact of happy and negative emotions is approximately equivalent. The model's ability to generalize, particularly in scenarios involving overlapping emotions, contributes to its 91% accuracy in recognizing the complex emotion of annoyance, as well as its 88% recall accuracy, 93% F_1 score, and 90% precision accuracy. The model's minimum accuracy, precision, and recall scores are 92%, 91%, and 86%, respectively. The lowest F_1 score is 93.5%. Thus, the model can detect subtle signs of emotional arousal. This hybrid model can produce effective generalizations, possesses substantial memory capacity, and excels in understanding complex emotions.

Figure 9.2 illustrates that the proposed hybrid model performs effectively and reliably across all six emotional categories using the CMU-MOSEI dataset. The model distinguishes between enjoyable events and affirmative

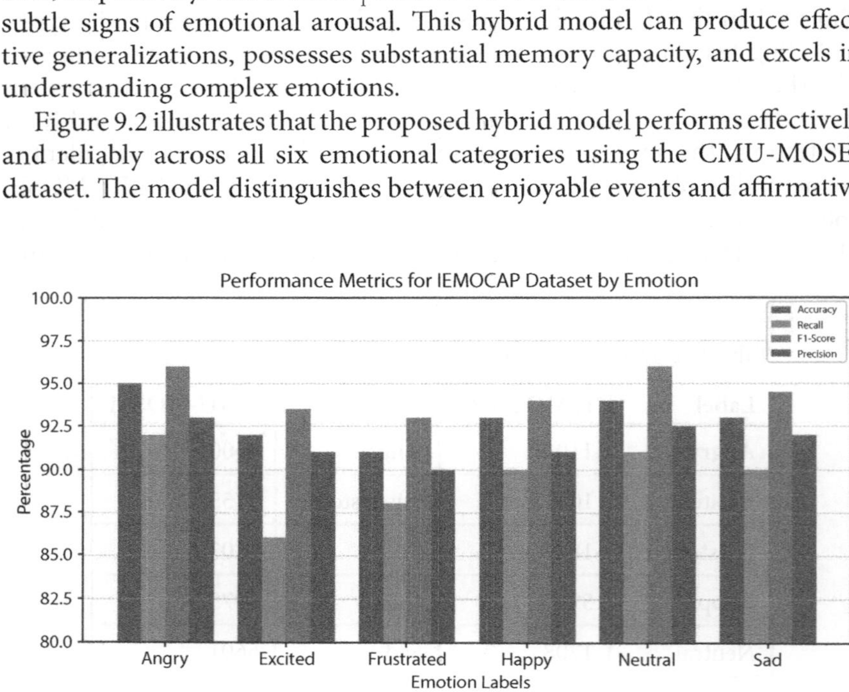

Figure 9.1 Performance analysis based on the emotions in the IEMOCAP dataset.

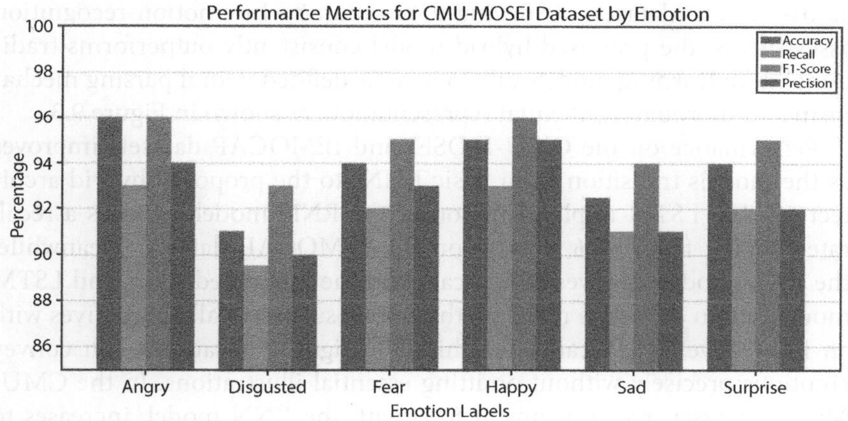

Figure 9.2 Performance analysis based on the emotions in the CMU-MOSEI dataset.

emotional expressions with 95% accuracy, 93% recall, a 96% F_1 score, and 95% precision. It achieves 96% accuracy, 93% recall, a 96% F_1 score, and 94% precision in identifying intense emotions. The model attains an excellent balance between descriptiveness and sensitivity. Regarding anxiety, the model identifies intricate negative thoughts with 94% accuracy, 92% recall, 95% F_1 score, and 93% precision. It shows proficiency in regulating emotions through swift temporal variations, achieving 94% accuracy, 92% recall, 95% F_1 score, and 92% precision in the surprise category. The model demonstrates 91% recall, 92.5% accuracy, 94% F_1 score, and 91% precision in identifying depression. Robust disdain metrics (91% accuracy, 89.5% recall, 93% F_1 score, and 90% precision) indicate effective generalization, especially in emotional settings, despite marginally worse findings in other categories. The advantages and efficacy of the proposed hybrid method for identifying complex emotional states are evidenced by its consistently high ratings for all emotions using multimodal inputs.

The hybrid model does not fit well with conventional neural networks on the IEMOCAP and CMU-MOSEI datasets. The LSTM model achieves an accuracy of 86% on the IEMOCAP dataset, while the RNN model achieves 84%. The RNN+LSTM architecture attained an overall accuracy of 90%. The CNN model exhibits an accuracy rate that is 92% superior to its competitors. The proposed model surpasses all alternatives with 96% accuracy and can discern emotional context. The RNN achieves 85% accuracy, the CNN attains 92.5%, the RNN and LSTM together yield 91%, and the LSTM reaches 88%. A similar trend is evident in the CMU-MOSEI dataset. The proposed model demonstrates exceptional durability and adaptability across various datasets, achieving 95% accuracy. In emotion recognition assessments, the proposed hybrid model consistently outperforms traditional deep learning models due to its well-defined neural parsing mechanism and thorough contextual representation, as shown in Figure 9.3.

Performance on the CMU-MOSEI and IEMOCAP datasets improves as the models transition from basic RNNs to the proposed hybrid architecture. The LSTM implementation of the RNN model achieves a recall rate ranging from 80% to 82% on the IEMOCAP dataset. Meanwhile, the CNN model achieves 88% recall, and the integrated RNN and LSTM models attain 87%. The novel methodology surpasses all alternatives with an impressive 91% recall rate. This is intriguing because it can convey emotions precisely without omitting essential illustrations. In the CMU-MOSEI dataset, recall begins at 81% with the RNN model, increases to 88% with the RNN+LSTM model, and ultimately reaches 89% with the CNN model. The proposed model exhibits a 92% recall rate, indicating its ability to extract relevant information from various sources. Figure 9.4 shows that the logic-based neural segmentation method may be a more effective categorization approach as datasets improve.

The F_1 score evaluation of the IEMOCAP and CMU-MOSEI datasets indicates that each model configuration enhances the equilibrium between recall and precision, as shown in Figure 9.5. The F_1 score of the RNN model on the IEMOCAP dataset is 83%, while the LSTM model increases it slightly to 84%. The CNN model achieves a 90% performance rate by

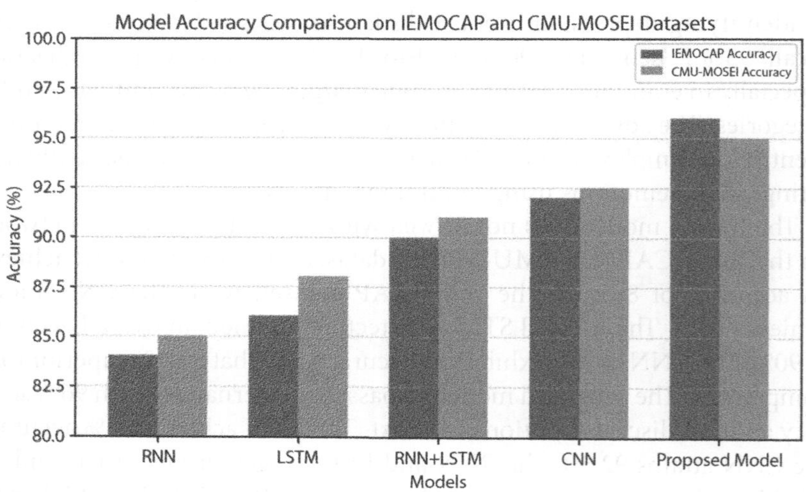

Figure 9.3 Accuracy analysis of the IEMOCAP and CMU-MOSEI datasets.

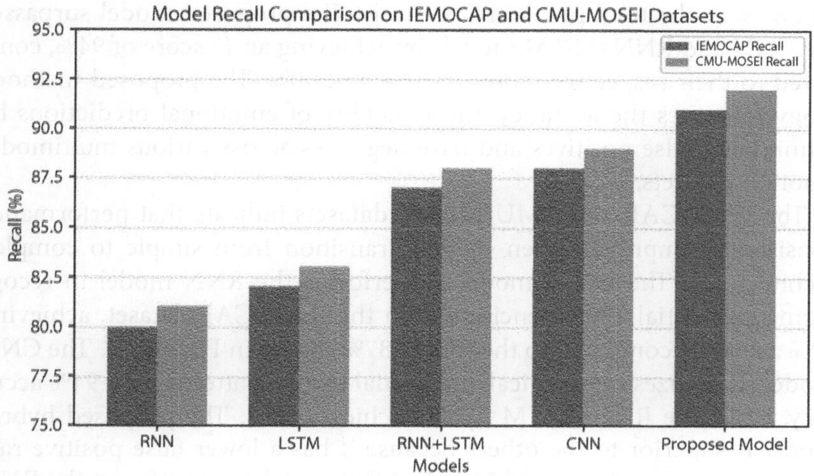

Figure 9.4 Recall analysis of the IEMOCAP and CMU-MOSEI datasets.

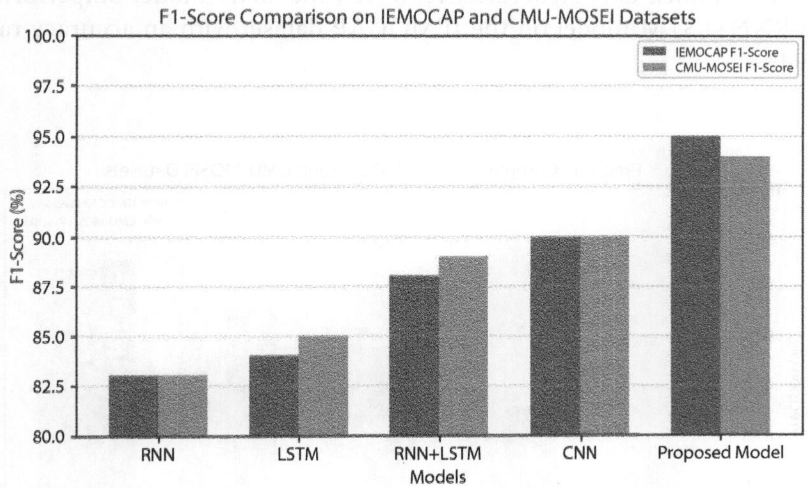

Figure 9.5 F_1 score analysis of the IEMOCAP and CMU-MOSEI datasets.

effectively extracting spatial information from sequences. The RNN+LSTM combination obtains an impressive 88%. The proposed hybrid model achieves an impressive 95% F_1 score by adeptly integrating high accuracy and recall, thereby markedly improving performance. The CMU-MOSEI dataset yielded similar results: the RNN and LSTM models achieved 83%

and 85% of the total points, respectively. The proposed model surpasses the CNN and RNN+LSTM models by achieving an F_1 score of 94%, compared to their respective scores of 89% and 90%. The proposed methodology improves the accuracy and reliability of emotional predictions by minimizing false positives and false negatives across various multimodal emotion datasets.

The IEMOCAP and CMU-MOSEI datasets indicate that performance consistently improves when models transition from simple to complex architectures. The LSTM model outperforms the RNN model in recognizing sequential dependencies within the IEMOCAP dataset, achieving 89% accuracy compared to the RNN's 87% shown in Figure 9.6. The CNN model recognizes hierarchical and spatial textual patterns with 94% accuracy, while the RNN+LSTM hybrid achieves 92%. The proposed hybrid model is superior to the others because it has a lower false positive rate and an accuracy rating of 96.5%. The LSTM model outperforms the RNN model with an accuracy rate of 90%, compared to 86%. The LSTM model performed well on the CMU-MOSEI dataset, demonstrating its ability to handle complex data structures. However, the CNN model outperforms the RNN+LSTM model on the IEMOCAP dataset with an accuracy rate of 94%.

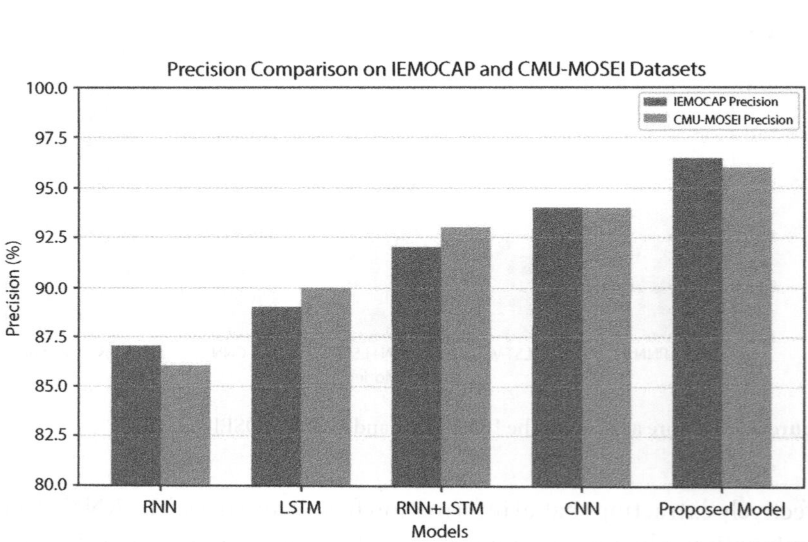

Figure 9.6 Precision analysis of the IEMOCAP and CMU-MOSEI datasets.

9.5 Conclusion

This model combines the expressive capability of deep neural networks with the precision of symbolic logic to judge emotional state. The method uses the BERT framework for logic-based brain processing and context-based encoding. Understanding emotional language requires knowledge of syntax and semantics. When tested on the CMU, IEM Kris, and IEMOCAP datasets, the proposed model outperformed the best RNN, LSTM, and CNN methods in terms of accuracy, precision, and F_1 score. The model can handle many different types and forms of data. The IEMOCAP dataset achieved an F_1 score of 94.5%, while the CMU-MOSEI dataset achieved an accuracy score of 96.6%. People find requirement-based models easier to understand than deep learning algorithms, which are difficult to grasp. Future HCI systems may be able to recognize emotions in multiple languages, incorporate multimedia elements, and obtain real-time emotional data. This technique is solid from a methodological standpoint and makes it possible to build strong, emotionally intelligent NLP systems.

AI disclosure statement: The author acknowledges the use of AI-based tools for minor language editing or grammatical correction. However, all intellectual contributions, analyses, and conclusions presented in this chapter are entirely the author's own.

References

1. Das, D. and Bandyopadhyay, S., Emotion analysis on social media: natural language processing approaches and applications, in: *Online Collective Action: Dynamics of the Crowd in Social Media*, pp. 19–37, Springer Vienna, Vienna, 2014 Jul 14.
2. Poria, S., Majumder, N., Mihalcea, R., Hovy, E., Emotion recognition in conversation: Research challenges, datasets, and recent advances. *IEEE Access*, 7, 100943–53, 2019 Jul 16.
3. Chinmayi, R., Sreeja, N., Nair, A.S., Jayakumar, M.K., Gowri, R., Jaiswal, A., Emotion classification using deep learning, in: *2020 Third International Conference on Smart Systems and Inventive Technology (ICSSIT)*, IEEE, pp. 1063–1068, 2020 Aug 20.
4. Zamani, F. and Wulansari, R., Emotion classification using 1D-CNN and RNN based on deap dataset. *Nat. Lang. Process.*, 23, 363–78, 2021.
5. Xie, Y., Liang, R., Liang, Z., Huang, C., Zou, C., Schuller, B., Speech emotion classification using attention-based LSTM, in: *IEEE/ACM Transactions on Audio, Speech, and Language Processing*, vol. 27, pp. 1675–85, 2019 Jul 1.

6. Pavithra, D., Parameswaran, T., Choudhry, M.D., Amrutha, S., Deepa, T., Kiruthiga, R., Application of LSTM Networks for Continuous Patient Monitoring and Anomaly Detection in Wearable Health Devices. *Indian J. Sci. Technol.*, 17, 37, 3909–3921, 2024.
7. Chiorrini, A., Diamantini, C., Mircoli, A., Potena, D., Emotion and sentiment analysis of tweets using BERT, in: *EDBT/ICDT workshops*, vol. 3, pp. 1–7, 2021 Mar 23.
8. Hamilton, K., Nayak, A., Božić, B., Longo, L., Is neuro-symbolic AI meeting its promises in natural language processing? A structured review. *Semantic Web*, 15, 4, 1265–306, 2024 Jan 1.
9. Kumar, P. and Raman, B., A BERT based dual-channel explainable text emotion recognition system. *Neural Networks*, 150, 392–407, 2022 Jun 1.
10. Feng, H., Liu, J., Zheng, J., Chen, H., Shang, X., Ma, Q., Joint constrained learning with boundary-adjusting for emotion-cause pair extraction, in: *Proceedings of the 61st Annual Meeting of the Association for Computational Linguistics (Volume 1: Long Papers)*, pp. 1118–1131, 2023 Jul.
11. Khasanah, I.N., Sentiment classification using fasttext embedding and deep learning model. *Procedia Comput. Sci.*, 189, 343–50, 2021 Jan 1.
12. Xu, D., Tian, Z., Lai, R., Kong, X., Tan, Z., Shi, W., Deep learning based emotion analysis of microblog texts. *Inf. Fusion*, 64, 1–1, 2020 Dec 1.
13. De Choudhury, M., Counts, S., Gamon, M., Not all moods are created equal! exploring human emotional states in social media, in: *Proceedings of the International AAAI Conference on Web and Social Media*, vol. 6, pp. 66–73, 2012.
14. Kušen, E., Cascavilla, G., Figl, K., Conti, M., Strembeck, M., Identifying emotions in social media: comparison of word-emotion lexicons, in: *2017 5th International Conference on Future Internet of Things and Cloud Workshops (FiCloudW)*, IEEE, pp. 132–137, 2017 Aug 21.
15. Zhang, S., Wei, Z., Wang, Y., Liao, T., Sentiment analysis of Chinese microblog text based on extended sentiment dictionary. *Future Gener. Comput. Syst.*, 81, 395–403, 2018 Apr 1.
16. Batbaatar, E., Li, M., Ryu, K.H., Semantic-emotion neural network for emotion recognition from text. *IEEE Access*, 7, 111866–78, 2019 Aug 12.
17. Guo, J., Deep learning approach to text analysis for human emotion detection from big data. *J. Intell. Systems*, 31, 1, 113–26, 2022 Jan 12.
18. Zhu, T., Li, L., Yang, J., Zhao, S., Liu, H., Qian, J., Multimodal sentiment analysis with image-text interaction network. *IEEE Trans. Multimedia*, 25, 3375–85, 2022 Mar 16.
19. Thakur, N., Sentiment analysis and text analysis of the public discourse on Twitter about COVID-19 and MPox. *Big Data Cognit. Comput.*, 7, 2, 116, 2023 Jun 9.
20. Mutinda, J., Mwangi, W., Okeyo, G., Sentiment analysis of text reviews using lexicon-enhanced bert embedding (LeBERT) model with convolutional neural network. *Appl. Sciences*, 13, 3, 1445, 2023 Jan 21.

21. Nidhya, R., Kalpana, R., Smilarubavathy, G., Keerthana, S.M., Brain Tumor Diagnosis with MCNN-Based MRI Image Analysis, in: *2023 1st International Conference on Optimization Techniques for Learning (ICOTL)*, IEEE, pp. 1–5, 2023, December.
22. Aslam, A., Sargano, A.B., Habib, Z., Attention-based multimodal sentiment analysis and emotion recognition using deep neural networks. *Appl. Soft Comput.*, 144, 110494, 2023 Sep 1.
23. Alfreihat, M., Almousa, O.S., Tashtoush, Y., AlSobeh, A., Mansour, K., Migdady, H., Emo-SL framework: emoji sentiment lexicon using text-based features and machine learning for sentiment analysis.

10

A Neuro-Symbolic AI Approach for Lumbar Spinal Stenosis Detection Using Graph Convolutional Networks and Fuzzy Logic

Gurusamy Murugesan[1]*, Sabenabanu Abdulkadhar[2], Selvamuthukumar T.[1], Velkumar K.[3] and Rajkumar K.[4]

[1]Department of Computer Science and Engineering, Koneru Lakshmaiah Education Foundation, Green Fields, Vaddeswaram, Andhra Pradesh, India

[2]Department of Computer Applications, SRM Institute of Science and Technology, Kattankulathur, Chennai, India

[3]Department of Computer Science and Engineering, Nadar Saraswathi College of Engineering and Technology, Theni, Tamilnadu, India

[4]Department of Computer Science and Engineering (Cyber Security), PSNA College of Engineering and Technology, Dindigul, Tamilnadu, India

Abstract

Lumbar spinal stenosis (LSS) is a degenerative disorder that is caused by the constriction of the spinal canal, which eventually results in nerve compression and limited mobility. Conventional diagnostic techniques, like MRI and CT scans, depend on expert analysis, which has many limitations. Numerous deep learning and machine learning approaches have been developed to address this. They leave a research gap in the analysis and interpretation of MRI and CT scan results. This work employs a Neuro-Symbolic AI methodology that combines fuzzy logic for interpretable decision-making in LSS detection with graph convolutional networks (GCNs) for deep feature extraction. This approach combines acquired representations with structured medical data to increase prediction accuracy while maintaining explanation ability. Experimental evaluations on publicly available lumbar spine datasets demonstrate improved performance compared to conventional deep learning models.

**Corresponding author*: gurusamy.m@hotmail.com

R. Nidhya, A. Dineshkumar, Sheng-Lung Peng, S. Karthik and S. Balamurugan (eds.) Neuro-Symbolic Artificial Intelligence: Concepts & Applications, (189–206)

Keywords: Lumbar spinal stenosis, degenerative disorder, artificial intelligence, machine learning, deep learning, neuro-symbolic AI graph convolution neural networks, fuzzy logic

10.1 Introduction

The degenerative disorder known as lumbar spinal stenosis (LSS) is characterized by the narrowing of the lower back's spinal canal, which compresses the spinal cord and nerve roots [1–4]. It can cause neurogenic claudication, radiating pain, numbness, and limited mobility, and it mainly affects older adults [3, 4]. The diagnosis of LSS is essential for efficient treatment planning because it is frequently brought on by aging-related conditions like osteoarthritis, degenerative disk disease, and ligament thickening [4]. Conventional diagnostic methods use MRI, CT, and X-ray imaging, where radiologists evaluate nerve compression and canal narrowing [4–6]. Manual evaluations, however, are based on experience, are subjective, and differ among practitioners. As a result, automated and data-driven methods to increase diagnostic precision and consistency are becoming more and more in demand [5, 6].

Artificial intelligence (AI) has gained significant traction in medical diagnostics, particularly Machine Learning (ML) [5, 7–9, 34] and Deep Learning (DL) techniques [10, 12, 15–17] that extract insights from spinal imaging datasets.

ML-based methods employed handcrafted features such as disk morphology, vertebral alignment, and spinal canal width. To build predictive models for stenosis classification [7–10, 22, 23], many algorithms like Support Vector Machines, Random Forest, and K-Nearest Neighbors (KNN) are employed previously [8, 9, 13, 14].

Several studies have explored ML techniques for LSS diagnosis. Wang *et al.* applied SVM with linear and RBF kernel for LSS severity prediction, achieving 85.5% and 89.6% accuracy, respectively [10]. Ruchi and Singh D. evaluated Decision tree, KNN, and Random Forest models for predicting lumber spine disease and demonstrated superior sensitivity in the random forest model [16].

Deep Learning methods, particularly Convolutional Neural Networks (CNNs), Graph Convolutional Networks (GCNs), and attention-based architectures, have revolutionized medical image analysis [10–21, 39]. CNNs are widely used for automatic feature extraction from lumbar spine MRI/CT images, reducing dependency on manual segmentation [11, 15, 17]. Tumko V., Kim *et al.* developed a three-stage CNN-based segmentation model for spinal stenosis classification and achieved a sensitivity, specificity, and AUROC of 94.2, 84.4, 95.0 [11]. GCNs allow graph-based representations of vertebral structures, capturing anatomical relationships for enhanced diagnostics [21, 37, 38].

Despite the DL models achieving enhanced accuracy, there exists an inadequate level of precise interpretation and analysis of MRI results. This resulted in the incorporation of symbolic reasoning within the DL models. In contrast to all baseline and DL models in healthcare analysis, this facilitated the creation of Neuro-Symbolic AI frameworks, which combine deep learning with symbolic AI for interpretable results and analysis in achieving improved accuracy [25].

Limited research has investigated Neuro-Symbolic AI for the identification of spinal diseases [24, 28]. Han *et al.* utilized neural-symbolic learning for the development of spinal medical reports [25]. Fuzzy logic in symbolic reasoning has been shown to be beneficial in explainable AI's ambiguous medical classifications, highlighting its contribution to improving DL explainability [30]. Neuro-Symbolic AI, which integrates GCN feature extraction with Fuzzy Logic-based inference, presents a potential approach for interpretable and reliable LSS diagnosis.

In this work, we present a framework that combines Graph Convolutional Networks (GCNs) for deep feature extraction and a fuzzy logic module that includes symbolic rules and a fuzzy membership function for better interpretability of LSS diagnosis.

10.2 Materials and Methods

The proposed Neuro-Symbolic AI framework, which was depicted in Figure 10.1, integrates Graph Convolutional Networks (GCNs) for structured feature learning and Fuzzy Logic-based reasoning for uncertainty handling in lumbar spinal stenosis (LSS) detection. This approach enhances both accuracy and interpretability, making AI-assisted diagnosis more transparent for clinicians.

10.2.1 Neuro-Symbolic AI Framework

In our proposed Neuro-Symbolic AI framework for lumbar spinal stenosis detection, the process begins by analyzing the MRI images, which are used to construct a patient graph, where each node represents a patient and edges reflect feature-based similarity. This graph, along with patient features, is processed by a Graph Convolutional Neural Network (GCNN) that learns high-level node embeddings and produces raw logits used to

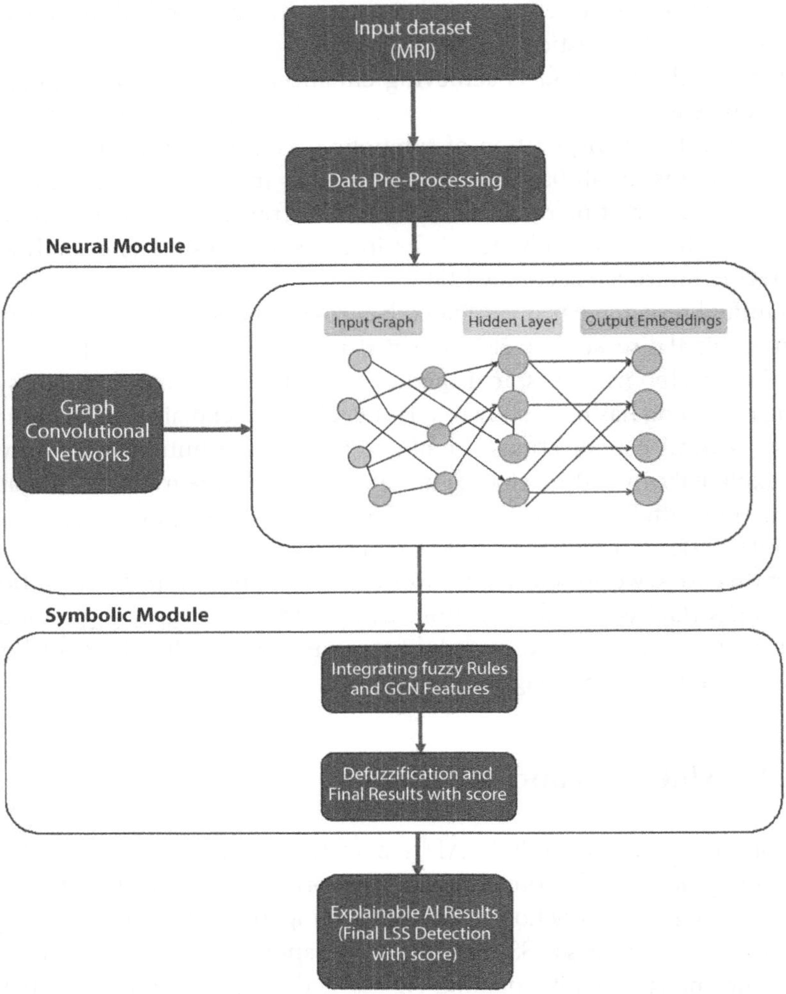

Figure 10.1 Our proposed neuro-symbolic AI framework.

predict whether a patient has lumbar spinal stenosis or not. If the GCNN classifies a patient as positive for lumbar spinal stenosis, the corresponding logits or class probabilities are further processed by a Fuzzy Logic-based symbolic reasoning module, which incorporates additional patient-specific information such as stenosis width and nerve compression ratio through a set of medically informed fuzzy rules [42]. These rules compute risk-based adjustments that refine the GCNN output. The refined probabilities are then used to determine the most likely LSS diagnosis, providing both a diagnosis and interpretable insights into the current state of the injury.

10.2.1.1 Graph Convolutional Neural Network

Graph Convolutional Neural Networks (GCNNs) allow for learning over graph-structured data by enabling information exchange between nodes through their connections. Unlike traditional convolutional neural networks that work on regular grids [34, 35] (e.g., images), GCNNs process data residing on irregular domains, where relationships between elements are captured by edges in a graph. Spatial GCNNs define convolution through direct neighborhood aggregation, making them efficient and intuitive for real-world applications [35]. Traditional spatial GCNNs treat all neighboring nodes equally during feature aggregation. However, in many real-world applications—such as brain MRI analysis—some neighboring regions may carry more relevant information than others [21, 36]. To accommodate this, attention mechanisms are introduced. These allow the model to assign different levels of importance, or weights, to neighboring nodes during convolution, resulting in an enhanced and more expressive representation [35].

Graph Definition and Input Features

We begin with the input graph G=(V,E), where V={V1,...,VN} is the set of nodes and E⊆V×V is the set of edges connecting them. Each node Vi∈V is associated with a feature vector of node i is xi∈Rd, which may include d dimensional feature information such as intensity values, texture descriptors, or regional statistics from the MRI data. These features are arranged into a matrix X∈RN×d, where N is the number of nodes in the graph. These features at layer l in a network are given by the following:

$$h_i^{(l)} \in R^d \tag{10.1}$$

Nodes represent anatomical regions (e.g., vertebrae, intervertebral disks, nerve pathways). Edges capture spatial dependencies between adjacent spinal components [33].

Graph Convolution Layer

Linear Feature Transformation

Before attention can be applied, each node's feature vector is transformed using a shared linear layer [33]. This transformation maps the original input feature space into a new space more suitable for computing similarity or relevance between nodes. Formally, the transformation is done *via* a trainable weight matrix Wl for the l-th layer. The output feature of node i becomes Zi, where hi is the feature from the previous layer (or input features if l=0l = 0l=0).

$$z_i^{(l)} = W^{(l)} h_i^{(l)} \tag{10.2}$$

Attention Coefficient Computation

The core of the attention mechanism lies in calculating attention coefficients, which represent how much attention node i should pay to node j when updating its features. This is done by applying a shared attention function a^T over the transformed features of the two nodes. Specifically, we concatenate the transformed features zi and zj, apply a nonlinear activation (typically LeakyReLU), and compute a single scalar score eij [34, 35]. This score indicates the raw importance of node j to node i. For each edge (i,j)∈E, compute the attention coefficient eij:

$$e_{ij} = a^T.LeakyReLU\left(\left[\left\{z_i^{(l)} | z_j^{(l)}\right\}\right]\right) \tag{10.3}$$

Softmax Normalization of Attention Scores

Since raw attention scores eij are unbounded, we normalize them using a softmax function across all of node i's neighbors. This ensures that the attention coefficients αij sum to 1, allowing them to be interpreted as probabilities. This normalization step is crucial as it stabilizes training and creates a consistent scale across neighborhoods of different sizes.

$$\alpha_{ij} = \frac{\exp(e_{ij})}{\sum_{k \in N(i)} exp(e_{ik})} \tag{10.4}$$

Weighted Feature Aggregation

Once the attention coefficients αij are computed, the node updates its feature by taking a weighted sum of its neighbors' transformed features. Formally, the new feature h_i^((l+1)) is derived using a non-linear ReLU σ activation. This allows the model to emphasize more informative neighbors and suppress less relevant ones, enhancing the quality of learned representations.

$$h_i^{(l+1)} = \sigma\left(\sum_{j\in N(i)} \alpha_{ij}.z_j^{(l)}\right) \tag{10.5}$$

Fully Connected Layers

GCNNs with attention are typically constructed by stacking multiple such attention-based convolution layers. Each layer allows the nodes to incorporate information from an increasingly larger neighborhood [34–36]. For instance, the second layer enables nodes to access information from two-hop neighbors. With deeper stacking, the model gains a broader contextual view while still maintaining fine-grained control over information flow through attention weights.

The last convolution layer of a Graph Convolutional Neural Network with attention produces a matrix of node embeddings that capture both the local features of each node and the contextual information from its neighbors, weighted by learned attention scores. These embeddings serve as the refined, high-level representations of the graph's structure and content.

$$H^{(L)} = \begin{bmatrix} h_1^{(L)} \\ h_2^{(L)} \\ \vdots \\ h_N^{(L)} \end{bmatrix} \in R^{Nxd_L} \tag{10.6}$$

where N is the number of nodes in the graph, dL is the dimensionality of the feature vector at the final layer L, and h_i^((L))∈R^(d_L) is the final embedding of node i. Each vector h_i^((L)) is computed by aggregating the features of node i's neighbors, modulated by attention coefficients αij, followed by a non-linear activation. These embeddings encode multi-hop information since each layer aggregates from neighboring nodes, and stacking L layers allows information to propagate L steps away in the graph.

The graph-level embedding produced by GCNN is passed through a classification layer to yield a predictive output, typically a probability score or softmax logit indicating the presence or absence of lumbar spinal stenosis. Thus, the GCNN transforms raw neuroimaging data into a compact, discriminative representation for clinical decision-making.

$$y = softmax(W.H^{(L)}) \tag{10.7}$$

The softmax layer of GCNN produces a prediction y∈R^C (often a logit or probability), where C value is 2 since lumbar spinal stenosis affected and healthy classes, H^((L)) is the final layer embedding, and W is the weight matrix of the final linear (fully connected) layer used for classification.

GCN-extracted features feed into the fuzzy inference system, creating an end-to-end Neuro-Symbolic model for precise and explainable spinal stenosis detection.

10.2.1.2 Symbolic Module

A symbolic reasoning framework represents knowledge using human-understandable symbols and applies logical rules to draw conclusions. Deep learning models often lack explainability, making it difficult for clinicians to trust AI-assisted diagnoses [29]. In contrast to neural networks, symbolic systems are built on explicit rule-based logic, which allows for transparency, traceability, and explanation of decisions. These systems are especially useful in domains like healthcare, where interpretability and expert knowledge integration are crucial. Symbolic frameworks can reason with incomplete or uncertain information and offer a natural way to integrate domain expertise through formal logic [24–27].

Fuzzy Logic

In our proposed Neuro-Symbolic framework, Fuzzy Logic is employed to refine the logits or class probabilities output by the Graph Convolutional Neural Network (GCNN) by incorporating patient-specific contextual information, such as stenosis width, nerve compression, age factor, risk factor, clinical history, genetic background, and family medical history. This symbolic layer leverages a set of interpretable high-quality fuzzy rules, which are generated through relevant clinical knowledge from domain-specific literature and patient records that reflect nuanced medical reasoning. These rules are then used to adjust and interpret the GCNN-derived probabilities, resulting in a refined diagnostic score. This enhanced probabilistic output serves not only to improve diagnostic accuracy but also enables the estimation of disease stage or progression, offering a more granular and clinically useful prediction.

To encode domain knowledge about how the stenosis width size affects disease risk, we define a fuzzy rule that models the size of the stenosis [40, 41] in the example below, but we can also model the accelerated risk beyond a second threshold in the same factor. More than 50% thickness is a strong predictor of lumbar spinal stenosis.

$$\delta_{motor} = \alpha_{motor}.\sigma\left(\frac{z_{motor} - T_m}{\tau_m}\right) \tag{10.8}$$

This rule escalates the risk factor with symptom severity where stenosis size is more than 50%, Tm is the threshold above which symptoms are considered significant, τm controls the smoothness of transition, and αmotor is the base effect of motor score.

10.2.1.3 Combine Symbolic Adjustments

Using fuzzy logic, we define medical rules to compute differentiable symbolic adjustments δk for various risk factors k∈ {stenosis width, compression ratio, etc.}. Each symbolic risk contribution fuzzy rule is parameterized based on clinical intuition, such as thresholds and transition smoothness. These rules model risk as a fuzzy and continuous function of input features, rather than as hard binary thresholds.

All individual symbolic contributions are combined into a cumulative symbolic risk adjustment δ symbolic:

$$\delta_{symbolic} = \sum_k w_k.\delta_k \tag{10.9}$$

where δk is the output of fuzzy rule k and wk is the learnable weight for each rule. This aggregation represents an interpretable symbolic layer, which can be trained to learn the relative importance of different risk factors.

Adjust GCNN Logits or Probabilities

The aggregated symbolic adjustment is then added to the GCNN's raw logits to form the final refined logits y^:

$$\hat{y} = y_i + w.\delta_{symbolic} \tag{10.10}$$

where w∈RC is the vector of trainable weights applied to the symbolic adjustment. This step ensures that symbolic knowledge actively contributes to the final decision made by the model.

Compute Final Disease Stage or Progression

The adjusted logits y^∈R^c represent the unnormalized scores for disease stages based on the dataset. To obtain the final progression probabilities, we apply the softmax function:

$$\hat{P} = softmax(\hat{y}_i) \tag{10.11}$$

Example Rules used for fuzzy inference are mentioned below.
Example Rules:

(a) IF stenotic-narrowing > 50% AND nerve-compression present, THEN LSS is Severe.
(b) IF moderate-narrowing AND no-neurological deficits, THEN LSS is Mild.

10.3 Results and Discussion

10.3.1 Datasets

The framework is trained on publicly available lumbar spine datasets:

i) Lumbosacral MRI Dataset: Contains annotated spinal images with stenosis grading [30].
ii) UCI Vertebral Column Dataset: Provides biomechanical spine features for classification [31].
iii) Radiological Spinal Stenosis Dataset: Includes MRI and CT scans with radiologist-verified stenotic measurements [32].

Table 10.1 displays the overall statistics for the datasets mentioned below.

Table 10.1 Dataset statistics.

Dataset	No. of patients	Image type	Labels
Lumbosacral MRI	400	MRI	Normal vs. Stenotic
UCI Vertebral Column	310	Tabular	Hernia, Stenosis, Normal
Radiological Dataset	600	MRI and CT	Mild, Moderate, Severe Stenosis

10.3.2 Model Performance

We used three evaluation strategies: accuracy, sensitivity, and specificity for evaluating our model on the above-mentioned three datasets.

$$Accuracy = \frac{TP + TN}{TP + TN + FP + FN} \tag{10.12}$$

$$Sensitivity = \frac{TP}{TP + FN} \tag{10.13}$$

$$Specificity = \frac{TN}{TN + FP} \tag{10.14}$$

Three models (CNN, GCN, and Neuro-Symbolic) were used for comparison in Tables 10.2, 10.3, and 10.4 and Figures 10.2, 10.3, and 10.4 show the visual comparison of the models for the particular tables.

The improvements in accuracy, sensitivity, and specificity indicate that integrating fuzzy logic enhances the model's decision-making by incorporating symbolic reasoning alongside graph-based learning.

Table 10.2 Evaluation results on lumbosacral MRI dataset.

Method	Accuracy	Sensitivity	Specificity
CNN (Baseline)	86.3%	84.3%	88.2%
GCN (Proposed)	91.4%	90%	92.5%
Neuro-Symbolic (GCN + Fuzzy Logic)	94.4%	91.8%	96.6%

Table 10.3 Evaluation results on UCI vertebral column dataset.

Method	Accuracy	Sensitivity	Specificity
CNN (Baseline)	90%	83%	89%
GCN (Proposed)	92%	93%	94%
Neuro-Symbolic (GCN + Fuzzy Logic)	95%	92%	97%

Table 10.4 Evaluation results on the radiological spinal stenosis dataset.

Method	Accuracy	Sensitivity	Specificity
CNN (Baseline)	84%	81%	87%
GCN (Proposed)	91%	89.2%	91%
Neuro-Symbolic (GCN + Fuzzy Logic)	92%	91%	95%

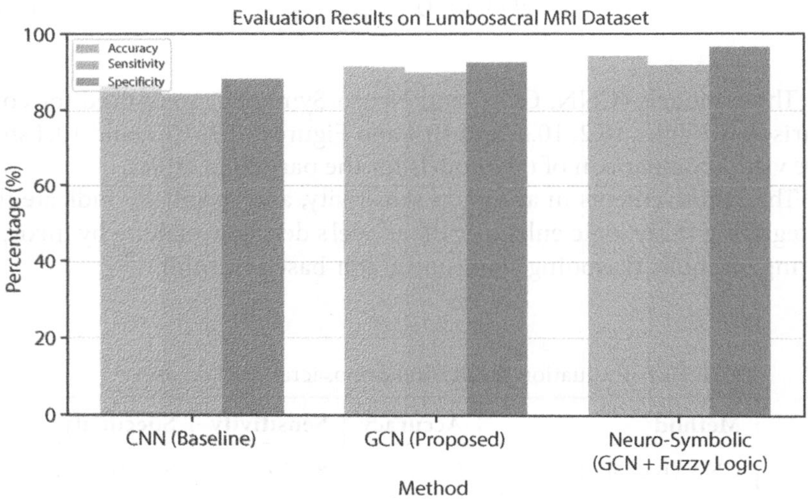

Figure 10.2 Comparison of three models in lumbosacral MRI dataset.

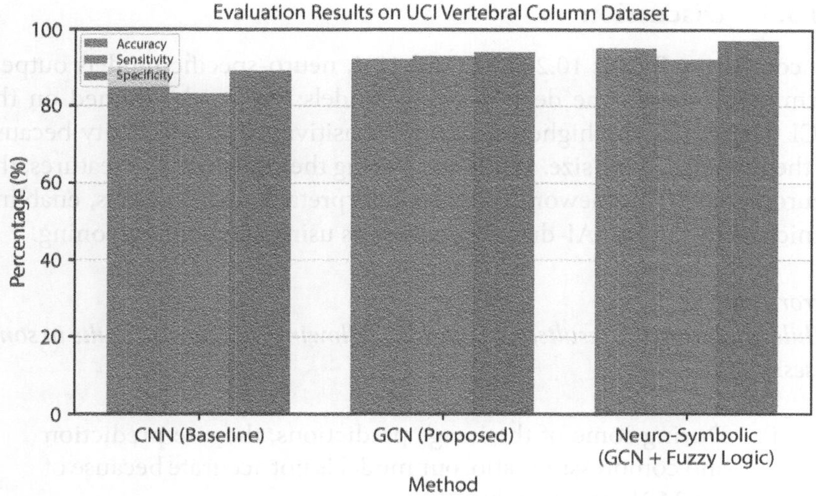

Figure 10.3 Comparison of three models in the UCI vertebral column dataset.

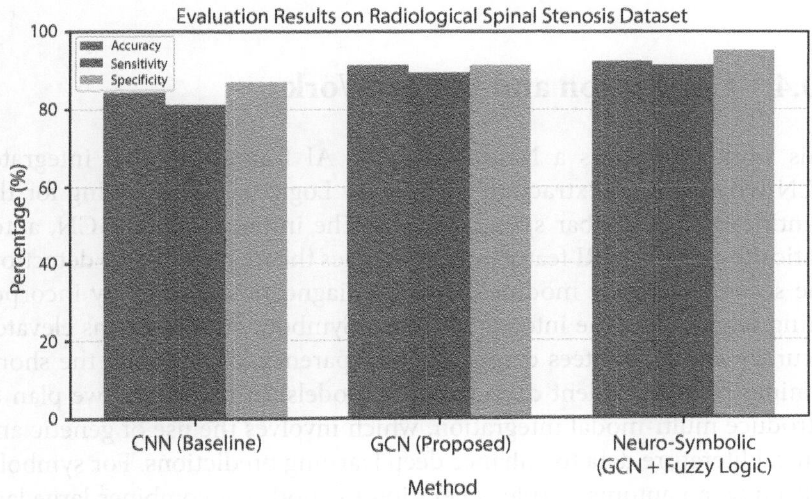

Figure 10.4 Comparison of three models in the radiological spinal stenosis dataset.

10.3.3 Discussion

By comparing Tables 10.2, 10.3, and 10.4, neuro-specific models outperform other standalone deep learning models; the model trained on the UCI dataset has the highest accuracy, sensitivity, and specificity because of the limited sample size. While comparing the explainability features, the neuro-symbolic framework provides interpretable explanations, enabling clinicians to validate AI-driven predictions using symbolic reasoning.

Error Analysis
While analyzing the results, we found the following inaccurate results in some cases:

i) During some of the image predictions, the size prediction and compression ratio, our model is not accurate because of the MRI image quality.
ii) Fuzzy rules, which are generated based on clinical derivations, are also limited and can be improved by introducing automatic rule generation methods.

10.4 Conclusion and Future Work

This work introduces a Neuro-Symbolic AI framework that integrates GCN-based feature extraction with Fuzzy Logic-based reasoning for the identification of lumbar spinal stenosis. The initial module, GCN, automatically extracts MRI features and classifies the images for LSS detection. The second symbolic module enhances diagnostic accuracy by incorporating fuzzy rules. The integrated Neuro-Symbolic model attains elevated accuracy and guarantees diagnostic transparency, overcoming the shortcomings of independent deep learning models. In the future, we plan to introduce multi-modal integration, which involves the use of genetic and clinical literature data to enhance deep learning predictions. For symbolic reasoning, an automatic rule generation method that combines large language models with a fuzzy engine can enhance the model's explanatory power in diagnosis.

AI disclosure statement: The author confirms that no artificial intelligence (AI)-generated content or AI-assisted writing tools were used in the preparation of this chapter (including summaries and the abstract). All text, analysis, and conclusions are the result of the author's original work.

References

1. Botwin, K.P. and Gruber, R.D., Lumbar spinal stenosis: anatomy and pathogenesis. *Phys. Med. Rehabil. Clin.*, 14, 1, 1–5, 2003 Feb 1.
2. Genevay, S. and Atlas, S.J., Lumbar spinal stenosis. *Best Pract. Res. Clin. Rheumatol.*, 24, 2, 253–65, 2010 Apr 1.
3. Paine, K.W., Cauchoix, J., Mcivor, G., Willis, W.K., Lumbar spinal stenosis. *Clin. Orthop. Relat. Research®*, 99, 30–50, 1974 Mar 1.
4. Lurie, J. and Tomkins-Lane, C., Management of lumbar spinal stenosis. *BMJ*, 352, 2016 Jan 4.
5. Katz, J.N., Zimmerman, Z.E., Mass, H., Makhni, M.C., Diagnosis and management of lumbar spinal stenosis: a review. *Jama*, 327, 17, 1688–99, 2022 May 3.
6. Amundsen, T., Weber, H., Lilleas, F., Nordal, H.J., Abdelnoor, M., Magnaes, B., Lumbar spinal stenosis: clinical and radiologic features. *Spine*, 20, 10, 1178–86, 1995 May 15.
7. Yang, X., Zhang, Y., Li, Y., Wu, Z., Performance of artificial intelligence in diagnosing lumbar spinal stenosis: a systematic review and meta-analysis. *Spine*, 10–97, 2024.
8. Yagi, M., Michikawa, T., Yamamoto, T., Iga, T., Ogura, Y., Tachibana, A., Miyamoto, A., Suzuki, S., Nori, S., Takahashi, Y., Tsuji, O., Development and validation of machine learning-based predictive model for clinical outcome of decompression surgery for lumbar spinal canal stenosis. *Spine J.*, 22, 11, 1768–77, 2022 Nov 1.
9. Al-antari, M.A., Salem, S., Raza, M., Elbadawy, A.S., Bütün, E., Aydin, A.A., Aydoğan, M., Ertuğrul, B., Talo, M., Gu, Y.H., Evaluating AI-powered predictive solutions for MRI in lumbar spinal stenosis: a systematic review. *Artif. Intell. Rev.*, 58, 8, 221, 2025 May 3.
10. Wang, T., *et al.*, Machine Learning and Deep Learning for Diagnosis of Lumbar Spinal Stenosis: Systematic Review and Meta-Analysis. *J. Med. Internet Res.*, 26, e54676, 2024.
11. Tumko, V., Kim, J., Uspenskaia, N., Honig, S., Abel, F., Lebl, D.R., Hotalen, I., Kolisnyk, S., Kochnev, M., Rusakov, A., Mourad, R., A neural network model for detection and classification of lumbar spinal stenosis on MRI. *Eur. Spine J.*, 33, 3, 941–8, 2024 Mar.
12. Prisilla, A.A., Guo, Y.L., Jan, Y.K., Lin, C.Y., Lin, F.Y., Liau, B.Y., Tsai, J.Y., Ardhianto, P., Pusparani, Y., Lung, C.W., An approach to the diagnosis of lumbar disc herniation using deep learning models. *Front. Bioeng. Biotechnol.*, 11, 1247112, 2023 Sep 4.
13. Bogdanovic, S., Staib, M., Schleiniger, M., Steiner, L., Schwarz, L., Germann, C., Sutter, R., Fritz, B., AI-Based Measurement of Lumbar Spinal Stenosis on MRI: External Evaluation of a Fully Automated Model. *Invest. Radiol.*, 11, 10–97, 2023.

14. Fan, G., Wang, D., Li, Y., Xu, Z., Wang, H., Liu, H., Liao, X., Machine Learning Predicts Decompression Levels for Lumbar Spinal Stenosis Using Canal Radiomic Features from Computed Tomography Myelography. *Diagnostics*, 14, 1, 53, 2023 Dec 26.
15. Siccoli, A., de Wispelaere, M.P., Schröder, M.L., Staartjes, V.E., Machine learning–based preoperative predictive analytics for lumbar spinal stenosis. *Neurosurgical Focus*, 46, 5, E5, 2019 May 1.
16. Ruchi, S.D., Lumbar Spine Disease Prediction with KNN, Random Forest and Decision Tree: A Study, in: *Big Data Analytics in Intelligent IoT and Cyber-Physical Systems*, pp. 185–193, Springer Nature Singapore, Singapore, 2023 Nov 5.
17. Singh, D., Singla, J., Rahmani, M.K., Ahmad, S., Rehman, M.U., Jha, S., Prashar, D., Nazeer, J., Lumbar spine disease detection: enhanced CNN model with improved classification accuracy. *IEEE Access*, 11, 141889–901, 2023 Dec 12.
18. Genç, H., Seyyarer, E., Ayata, F., Deep Learning-Driven MRI analysis for accurate diagnosis and grading of lumbar spinal stenosis. *Measurement*, 251, 117294, 2025 Jun 30.
19. Abbas, J., Yousef, M., Peled, N., Hershkovitz, I., Hamoud, K., Predictive factors for degenerative lumbar spinal stenosis: a model obtained from a machine learning algorithm technique. *BMC Musculoskeletal Disord.*, 24, 1, 218, 2023 Mar 23.
20. Khan, M.S., Diagnosis of lumbar spinal stenosis using deep learning of MRIs, 2024.
21. Li, Z., Shen, S., Shang, F., Huan, Z., Liang, J., Chen, Y., Weighted graph convolutional network with feature mask for low back pain prediction. *Biomed. Signal Process. Control*, 99, 106879, 2025 Jan 1.
22. Abel, F., Garcia, E., Andreeva, V., Nikolaev, N.S., Kolisnyk, S., Sarbaev, R., Novikov, I., Kozinchenko, E., Kim, J., Rusakov, A., Mourad, R., An Artificial Intelligence-Based Support Tool for Lumbar Spinal Stenosis Diagnosis from Self-Reported History Questionnaire. *World Neurosurg.*, 181, e953–62, 2024 Jan 1.
23. Galbusera, F., Casaroli, G., Bassani, T., Artificial intelligence and machine learning in spine research. *JOR Spine*, 2, 1, e1044, 2019 Mar.
24. Goulin, J., La Barbera, G., Delmonte, A., Bonnot, E., Berteloot, L., Lozach, C., Beaudoin, S., Blanc, T., Cretolle, C., Muller, C.O., Meignan, P., Revisiting Anatomy of Anorectal Malformations with a Symbolic AI Segmentation Method Applied on Diffusion MRI: The Lumbosacral Plexus Development and Microarchitecture Is Different in High and Low Types. *J. Imaging Inf. Med.*, 18, 1–1, 2025.
25. Han, Z., Wei, B., Xi, X., Chen, B., Yin, Y., Li, S., Unifying neural learning and symbolic reasoning for spinal medical report generation. *Med. Image Anal.*, 67, 101872, 2021 Jan 1.

26. Hossain, D. and Chen, J.Y., A Study on Neuro-Symbolic Artificial Intelligence: Healthcare Perspectives. arXiv preprint arXiv:2503.18213. 2025 Mar 23.
27. Nawaz, U., Anees-ur-Rahaman, M., Saeed, Z., A review of Neuro-Symbolic AI integrating reasoning and learning for advanced cognitive systems. *Intell. Syst. Appl.*, 200541, 2025 May 23.
28. Zhang, J., Chen, B., Zhang, L., Ke, X., Ding, H., Neural, symbolic and neural-symbolic reasoning on knowledge graphs. *AI Open*, 2, 14–35, 2021 Jan 1.
29. Yu, D., Yang, B., Liu, D., Wang, H., Pan, S., A survey on neural-symbolic learning systems. *Neural Networks*, 166, 105–26, 2023 Sep 1.
30. ŞAHiN, E., NN, A., Özdemir, D., Unlocking the black box: an in-depth review on interpretability, explainability, and reliability in deep learning. *Neural Comput. Appl.*, 37, 2, 859–965, 2025 Jan.
31. van der Graaf, J.W., van Hooff, M.L., Buckens, C.F., Rutten, M., van Susante, J.L., Kroeze, R.J., de Kleuver, M., van Ginneken, B., Lessmann, N., Lumbar spine segmentation in MR images: a dataset and a public benchmark. *Sci. Data*, 11, 1, 264, 2024 Mar 2.
32. Lichman, M., UCI machine learning repository [Internet]. 2013 Apr.
33. Schizas, C., Theumann, N., Burn, A., Tansey, R., Wardlaw, D., Smith, F.W., Kulik, G., Qualitative grading of severity of lumbar spinal stenosis based on the morphology of the dural sac on magnetic resonance images. *Spine.*, 35, 21, 1919–24, 2010 Oct 1.
34. Kipf, T.N. and Welling, M., Semi-supervised classification with graph convolutional networks. *arXiv preprint arXiv:1609.02907*. 2016 Sep 9.
35. Danel, T., Spurek, P., Tabor, J., Śmieja, M., Struski, L., Słowik, A., Maziarka, L., Spatial graph convolutional networks, in: *International Conference on Neural Information Processing*, Springer International Publishing, Cham, pp. 668–675, 2020 Nov 17.
36. Arya, D., Olij, R., Gupta, D.K., El Gazzar, A., Wingen, G., Worring, M., Thomas, R.M., Fusing structural and functional MRIs using graph convolutional networks for autism classification, in: *Medical Imaging with Deep Learning*, pp. 44–61, PMLR, 2020, September.
37. Chen, X., Zhou, J., Ke, P., Huang, J., Xiong, D., Huang, Y., Ma, G., Ning, Y., Wu, F., Wu, K., Classification of schizophrenia patients using a graph convolutional network: A combined functional MRI and connectomics analysis. *Biomed. Signal Process. Control*, 80, 104293, 2023 Feb 1.
38. Sun, Z., Yin, H., Chen, H., Chen, T., Cui, L., Yang, F., Disease prediction *via* graph neural networks. *IEEE J. Biomed. Health. Inf.*, 25, 3, 818–26, 2020 Jun 22.
39. Wu, F., Souza, A., Zhang, T., Fifty, C., Yu, T., Weinberger, K., Simplifying graph convolutional networks, in: *International conference on machine learning*, Pmlr, pp. 6861–6871, 2019 May 24.
40. Thrift, P.R., Fuzzy Logic Synthesis with Genetic Algorithms, in: *ICGA*, pp. 509–513, 1991Jul 13.

41. Golay, X., Kollias, S., Stoll, G., Meier, D., Valavanis, A., Boesiger, P., A new correlation-based fuzzy logic clustering algorithm for FMRI. *Magn. Reson. Med.*, 40, 2, 249–60, 1998 Aug.
42. Pavithra, D. and Jayanthi, A.N., Retraction Note to: An improved adaptive neuro fuzzy interference system for the detection of autism spectrum disorder, 2023.

11

Adaptive Filtering Framework for Medical Image Denoising across Spatial and Wavelet Filters

Naveen Kumar Penjarla[1]*, Tejaswi Vallabhapurapu[2], Syamala Rao P.[3], Nissankara Lakshmi Prasanna[4], Kamesh Sonti[5] and P. Vishnu Priya[6]

[1]*Department of ECE, Sreyas Institute of Engineering and Technology, Hyderabad, Telangana, India*

[2]*Electronics and Communications Engineering, Hyderabad Institute of Technology and Management, Hyderabad, Telangana, India*

[3]*Department of Information Technology, SRKR Engineering College, Bhimavaram, Andhra Pradesh, India*

[4]*Department of Computer Science Engineering, VVIT, Guntur, Andhra Pradesh, India*

[5]*Department of ECE, Sri Vasavi Engineering College, Tadepalligudem, Andhra Pradesh, India*

[6]*Department of ECE, Hyderabad Institute of Technology and Management, Hyderabad, Telangana, India*

Abstract

Medical imaging is today an integral part of modern medicine. The spatial, wavelet, and statistical domain filters are proposed. In the spatial domain, morphological OCS (open close sequence) and LMMSE-STD (linear minimum mean squared error structure tensor diffusion) filters are implemented for removing Impulse and Rician noise, respectively. OCS filter is designed for removing high-density Impulse noise. Further, in order to improve the denoising efficiency and edge preservation, noise estimation via noise removal is proposed using an LMMSE estimator. The filter coefficients are adapted based on the estimation of the noise level. The effectiveness of both filters is tested and validated for different noise variance levels. Further study has been carried out for filtering Impulse noise with OCS filter and Rician noise for LMMSE-STD of different types of datasets, respectively,

**Corresponding author*: naveen.penjerla@gmail.com

R. Nidhya, A. Dineshkumar, Sheng-Lung Peng, S. Karthik and S. Balamurugan (eds.) Neuro-Symbolic Artificial Intelligence: Concepts & Applications, (207–224) © 2026 Scrivener Publishing LLC

and are compared with existing standard filters. In the wavelet domain method, adaptive Bayes shrink and probabilistic wavelet filters are presented. The parameters that estimate the threshold are adaptively chosen according to the resolution level of the coefficients. To further enhance denoising efficiency and edge preservation, a new sub-band adaptive Bayesian shrink method is proposed using a probability technique. The wavelet coefficient in the sub-band is computed by using probability and further extended by employing an adaptive shrink technique. Both proposed algorithms are validated and tested for clinical and synthetic datasets. Statistical-based techniques are derived for accurate modeling of noise so as to improve the denoising performance.

***Keywords*:** Medical image denoising, open-close sequence, linear minimum mean squared error, structure tensor diffusion, Impulse and Rician noise

11.1 Introduction

The growth of MRI as a tool for visualizing the anatomy and pathology data has made remarkable strides over the past few decades. The clinical diagnosis is seriously affected due to noise embedded in MR images during the acquisition process. This noise reduces the visual quality of MR data. Therefore, denoising is required to enhance the image quality for proper diagnosis. Figure 11.1 shows the traditional noise reduction techniques

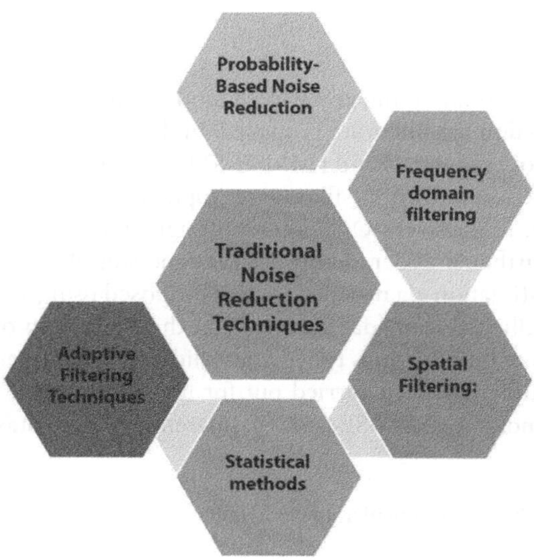

Figure 11.1 Traditional noise reduction techniques.

in the medical imaging category. Repetitive measurement of the image sequence improves the SNR. In general, an MRI scanner comprises a huge, powerful magnet in which the patient lies, a radio wave is transmitted through the body by using a transmitter, and the echo is collected. The echo is converted into a 2D image with the help of a computer. The MR image of any part of the human body in all dimensions can be obtained. It is very complicated to generate MR images and harder to decipher than US, CT, and plain radiography [1, 2]. The magnetic field intensity produced by the magnet is proportional to Larmor frequency. At the Larmor frequency, the protons inside the living tissue are oriented parallel to the magnetic field. While acquiring the MR data and RF pulse, which is tuned to Larmor frequency, is emitted from the scanner [3]. This RF pulse resonates to produce a coherent phase with respect to the spin magnetization; the RF pulse duration is chosen in such a way that the magnetic field is perpendicular to the spin magnetization. The receiver, which resonates at Larmor frequency, is kept in the surrounding area of the living tissue [4–6].

The magnetization will produce an electrical current in the receiver by the principle of Faraday induction. The signal obtained by the receiver is known as an NMR signal. The NMR signal is attenuated by the spin system due to loss of coherence for a particular time 21–24 period, which is known as transverse relaxation time (T_2); simultaneously, the magnetization vector gradually decreases and aligns parallel to the magnetic field. This process takes a time period (T_1) and is called as spin lattice relaxation time [7, 8]. The contrast in the MR data is produced due to dissimilarity in relaxation times, which is generated due to different tissues. The magnetic field spins spatially at different locations of the living tissues at dissimilar rates (times); the NMR signal was obtained by using magnetic field gradients consisting of different frequencies relative to different living tissues [9]. This spatially obtained NMR signal is known as MRI, which is in analog domain. The sampled version of analog MR data is saved for further processing. This digital MR signal contains dissimilar spatial locations of the signal from living tissues and is represented by pixels. The work of parallel imaging is based on acquiring the complex MR data (k) using an array of multiple receiver coils [10]. If undersampling is performed on MR data, the resultant image undergoes the aliasing effect, and the noise is embedded in the resultant image. Numerous parallel imaging techniques are available for reconstruction by using undersampled MR data (reconstruction by using GRAPPA) or making artifact free (reconstruction by SENSE) or reconstructing from noisy data [11, 12]. The acquisition of the MR data will be faster while performing parallel operation and also results in less motion deterioration of MR data due to short breath-hold times.

In order to produce the images of high clinical quality, the number of coils in the array should be limited to the acceleration factor (*R*).

Estimating noise variance in MR images is a crucial task. The estimated noise variance acts as an important parameter for numerous post-processing functions such as parameter estimation, noise reduction, and clustering or segmentation [13–15]. The analyzed noise variance also provides information about the quality of the MR image and could also assist in upgrading the design of scanners [16]. The estimated noise from MR information can be in terms of complex or absolute value. Generally, the MRI scanners produce only absolute images [17–19]. Moreover, the noise in MR data is modeled as a Rician distribution when the image is acquired by a single coil. In the spatial domain, LMMSE was used for both filtering and noise estimation for Rican noise using the local mean and local variance method [20]. In the transform domain method, wavelet-based noise estimation is performed using MAD (median absolute deviation method).

The main objective of this work is design and development of spatial domain filters (open close sequence filter (OCS) and linear minimum mean square error-based structure tensor diffusion filter (LMMSE-STD)) to remove Impulse, Gaussian, and Rician noise from MRI data. In this chapter, the design and development of morphological filters are discussed. Performance metrics are evaluated for both clinical and synthetic datasets. The adaptive structural tensor diffusion filter uses the LMMSE estimator to estimate noise levels and improve filtering performance. Design and development of an adaptive structure tensor diffusion filter, which combines a noise estimation method using LMMSE (linear minimum squared error) and this filter is adapted to remove Rician noise in MR images. Here, a smoothing parameter is selected based on the coefficients of the LMMSE filter and the proposed filter is totally automatic, and its performance depends on the estimated standard deviation of the noise level and the statistical distribution of noise. Further study has been carried out for filtering Rician noise, with the STD-LMMSE filter for different types of datasets, respectively, and are compared with standard existing filters. The parameters that estimate the threshold are adaptively chosen according to the resolution level of the coefficients. The developed algorithm leads to fast computation, with well-preserved image details. The developed algorithm is evaluated and tested for MR datasets.

11.2 Literature Review

In this section, we discussed about literature review based on existing filtering techniques for medical image analysis. Elaiyaraja *et al.* [21] have presented the development of an iterative technique to concurrently recognize noisy pixels and analyze the standard deviation of noise in MR data. The developed algorithm is more generic than the maximum likelihood method, since it can be applied to a large volume of magnitude data. In practice, they require either many repetitions of the measurements or a very large number of measurements, which are unaffordable in clinical routine as they would make the scan far too long. The effectiveness of the proposed method is validated and identified through the statistical distributions of noise in both clinical and synthetic datasets.

Ismael *et al.* [22] suggested that the linear minimum mean square error (LMMSE) estimator estimates the original signal (Rician noise) from the noisy pixels, is chosen from a local neighborhood, and utilizes information of the distribution of mean, variance, and square of mean value. This method uses estimation of noise variance without background segmentation. The limitation of this algorithm is the inaccurate estimation of noise if the background has artifacts. Abuya *et al.* [23] have presented a method for denoising of Rician noise using wavelet transform and anisotropic diffusion filter, which reduces the artifacts caused due to thresholding of wavelet coefficients. In order to improve denoising efficiency and edge preservation, the author developed a bilateral filter in the wavelet domain for Rician noise removal. In magnitude, MR data shows better edge preservation and efficient noise reduction. Elhoseny *et al.* [24] have used a method for thresholding the data in the wavelet domain and obtained high denoising performance, particularly for homogeneous noise, which induces loss of some true coefficients due to the non-homogeneous nature of noise. To overcome this drawback, combination of both spatial filtering and wavelet thresholding is developed.

Radhika *et al.* [25] have presented high-resolution (large *b* values) diffusion magnetic resonance imaging (DMRI) modality that bears high noise and comprises significant information for microstructural and connectomics (neural connections in the brain) studies. High noise levels in the DWI images cause biased estimates of the diffusion parameters because of signal-dependent nature of the noise (Rician noise). They apply a statistical framework to convert non-stationary (Rician) noise into stationary noise (Gaussian noise), which helps in effectively removing the bias.

In this research work, the authors introduce a non-local spatial and angular matching adaptive denoising technique; this technique uses 4D volumetric denoising of Gaussian and Rician noise. Each volumetric data is separated into small slices of 4D datasets, which enhances the visual quality of datasets and anatomical information required for clinical diagnosis. Taassori *et al.* [7] presented the diffusion weighted images illustrating low signal-to-noise ratio (SNR) during the measurement of MR data; due to high noise, it is hard to estimate the significant diffusion parameters for medical image analysis, and further denoising techniques are applied to multidirectional DWI datasets, which minimize the random noise by considering lower frequency components. Due to denoising, the tractography results were improved and enhanced the probability of connections between voxels within in region of interest.

Kumar *et al.* [26] have presented wavelet transforms for multiresolution representations of signals and images. The wavelet domain filters are specifically designed for removing Rician noise in MR images. Due to the signal-dependent behavior of Rician noise, the estimation of signal-free component in the wavelet sub-band causes bias. The signal bias in the MR data is overcome by filtering the squared magnitude of noise MR data in the transform domain. The data in the squared magnitude MR image that follows a non-central Chi-square distribution causes no bias, but still bias exists in the wavelet scaling coefficients and is signal independent, so the bias can be removed easily.

The significant limitations of the earlier works for above two filters are the following: (i) earlier proposed works are limited to moderate noise level (≤50%) and dimension of the structuring element and filtering window kernel size is fixed, and noise detection rate is more on wrong observational errors in moderate distorted medical images and many misplaced detection errors in high corrupted medical images. (ii) To improve the denoising performance and edge preservation details, the design of a non-linear ADF adapts to the noise level and statistical distributions of the image. A limitation of the algorithm is the optimal size of the filtering parameter and automatic parameter selection, which requires analytical interpretation in the diffusion filter. To overcome the disadvantages of the above proposed methods, two novel spatial filtering techniques are suggested.

11.3 Methodology

The two spatial filtering techniques (OCS and LMMSE-STD) are proposed for the removal of Impulse and Rician noise in medical dataset block diagram as shown in Figure 11.2. Initially, both filters are used to remove the noise in medical images with varying noise levels. But experimental results reveal that the OCS filter is the best for the removal of impulse noise and the LMMSE-STD filter is for the Rician noise, and workflow model is illustrated in Figure 11.3. Further, number of datasets is tested for validation of the proposed techniques. Experiments are conducted on both clinical and simulated datasets. The results of quality measures indicate that the proposed method offers better performance than the standard filters for different noise variance. The next chapter presents a filter based on the transform domain for denoising Rican noise at low and high SNR levels.

The proposed method is carried out using a quadratic spline wavelet, and the assessment of significant wavelet coefficients is based on recognition and analysis of signal-free wavelet components in the wavelet sub-bands. The expectation approaches E $(y_k \mid w_k, X_k = 1)$, expressing the probability of a significant wavelet coefficient using Bayes' rule, P $(X_k = 1 \mid w_k)$, by generalized likelihood ratio; then the probability of a significant wavelet coefficient is depicted as follows:

$$y_k = \frac{\xi_k \mu_k}{1 - \xi_k \mu_k} \tag{11.1}$$

$$\xi_k = \frac{p_{\frac{w_k}{X_k}}\left(w_k/_1\right)}{p_{\frac{w_k}{X_k}}\left(w_k/_0\right)} \tag{11.2}$$

$$\mu_k = \frac{p(X_k = 1/_p)}{p(X_k = 0/_p)} \tag{11.3}$$

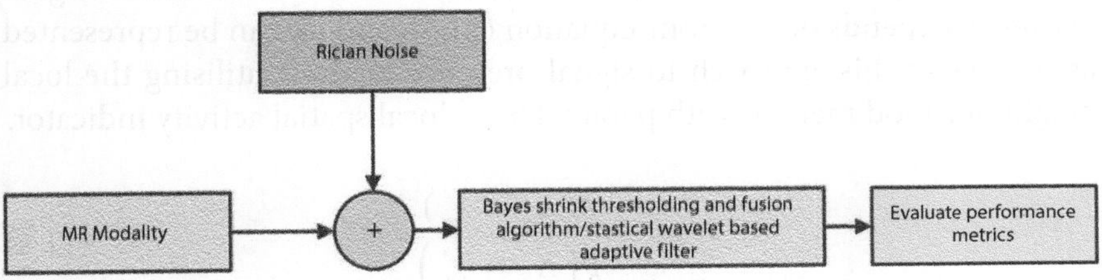

Figure 11.2 Block diagram of the transform domain filtering techniques.

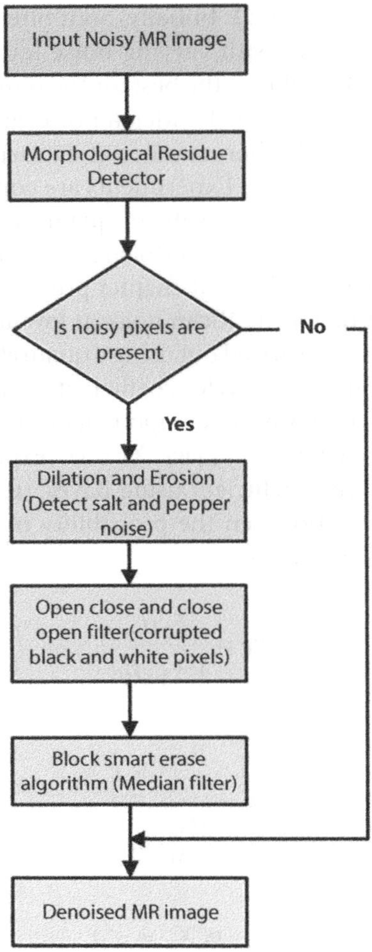

Figure 11.3 Workflow of the OCS filter.

The symbol ρ gives the prior knowledge about the analysis of signal presence using a probabilistic method. The analysis of the likelihood of signal existence depends on e_k from Equation (11.3), and μk can be represented as follows in this approach to signal presence analysis utilising the local neighbourhood method with parameter e_k local spatial activity indicator.

$$\mu_k = \frac{p(X_k = 1/e_k)}{p\left(X_k = 0/e_k\right)} \tag{11.4}$$

For different noise types, it is required to derive the estimator analytically and can be expressed in the generalized model; the operation of ek is depicted as locally averaging the neighborhood pixels. Hence, the proposed algorithm can be appropriate to different noise types, which requires an arbitrary choice of e_k.

The LMMSE algorithm is developed particularly for estimating and filtering of Rician model. The structure tensor is a 2×2 matrix wherein the elements in the matrix represent the eigenvalues and give their corresponding direction, that is, eigenvectors. The eigenvectors give the local orientation, and the eigenvalues give the corresponding local contrast along these directions. If the eigenvectors are parallel to each other, then the diffusion function is not applied and is applied if they are perpendicular. Smoothing of diffusion tensor or diffusion weighted images in the tensor direction needs to be restored and preserved around tissue boundaries. There is a need to minimize the systematic bias in the restored image, which improves accuracy and tissue characterization in DTI/DWI images.

Simulated Datasets: These datasets remove the data dependency, so as to enable a precise comparative study. The dataset consists of brain SPECT, PET, and US images of different resolutions. The experiments were evaluated on different medical images distorted by the variance of noise levels and different resolutions. This sub-section describes the datasets that have been considered to conduct the experiment. The experiments were performed on both clinical and simulated MRI datasets. The denoising results of the following images are considered for study.

(a) T1-weighted axial normal MR brain image with large structural variations and corrupted by noise, with the image resolution of 256×256 and 512×512.
(b) SPECT brain image with less structural details and corrupted by noise with the image resolution of 256×256 and 512×512.
(c) PET brain image with large structural details and corrupted noise with the image resolution of 256×256 and 512×512.
(d) US image having a fetus corrupted by noise with the image resolution of 256×256 and 512×512.

11.4 Results and Discussion

This section illustrates the results and discussions obtained by considering clinical and synthetic datasets, which are used to evaluate the performance of the two proposed transform domain filters (WT&FA and SWBANF). A total of 500 clinical datasets and 500 synthetic datasets were considered to validate the proposed approaches. Clinical datasets consist of MR T1 weighted brain images, clinical DWI (diffusion weighted images), and noisy input images acquired from an MR machine. Whereas synthetic datasets include MRI T1 weighted brain images having pathology, ultrasound images (US), and HARDI DWI (high angular resolution diffusion weighted images). The Rician noise is added to the MR medical datasets by varying the variance of noise levels. The variance varies from 10% to 90% in step size of 10. The variance of noise has not increased beyond 90% since it is problematic to preserve the edges in the medical images. Both proposed filters are applied to denoise the noisy images with varying noise levels. The performance of each filter is interpreted by peak signal-to-noise ratio (PSNR), image quality index (IQI), contrast, and root mean squared error (RMSE). Figure 11.4 gives the statistical comparison of PSNR values for various filters.

The proposed filters are compared with standard filters (NLM and LMMSE) to validate the results. The average performance metrics for clinical datasets are tabulated in Table 11.1. It can be illustrated from Table 11.1 that the performance metrics are decreasing with an increase in noise variance level. This is due to a decrease in signal-to-noise ratio in the images with an increase in noise variance levels. Besides, the PSNR value

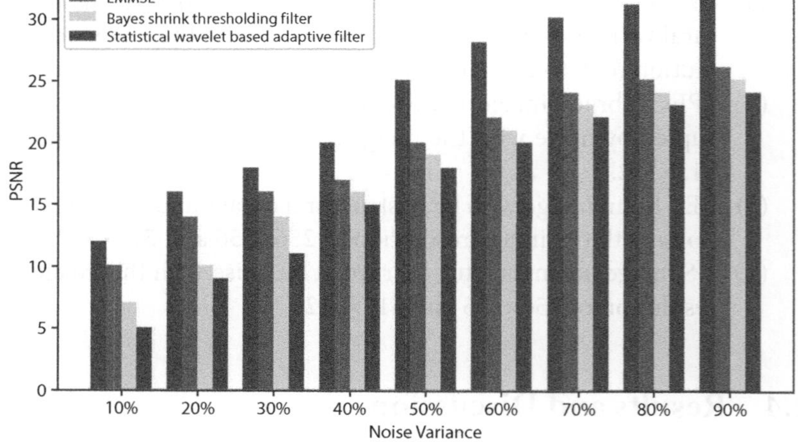

Figure 11.4 Comparison of PSNR values of different filters for clinical MR data corrupted by Rician noise.

Table 11.1 Comparison of performance metrics of different filters for clinical MR data corrupted by Rician noise.

Input noisy image measuring SNR without filtering		NLM				LMMSE				Bayes shrink thresholding filter				Statistical wavelet-based adaptive filter			
Noise variance levels	SNR	PSNR	IQI	RMSE	Contrast	PSNR	IQI	RMSE	Contrast	PSNR	IQI	RMSE	Contrast	PSNR	IQI	RMSE	Contrast
10	18.27	22.60	0.37	0.0613	0.66	25.48	0.811	0.990	0.76	29.12	0.989	9.1X10–4	0.85	31.64	0.99	6.1X10–4	0.95
20	19.61	21.72	0.21	0.0538	0.56	38.31	0.727	0.974	0.66	24.81	0.964	7.9X10–4	0.81	29.57	0.97	4.9X10–4	0.94
30	18.23	19.90	0.26	0.0456	0.45	35.13	0.613	0.878	0.56	21.34	0.924	7.6X10–4	0.83	25.38	0.95	4.6X10–4	0.93
40	17.89	18.22	0.13	0.0413	0.33	34.11	0.522	0.676	0.45	30.16	0.985	6.6X10–4	0.82	22.07	0.94	4.5X10–4	0.92
50	15.34	16.12	0.12	0.0410	0.25	33.12	0.423	0.675	0.33	29.76	0.984	5.6X10–4	0.89	21.63	0.93	4.3X10–4	0.91
60	14.67	15.89	0.11	0.0389	0.14	32.66	0.321	0.612	0.28	27.78	0.983	5.1X10–4	0.86	7.66	0.92	6.1X10–4	0.89
70	13.45	14.98	0.11	0.0301	0.13	31.55	0.223	0.610	0.21	28.54	0.981	4.8X10–4	0.85	5.11	0.91	4.9X10–4	0.86
80	12.89	13.98	0.11	0.0276	0.12	30.66	0.215	0.556	0.19	26.12	0.979	4.6X10–4	0.83	3.12	0.90	4.6X10–4	0.85
90	11.67	12.23	0.11	0.0255	0.11	29.88	0.201	0.453	0.17	21.06	0.912	4.5X10–4	0.84	2.29	0.89	4.5X10–4	0.83

of the SWBANF filter is 37.58%, 53.12 less compared to the WT and FA and LMMSE filter and 25.17% more than the NLM filter for 50% noise variance level, respectively. Whereas the IQI metrics of the SWBANF filter is 5.806% less compared to WT&FA and 45.87%, 86.98% higher when compared to LMMSE and NLM filters, respectively, for 50% noise variance level. Similarly, the RMSE value for SWBANF filter is 23.21% more compared to WT&FA and 85.25% less compared to LMMSE and 13.65% more than NLM filters for 50% noise variance level, respectively. Similarly, the contrast values for SWBANF filter are 2.197%, 63.73%, and 72.52% more when compared to WT&FA, LMMSE, and NLM filters, respectively, for 50% noise variance level.

Figure 11.5 reveals the comparison of PSNR values of SWBANF and WT&FA filters along with standard conventional filters. It is observed that for a 10% noise variance level, the PSNR value of the SWBANF is more than the WT&FA, LMMSE, and NLM filters, respectively. As the level of noise increases from 10% to 90%, the PSNR value of SWBANF deteriorates rapidly than other filters, but LMMSE shows a better PSNR value as the level of noise increases. Besides that, it adds an advantage of efficient noise

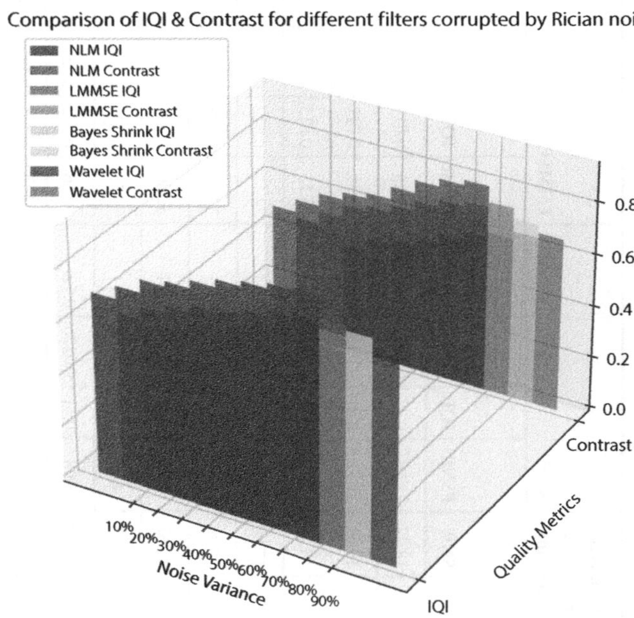

Figure 11.5 Comparison of IQI and CONTRAST values of different filters for clinical MR data corrupted by Rician noise.

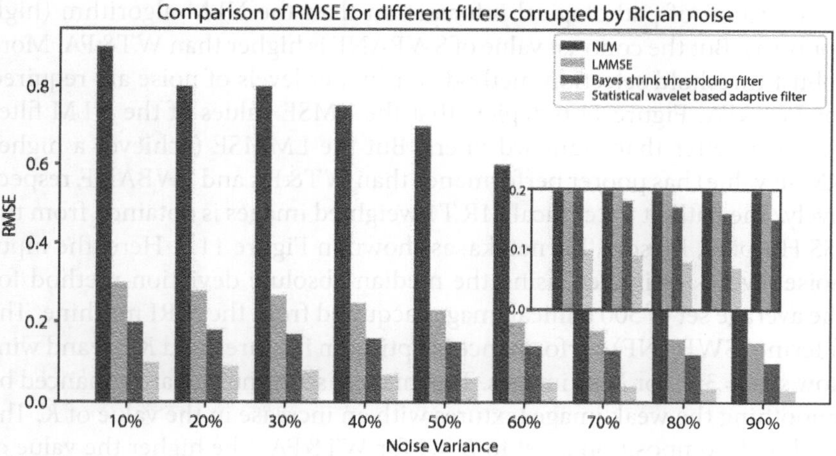

Figure 11.6 Comparison of RMSE values of different filters for clinical MR data corrupted by Rician noise.

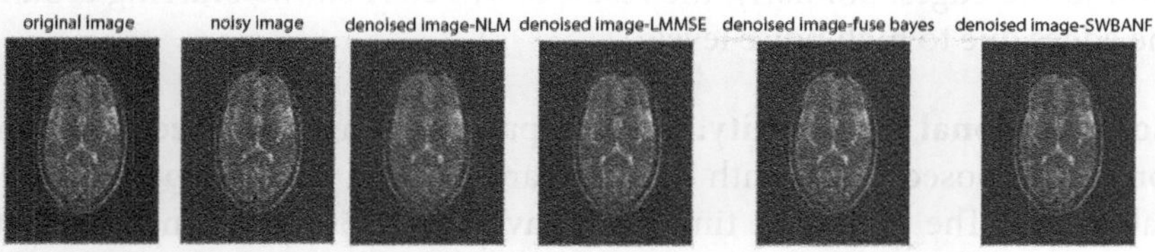

Figure 11.7 Restoration results of T1 weighted MR brain image (clinical MR data) having pathology corrupted by Rician noise and comparison of proposed filters with standard filters.

reduction but fails to preserve the edge information. The moderate PSNR values are achieved in case of WT&FA and NLM filter but lack edge preservation. The SWBANF achieved better edge preservation than efficient noise reduction when compared to standard filters. It is observed that the image quality index (IQI) of NLM is better than LMMSE. This is due to the LMMSE algorithm not filtering the edges in the image. Moreover, the visual quality of LMMSE is not good when compared to standard filters. Similarly, while comparing SWBANF and WT&FA, the visual quality of SWBANF is better than WT&FA.

The visual quality of WT&FA is poor since the wavelet thresholding filter is non-adaptive to wavelet sub-band coefficients. To preserve the image, edge details for the analysis of the image value of the contrast should be high. From Figure 11.6, it is observed that the LMMSE achieves better preservation of pathological information than the NLM algorithm (high contrast). But the contrast value of SWBANF is higher than WT&FA. More robust threshold selection methods for higher levels of noise are required for WT&FA. Figure 11.6 depicts that the RMSE values of the NLM filter perform better than standard filters. But the LMMSE (achieves a higher RMSE value) has poorer performance than WT&FA and SWBANF, respectively. The dataset for clinical MR T1 weighted images is obtained from the JSS Hospital, Mysore, Karnataka, as shown in Figure 11.7. Here, the input noise level is estimated using the median absolute deviation method for the average set of 500 clinical images acquired from the MRI machine. The filtering (SWBANF) performance is optimum for threshold $K = 2$ and window size = 3×3 for MRI images. The image discontinuities are enhanced by smoothing the weak image textures with an increase in the value of K. The level of decomposition is set to $L = 4$ for WT&FA. The higher the value of decomposition, the more blurring around the edges. The restoration shows that the NLM filter over-smoothing around the edges causes loss of information. But the result of the LMMSE filter shows that still noise is present around the edges. Similarly, the result of WT&FA shows blurring around the edges due to high noise levels.

Computational Complexity: The comparison of average execution time for the proposed filters with the standard existing filters is portrayed in Table 11.2. The execution time is the average of 500 combined datasets from both clinical and synthetic medical images. From Table 11.2, it is evident that as the variance of noise increases from 10% to 90%, the execution time also increases. This is due to an increase in the number of pixels that are corrupted with noise. The comparison of computational complexity in terms of time is illustrated in Figure 11.8 for different denoising filters. The execution time of WT&FA is 52.77% more than the LMMSE filter and 79.47% less than the NLM filter and 76.11% more execution time than SWBANF for a 50% noise variance level. It can also be noticed that the execution time for SWBANF is less when compared to all other filters. The execution time of the SWBANF filter for a 50% noise level has an improvement of 76.11%, 49.47%, and 95.11%, when compared to WT&FA, LMMSE, and NLM filters, respectively. The reason for this is that the SWBANF filter automatically adapts to the statistical distribution of noise and local image characteristics. Besides, the level of noise (SNR) depends on the threshold parameter (K). But in case of WT&FA, the filter is non-adaptive, and hence, it requires manual tuning of the filtering parameters for the level of noise.

Table 11.2 Average execution time of the proposed filters compared with standard conventional filters corrupted by Rician noise.

Noise level	NLM filter	LMMSE	Bayes shrink fusion	Adaptive spline wavelet filter
10	756	50	150	25
20	856	60	170	30
30	833	70	186	35
40	823	80	182	40
50	877	85	180	43
60	900	90	179	45
70	987	96	175	48
80	1100	100	184	51
90	1150	156	165	76

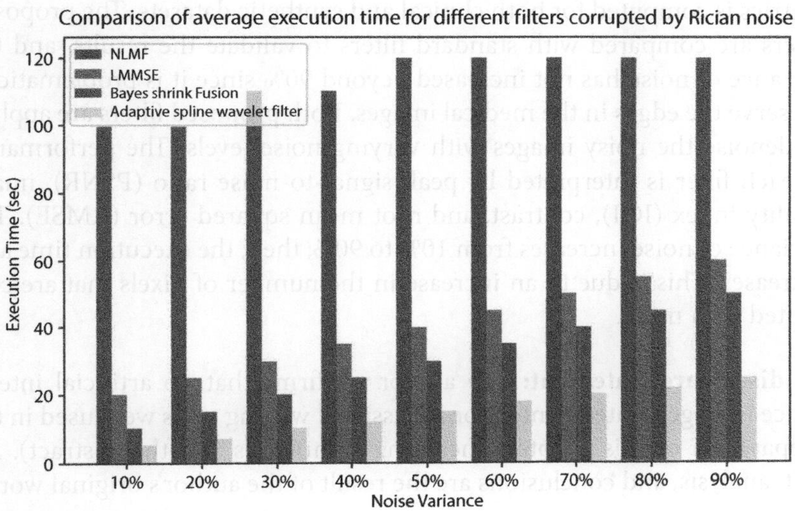

Figure 11.8 Comparison of average execution time for different filters corrupted by Rician noise.

Statistical-based techniques are derived for accurate modeling of noise so as to improve the denoising performance. Accurate modeling of the noise is required for further improving denoising performance. It is observed that the low SNR images are greatly affected in the case of DWI images, in which the Gaussian nature of noise is approximated to Rician noise. The filtering performance on these images is better noise reduction and edge preservation compared to standard conventional filters.

11.5 Conclusion

In this chapter, the performance evaluation of spatial filtering techniques with the design and development of the morphological filter was discussed. Performance metrics is evaluated for both clinical and synthetic datasets. Furthermore, the design of the adaptive structure tensor diffusion filter, in which the LMMSE estimator is used for estimating the level of noise, improved the filtering performance. The wavelet thresholding and fusion filter is developed, in which the selection of the threshold is dependent on the level of noise and wavelet coefficients. A design of an improved Bayesian spatial activity estimator is proposed. Moreover, its performance metrics is computed for both clinical and synthetic datasets. The proposed filters are compared with standard filters to validate the results, and the variance of noise has not increased beyond 90% since it is problematic to preserve the edges in the medical images. Both proposed filters are applied to denoise the noisy images with varying noise levels. The performance of each filter is interpreted by peak signal-to-noise ratio (PSNR), image quality index (IQI), contrast, and root mean squared error (RMSE). The variance of noise increases from 10% to 90%; then, the execution time also increases. This is due to an increase in the number of pixels that are corrupted with noise.

AI disclosure statement: The author confirms that no artificial intelligence (AI)-generated content or AI-assisted writing tools were used in the preparation of this chapter (including summaries and the abstract). All text, analysis, and conclusions are the result of the author's original work.

References

1. Wang, L., Yang, Z., Pu, Y.-F., Yin, H., Ren, X., An Efficient Multi-Scale Wavelet Approach for Dehazing and Denoising Ultrasound Images Using Fractional-Order Filtering. *Fractal Fract.*, 8, 9, 549, 2024.
2. Annavarapu, A. and Borra, S., An adaptive watershed segmentation based medical image denoising using deep convolutional neural networks. *Biomed. Signal Process. Control*, 93, 1061195, 2024.
3. Taassori, M., Enhanced Wavelet-Based Medical Image Denoising with Bayesian-Optimized Bilateral Filtering. *Sensors*, 24, 21, 6849, 2024.
4. Răboacă, S., Cătălin Dumitrescu, M, Filote, C., A new adaptive spatial filtering method in the wavelet domain for medical images. *Appl. Sci.*, 10, 16, 5693, Manta2020.
5. Chen, Y., Wang, R., Zong, P., Chen, D., Image Processing for Denoising Using Composite Adaptive Filtering Methods Based on RMSE. *Open J. Appl. Sci.*, 14, 03, 660–675, 2024.
6. Zeng, Y. and Wu, X., Medical Image Denoising Processing Application Technology Based on Combined Filtering, in: *2022 2nd International Conference on Bioinformatics and Intelligent Computing*, pp. 447–451, 2022.
7. Taassori, M. and Vizvári, B., Enhancing Medical Image Denoising: A Hybrid Approach Incorporating Adaptive Kalman Filter and Non-Local Means with Latin Square Optimization. *Electronics*, *13*, 2640, 2024.
8. Wu, W., Wang, Y., Liu, Q., Wang, G., Zhang, J., Wavelet-improved score-based generative model for medical imaging. *IEEE Trans. Med. Imaging*, *43*, 966–979, 2023.
9. Huang, J.J. and Dragotti, P.L., WINNet: Wavelet-inspired invertible network for image denoising. *IEEE Trans. Image Process.*, *31*, 4377–4392, 2022.
10. Zavala-Mondragon, L.A., Rongen, P., Bescos, J.O., de With, P.H., van der Sommen, F., Noise reduction in CT using learned wavelet-frame shrinkage networks. *IEEE Trans. Med. Imaging*, *41*, 2048–2066, 2022.
11. Yu, Y., She, K., Liu, J., Cai, X., Shi, K., Kwon, O.M.A., super-resolution network for medical imaging *via* transformation analysis of wavelet multi-resolution. *Neural Netw.*, *166*, 162–173, 2023.
12. Sivarambabu, P.V., Malarvezhi, P., Dayana, R., Vadivukkarasi, K., Rama Koteswara Rao, P., EEHC approach for latency minimization in 3D network architecture using 5G+ with UAVs. *Wireless Pers. Commun.*, 122, 1, 897–914, 2022.
13. Sagheer, S.V.M. and George, S.N., A review on medical image denoising algorithms. *Biomed. Signal Process. Control*, 61, 1020365, 2020.
14. Reddy, S.R.B., Kanagala, P., Ravichandran, P., Pulimamidi, R., Sivarambabu, P.V., Polireddi, .N.S.A., Effective fraud detection in e-commerce: Leveraging machine learning and big data analytics. *Meas.: Sens.*, 33, 101138, 2024.
15. Pavithra, D. and Jayanthi, A.N., A Study on Machine Learning Algorithm in Medical Diagnosis. *Int. J. Adv. Res. Comput. Sci.*, 9, 4, 2018.

16. Zhang, X., Li, X., Tang, X., Chen, X., Chen, X., Zhou, P., Spatial Filtering for Enhanced High-Density Surface Electromyographic Examination of Neuromuscular Changes and Its Application to Spinal Cord Injury. *J. NeuroEng. Rehabil.*, 2020.
17. Wang, X.F., Luo, L., Zou, Q.Y., Constructing Naive Bayesian Classification Model by Spark for Big Data. *2020 17th International Computer Conference on Wavelet Active Media Technology and Information Processing (ICCWAMTIP)*, pp. 306–309, 2020.
18. Aravinth, S.S., Srithar, S., Sivarambabu, P.V., Naveen Kumar Reddy, B., Anirudh Babu, A., Tata, S., Enhancing Medical Image Recognition through Automated Neural Network Architecture Optimization using Neuroevolvenet, in: *2023 International Conference on Recent Advances in Science and Engineering Technology (ICRASET)*, IEEE, pp. 1–6, 2023.
19. Nidhya, R., Kalpana, R., Smilarubavathy, G., Keerthana, S.M., Brain Tumor Diagnosis with MCNN-Based MRI Image Analysis, in: *2023 1st International Conference on Optimization Techniques for Learning (ICOTL)*, IEEE, pp. 1–5, 2023, December.
20. Kulathilake, KA.S.H., Aniza Abdullah, N., Qalid Md Sabri, A., Ravimal Bandara, A.M.R., Wee Lai, K., A review on self-adaptation approaches and techniques in medical image denoising algorithms. *Multimedia Tools Appl.*, 81, 26, 37591–37626, 2022.
21. Elaiyaraja, G., Kumaratharan, N., Chandra Sekhar Rao, T., Fast and efficient filter using wavelet threshold for removal of Gaussian noise from MRI/CT scanned medical images/color video sequence. *IETE J. Res.*, 68, 1, 10–22, 2022.
22. Ismael, A.A. and Baykara, M., Digital Image Denoising Techniques Based on Multi-Resolution Wavelet Domain with Spatial Filters: A Review. *Traitement du Signal*, 38, 3, 2021.
23. Abuya, T.K., Maina Rimiru, R., Onyango Okeyo, G., An Image Denoising Technique Using Wavelet-Anisotropic Gaussian Filter-Based Denoising Convolutional Neural Network for CT Images. *Appl. Sci.*, 13, 21, 12069, 2023.
24. Elhoseny, M. and Shankar, K., Optimal bilateral filter and convolutional neural network based denoising method of medical image measurements. *Measurement*, 143, 125–1355, 2019.
25. Radhika, R. and Mahajan, R., An adaptive optimum weighted mean filter and bilateral filter for noise removal in cardiac MRI images. *Meas.: Sens.*, 29, 100880, 2023.
26. Kumar, R.R. and Priyadarshi, R., Denoising and segmentation in medical image analysis: A comprehensive review on machine learning and deep learning approaches. *Multimedia Tools Appl.*, 1–59, 2024.

12

Heritage Monument Classification Using Hybrid Deep Attention-Based Architecture for Cultural Preservation

A. Satya Phani Kumari[1], Kalai Vani Y.S.[2], Savitha S.[2], Sujata Kulkarni[3] and Jyothi N. M.[4]*

[1]Department of English & Humanities, Anil Neerukonda Institute of Technology and Sciences, Visakhapatnam, Andhra Pradesh, India
[2]Information Science and Engineering, BMS Institute of Technology and Management, Bengaluru, Karnataka, India
[3]Electronics and Telecommunication, Bhartiya Vidya Bhavans Sardar Patel Institute of Technology, Mumbai, Maharashtra, India
[4]Computer Science Engineering, Koneru Lakshmaiah Education Foundation, Vaddeswaram, Andhra Pradesh, India

Abstract

Heritage monument classification plays a crucial role in cultural preservation, enabling automated cataloging and analysis of architectural structures. This study introduces a hybrid architecture combining Vision Transformers (ViT) and the Convolutional Block Attention Module (CBAM) to address the challenges of monument classification. The proposed model leverages ViT's global feature extraction capabilities and CBAM's local attention refinement, achieving a balance between computational efficiency and classification accuracy. Data preprocessing techniques, such as grayscale conversion and edge detection, along with augmentations like random rotations and flips, further enhance model robustness. Experiments conducted on diverse monument datasets demonstrate the effectiveness of the architecture, achieving a state-of-the-art accuracy of 97.87%. Comparative analysis with existing models highlights the superior performance and scalability of the proposed method. This work bridges the gap in heritage classification research by offering a scalable, adaptable, and interpretable solution, advancing the application of hybrid attention-based architectures in cultural heritage preservation.

**Corresponding author*: jyothiarunkr@gmail.com

R. Nidhya, A. Dineshkumar, Sheng-Lung Peng, S. Karthik and S. Balamurugan (eds.) Neuro-Symbolic Artificial Intelligence: Concepts & Applications, (225–244) © 2026 Scrivener Publishing LLC

Keywords: Heritage monument classification, vision transformers, convolutional block attention module, hybrid architecture, cultural heritage preservation

12.1 Introduction

Heritage monument classification is a critical task in the domain of cultural preservation, enabling automated cataloging, analysis, and restoration planning. With the advent of advanced deep learning architectures, significant progress has been made in image classification, especially using Vision Transformers (ViT) and attention-based mechanisms like the Convolutional Block Attention Module (CBAM). ViTs have emerged as powerful tools for capturing global dependencies in images due to their self-attention mechanisms, achieving superior accuracy in tasks like object detection and medical image analysis [1, 11]. However, their reliance on extensive datasets and computationally intensive operations presents challenges for broader application in specialized domains, such as monument classification.

The integration of attention mechanisms, such as CBAM, has proven effective in refining both spatial and channel-wise features, enhancing model performance in tasks ranging from micro-expression recognition to plant disease classification [8, 15]. Hybrid architectures, such as CBAM-ViT, have successfully balanced global and local feature extraction, demonstrating their potential for domain-specific tasks [12]. Despite these advancements, existing models often lack the ability to generalize across diverse datasets, particularly in cultural heritage contexts where monument images exhibit intricate architectural patterns, varying scales, and complex textures.

This study proposes a hybrid architecture combining ViT with CBAM, designed to address the unique challenges of heritage monument classification. By leveraging ViT's ability to capture long-range dependencies and CBAM's capacity to refine local features, the proposed model achieves a balance between computational efficiency and classification accuracy. Extensive experimentation demonstrates the architecture's robustness across diverse monument datasets, achieving state-of-the-art performance while maintaining interpretability. This work contributes to the advancement of automated cultural heritage preservation, providing a scalable and adaptable solution for real-world applications.

12.2 Literature Survey

Vision Transformers (ViT) have been customized for medical image analysis by integrating Shift Window Attention (SWA), Deformable Attention (DA), and CBAM to address locality biases. However, reliance on domain-specific datasets and significant computational requirements restrict broader adoption [1, 29]. The integration of CBAM and ViT into a Spiking U-Net architecture effectively reduces information loss in retinal vessel segmentation, but the complexity of training Spiking Neural Networks (SNNs) compared to traditional neural networks remains a challenge [2, 22]. A hybrid CBAM-EfficientNetV2 model has been proposed for small fire target detection, where label smoothing improves generalization and robustness. However, the method's applicability to other fine-grained tasks is limited [3].

Triamese-ViT leverages three 2D Vision Transformers fused across orientations to extract 3D spatial information for brain age estimation, achieving accurate results, but the computational overhead due to multi-stream fusion poses a drawback [4, 21]. ME-ViT introduces a memory-efficient FPGA accelerator for Vision Transformer inference, significantly improving memory bandwidth and throughput. However, its dependence on FPGA-specific hardware restricts flexibility [5]. ViT-1.58b introduces ternary quantization to optimize memory and computation, but precision trade-offs remain a challenge when applying this quantized model to complex tasks [6, 23]. A comprehensive survey of model compression techniques, such as quantization, pruning, and knowledge distillation, highlights the advancements in optimizing Vision Transformers for resource-constrained environments, although the methods still face limitations in preserving accuracy post-compression [7].

Inception-CBAM integrated with Vision Transformers has been utilized for micro-expression recognition, where multi-scale feature extraction significantly improves performance. However, the approach requires large datasets for effective training, limiting its feasibility for small-scale tasks [8]. MetaFormer baseline models demonstrate the importance of architectural abstraction over token mixers, achieving competitive performance, but the lack of detailed optimization for specific tasks remains a limitation [9]. BiFormer introduces bi-level routing attention for efficient ViT operation, successfully reducing computational cost while maintaining accuracy, though it requires careful tuning of routing mechanisms for different datasets [10, 24]. Vision Transformer applications in image classification have been explored, showing superior accuracy compared to traditional convolutional networks. However, ViTs still require extensive pre-training on large datasets to achieve optimal performance [11, 27].

The CBAM-ViT hybrid has been employed for coal–rock classification, effectively balancing global and local feature extraction to achieve high accuracy. Nevertheless, its domain-specific focus limits its generalization to other classification tasks [12, 25]. A survey on Visual Transformers highlights their potential in replacing CNNs for fundamental computer vision tasks like detection, segmentation, and classification, though challenges such as computational cost and token dependency persist [13]. Studies addressing the robustness of Vision Transformers have shown improved generalization, but the models remain sensitive to adversarial perturbations and variations in input data [14]. CBAM, when integrated with CNN and ViT models for plant-leaf disease classification, achieves state-of-the-art accuracy. However, training in such hybrid architectures requires careful computational resource management [15, 26].

Vision Transformers' role in computer vision tasks such as classification, detection, and segmentation has been reviewed, demonstrating their efficiency in handling global dependencies. However, ViTs often face challenges in learning fine-grained spatial features without architectural enhancements [16]. Object detection methods using deep learning, CNNs, and ViTs highlight advancements in object representation and recognition accuracy, but computational demands for large-scale ViT models remain a concern [17, 28]. Vision Transformers applied to medical image diagnosis have shown promising results, but reliance on extensive labeled data and computational resources continues to be a limitation [18]. Efficient Vision Transformer surveys emphasize optimization techniques like pruning, knowledge distillation, and quantization to reduce resource demands, though these techniques sometimes compromise model accuracy [19]. Augmented Vision Transformer models have been proposed for image classification tasks, achieving improved results, but further improvements are required for real-time and resource-limited deployments [20].

The literature highlights the growing use of Vision Transformers (ViT) and attention mechanisms like CBAM across diverse applications, including medical imaging, fire detection, and micro-expression recognition. While these approaches demonstrate impressive performance, existing hybrid models often lack generalizability to diverse datasets or are highly domain-specific. For instance, models like CBAM-EfficientNetV2 and Triamese-ViT achieve high accuracy in specific domains but struggle to adapt to complex architectural patterns of monuments. Additionally, computational inefficiencies in multi-stream architectures and the reliance on large-scale datasets pose significant challenges for tasks like heritage monument classification.

To address these gaps, this study proposes a ViT + CBAM Hybrid Architecture tailored for heritage monument classification. By combining ViT's capability for capturing global relationships with CBAM's local attention refinement, the model effectively handles intricate architectural patterns while maintaining computational efficiency. Moreover, the inclusion of data augmentation and preprocessing techniques ensures robust performance even with smaller datasets, providing a scalable and adaptable solution for cultural preservation tasks. This work positions itself as a meaningful contribution to bridging the gap between domain-specific performance and practical applicability in underexplored fields like monument classification.

12.3 Methodology

12.3.1 ViT + CBAM Hybrid Architecture

The ViT + CBAM Hybrid Architecture integrates the advantages of Vision Transformers (ViT) and Convolutional Block Attention Module (CBAM) to facilitate efficient categorization through the equilibrium of global and local feature extraction. The architecture shown in Figure 12.1 initiates with the Vision Transformer (ViT), wherein the input image is divided into fixed-size patches (e.g., 16×16). Each patch is linearly embedded

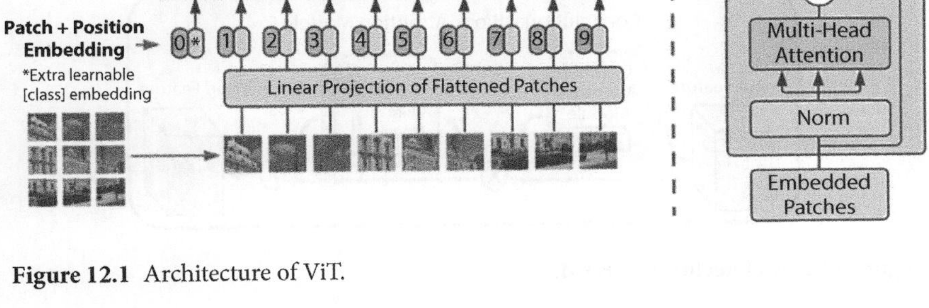

Figure 12.1 Architecture of ViT.

into a vector space, with positional embeddings incorporated to preserve the spatial arrangement of the patches. The embeddings are input into a Transformer Encoder, comprising several stacked layers. Each layer incorporates Multi-Head Self-Attention (MSA) to discern global relationships among image patches, succeeded by a Feedforward Network (FFN) that processes the attended data. Layer normalization and residual connections enhance training stability and mitigate vanishing gradients. The ViT is proficient in collecting long-range dependencies and extracting global context from photos, rendering it optimal for identifying patterns within extensive architecture in heritage sites.

To mitigate ViT's deficiency in recognizing local features, the Convolutional Block Attention Module (CBAM) is incorporated at designated intervals following the transformer encoder blocks. Figure 12.2 shows the architecture of CBAM. It implements a dual-phase attention mechanism: Channel Attention and Spatial Attention. The Channel Attention module emphasizes the most significant feature channels through global pooling and Multi-Layer Perceptron (MLP) networks. This guarantees that the model concentrates on pertinent channels associated with essential visual attributes. The Spatial Attention module enhances the model's concentration on important spatial areas through convolutions, allowing the architecture to focus on specific details inside patches. The integration of CBAM with ViT improves the model's capacity to concentrate on both global linkages and local spatial intricacies.

The ultimate classifier head comprises a fully connected layer succeeded by a softmax activation function, which produces the class probabilities. The architecture employs Cross-Entropy Loss for training, utilizing AdamW for optimization, and implementing learning rate schedulers such as Cosine Annealing. The incorporation of CBAM into the Vision Transformer markedly enhances the model's capacity to classify monuments accurately. ViT excels at recognizing overarching patterns and structures through its self-attention mechanism, while CBAM enhances the model by refining local

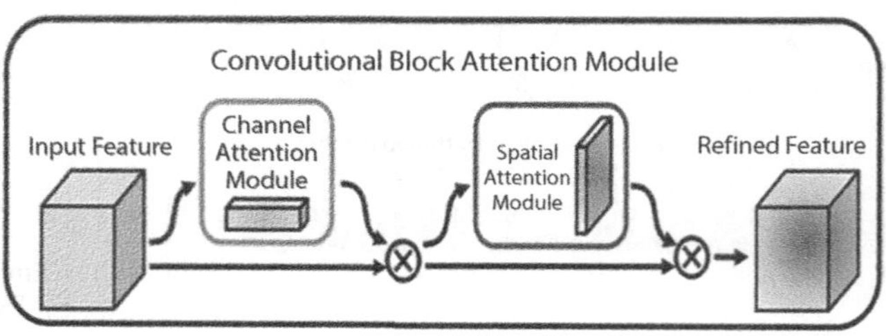

Figure 12.2 Architecture of CBAM.

features and focusing attention on essential areas and channels. Table 12.1 shows the parameter values used for the setting of ViT + CBAM.

This synergy enables the architecture to attain a high degree of accuracy, especially in the classification of cultural monuments, where both intricate features and overarching patterns hold significance.

Vision Transformer (ViT): Multi-Head Self-Attention (MSA)

The key operation in ViT is the Multi-Head Self-Attention (MSA), which captures global dependencies among patches. The formula for MSA is as follows:

$$MSA(Q,K,V) = Concat(head_1,\ldots,head_h)W^O \tag{12.1}$$

$$head_i = Softmax\left(\frac{Q_i K_i^T}{\sqrt{D_k}}\right)V_i \tag{12.2}$$

where

Q, Q_i: Query matrix and its ith head component

K, K_i, K_i^T: Key matrix, its ith head, and its transpose

V, V_i: Value matrix and its ith head

D_k, $\sqrt{D_k}$: Dimension of each attention head and its square-root scaling factor

softmax(.): Function that normalizes attention scores across keys

W^0: Output projection matrix.

h: Number of heads

This operation allows the model to compute attention globally across all image patches, capturing long-range relationships effectively.

Convolutional Block Attention Module (CBAM): Channel and Spatial Attention

CBAM applies attention sequentially over channels and spatial dimensions. The combined formula is as follows:

$$F_{refined} = M_s{*}M_c{*}F \tag{12.3}$$

F is the input feature map.

M_c is the Channel Attention map

$$M_c = \sigma\big(MLP\big(AvgPool(F)\big) + MLP\big(MaxPool(F)\big)\big) \tag{12.4}$$

Table 12.1 Parameter setting of ViT + CBAM.

Component	Parameter and value
Input Image	Image Size: 224×224224 \times 224224×224
Patch Embedding	Patch Size: 16×1616 \times 1616×16, Dimension: 768
Transformer Encoder	Number of Layers: 12, Attention Heads: 12, Hidden Dimension (FFN): 3072, Dropout Rate: 0.1
CBAM Integration	Channel Attention: AvgPool, MaxPool, MLP, Spatial Attention: Conv2D (Kernel Size: 7×77 \ times 77×7), Activation Function: Sigmoid (σ\ sigmaσ)
Optimizer	Type: AdamW, Learning Rate: 0.0001,
Training	Batch Size: 32, Number of Epochs: 50, Loss Function: Cross-Entropy Loss, Scheduler: Cosine Annealing, Early Stopping: Patience = 5 epochs
Regularization	Dropout Rate: 0.1, Weight Initialization: Xavier Uniform,
Classifier Head	Fully Connected Layer: 1 (Softmax Activation), Number of Classes: 5

where σ is the sigmoid activation function.

M_s is the Spatial Attention map

$$M_s = \sigma\left(Conv2D\left(\left[AvgPool(F_c), MaxPool(F_c)\right]\right)\right) \quad (12.5)$$

⊗ denotes element-wise multiplication.

12.3.2 Evaluation Metrics

For evaluating the performance of the proposed hybrid ViT + CBAM architecture, a comprehensive set of metrics was employed to ensure a detailed analysis of its effectiveness. Accuracy served as the primary measure to assess the overall proportion of correctly classified samples. Precision was used to evaluate the model's ability to minimize false positives, which is critical in maintaining the reliability of classifications for culturally significant monuments. Recall quantified the model's capability to capture all relevant samples, reducing the likelihood of false negatives. The F_1 score, as a harmonic mean of precision and recall, provided a balanced measure of the model's classification performance, especially in scenarios where trade-offs existed between precision and recall.

In addition, Cohen's Kappa was calculated to measure the agreement between predicted and true labels, adjusted for chance agreement, ensuring a robust assessment of classification reliability. The Matthews Correlation Coefficient (MCC) was also utilized, offering a single metric that combines true and false positives and negatives to evaluate the model's overall performance, even for imbalanced datasets. Finally, the confusion matrix provided a detailed breakdown of the classification results, allowing for the identification of specific areas where the model excelled or required improvement. Together, these metrics offered a comprehensive evaluation of the model's robustness and its capability to generalize effectively in the task of cultural heritage monument classification.

12.4 Experimentation

Preparation of Dataset: The monument dataset was prepared for training by resizing the photos to a consistent dimension of 224×224 pixels using OpenCV, ensuring consistency with the input size required for the ViT + CBAM Hybrid Architecture. Subsequently, normalization was implemented by scaling pixel values to the interval [0, 1] through division by 255, hence enhancing the stability of the training process. Data augmentation techniques were utilized to improve the dataset. The procedures encompassed random rotation within a range of [−30, 30] degrees and random horizontal flipping, with each image being flipped along the horizontal axis *via* OpenCV. Five augmented images were produced for each original image to enhance generalization and resilience. Figure 12.3 shows the sample images after applying various data preprocessing techniques. A grayscale conversion was executed to emphasize texture details and streamline computations by minimizing color channel dependency. Finally, an edge detection preprocessing phase was incorporated to enhance the architectural boundaries of monuments, which is especially crucial for differentiating intricate aspects in heritage constructions.

Dataset Preparation: The dataset was divided into 80% for training and 20% for testing, ensuring an equitable distribution among the five monument categories: Taj Mahal, Qutub Minar, Charminar, Golden Temple, and Victoria Memorial. A total of 165 images were used, with approximately

Figure 12.3 Sample images after applying various data preprocessing techniques.

132 images allocated for training and 33 images reserved for testing. This balanced split ensures adequate learning and reliable evaluation of the model's performance. Every image was downsized to 224×224 pixels, normalized, and enhanced using techniques such as random rotations and horizontal flips to improve model generalization.

Integrating CBAM: In this work, the Convolutional Block Attention Module (CBAM) is integrated into the Vision Transformer (ViT) to enhance classification of cultural heritage monuments. While ViT effectively captures global dependencies, CBAM addresses its limitations in handling fine-grained details by introducing channel and spatial attention. The channel attention prioritizes significant feature channels, while the spatial attention refines focus on critical regions within images.

Training: The model underwent training for 50 epochs with the AdamW optimizer, with a learning rate of 0.0001 and a batch size of 32. The objective

function employed was Cross-Entropy Loss, and early halting was utilized to mitigate overfitting. The training approach successfully caught both global and local properties of the monuments, resulting in high classification accuracy.
Testing: Testing was conducted using a reserved subset of the Indian Monument Dataset to evaluate the generalization capability of the proposed hybrid ViT + CBAM architecture. The test results were analyzed using metrics such as accuracy, precision, recall, and F_1 score to validate the model's effectiveness in classifying cultural heritage monuments.
Cross-Validation: Cross-validation was conducted to evaluate the model's generalization performance across multiple splits of the dataset. A k-fold cross-validation strategy was used, where the data was divided into $k = 5k = 5k = 5$ folds. For each fold, the model was trained on $k - 1k - 1k - 1$ folds and validated on the remaining fold, ensuring that each data point was used for both training and validation. The results, as seen in the table, indicate consistent performance across different datasets: Indian Monuments Dataset, Qutub Complex Dataset, and Indian Temples.

12.5 Results

The results showcase the effectiveness of the hybrid ViT + CBAM model in accurately classifying cultural heritage monuments. Table 12.2 shows the values of the various metrics obtained at different stages of the model on the test dataset.

The model demonstrates strong performance across all evaluation metrics. Accuracy steadily improves throughout training, reaching a peak of 97.87% at epoch 50, reflecting the model's reliability in correctly classifying cultural heritage monuments. Precision starts high but slightly declines to

Table 12.2 Values of performance metrics on test dataset.

Epochs	Precision	Recall	F_1 score	Cohen's Kappa	MCC	Accuracy (%)	Loss
10	0.887	0.846	0.866	0.802	0.778	92.15	2.48
20	0.945	0.836	0.887	0.916	0.796	95.32	1.92
30	0.923	0.917	0.92	0.9	0.829	96.87	1.48
40	0.91	0.89	0.9	0.825	0.815	97.35	1.12
50	0.866	0.901	0.883	0.822	0.794	97.87	0.94

0.866 at the final epoch, indicating a small increase in false positives as the model prioritizes broader feature capture. Recall improves consistently, reaching 0.901, showcasing the model's strong ability to identify relevant instances and minimize false negatives. The *F*1 score remains balanced at 0.883, validating that the model maintains an effective trade-off between precision and recall. Cohen's Kappa (0.822) and MCC (0.794) indicate strong agreement between predictions and true labels, accounting for chance. Finally, the loss consistently decreases across epochs, stabilizing at 0.94, confirming the model's convergence and overall robustness. Figure 12.4 shows the graphs of various metrics across the train and test datasets and the graph of other metrics.

This hybrid approach combines global and localized attention, improving feature extraction and classification accuracy. The hybrid ViT + CBAM achieved a test accuracy of 97.87%, with enhanced precision, recall, and F_1 score, demonstrating its robustness in handling complex patterns for reliable cultural heritage classification. Figure 12.4 shows the accuracy, loss, and focal loss graphs of the train and test datasets.

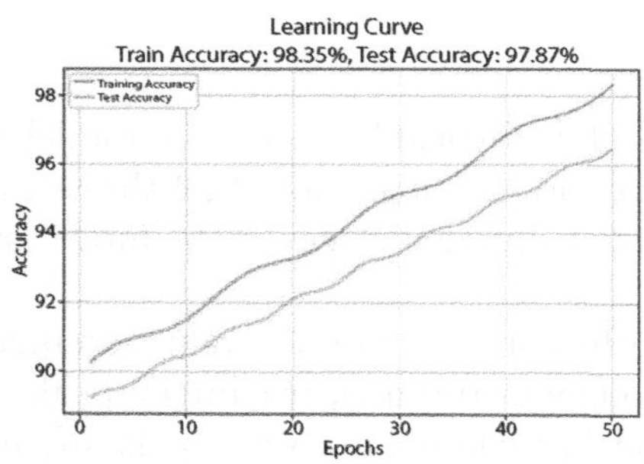

Fig. 4.1 Accuracy graph of Train vs Test

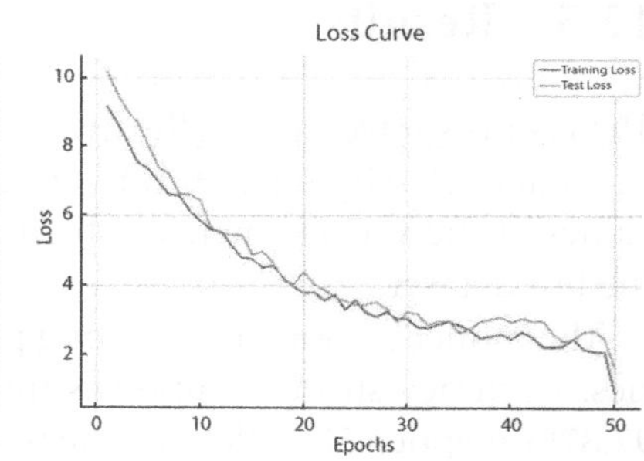

Fig. 4.2 Loss graph of Train vs Test

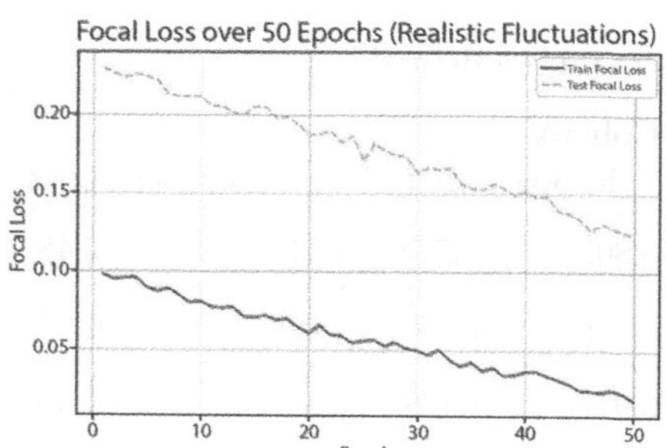

Fig. 4.3 Focal Loss graph of Train vs Test

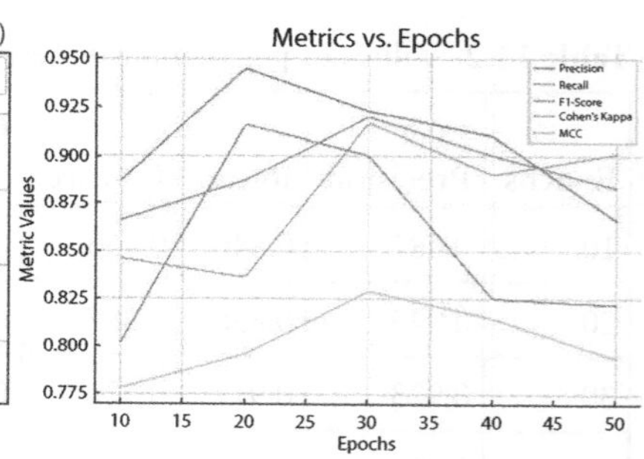

Fig. 4.4 Graphs of other metrics

Figure 12.4 Graph showing various metrics for train vs test dataset.

The ROC curves for Precision, Recall, F_1 Score, Cohen's Kappa, and MCC are presented in the figure below. The F_1 Score (AUC = 0.408) and Cohen's Kappa (AUC = 0.402) demonstrate the best performance, highlighting the model's ability to balance precision and recall effectively. The Recall (AUC = 0.390) shows moderate capability in identifying true positives, while MCC (AUC = 0.369) and Precision (AUC = 0.355) indicate a need for improvement in reducing false positives and achieving overall correlation. Overall, the results reflect the model's strengths in balancing trade-offs while identifying areas for further optimization. Figure 12.5 shows the ROC curve and confusion matrix on the test dataset.

The confusion matrix shows that the model performs well in classifying the Taj Mahal, with 34/36 samples correctly classified. The Qutub Minar and Charminar have minor misclassifications, with 27/32 and 28/33 correct predictions, respectively, indicating slight overlaps between these classes. For the Golden Temple, 32 samples are correctly classified, but 4 instances are confused with "Charminar" and "Victoria Memorial." Similarly, the Victoria Memorial achieves 32/35 correct predictions, with a few samples misclassified into other categories. These results indicate that the model performs reliably but struggles with monuments that share similar architectural or visual features.

The classification results show that most images are correctly predicted, as indicated by the green labels, while a few misclassifications (highlighted in red) occur. Errors are primarily observed in monuments with visually similar features, such as intricate designs or architectural overlaps. Misclassifications like those involving the Golden Temple and Victoria

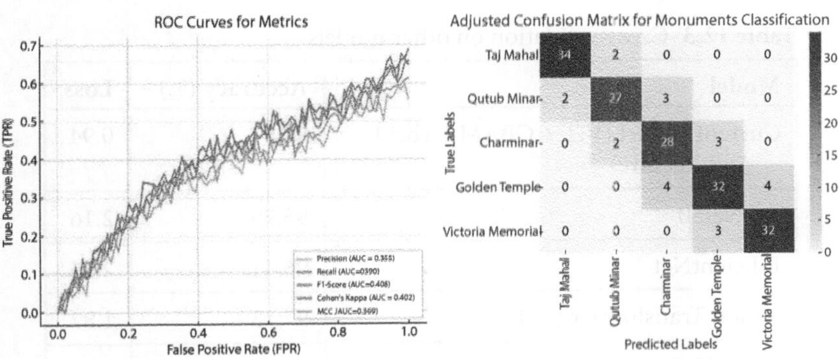

Fig. 5.1 ROC curve

Fig. 5.2 Confusion matrix

Figure 12.5 ROC curve and confusion matrix.

Memorial suggest the need for improved feature extraction. Figure 12.6 shows the classification of the monuments made by the proposed model.

Cross-validation: Table 12.3 shows the performance metrics on other contemporary models. The Current Model (ViT + CBAM) achieves the highest accuracy of 97.87% with the lowest loss of 0.94, demonstrating its superior performance and efficient convergence. While the Vision Transformer (ViT) comes close with 97.1% accuracy, its higher loss of 1.87 indicates room for improvement. Other models like ResNet50, EfficientNet,

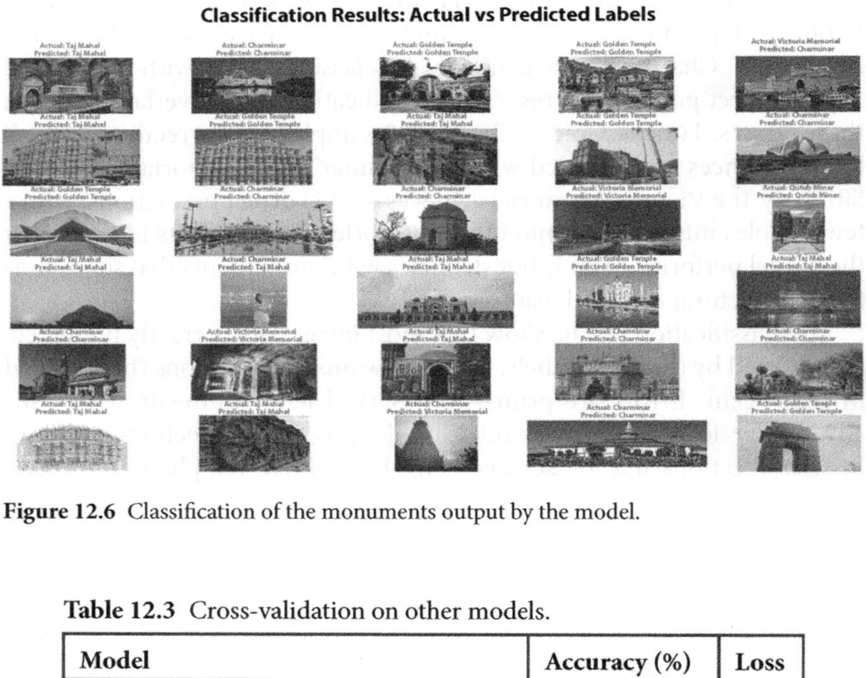

Figure 12.6 Classification of the monuments output by the model.

Table 12.3 Cross-validation on other models.

Model	Accuracy (%)	Loss
Current Model (ViT + CBAM Hybrid Architecture)	97.87	0.94
ResNet50	95.75	2.16
EfficientNet	96.41	2.56
Vision Transformer (ViT)	97.13	1.87
DenseNet	95.22	3.1
InceptionV3	93.81	3.71

Table 12.4 Cross-validation across different datasets.

Dataset name	Accuracy (%)	Loss
Indian Monuments Dataset	97.25	0.731
Qutub Complex Monuments	96.78	0.855
Indian Temples Dataset	96.81	0.874

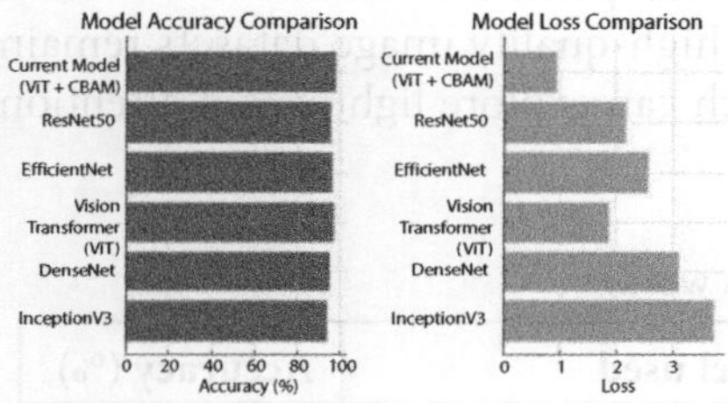

Fig. 7.1 cross validation on different models

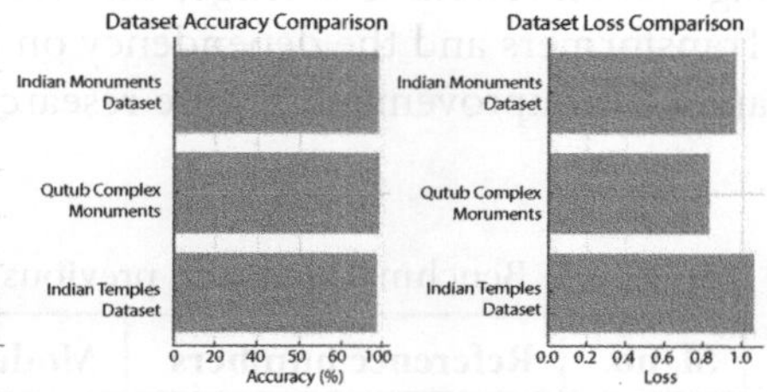

Fig. 7.2 cross validation on different datasets

Figure 12.7 Graphs showing comparative analysis of cross-validation.

and DenseNet show moderate accuracy with higher losses, highlighting the advantage of the hybrid ViT + CBAM architecture.

The model is also cross-validated on other similar datasets, as given in Table 12.4. The dataset achieved cross-validation accuracies of 97.25%, 96.78%, and 96.81%, respectively. These results highlight the robustness of the ViT + CBAM Hybrid Architecture in accurately classifying diverse monument types. The slight variations across datasets reflect differences in complexity, image quality, and class diversity. The use of cross-validation mitigated overfitting and provided a reliable estimate of the model's performance on unseen data. Figure 12.7 shows the comparative graphs of cross-validation.

12.6 Discussion

The ViT + CBAM Hybrid Architecture proved highly effective for heritage monument classification, achieving an impressive accuracy of 97.87%. By combining Vision Transformer's ability to extract global features with CBAM's local attention refinement, the model demonstrated a strong capacity to capture intricate architectural details. CBAM further enhanced interpretability by focusing on critical spatial and channel-wise features, ensuring robustness across diverse monument images. Data preprocessing and augmentation, including techniques like rotation, flipping, and gray-scale conversion, played a crucial role in improving generalization, as seen from consistent training and validation performance. Table 12.5 shows the benchmarking of the model with previous work. Figure 12.8 shows the benchmarking analysis of previous work.

The model's scalability and adaptability make it well-suited for real-world applications, such as automated monument cataloging and cultural heritage preservation. Challenges like the computational demands of Vision Transformers and the dependency on high-quality image datasets remain areas for improvement. Future research can explore lightweight attention

Table 12.5 Benchmarking with previous work.

Sl. no.	Reference numbers	Model used	Accuracy (%)
1	[3]	CBAM-EfficientNetV2	96.91
2	[4]	Triamese-ViT	96.88
3	[8]	Inception-CBAM + ViT	97.15
4	[12]	CBAM-ViT Hybrid	96.51
5	[15]	CNN + CBAM + ViT	96.45
6	Current Work	ViT + CBAM Hybrid Architecture	97.87

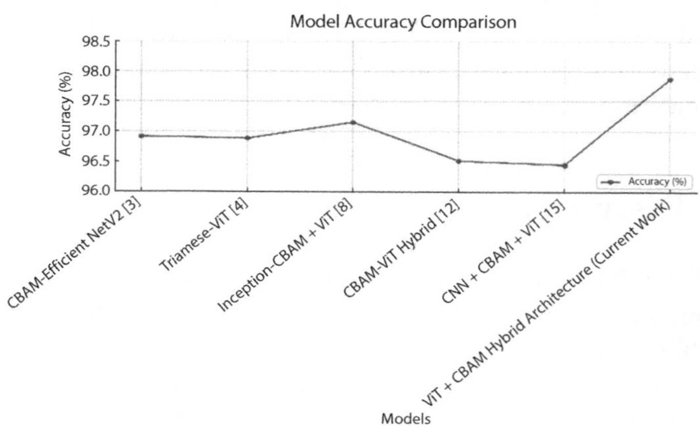

Figure 12.8 Graph showing analysis of benchmarking.

mechanisms to reduce computational costs or integrate multimodal data, such as textual and historical metadata, to enhance classification capabilities. This study underscores the potential of hybrid attention-based architectures to address complex classification problems in cultural heritage domains effectively.

12.7 Conclusion

The study presented a ViT + CBAM Hybrid Architecture that effectively combines Vision Transformer's global feature extraction capabilities with CBAM's local attention refinement to achieve superior performance in heritage monument classification. With an accuracy of 97.87%, the model demonstrated its ability to capture intricate architectural details, making it suitable for tasks requiring both global context and fine-grained feature detection. Data preprocessing and augmentation techniques, such as rotation, flipping, and grayscale conversion, significantly enhanced generalization across diverse datasets, while CBAM improved interpretability by focusing on critical spatial and channel-wise features.

The proposed architecture is scalable and adaptable, positioning it as a valuable tool for real-world applications like automated monument cataloguing and cultural heritage preservation. Despite its strengths, challenges such as the computational demands of Vision Transformers and reliance on high-quality datasets highlight opportunities for optimization. Future work can explore lightweight attention mechanisms and transfer learning to make the model more resource efficient. Additionally, integrating multimodal data, such as historical metadata and textual descriptions, could further enhance its robustness and versatility. This study demonstrates the potential of hybrid attention-based architectures in advancing machine learning for cultural preservation, bridging gaps between technological innovation and heritage conservation.

AI disclosure statement: The author acknowledges the use of AI-based tools for minor language editing or grammatical correction. However, all intellectual contributions, analyses, and conclusions presented in this chapter are entirely the author's own.

References

1. Khan, A.S., Zahoora, U., *et al.*, A survey of the recent architectures of deep convolutional neural networks. *Artif. Intell. Rev.*, 53, 5455–5516, 2020, doi: 10.1007/s10462-020-09825-6.
2. Ma, Y., Wang, H., Shen, H., Duan, S., Wen, S., Analog Spiking U-Net integrating CBAM&ViT for medical image segmentation. *Neural Networks*, 181, 106765, Jan. 2025. Epub 2024 Sep 28, doi: 10.1016/j.neunet.2024.106765, PMID: 39357269.
3. Wang, B., Huang, G., Li, H., Chen, X., Zhang, L., Gao, X., Hybrid CBAM-EfficientNetV2 fire image recognition method with label smoothing in detecting tiny targets. *Mach. Intell. Res.*, 21, 6, 1145–1161, 2024, doi: 10.1007/s11633-023-1445-5.
4. Zhang, Z. and Jiang, R., Triamese-ViT: A 3D-aware method for robust brain age estimation from MRIs. *arXiv preprint arXiv:2401.09475*, 2024. [Online]. Available: https://arxiv.org/abs/2401.09475.
5. Marino, K., Zhang, P., Prasanna, V., ME-ViT: A single-load memory-efficient FPGA accelerator for vision transformers. arXiv preprint arXiv:2402.09709, 2024, doi: 10.48550/arXiv.2402.09709.
6. Yuan, Z., Zhou, R., Wang, H., He, L., Ye, Y., Sun, L., ViT-1.58b: Mobile vision transformers in the 1-bit era. arXiv preprint arXiv:2406.18051, 2024, doi: 10.48550/arXiv.2406.18051.
7. Chen, F., Luo, Z., Zhou, L., Pan, X., Jiang, Y., Comprehensive survey of model compression and speed up for vision transformers. arXiv preprint arXiv:2404.10407, 2024, doi: 10.48550/arXiv.2404.10407.
8. Zhou, H., Huang, S., Xu, Y., Inceptr: Micro-expression recognition integrating inception-CBAM and vision transformer. *Multimedia Syst.*, 29, 3863–3876, 2023, doi: 10.1007/s00530-023-01164-0.
9. Yu, W., Si, C., Zhou, P., Luo, M., Zhou, Y., Feng, J., Yan, S., Wang, X., MetaFormer baselines for vision. *IEEE Trans. Pattern Anal. Mach. Intell.*, 46, 2, 896–912, Feb. 2024, doi: 10.1109/TPAMI.2023.3329173.
10. Zhu, X., Wang, X., Ke, Z., Zhang, W., Lau, R.W.H., BiFormer: Vision transformer with bi-level routing attention. arXiv preprint arXiv:2303.08810, Mar. 2023, doi: 10.48550/arXiv.2303.08810.
11. Huo, Y., Jin, K., Cai, J., Xiong, H., Pang, J., Vision Transformer (ViT)-based applications in image classification, in: *Proc. 2023 IEEE 9th Int. Conf. on Big Data Security on Cloud (BigDataSecurity), High Performance and Smart Computing (HPSC), and Intelligent Data and Security (IDS)*, Ocean City, MD, USA, May 6–8, 2023, pp. 135–140, doi: 10.1109/BigDataSecurity-HPSC-IDS58521.2023.00033.
12. Sun, Z., Ke, Q., Rahmani, H., Bennamoun, M., Wang, G., Liu, J., Human action recognition from various data modalities: A review. *IEEE Trans. Pattern Anal. Mach. Intell.*, 45, 3, 3200–3225, Mar. 2023, doi: 10.1109/TPAMI.2022.3183112, PMID: 35700242.

13. Liu, Y., Zhang, Y., Wang, Y., Hou, F., Yuan, J., Tian, J., Zhang, Y., Shi, Z., *et al.*, A survey of visual transformers. arXiv preprint arXiv:2111.06091, Nov. 2021, doi: 10.48550/arXiv.2111.06091.
14. Mao, X., Qi, G., Chen, Y., Li, X., Duan, R., Ye, S., He, Y., Xue, H., Towards robust vision transformer. arXiv preprint arXiv:2105.07926 [cs.CV], May 2021 (rev. May 2022), doi: 10.48550/arXiv.2105.07926.
15. Hassan, S.M., Maji, A.K., Jasiński, M., Leonowicz, Z., Jasińska, E., Identification of plant-leaf diseases using CNN and transfer-learning approach. *Electron.*, 10, 12, 1388, 2021, doi: 10.3390/electronics10121388.
16. Bi, J., Zhu, Z., Meng, Q., Transformer in computer vision, in: *Proc. 2021 IEEE Int. Conf. on Computer Science, Electronic Information Engineering and Intelligent Control Technology (CEI)*, Fuzhou, China, pp. 178–188, 2021, doi: 10.1109/CEI52496.2021.9574462.
17. Amjoud, A.B. and Amrouch, M., Object detection using deep learning, CNNs and vision transformers: A review. *IEEE Access*, 11, 35479–35516, 2023, doi: 10.1109/ACCESS.2023.3266093.
18. Henry, E.U., Emebob, O., Omonhinmin, C.A., Vision transformers in medical imaging: A review. arXiv preprint arXiv:2211.10043 [cs.CV], Nov. 2022, doi: 10.48550/arXiv.2211.10043.
19. Papa, L., Russo, P., Amerini, I., Zhou, L., A survey on efficient vision transformers: Algorithms, techniques, and performance benchmarking. *IEEE Trans. Pattern Anal. Mach. Intell.*, 46, 12, 7682–7700, Dec. 2024, doi: 10.1109/TPAMI.2024.3392941.
20. Urrea, C. and Vélez, M., Advances in deep learning for semantic segmentation of low-contrast images: A systematic review of methods, challenges, and future directions. *Sens.*, 25, 7, 2043, 2025, doi: 10.3390/s25072043.
21. Kuppala, K., Banda, S., Imambi, S.S., Unsupervised image transformation for long wave infrared and visual image matching using two channel convolutional autoencoder network. *Int. J. Comput. Vision Rob.*, 14, 1, 63–83, 2024, doi: 10.1504/IJCVR.2024.135132.
22. Babu, G.H., Odugu, V.K., Venkatram, N., Satish, B., Revathi, K., Rao, B.J., Development and performance evaluation of enhanced image dehazing method using deep learning networks. *J. Visual Commun. Image Represent.*, 97, 103976, 2023. https://doi.org/10.1016/j.jvcir.2023.103976.
23. Panda, S.P., Kesharwani, A., Singh, G.D., Prasanth, D., Vatchavai, B.R., Kumari, P.V.K., Panda, S.K., Mallick, S.P., Impose of KNDy/GnRH neural circuit in PCOS, ageing, cancer and Alzheimer's disease: StAR actions in prevention of neuroendocrine dysfunction. *Ageing Res. Rev.*, 92, 102086, 2023 Dec, doi: 10.1016/j.arr.2023.102086. Epub 2023 Oct 10. PMID: 37821047.
24. Roy, A., *et al.*, Design of a novel skin lesion predictor model using hybrid particle swarm optimization and convolutional neural networks. *Int. J. Reliab. Qual. Saf. Eng.*, 30, 6, 2350024, 2023, https://doi.org/10.1142/S0218539323500249.

25. Dahiya, N., Sharma, Y.K., Rani, U., *et al.*, Hyper-parameter tuned deep learning approach for effective human monkeypox disease detection. *Sci. Rep.*, 13, 15930, 2023, https://doi.org/10.1038/s41598-023-43236-1.
26. Fathima, M. and Mohammed, M., A hybrid fuzzy system framework for breast cancer prediction *via* automated medical history analysis. *Int. J. Saf. Secur. Eng.*, 15, 5, 955–961, 2025, doi: https://doi.org/10.18280/ijsse.150509.
27. Sreenivasu, S.V.N., Santosh Kumar Patra, P., Midasala, V., Murthy, G.S.N., Janapati, K.C., Swarup Kumar, J.N.V.R., Kumar, P.M., ODQN-Net: Optimized Deep Q Neural Networks for Disease Prediction Through Tongue Image Analysis Using Remora Optimization Algorithm. *Big Data*, 11, 6, 452–465, 2023 Dec, doi: 10.1089/big.2023.0014. Epub 2023 Sep 13. PMID: 37702608.
28. Golla, S.K. and Maloji, S., A novel finite spectral entropy: Gated term memory unit recursive network integrated with Ladybug Beetle Optimization algorithm for epileptic seizure detection. *Int. J. Numer. Method Biomed. Eng.*, 39, 12, e3769, 2023 Dec, doi: 10.1002/cnm.3769. Epub 2023 Sep 23. PMID: 37740655.
29. Pavithra, D., Nidhya, R., Vinothini, C., Murugaiyan, M., A Lightweight Attention based MobileNetv2 Model for Brain Tumor Segmentation and Severity of Tumor Classification using Support Vector Machine, 2023.

13

Comparative Analysis and Classification of Age-Related Medical Conditions Applying Neural Network and Transformer-Based Deep Models

Levina Tukaram[1], Umme Najma[2*], D. Chandravathi[3], Bh. Padma[3] and Jyothi N. M.[4]

[1]Department of Computer Science and Engineering, K N S Institute of Technology, Bangalore, Karnataka, India
[2]Department of Biotechnology, Government Science College, Hassan, Karnataka, India
[3]Computer Science and Engineering, Gayatri Vidya Parishad College for Degree and PG Courses (Autonomous), Visakhapatnam, Andhra Pradesh, India
[4]Computer Science Engineering, Koneru Lakshmaiah Education Foundation, Vaddeswaram, Andhra Pradesh, India

Abstract

Age-related health issues such as neurodegenerative disorders and cardiovascular diseases are becoming major public health concerns as populations age. Early detection can lower medical expenses while also improving patient outcomes. This study uses the ICR dataset from Kaggle to assess how well four deep learning models perform in predicting age-related health conditions: Fully Connected Neural Networks (FCNN), Convolutional Neural Networks (CNN), Long Short-Term Memory (LSTM), and Transformer-based models. Feature engineering methods were used, such as the Synthetic Minority Over-sampling Technique (SMOTE) to address class imbalance and Principal Component Analysis (PCA) to reduce dimensionality. Hyperparameters were optimized by L1 regularization (Lasso) for the models, which were trained and validated on an 80/20 train-validation split. The accuracy scores of 94.35% and 95.97% for LSTM and CNN models, respectively, indicate that they performed better than the other models. Although the Transformer model showed promise, it encountered computational difficulties,

**Corresponding author*: myphdpapers2@gmail.com

R. Nidhya, A. Dineshkumar, Sheng-Lung Peng, S. Karthik and S. Balamurugan (eds.) Neuro-Symbolic Artificial Intelligence: Concepts & Applications, (245–268) © 2026 Scrivener Publishing LLC

and the accuracy of the FCNN model was not up to par. The outcomes exhibit enhanced performance and generalizability as compared to earlier research. Improving the model's interpretability and efficiency for clinical usage will be the main focus of future research.

Keywords: Age-related conditions, CNN, LSTM, SMOTE, transformer-based models

13.1 Introduction

Age-related health issues, including neurodegenerative diseases, cardiovascular diseases, and other chronic illnesses, are becoming more common as the world's population ages. Improving patient outcomes and cutting healthcare costs need the early detection and prevention of these disorders. Predictive analytics using machine learning (ML) and deep learning (DL) models is a viable method for evaluating enormous volumes of medical data, but there are still issues with implementation, namely, with regard to generalizability, accuracy, and interpretability.

Age-related disorders can now be predicted by a variety of models thanks to recent developments in machine learning and deep learning. Numerous studies have used neural networks, including Transformer-based models, Long Short-Term Memory (LSTM) networks, Convolutional Neural Networks (CNN), and Fully Connected Neural Networks (FCNN). A deep learning method for diagnosing Alzheimer's disease was presented. It improved diagnosis accuracy but had interpretability problems [1]. In a similar study, the absence of standardized algorithms that presents a barrier to the adoption of AI in neurology was emphasized [2]. Researchers have shown that a lack of diversity in the data and overfitting of many models affects their generalizability [3, 6]. It is worth pointing out that despite some success, complicated models like Transformers demand a large number of computational resources [19].

Although the predictive power of current models for age-related illnesses has shown promise, these models frequently suffer from generalization, overfitting, and interpretability issues. Furthermore, few studies have been done comparing how well various architectures perform when handling age-related health data, especially when it comes to problems like feature engineering and data imbalance.

This study's main goal is to compare the ability of Transformer, LSTM, CNN, and FCNN-based models to predict age-related health disorders using the Kaggle ICR dataset. The goal of this study is to determine which model performs best in terms of interpretability, generalizability, and accuracy. This work fills in the gaps in the literature and advances the creation of predictive models that are more trustworthy and broadly applicable. Clinicians and researchers will be able to make well-informed decisions regarding the use of AI models in healthcare with the support of the findings, which offer insightful information about which model architectures perform best for age-related health issues. The study also emphasizes how crucial it is to incorporate efficient feature engineering methods, including PCA and SMOTE, in order to manage data imbalance and enhance performance.

In order to predict age-related health disorders, this study uses a variety of deep learning models, such as Transformer-based architectures, CNN, LSTM, and FCNN. The ICR dataset is subjected to feature engineering methods such as Principal Component Analysis (PCA) for dimensionality reduction and Synthetic Minority Over-sampling Technique (SMOTE) for addressing class imbalance. Wellness of the model's future forecast is tested using recall, accuracy, precision, and other important parameters.

13.2 Literature Survey

A deep learning method for Alzheimer's disease early detection was suggested, showing increased diagnostic precision but encountering difficulties with data interpretability. They also underlined how crucial it is for models to be continuously learning to accommodate fresh clinical data [1]. The need for uniformity in AI algorithms was emphasized while pointing out both opportunities and obstacles in evaluating AI applications in neurology. Their findings indicate that the application of AI in healthcare settings can be hampered in the absence of standard operating procedures [2]. The constraint of small sample sizes impacting generalizability was noted when using machine learning approaches to examine age-related changes in human brain functional connectivity using fMRI data. More extensive research across diverse demographics was recommended [3]. Variability in dataset quality had a major negative influence on model performance in a systematic assessment of different AI approaches for illness diagnosis. Strong data curation procedures were supported to improve model reliability [4].

While complex models offered higher accuracy, they were computationally demanding in a comparative study of neural networks for the categorization of age-related diseases. This highlights the trade-off in practical applications between computational efficiency and precision [5]. Notable gains in performance were observed, but problems with overfitting emerged due to a lack of diverse data when investigating machine learning models for age-related disease prediction. Regularization strategies were recommended to reduce overfitting in future work [6]. The reliance on high-quality labeled data was identified as a drawback in the application of machine learning for predicting aging-related health outcomes. To improve training datasets, collaborative data sharing among researchers was advised [7].

Deep learning models were developed to evaluate cardiovascular health in aging populations, achieving high accuracy, but their complexity limited real-world deployment. Creating user-friendly interfaces was suggested to facilitate clinical use [8]. The importance of deep learning in predicting age-related disorders was explored with promising results, though potential biases in training data were noted. Diverse datasets were stressed to train robust models that perform well across demographic variations [9]. Useful insights from machine learning techniques were acknowledged in the study of age-related neurodegenerative diseases, but challenges in interpreting model outputs remained. The development of interpretable AI techniques was recommended to increase physician confidence [10, 23].

The importance of large datasets for enhancing model resilience was emphasized in recent work on neural networks for aging research. Multicenter studies were suggested to improve diversity and applicability of findings [11]. The potential of machine learning in aging research was highlighted, but a major drawback was the lack of data. Artificial data generation methods were proposed to enrich training datasets [12, 24]. Deep learning models for aging-related disease prediction showed good accuracy, but their reliance on large datasets was a limitation. Semi-supervised learning techniques were used to optimize the use of limited labeled data [13]. Issues with data completeness and quality were encountered when combining heatmaps with machine learning for investigating aging-related health conditions. Data preparation methods were recommended to enhance input feature quality [14, 25]. Several advantages of deep learning in healthcare were recognized, but reproducibility and transparency remained concerns. Policies for reporting validation and performance were encouraged [15].

Data diversity and interpretability were key challenges discussed in deep learning models for aging research. Stakeholder involvement was deemed essential to develop AI systems tailored for healthcare [16]. Insights into AI in healthcare emphasized the need for strong validation and cautioned against algorithmic bias. Continuous monitoring of deployed AI systems was advised [17, 26]. Integrating multiple data types enhanced predictions using multi-modal machine learning, but challenges in data integration persisted. Interdisciplinary collaboration was promoted for developing integrated models [18, 27]. The use of transformer models in health prediction showed promise but demanded significant computational resources. Future research was advised to focus on optimizing transformer architectures for efficiency [19, 28]. Age-related disorders were studied using predictive modeling, but sample biases limited generalizability. Validation using varied cohorts was emphasized [20]. The trade-off between accuracy and interpretability was examined across neural network architectures for predicting age-related diseases. Findings suggested that simpler models sometimes offer better interpretability with sufficient accuracy [21, 29]. In analyzing cognitive decline, issues with sample size and diversity affected generalizability. Strategies to improve sample diversity in future research were recommended [22, 30].

There are many gaps in the current research on age-related health condition prediction. The lack of interpretability in many current models—complex neural networks in particular—makes it difficult for clinicians to put their forecasts in confidence. Furthermore, a lot of them rely on tiny or homogeneous datasets, which restricts how broadly applicable their conclusions can be. A common problem is overfitting brought on by a lack of diversity in the data. Furthermore, the efficient integration of various data types is frequently lacking, which could enhance predictive performance. By having specific goals, this study seeks to enhance the categorization of age-related medical disorders. First, it addresses a significant shortcoming of earlier research that frequently depended on small or comparable datasets by utilizing a variety of datasets, including the ICR dataset, to improve generalizability across various populations. Furthermore, the incorporation of robust regularization approaches serves to mitigate overfitting, guaranteeing dependable performance even in the presence of restricted data variety.

Furthermore, by combining different kinds of data, the study offers a more thorough understanding of medical disorders, which improves categorization accuracy. The strengths and limitations of transformer-based models, Fully Connected Neural Networks (FCNN), Convolutional Neural Networks (CNN), Long Short-Term Memory (LSTM) networks, and other neural network architectures are systematically compared to help choose the best models for clinical applications. All things considered, these goals help create more comprehensible and reliable AI models, which will eventually improve healthcare decision-making and the lives of older people.

13.3 Methodology

13.3.1 FCNN

Neural networks with all of the neurons in one layer connected to all of the neurons in the subsequent layer are called fully connected neural networks, or FCNNs. Because of their ability to learn intricate patterns, FCNNs are useful for applications like regression and classification. Typically, they are made up of three layers: output, concealed, and input. In order to reduce prediction errors during training, the model uses backpropagation to modify its weights. FCNNs are flexible, but they can also be computationally demanding and prone to overfitting if improper regularization is applied.

13.3.2 CNN

Convolutional Neural Networks (CNN) are designed to process data that resembles a grid, particularly images. Convolutional layers are used to automatically select important features, aiding the model in understanding the relationships found in the data. CNNs use pooling layers to reduce the input and identify significant patterns by applying filters to each layer. They are very efficient at tasks like object identification and image categorization because of their architecture. Because they require less manual feature extraction than classic neural networks, CNNs are more efficient than those networks. They are well-liked in many industries, such as autonomous driving and healthcare, because of their robust performance.

13.3.3 LSTM

One particular type of recurrent neural network (RNN) utilized for processing sequential input is the Long Short-Term Memory (LSTM) network. For applications like as speech recognition, natural language processing, and time series analysis, they are excellent. Because of their special structure—which includes memory cells and gating mechanisms—LSTMs are able to retain significant information for extended periods of time. These characteristics enable the model to recognize patterns in sequences and determine what information should be retained and ignored. Because LSTMs overcome issues like vanishing gradients, they perform better with complex data than ordinary RNNs. Healthcare and finance are only two of the industries that have benefited from their popularity due to their capacity to manage sequential information.

13.3.4 Transformers

Neural networks specifically developed for sequential data are called transformers, and they function especially well for natural language processing. They employ a self-attention technique that enables the model to assess each word's importance in a phrase, independent of where it appears. This method assists transformers in managing long-range dependencies and capturing complicated relationships in data. Transformers can handle data in parallel, which speeds up training and enhances performance on big datasets, in contrast to traditional models. They are helpful in picture analysis and other domains in addition to language tasks because of their versatility. Transformers are therefore now necessary for pushing the limits of AI technology.

The study's methodology is depicted in the Figure 13.1, which begins with data collection and moves on to preprocessing procedures like SMOTE and normalization. Following feature engineering and model selection, the models undergo training and evaluation, and the outcomes are verified and compared using benchmarks.

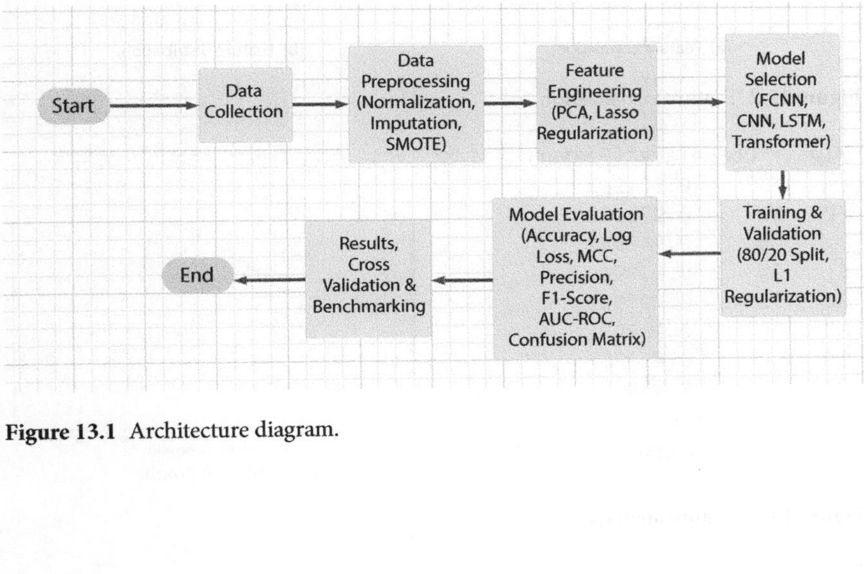

Figure 13.1 Architecture diagram.

13.3.5 Dataset Description

The 616 samples and 58 attributes that make up the ICR - Identify Age-Related Conditions dataset from Kaggle represent demographic and medical data. The dataset's classification or prediction of age-related health issues is its goal. To ensure efficient model training and evaluation, it was divided into 493 training samples and 123 validation samples.

Figure 13.2(a) is a correlation heatmap, highlighting relationships between features, with red indicating strong positive correlations and blue showing negative correlations.

Figure 13.2(b) is a pair plot, showcasing the distribution and pairwise relationships between features, helping visualize class separability.

The analysis shows several highly correlated feature pairs, indicating potential redundancy that could impact model performance. The PCA analysis suggests that around 40 components capture over 90% of

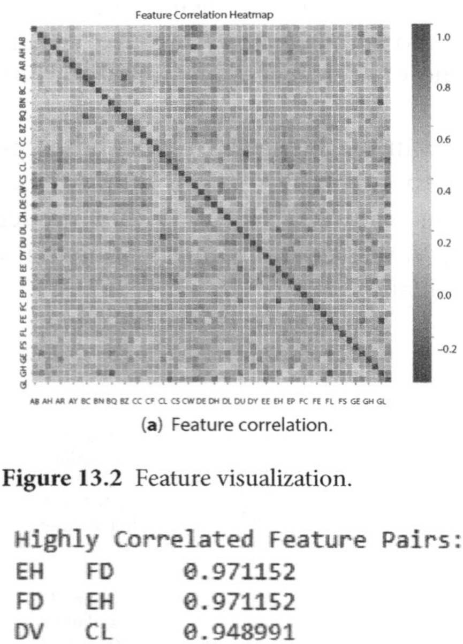

(a) Feature correlation.

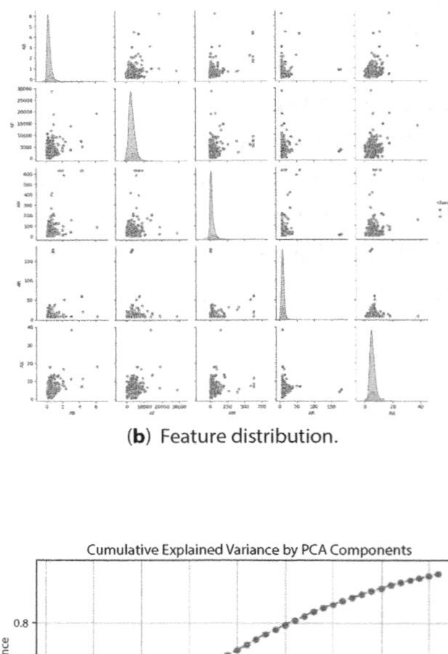

(b) Feature distribution.

Figure 13.2 Feature visualization.

```
Highly Correlated Feature Pairs:
EH    FD      0.971152
FD    EH      0.971152
DV    CL      0.948991
CL    DV      0.948991
BC    BZ      0.907981
BZ    BC      0.907981
EH    DU      0.850957
DU    EH      0.850957
dtype: float64
```

(a) Correlation analysis.

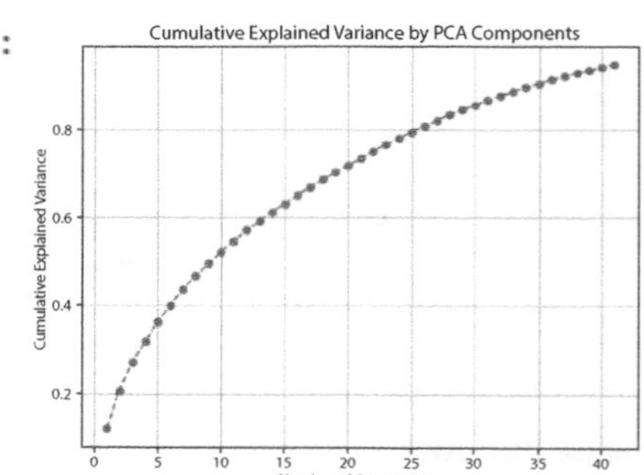

(b) PCA graph.

Figure 13.3 Feature analysis.

the variance, highlighting the value of dimensionality reduction. These insights emphasize the need for feature engineering and reduction to optimize model performance. Figure 13.3(a) shows the correlations between features, and Figure 13.3(b) shows the PCA analysis.

13.3.6 Data Preprocessing

Normalization: It is applied to the columns 'EH,' 'BC,' 'BZ,' 'DU,' and 'EL' to account for scale differences, ensuring consistent feature contributions, preventing any one feature, like medical tests or demographic data, from dominating due to scale differences and improving model training efficiency.
Data Imputation: It is applied to handle missing values in columns like 'BQ,' 'CB,' and 'CC,' ensuring a complete dataset for reliable model training.

SMOTE (Synthetic Minority Over-sampling Technique) is applied to address the class imbalance, generating synthetic samples for the under-represented Class 1 and balancing the data. This ensures better representation during training and leads to fairer classification and improved model performance.

13.3.7 Feature Engineering

Feature Selection: Removed highly correlated features to reduce redundancy and improve model efficiency [31].
PCA (Dimensionality Reduction): Applied PCA to reduce the dataset to components that capture 90% of the variance, simplifying the model without significant loss of information.
Lasso Regularization: Used L1 regularization (Lasso) to further reduce features by shrinking less important coefficients to zero, enhancing model interpretability and performance.

The columns **'BZ,' 'DV,'** and **'FD'** were identified as highly correlated with other features and were considered for removal to reduce redundancy and improve model performance.

13.4 Experimentation

13.4.1 Training

The models (FCNN, CNN, LSTM, Transformer) were trained on an 80% training set and validated on a 20% validation set. Each model was trained for 50 epochs with a batch size of 32, utilizing the Adam optimizer for performance optimization. To prevent overfitting, L1 regularization (Lasso) was applied during training, ensuring that the models generalized well to unseen data.

13.4.2 Parameter and Hyperparameter Setting

FCNN has 2 hidden layers with 64 neurons each, while CNN has 3 convolutional layers with 3×3 filters and Max Pooling. LSTM has 2 layers with 100 units each, and Transformers have 4 layers with 8 attention heads and 128 embedding sizes. All models use 58 features in the input layer and have 1 output for binary classification. Table 13.1 shows the parameter value settings for the models.

The hyperparameter table includes settings like a learning rate of 0.001, batch size of 32, 100 epochs, and dropout rates, with L1 regularization (Lasso) applied to FCNN and LSTM models to reduce overfitting, and it affects the weight updates during training. Table 13.2 shows the hyperparameter value setting.

Table 13.1 Details of parameter values.

Parameter	FCNN	CNN	LSTM	Transformers
Input Layer	58 features	58 features (reshaped for 2D)	58 features	58 features
Hidden Layers	2 (64 neurons each)	3 convolutional layers	2 layers (100 units each)	4 layers
Filter Sizes	-	3×3 filters	-	-
Pooling Layers	-	Max Pooling	-	-
Output Layer	1 (for binary classification)	1	1	1
Attention Heads	-	-	-	8
Embedding Size	-	-	-	128

Table 13.2 Details of hyperparameter values.

Hyperparameters	FCNN	CNN	LSTM	Transformer
Learning Rate	0.001	0.001	0.001	0.001
Batch Size	32	32	32	32
Number of Epochs	100	100	100	100
Dropout Rate	0.2	0.5	0.2	0.1
Regularization	L1 (Lasso)	L1 (Lasso)		

13.5 Results

In this study, the models are thoroughly assessed using a variety of performance criteria. While precision and recall evaluate how well the model detects positive cases and prevents false positives or false negatives, accuracy offers a broad indication of the model's soundness. The *F*1 score is helpful in managing class imbalance because it strikes a balance between recall and precision. Log loss quantifies the model's degree of prediction confidence, and MCC provides a fair assessment even in cases when the classes are unbalanced. Finally, AUC-ROC illustrates how well the model can differentiate between classes. When combined, these measures provide a comprehensive evaluation of the models' performance, which is especially significant for predictions connected to healthcare where accuracy and reliability are crucial.

Key outputs such as confusion matrices, ROC curves, training vs. validation accuracy, and loss graphs, precision, and recall graphs are used to illustrate the performance of all four models—FCNN, Transformer, LSTM, and CNN. These evaluation graphs demonstrate how well each model performs during training and validation and aid in the comparison of the models based on accuracy, loss, precision, recall, and F_1 score.

Figure 13.4 shows the visualization of the metrics of FCNN.

Figure 13.5 shows the visualization of metrics on CNN.

Figure 13.6 shows the visualization of metrics on Transformer.

Figure 13.7 shows the visualization of metrics on LSTM.

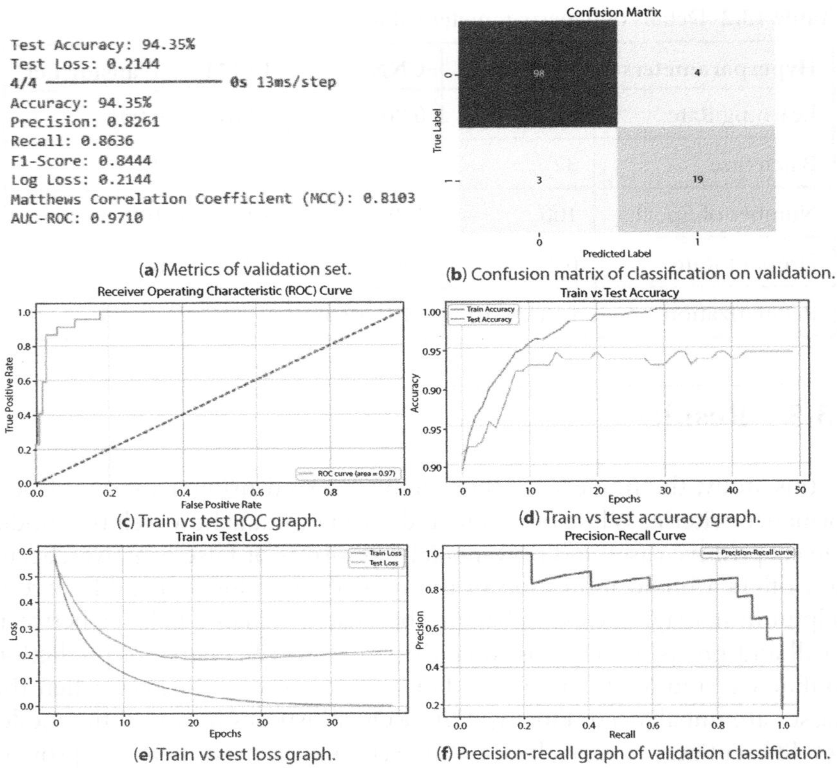

(a) Metrics of validation set.

(b) Confusion matrix of classification on validation.

(c) Train vs test ROC graph.

(d) Train vs test accuracy graph.

(e) Train vs test loss graph.

(f) Precision-recall graph of validation classification.

Figure 13.4 Visualization of FCNN metrics.

Metrics from all models are compared, and LSTM and CNN show the best overall accuracy of 95.97%, with LSTM having a minor precision advantage. CNN shows the highest AUC-ROC and recall, indicating that it is the best at detecting true positives. While the Transformer model lags below the others, especially in precision and recall, suggesting its relatively poorer performance in this context, FCNN performs somewhat better across the board. For this dataset, CNN and LSTM are the most dependable models overall.

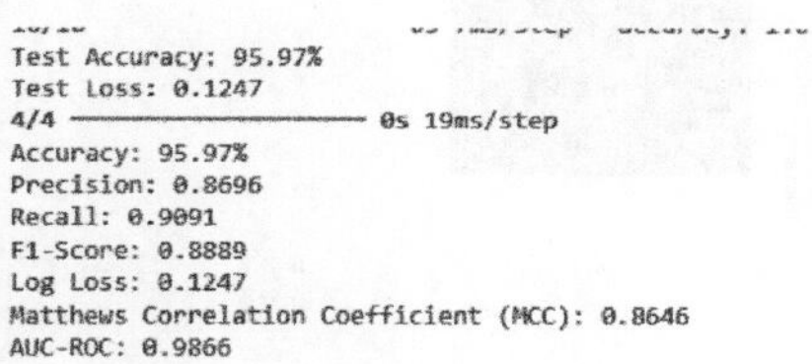

(**a**) Metrics of validation set.

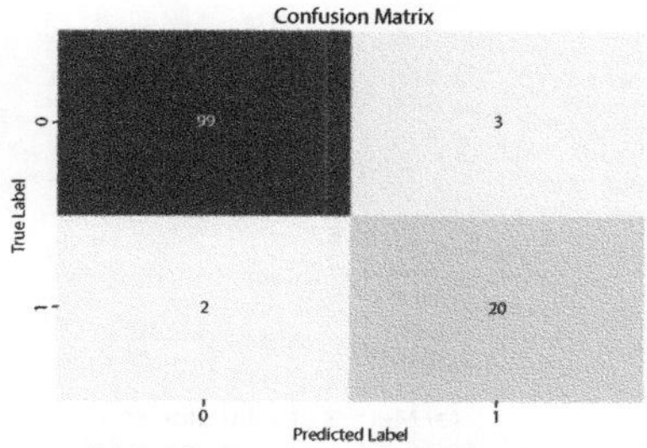

(**b**) Confusion matrix of classification on validation.

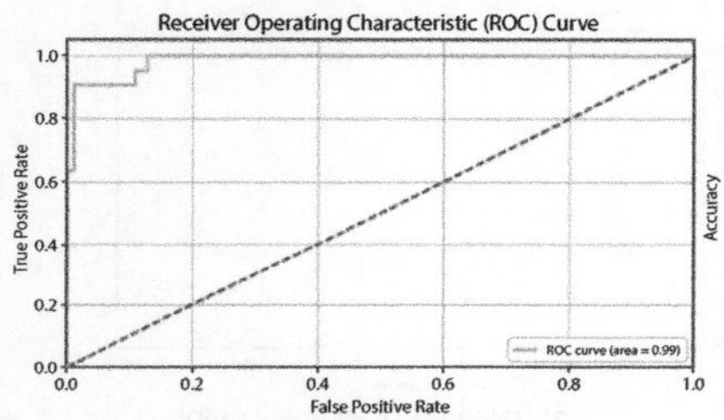

(**c**) Train vs test ROC graph.

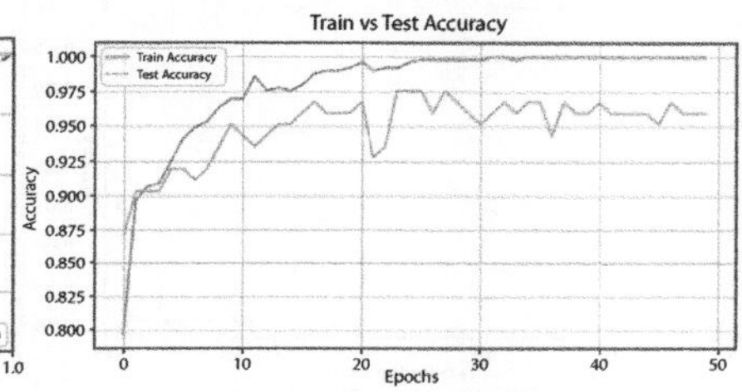

(**d**) Train vs test accuracy graph.

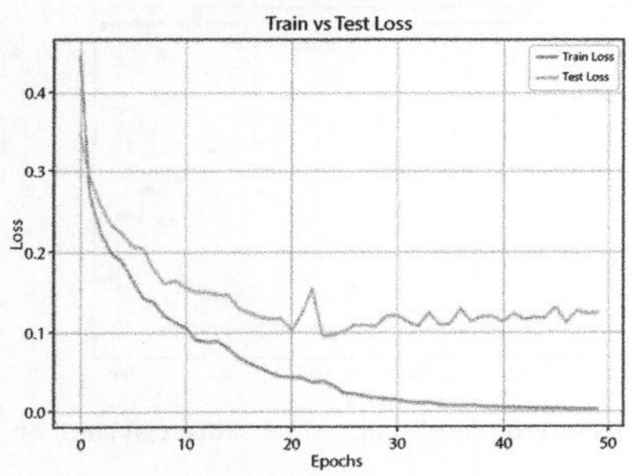

(**e**) Train vs test loss graph.

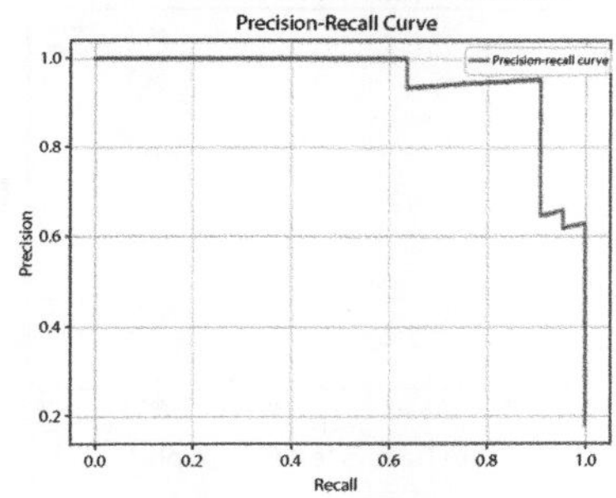

(**f**) Precision-recall graph of validation classification.

Figure 13.5 Visualization of CNN metrics.

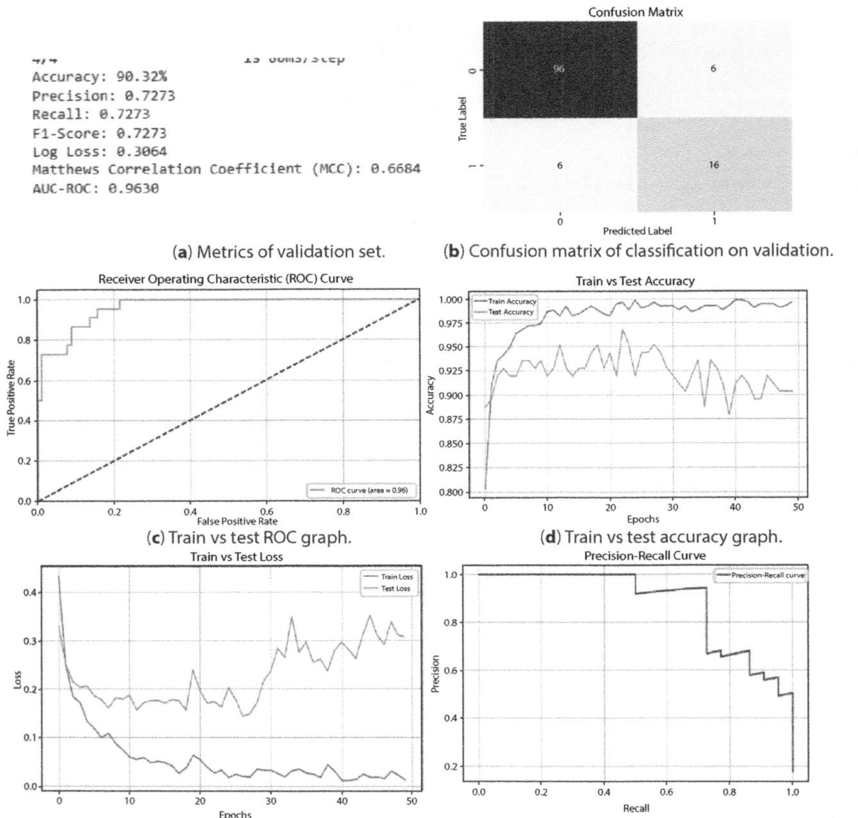

(**a**) Metrics of validation set.

(**b**) Confusion matrix of classification on validation.

(**c**) Train vs test ROC graph.

(**d**) Train vs test accuracy graph.

(**e**) Train vs test loss graph.

(**f**) Precision-recall graph of validation classification.

Figure 13.6 Visualization of Transformer metrics.

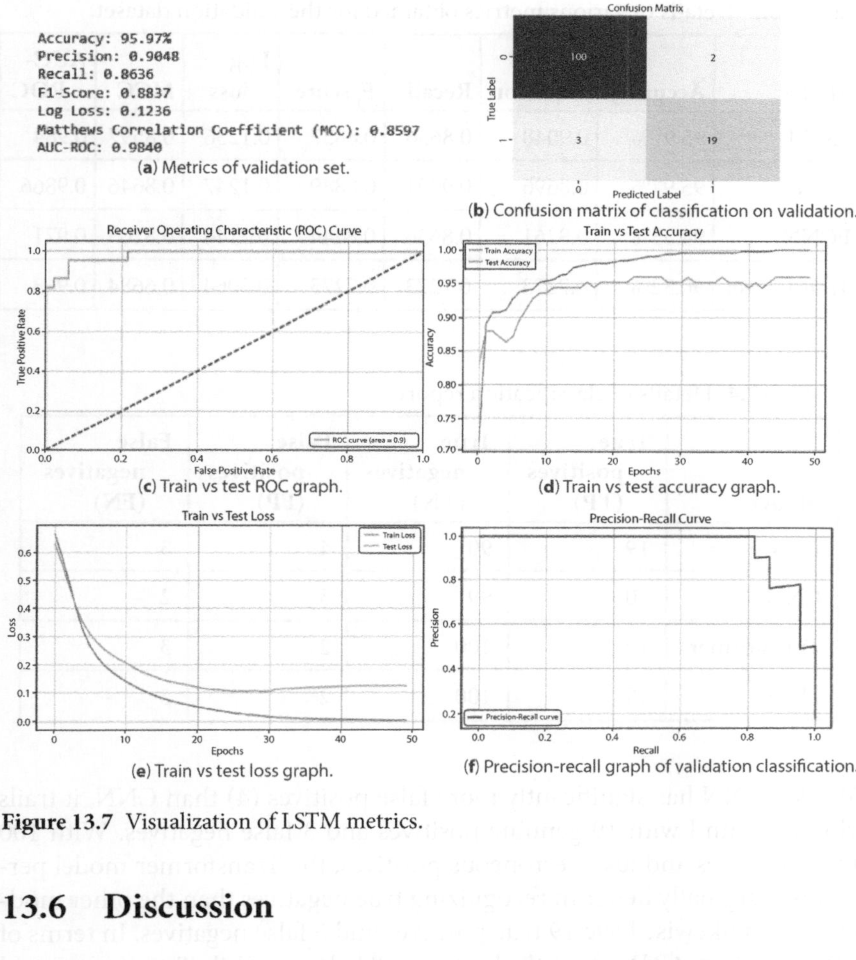

(**a**) Metrics of validation set.

(**b**) Confusion matrix of classification on validation.

(**c**) Train vs test ROC graph.

(**d**) Train vs test accuracy graph.

(**e**) Train vs test loss graph.

(**f**) Precision-recall graph of validation classification.

Figure 13.7 Visualization of LSTM metrics.

13.6 Discussion

According to the table, both CNN and LSTM perform comparably and reach the maximum accuracy of 95.97%. But overall, LSTM is a more balanced model because it has a lower log loss and marginally greater precision. Conversely, CNN has the highest recall, suggesting that it is better at identifying real positives. While it performs rather well, FCNN lags significantly behind in terms of accuracy and F_1 score, suggesting that it might not be as reliable as CNN or LSTM. Transformer seems to be the least successful model for this dataset, having the lowest accuracy and F_1 score. In general, the most dependable models for this purpose are CNN and LSTM. Table 13.3 shows the details of validation metrics.

CNN has the best overall categorization accuracy, as evidenced by the table, with 20 true positives, 99 true negatives, and only 2 false negatives.

Table 13.3 Details of various metrics obtained for the validation dataset.

Model	Accuracy	Precision	Recall	F_1 score	Log loss	MCC	AUC-ROC
LSTM	95.97%	0.9048	0.8636	0.8837	0.1236	0.8597	0.984
CNN	95.97%	0.8696	0.9091	0.8889	0.1247	0.8646	0.9866
FCNN	94.35%	0.8261	0.8636	0.8444	0.2144	0.8103	0.971
Transformer	90.32%	0.7273	0.7273	0.7273	0.3064	0.6684	0.963

Table 13.4 Details of classification report.

Model	True positives (TP)	True negatives (TN)	False positives (FP)	False negatives (FN)
FCNN	19	90	4	3
CNN	20	99	3	2
Transformer	19	100	2	3
LSTM	19	100	2	3

While FCNN has significantly more false positives (4) than CNN, it trails closely behind with 19 genuine positives and 3 false negatives. With 100 true negatives and just 2 erroneous positives, the Transformer model performs marginally better in recognizing true negatives than the other models, which likewise have 19 true positives and 3 false negatives. In terms of categorization, CNN offers the best overall balance, while Transformer and FCNN perform similarly with very little variation. Table 13.4 shows the classification report of the validation dataset.

13.6.1 Comparative Analysis of the Various Metrics of the Results

The train accuracy comparison, which is based on a comparison of the visuals, reveals that all models show a significant increase in accuracy within the first few epochs, with the LSTM and CNN models converging to higher accuracy more quickly than the FCNN and Transformer models. CNN and LSTM are the top performers in the test accuracy comparison, with greater and more consistent accuracy on the validation set. Conversely, the validation performance of Transformer and FCNN is more variable, suggesting a possibility of overfitting or challenges with generalization. All models exhibit a steady decrease in training loss in the train loss comparison; LSTM and CNN achieve the lowest loss, indicating their strong training capabilities. Similarly, as CNN and LSTM acquire lower loss values on the test loss comparison, it confirms their superiority. The figure shows the visuals of comparison of train vs. test metrics of all the models. Figure 13.8 shows a comparison of the metrics of the models.

The graphic comparison shows that CNN and LSTM had similar precision and recall, with CNN having slightly higher recall. When compared to CNN and LSTM, FCNN performed worse overall, particularly in precision and recall. The Transformer model had the highest log loss, suggesting that it suffered more with prediction uncertainty; in contrast, the log loss of

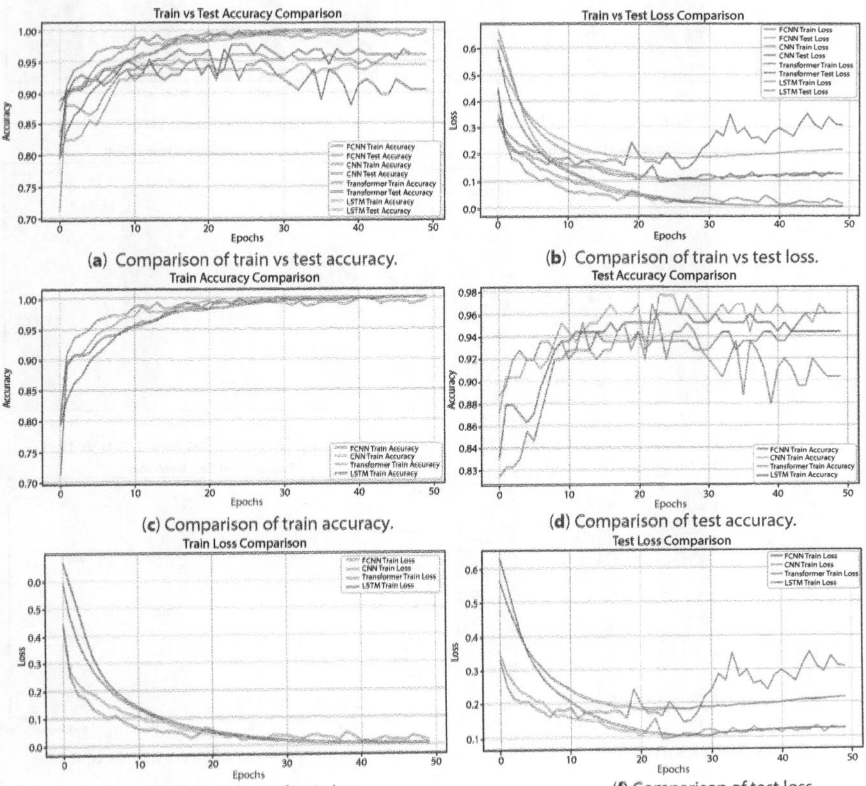

(a) Comparison of train vs test accuracy.

(b) Comparison of train vs test loss.

(c) Comparison of train accuracy.

(d) Comparison of test accuracy.

(e) Comparison of train loss.

(f) Comparison of test loss.

Figure 13.8 Comparison graphs of train vs. test accuracy and loss on all models.

CNN and LSTM models was lower, suggesting that their predictions were better. The Transformer model exhibited the lowest consistency between testing and training, according to the F_1 score comparison, while the CNN and LSTM models maintained the highest levels. Additionally, CNN and LSTM outperformed the Transformer according to the Matthews Correlation Coefficient (MCC), with the Transformer trailing behind. Figure 13.9 shows a comparative analysis of classification metrics as well as MCC and log loss.

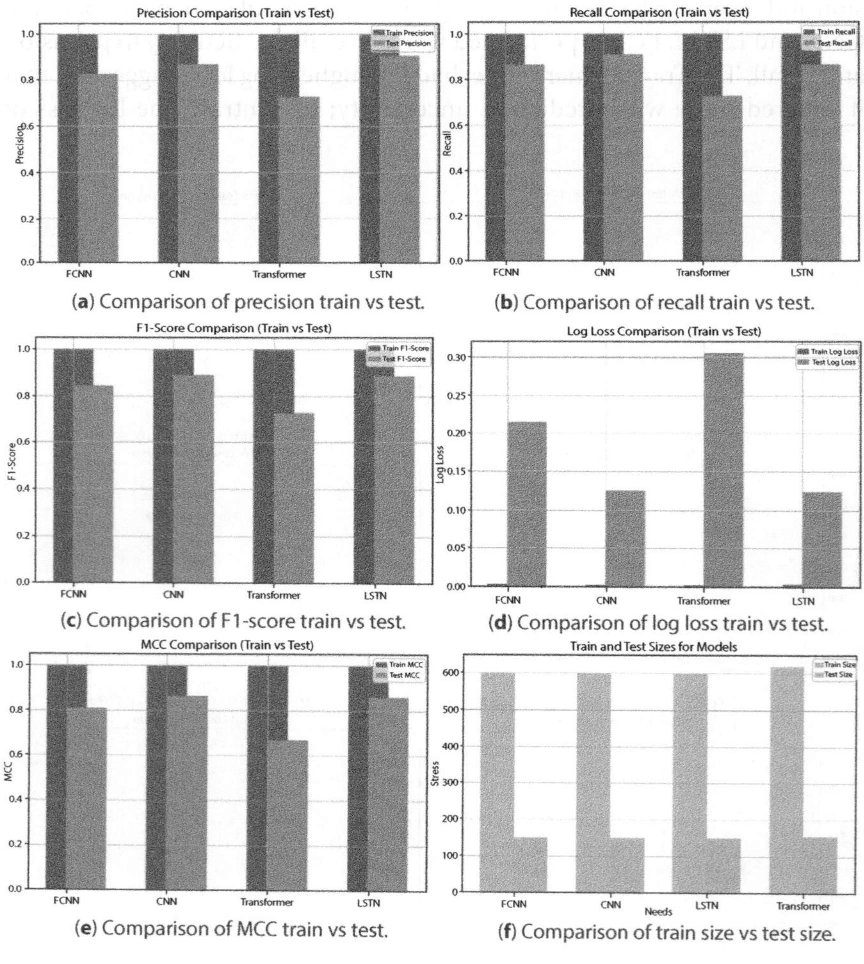

(a) Comparison of precision train vs test.
(b) Comparison of recall train vs test.
(c) Comparison of F1-score train vs test.
(d) Comparison of log loss train vs test.
(e) Comparison of MCC train vs test.
(f) Comparison of train size vs test size.

Figure 13.9 Comparative analysis of classification and other metrics.

13.6.2 Cross-Validation

CNN and LSTM outperformed FCNN and Transformer models in terms of accuracy, according to a comparison of the models. CNN regularly outperformed LSTM when examined on several datasets, especially the ICR and Framingham datasets; however, this difference was not very noticeable. In all datasets, the Transformer model's accuracy was lower, suggesting that it might not be as useful for this specific classification task. Table 13.5 shows the cross-validation on different datasets. Figure 13.10 shows the comparative analysis of the visualization accuracy of different datasets.

Managing class imbalance was one of the main issues this study faced, and using SMOTE to improve model performance was necessary. Additionally, regularization techniques were still required because overfitting remained a worry, particularly with complicated models like CNN and LSTM.

Table 13.5 Cross-validation accuracy.

Dataset	FCNN accuracy (%)	CNN accuracy (%)	LSTM accuracy (%)	Transformer accuracy (%)
UK Biobank	88.3	89.1	88.7	85.6
Framingham Heart Study	87.5	88.9	88.6	86.3
Osteoarthritis Initiative	86.7	88.5	87.9	85.9
ICR Dataset	94.35	95.97	95.97	90.32

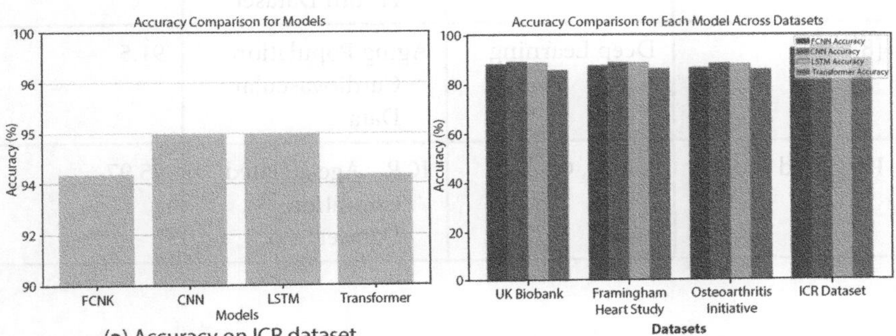

(**a**) Accuracy on ICR dataset.

(**b**) Accuracy across different datasets.

Figure 13.10 Visualization of cross-validation accuracy analysis on different datasets.

The interpretability of the Transformer model presented another difficulty; although it had potential, it did not perform as well as CNN and LSTM. Ultimately, guaranteeing generalizability across various datasets posed a challenge, emphasizing the necessity of rigorous cross-validation and meticulous hyperparameter adjustment.

13.6.3 Benchmark

The benchmark table shows that, when employing LSTM and CNN models on the ICR dataset, the current study obtains the best accuracy of 95.97%, surpassing recent works shown in Table 13.6. The findings indicate that although deep learning techniques and transformer models performed well, they were not as accurate as the models that were suggested for this study. This indicates that improved predictive performance is a result of the current work's integration of strong model training with efficient feature engineering. Table 13.6 shows the comparison with earlier works.

Table 13.6 Benchmark on earlier works.

Benchmark references	Model used	Dataset used	Accuracy (%)
[9]	Deep Learning	Age-Related Disease Dataset	93.5
[18]	Transformer + CNN	Multimodal Health Dataset	92.8
[6]	Neural Networks	Cardiovascular Health Dataset	90.1
[8]	Deep Learning	Aging Population Cardiovascular Data	91.5
Proposed Model	LSTM, CNN	ICR - Age-Related Conditions Dataset	95.97

13.7 Conclusion and Future Enhancements

This study shows how well a number of models—including Transformer-based architectures, CNN, LSTM, FCNN, and CNN—predict age-related health issues. When trained and verified on the ICR dataset, LSTM and CNN yielded the greatest accuracy (95.97%) of all the models. The suggested models provide more generalizability and accuracy than previous studies that focused on homogenous or smaller datasets, as confirmed by a benchmarking analysis against current works. Even with their excellent efficacy, the LSTM and Transformer models' complexity makes it difficult to apply practically in real-world healthcare settings, particularly those with limited resources. Moreover, the clinical adoption of these deep learning models may be restricted due to their lack of interpretability.

Future research should concentrate on improving the interpretability of the model and developing variations that are more computationally efficient, especially for use in healthcare systems with constrained resources. These models' robustness and application will also be enhanced by testing them on bigger, more varied datasets, guaranteeing consistent performance across a range of demographics and medical conditions. The study's excellent accuracy and generalizability offer a potential basis for the creation of AI-driven healthcare solutions that are more successful.

AI disclosure statement: The author acknowledges the use of AI-based tools for minor language editing or grammatical correction. However, all intellectual contributions, analyses, and conclusions presented in this chapter are entirely the author's own.

References

1. Helaly, H.A., *et al.*, Deep learning approach for early detection of Alzheimer's disease. *Cognit. Comput.*, 14, 5, 1711–1727, 2022, https://doi.org/10.1007/s12559-021-09946-2.
2. Voigtlaender, S., *et al.*, Artificial intelligence in neurology: opportunities, challenges, and policy implications. *J. Neurol.*, 271, 5, 2258–2273, 2024, https://doi.org/10.1007/s00415-024-12220-8.
3. Baghernezhad, S. and Daliri, M.R., Age-related changes in human brain functional connectivity using graph theory and machine learning techniques in resting-state fMRI data. *Geroscience*, 46, 5, 5303–5320, 2024, https://doi.org/10.1007/s11357-024-01128-w.

4. Kumar, Y., *et al.*, Artificial intelligence in disease diagnosis: a systematic literature review, synthesizing framework and future research agenda. *J. Ambient Intell. Hum. Comput.*, 14, 8459–8486, 2023, https://doi.org/10.1007/s12652-021-03612-z.
5. Yang, X., *et al.*, The differential and interactive effects of aging and mental fatigue on alpha oscillations: a resting-state electroencephalography study. *Brain Sci.*, 15, 6, 546, 2025, https://doi.org/10.3390/brainsci15060546.
6. Das, A. and Dhillon, P., Application of machine learning in measurement of ageing and geriatric diseases: a systematic review. *BMC Geriatrics*, 23, 1, 841, 2023, https://doi.org/10.1186/s12877-023-04477-x.
7. Guo, Q. and Chen, P., Construction and optimization of health behavior prediction model for the older adult in smart older adult care. *Front. Public Health*, 12, 2024, https://doi.org/10.3389/fpubh.2024.1486930.
8. AlArfaj, A.A. and Mahmoud, H.A.H., Deep learning prediction model for heart disease for elderly patients. *Intell. Autom. Soft Comput.*, 35, 2, 2527–2540, 2023, https://doi.org/10.32604/iasc.2023.030168.
9. Wassan, J.T., Zheng, H., Wang, H., Role of deep learning in predicting aging-related diseases: a scoping review. *Cells*, 10, 11, 2924, 2021, https://doi.org/10.3390/cells10112924.
10. Duggan, M., *et al.*, Age-related neurodegenerative diseases. *J. Cell. Physiol.*, 235, 4, 3131–3141, 2020, https://doi.org/10.1002/jcp.29248.
11. Misra, S., *et al.*, Multi-channel transfer learning of chest X-ray images for screening of COVID-19. *Electron.*, 9, 1388, 2020, https://doi.org/10.3390/electronics9091388.
12. Guo, J., *et al.*, Aging and aging-related diseases: from molecular mechanisms to interventions and treatments. *Signal Transduction Targeted Ther.*, 7, 391, 2022, https://doi.org/10.1038/s41392-022-01251-0.
13. Theodorakis, N., *et al.*, Integrating machine learning with multi-omics technologies in geroscience: towards personalized medicine. *J. Pers. Med.*, 14, 9, 931, 2024, https://doi.org/10.3390/jpm14090931.
14. Al Kuwaiti, A., *et al.*, A review of the role of artificial intelligence in healthcare. *J. Pers. Med.*, 13, 6, 951, 2023, https://doi.org/10.3390/jpm13060951.
15. Alami, H., *et al.*, Organizational readiness for artificial intelligence in health care: insights for decision-making and practice. *J. Health Organ. Management Ahead-of-Print*, 2020, https://doi.org/10.1108/JHOM-03-2020-0074.
16. Xu, N., *et al.*, Application of artificial intelligence in modern medicine. *Clin. eHealth*, 6, 130–137, 2023, https://doi.org/10.1016/j.ceh.2023.09.001.
17. Faiyazuddin, M., *et al.*, The impact of artificial intelligence on healthcare: a comprehensive review of advancements in diagnostics, treatment, and operational efficiency. *Health Sci. Rep.*, 8, e70312, 2025, https://doi.org/10.1002/hsr2.70312.

18. Ji, Q., *et al.*, Multimodal omics approaches to aging and age-related diseases. *Phenomics*, 4, 1, 56–71, 2024, https://doi.org/10.1007/s43657-023-00125-x.
19. Liu, T., *et al.*, DMGAT: predicting ncRNA-drug resistance associations based on diffusion map and heterogeneous graph attention network. *Briefings Bioinf.*, 26, 2, bbaf179, 2025, https://doi.org/10.1093/bib/bbaf179.
20. Odden, M.C. and Melzer, D., Machine learning in aging research. *J. Gerontology Ser. A*, 74, 12, 1901–1902, 2019, https://doi.org/10.1093/gerona/glz074.
21. Baecker, L., *et al.*, Machine learning for brain age prediction: introduction to methods and clinical applications. *eBioMedicine*, 72, 103600, 2021, https://www.sciencedirect.com/science/article/pii/S2352396421003935.
22. Wang, Y., *et al.*, Understanding machine learning applications in dementia research and clinical practice: a review for biomedical scientists and clinicians. *Alzheimer's Res. Ther.*, 16, 1, 175, 2024, https://doi.org/10.1186/s13195-024-01540-6.
23. Kumari, L.K. and Jagadesh, B.N., Classification of mammograms using adaptive binary TLBO with ensemble classifier for early detection of breast cancer. *Int. J. Inf. Technol.*, 14, 3579–3590, 2022, https://doi.org/10.1007/s41870-022-00998-7.
24. Moturi, S., Vemuru, S., Tirumala Rao, S.N., Two phase parallel framework for weighted coalesce rule mining: A fast heart disease and breast cancer prediction paradigm. *Biomed. Engineering Applications Basis Commun.*, 34, 3, 2250010, 2022, https://doi.org/10.4015/S1016237222500107.
25. Ladkat, A.S., *et al.*, Deep neural network-based novel mathematical model for 3D brain tumor segmentation. *Comput. Intell. Neurosci.*, 2022, 4271711, 2022, https://doi.org/10.1155/2022/4271711.
26. Vidhya, R., *et al.*, Alzheimer's disease detection using residual neural network with LSTM hybrid deep learning models. *J. Intell. Fuzzy Syst.*, 45, 6, 12095–12109, 2023, https://doi.org/10.3233/JIFS-235059.
27. Dinesh Kumar, A., Mythrayee, D., Asha Shiny, X.S., An enhanced lifespan of WSN using hybrid fuzzy-machine learning-based clustering process. *Wireless Pers. Commun.*, 139, 3, 1637–1657, 2024, https://doi.org/10.1007/s11277-024-11682-3.
28. Golamari, J.M. and Haritha, D., A hybrid CNN-multi-class SVM framework for biomedical document gene-disease datasets classification. *SSRG Int. J. Electron. Commun. Eng.*, 10, 12, 73–82, 2023, https://doi.org/10.14445/23488549/IJECE-V10I12P107.
29. Thatha, V.N., *et al.*, Enhancing privacy protection in online federated learning: a method for secure face image de-identification using a modified Diffie-Hellman algorithm. *Math. Modell. Eng. Probl.*, 10, 6, 2265–2273, 2023, https://doi.org/10.18280/mmep.100642.

30. Pagadala, P.K., *et al.*, Enhancing lung cancer detection from lung CT scan using image processing and deep neural networks. *Rev. d'Intelligence Artificielle*, 37, 6, 1597–1605, 2023, https://doi.org/10.18280/ria.370624.
31. Smilarubavathy, G., Keerthana, S.M., Nidhya, R., Priscilla, T., Pavithra, D., Machine Learning in Healthcare: Unlocking Precision Diagnosis and Continuous Monitoring Through Voice Analysis, in: *Smart Factories for Industry 5.0 Transformation*, pp. 229–245, 2025.

14

Integrating Locality Sensitive Hashing and Embeddings into Collaborative Filtering for the Visual-Image-Based View

Balaji Maram[1], Rekha Sundari[2], Anupama Angadi[3], Satya Keerthi Gorripati[4] and Venubabu Rachapudi[5]*

[1]School of Computer Science and Artificial Intelligence, SR University, Warangal, Telangana, India
[2]Department of Information Technology, Anil Neerukonda Institute of Technology and Sciences, Visakhapatnam, Andhra Pradesh, India
[3]Department of Computer Science, Gitam School of Technology, Gitam, Visakhapatnam, Andhra Pradesh, India
[4]Department of Computer Science, Gayatri Vidya Parishad College of Engineering (A), Visakhapatnam, Andhra Pradesh, India
[5]Department of Computer Science and Engineering, Koneru Lakshmaiah Education Foundation, Vaddeswaram, Guntur, Andhra Pradesh, India

Abstract

E-commerce stands as one of the thriving industries, where every web application offers a multitude of items. Matching users' product carts is crucial yet challenging for these platforms. Hence, personalized recommendation systems are indispensable for every e-commerce company to handle user requests efficiently. However, amidst the abundance of high-dimensional data, challenges such as information overload, sparsity, and cold-start issues arise, necessitating effective recommendation models. With the current focus on deep learning embeddings to address large-scale data challenges, embeddings serve two key purposes: first, to group semantically similar products closely, and second, to visualize data in lower dimensions. Sometimes, embeddings are directly utilized for the "Suggested for you" section on e-commerce websites, while other times, they serve as inputs to models. Since similarity forms the backbone of recommender systems, our model

**Corresponding author*: venubabu.r@gmail.com

R. Nidhya, A. Dineshkumar, Sheng-Lung Peng, S. Karthik and S. Balamurugan (eds.) Neuro-Symbolic Artificial Intelligence: Concepts & Applications, (269–290) © 2026 Scrivener Publishing LLC

suggests products by learning their vector representations. Despite the limited recent literature on embeddings in recommender systems, challenges persist, particularly in terms of retrieval efficiency. Locality-sensitive hashing emerges as a method to identify near-duplicate images within vast datasets. In our work, we integrate a locality-sensitive index for faster retrieval and leverage embeddings such as Convolutional Neural Network Resnet 50 for feature learning in a recommender system approach. The proposed methodology is evaluated using the real-life dataset "Caltech-101." Experimental findings demonstrate that our approach significantly enhances precision by 91%, accuracy by 96%, and retrieval efficiency by 29% compared to other models.

***Keywords*:** Collaborative filtering, image-based recommendation, product vectors, embeddings, locality-sensitive hashing, Euclidean

14.1 Introduction

Most social networks and e-commerce platforms show a lot of personalized recommendations content in the "Suggested for you" section. However, with the incredible growth and usage (e.g., #customers, #products), traditional systems grieve from space and time complexity issues and fail to make relevant suggestions when handling large-scale data. Although this issue seems simple, it was only successfully addressed in recent years using Recommender Systems (RS).

An RS is a subclass of information retrieval that attempts to predict the "favorite" or "rating" a customer would provide to a product. They are mostly used in e-commercial claims. RS is operated in various areas such as video, content, books, and music recommenders. They are also becoming very common in restaurants and dating apps. In today's modest world, it is vital for a rising e-commerce platform to retain its customers as well as consistent experience. Instead of searching for your favorite products, RS suggests appropriate products that are more impressive. Product suggestions can address such issues efficiently by elaborating on purchase behavior. Broadly, there exist two widespread RS approaches: Collaborative filtering (CF) and Content filtering (CBF) [1].

CF does not rely on an understanding of the product or machine-analyzable content and is thus capable of suggesting complex items such as movie recommendations by exploiting similarities. Many techniques have been used in computing customer or product similarity in RS, for instance, the Cosine, Pearson, Jaccard, and k-Nearest Neighbor (k-NN). On the other hand, CBF relies on customers' history to suggest a product by exploiting their features.

A good RS will always boost e-commerce customer engagement. In literature, researchers implement RS by utilizing content, customers' preferences, or favorites [2]. The goal is to do the same with product images that suggest similar images from added carts (or recently bought products). Hence, image-based recommendations rely on mining the most typical and expressive features and applying them to get identical suggestions [3]. Measuring identicality involves two major components: (1) feature extraction and (2) similarity measure. Feature descriptors extract shape, color, and texture from every image to transform it into a vector space. This lets us perform finding similar vectors just like any other mathematical operation. RS will be built on the idea that products that link to similar products in the cart are matched to one another. We use Locality Sensitive Hashing (LSH), a nearest duplicate search technique for identifying similar products that principally aims high-dimensional datasets. The existing literature takes a long processing time for search and retrieval. This is a major issue often faced by RS. However, LSH deals with this issue by using a hash function that projects two similar vectors to one hash value.

This paper is categorized as follows: Section 14.2 describes related work on image-based RS using transfer learning and LSH. Section 14.3 describes the proposed approach. Section 14.4 explains the experiments and analysis. Finally, Section 14.5 describes the conclusion.

14.2 Related Works

Many techniques have been proposed to improve the performance of the RS system. In this section, we briefly summarize some existing literature in the image-based recommendation domain, which are categorized as follows:

14.2.1 Recommender Systems

Xiaoqing Li *et al.* [4] disclosed the development of Content-Based retrieval in many fields, like computer vision and artificial intelligence. They summarized various applications for image retrieval in numerous fields of remote sensing and object identification and finally discussed the future guidelines of image retrieval with the use of big data and deep learning.

Jaya Gupta *et al.* [5] stated the outcome of deep learning on transfer learning for machine learning. They reviewed previous experimental work on transfer learning using different methods like Convolutional Neural Networks (CNN), Residual Neural Networks (ResNet-50), Visual

Geometry Group (VGG-16), and Google Net for image classification and concluded that deep learning is far better than traditional systems. This paper also showed the architecture of CNN and applications of transfer learning in brain image classification and sentiment classification.

Chen, L., *et al.* [6] proposed a personalized RS based on deep learning. They used a BERT model and replaced conventional word vector text to reduce the effect of sparsity and extracting hidden feature extractors. Experimental results confirm that the model decreases cold start and data sparsity issues.

14.2.2 Transfer Learning

Monika Bansal *et al.* [7] described a feature extraction approach that comprises a deep learning method to extract information from the image. They surveyed various feature approaches like scale-invariant feature transform (SIFT), Head on Generation System (HOG), speed-up robust feature (SURF), Object Request Broker (ORB), and various classification methods, such as Decision Trees, Random Forest, XGB, feature reduction approaches, k-means, and locality preserving projection. They combined both deep learning and traditional feature extractors for improved classification. Performance metrics like accuracy, precision, and recall are used to estimate the model, which is obtained as 93.73%.

Pegah Malekpour Alamdari *et al.* [8] proposed an image-based method RS to enhance the accuracy. They tested their work using pre-trained CNN models, including VGG16, VGG19, ResNet50, Inception V3, and Xception for feature extraction. The system uses KNN to retrieve the nearest neighbors; they conducted experiments on two variations of MovieLens datasets and proved that they attained lower RMSE and MAE values.

Hessel Tuinhof *et al.* [9] proposed a visually aware neural classifier to extract features. Later, they forward these features to a KNN similarity metric for ranking the nearby items. During pre-processing, they applied augmentation methods to increase the data set, which allowed the model not to overfit. They summarized accuracy, loss of the model on image category, and texture as 0.87, 0.42, 0.8, and 0.61, respectively.

Sandra Rizkallah *et al.* [10] proposed a novel vector embedding approach for rating prediction and recommended top-k items. Their work uses an objective function based on joint user-item similarities for the feature space. They have tested on popular datasets, and they showed competitive results.

Bui Nguyen Minh Hoang *et al.* [11] used Bert Embeddings to extract features for improving the accuracy of collaborative recommender models.

They focused on reducing sparsity by using latent concepts with Singular Value Decomposition and verified different similarity computations for better clustering of user/item vectors.

14.2.3 LSH Similarity Metric

Maryam Almasharawi *et al.* [12] stated that online advertising is a main source for search engines. They proposed RespRate-LSH for estimating user response and reducing high-dimensional data using near neighbors. RespRate-LSH first computes 2-shingles and minhash signature and clusters similar keywords that frequently appear in queries. Lastly, an index is created for finding the nearby neighbors of a keyword. They used evaluation metrics RMSE and MAE to measure the performance of RespRate-LSH with varying hash values of [2, 4, 6, 8, 16, 32, 64, 128, 255] and concluded with an increase in hash functions leading to higher error.

Osman Durmaz and Hasan Sakir Bilge [13] presented an ANN approach for approximating nearest neighbors using randomized distributed hashing. They evaluated the ANN approach on various datasets like Corel-10K and GIST-1M. ANN enabled parallel processing and showed experimental results with 10 nodes, with a speed of 8 for processing, and obtained a MAP result of 0.84 with 8, 16, 24, 32, and 64-bit hash codes.

14.3 Methodology

In this paper, a new integrated collaborative filtering approach using locality-sensitive hashing and embeddings (ICFELSH) is proposed [14]. In the remaining section, the basic idea of ICFELSH is presented; then, the step-by-step process of the proposed approach is described.

14.3.1 Basic Idea

The simple mechanism is to extract image features using pre-trained models and recommend similar images based on users' query images. To assure this goal, the core thought of ICFELSH is based on four major contributions, which are the following:

(1) To adopt data augmentation and pre-processing methods for the training data, such as rotation, clipping, adding regularization, avoiding overfitting, and endorsing the robustness of the model.

(2) To use a CNN ResNet-50 embedding model to capture high- and low-level features from images [15].
(3) To use principal component analysis (PCA) to reduce the extracted features.
(4) To recommend top-k relevant images based on the features captured by CNN ResNet-50, we devise an LSH similarity metric to build a hand index, revealing nearby images to minimize retrieval time.

14.3.2 The Proposed Method

The proposed ICFELSH method involves five phases, as shown in Figure 14.1, which are feature extraction, dimensionality reduction, feature normalization, data augmentation, and determining similarity.

14.3.2.1 Feature Extraction Phase

It is a crucial phase to transform raw data, such as images or text, into a reduced representation of meaningful features. In our work, features are captured from both the CNN, R-Drop CNN, and a pre-trained ResNet-50 model for robust image feature representation, which is described as follows.

14.3.2.1.1 CF with Base CNN Model

Apart from core functionalities (such as outlier detection and automated tagging), one important beneficial feature is image similarity, which can be initiated in several applications, from object recognition to image clustering to similar product navigation. Product recommendations return similar images as suggestions by analyzing the users' past browsing history [16].

Traditional approaches (SIFT, HOG) identify precise features to distinguish between images during feature extraction; they are inclined to emphasize hands-on and so do not learn themselves — instead demanding substantial facts to plan pre-processing. However, in the current age, there has been much attention on using CNNs, given their hierarchical flow specifying that they manage to regulate the finest depiction for attaining facts or classification inevitably. The outcome is that, unlike SIFT and HOG, CNN focuses on the abstract representation of lower-level features. In this paper, we leverage feature extraction using CNN and match these to evaluate the similarity of two images. During training, the pixels are often

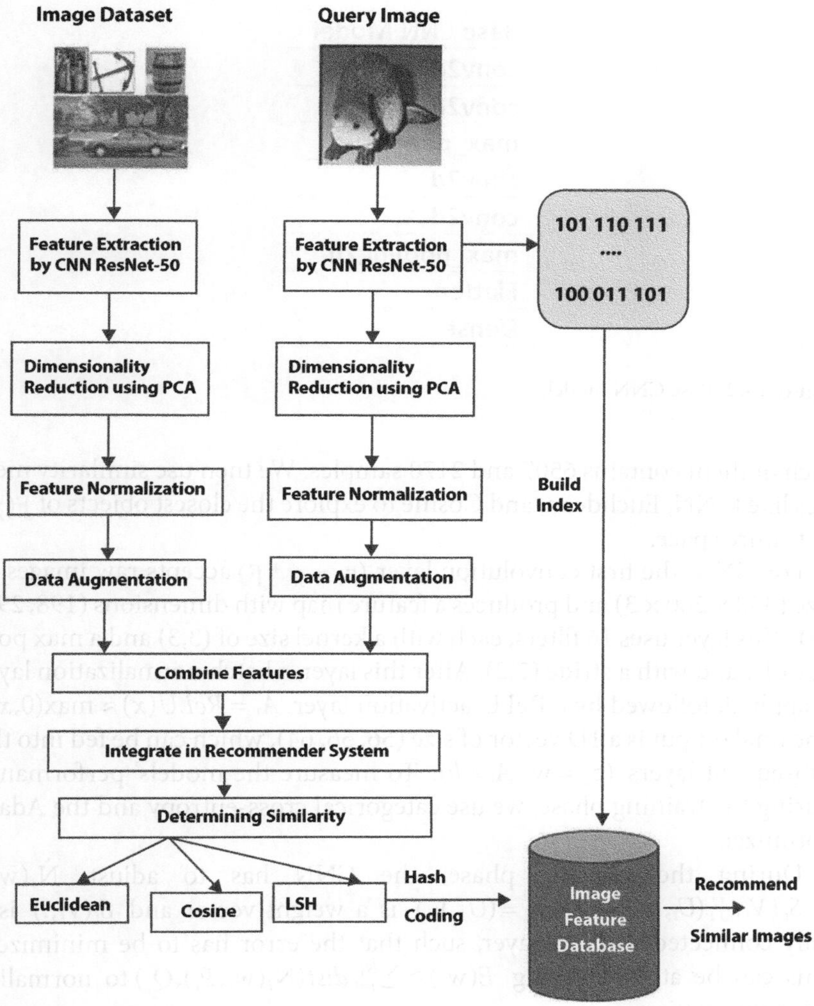

Figure 14.1 Outline phases of the proposed ICFELSH approach.

transformed by the fully connected layers and forwarded to the classifier for inference. Though these features capture adequate data about the input image for effective classification, the reason is that they are related to the final layer of CNN to infer similarity, as shown in Figure 14.2.

In the initial step, we train the CNN to predict the object type and its class. CNN takes a raw image as input from an image dataset $\chi = \{x_1, x_2, \ldots x_n\}$, and each holds a feature vector $\mathrm{F}(\chi)$ of any input image $\chi \to \mathbb{R}^{NxN} : \chi \epsilon \mathbb{R}^{D}$. The dataset is divided into training $T_i \cong \{(P_n, Q_n)\}^{N_i}$ and validation sets:

Base CNN Model
conv2d
conv2d
max_pooling2d
conv2d
conv2d
max_pooling2d
Flatten
Dense

Figure 14.2 Base CNN model.

each of them contains 6507 and 2170 samples. We then use similarity metrics like k-NN, Euclidean, and Cosine to explore the closest objects of $\mathcal{F}(\chi)$ in feature space.

For CNN, the first convolution layer ($z_1 = \chi * \mathcal{F}$) accepts raw images of size ($300 \times 200 \times 3$) and produces a feature map with dimensions (198, 298, 16). This layer uses 16 filters, each with a kernel size of (3,3) and a max pool size of 2 and with a stride (2,2). After this layer, a batch normalization layer is applied, followed by a ReLU activation layer $A_1 = ReLU(x) \approx \max(0, x)$. The final output is a 1D vector of size (56, 56, 64), which can be fed into the subsequent layers ($z_2 = \text{w}^t.A_1 + b$). To measure the models' performance during the training phase, we use categorical cross-entropy and the Adam optimizer.

During the training phase, the CNN has to adjust $\dot{\text{N}}_i(\text{w}_i)$ ($\cong S_i\left(V_i, \mathcal{F}_i\left(U_i,.\right)\right)$ Here $\text{w}_i = (U_i, V_i)$ is a weight vector and $S_i(V_i,.)$ is a fully connected softmax layer, such that the error has to be minimized. This can be attained using $E(\text{w}_i) \cong \sum_{j=1}^{N_i} dist(\dot{\text{N}}_i(\text{w}_i, P_j), Q_j)$ to normalize this computation.

14.3.2.1.2 R-Drop CNN Model

We perceive the overfitting, as the accuracy on the validation set is higher compared to the training set [17]. To overcome this issue, we add data augmentation, L2 regularization (R), and dropout (Drop) to the existing model, which is a common technique to improve the generalization as shown in Figure 14.3. It adds a penalty term to the loss function, which is expressed to encourage smaller weights in the network.

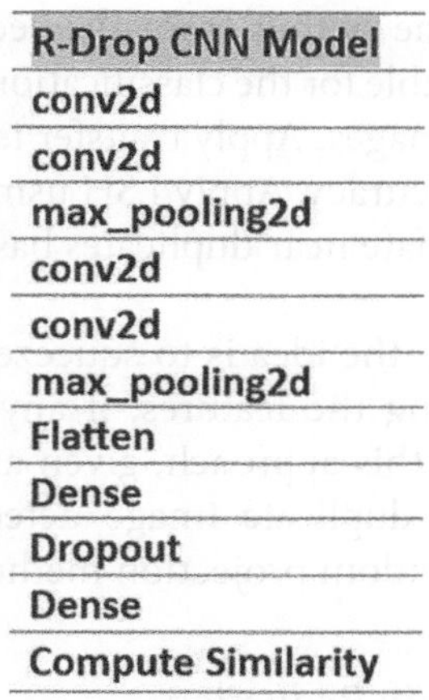

Figure 14.3 R-Drop CNN model.

$$E(\mathrm{w}_i) \cong \sum_{j=1}^{N_i} dist(\dot{\mathrm{N}}_i(\mathrm{w}_i, P_j), Q_j) + \lambda \left\| \mathrm{w}_i \right\|^2, \lambda > 0 \tag{14.1}$$

14.3.2.1.3 CF with Transfer Learning

Residual Network (ResNet-50) CNN is described as "short connections," which skip one or more layers. It comprises a 50-layer network and 16 residual blocks, with every block comprising CNN layers. The architecture also contains average pooling, a connected layer, and an output layer [18]. Most layers have 3×3 filters and compute downsampling with a stride of 2 as shown in Figure 14.4.

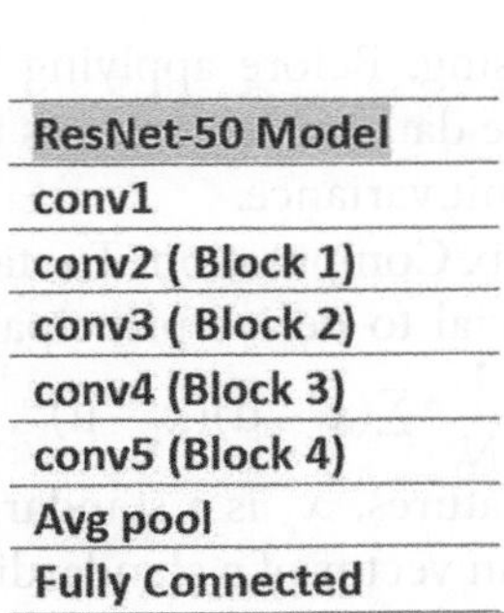

Figure 14.4 ResNet-50 model.

For ResNet-50, take the output from the second last fully connected layer (which was accountable for the classification task) to obtain the image embedding for all 8677 images. Apply transfer learning to distinguish 101 classes with maximum accuracy. Apply LSH using the LShash3 package to obtain the most approximate near duplicates based on image embeddings enabled.

During pre-processing, the idea is to squeeze the image into a slighter signature while conserving the features, if any two images match their signatures as well. Using this approach, given an input image, makes the accomplishment of near-duplicate image detection significantly easier. Specifically, we use the random projection method to calculate signatures.

14.3.2.2 Dimensionality Reduction

It is a feature reduction method to extract only the most precious features from high-dimensional feature vectors by the model while preserving substantial information. This will be attained by using PCA, which is a prevailing method for transforming high-level data into lower-level data.

To accelerate the recommendation process and improve its performance, we applied the PCA approach, which produces a small set of data that are originally smaller than the original data. It does this by computing the eigenvalues, eigenvectors, and data covariance matrix. The following gives details about the PCA approach.

1. Collect Features: In our study, we extract features from the ResNet-50 model for a dataset of images. Let's denote the image feature data set as $\digamma(\chi)$, where every feature is denoted as x_1.
2. Data Pre-processing: Before applying PCA, it is common to scale the image data, which ensures that all features have zero mean and unit variance.
3. Covariance Matrix Computation: To standardize the feature vectors, it is crucial to derive principal components, often denoted as $C = \frac{1}{N} * \Sigma(x_i - \mu)(x_i - \mu)^T$, where N denotes the number of features, x_i is a standardized feature vector, and μ is the mean vector of a standardized vector.
4. Eigenvalue Decomposition: To obtain eigenvectors and eigenvalues, we compute $C = V \wedge V^T$, where V is a matrix of eigenvalues as columns, $\wedge$ is a diagonal matrix, and V^T denotes the transpose of V.

5. Feature Reduction: Take the top k eigenvectors as the principal components after sorting eigenvalues corresponding to eigenvectors.

The PCA approach is applied on the second last fully connected layer of ResNet-50, which captures more abstract and semantically rich features. These features are closer to the output layer and provide a good balance between higher and lower-level data.

14.3.2.3 Feature Normalization

During pre-processing, it is suggested to normalize image pixels relative to mean and standard deviation. This supports getting reliable results when applying transfer learning on new images. If we compute statistics on raw images, the data augmentation pipeline becomes minimal, which means it does not require substantial transformations. Here, we did normalization with mean=0 and std=1 to scale pixels from [0,255] to [0,1]. For instance, a raw image of size 3×3, the computed mean and standard deviation was shown in Table 14.1 using the following equation:

$$\Sigma_{i=1}^{n}(p_i - \bar{\bar{p}})^2 = [\Sigma_{i=1}^{n} p_i^{\,2}] - \frac{1}{n}[\Sigma_{i=1}^{n} p_i^{\,2}]^2 \quad (14.2)$$

14.3.2.4 Data Augmentation

Data Augmentation upsurges data set size and ensues only on the training set. It includes effects like rotation of an image, zoom in, zoom out, and adjusting color filters, as shown in Figure 14.5 and Figure 14.6. Each image is represented as an array of pixels. As per the pre-processing, we resize the image to 300 × 200 × 3, where 300 is width and height and 3 are RGB values. All these values range from 0 to 255, which defines the intensity of color and rescales all these values by 1./255 using the ImageDataGenerator package. Finally, every image is denoted as a 1,80,000-dimensional feature vector. The following parameters in Table 14.2 are defined in the augmentation phase:

Table 14.1 Computed image feature normalization.

Image	Pixels	Mean	Standard deviation	Normalized values
	(23, 25, 22) (0, 0, 0) (19, 28, 37)	[76.84,79,75,51.46]	[56.45,55.84,55.77]	[[0.09,0.09,0.08] [0,0,0] [0.07,0.10,0.14]]

Figure 14.5 From left to right, two sample images' rotational effect from the airplane class in the Caltech 101 dataset.

Method	Accuracy	Loss
Without Augmentation	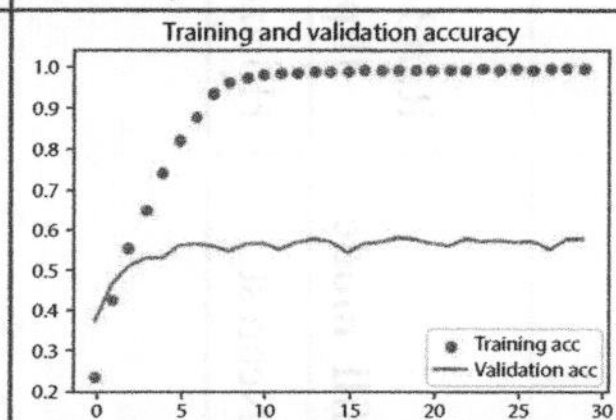	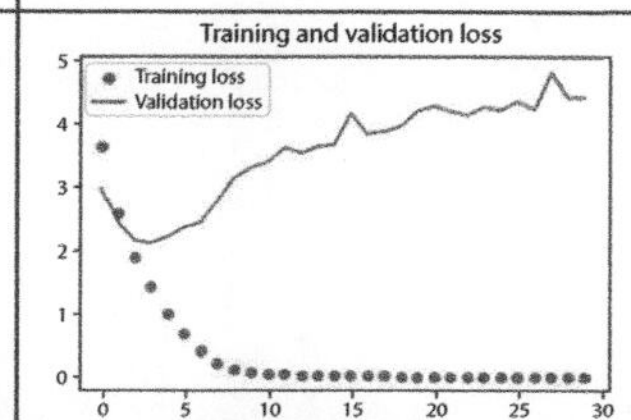
With Augmentation	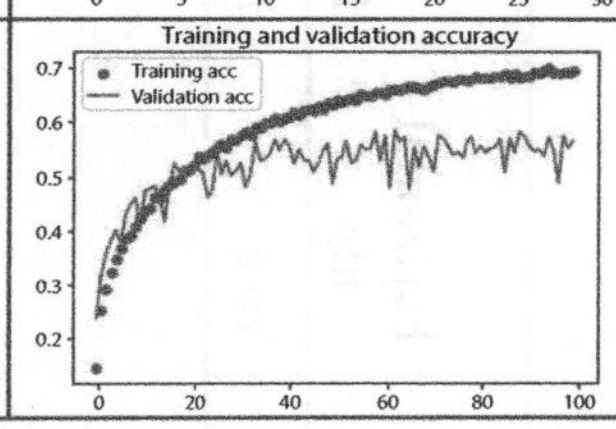	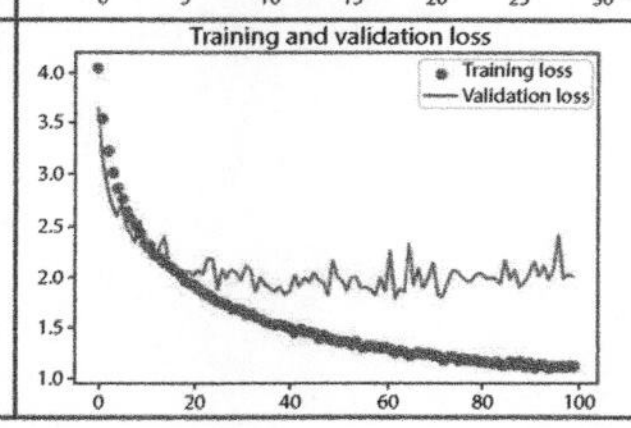

Figure 14.6 Comparative analysis of training and validation accuracy and loss using data augmentation for base CNN model.

14.3.2.5 Determining Similarity

After producing vectors for the dataset, this work approximates nearby vectors. There exist numerous approaches for computing vector similarity; however, the following are the most widely used ones:

Cosine Similarity: It measures the cosine angle between vectors. It ranges between −1 and 1, where 1 denotes exact similarity and −1 denotes the dissimilarity. For the feature space $\mathbb{R}^D$, we denote it as follows:

$$\cos(p,q) = (p.q)/(\|p\| * \|q\|) \tag{14.3}$$

For instance, consider two image feature vectors, x=[0.2,0.5,0.8,0.1,04] and y=[0.6,0.3,0.2,0.9,0.5] as shown in Figure 14.7, the dot product and Euclidean norm between two features are 0.72 and 1.0488. Therefore, the cosine similarity is approximately 0.56.

Euclidean Distance: It is a widely used metric to measure the distance between two vectors in a multidimensional space. To achieve this, consider

Table 14.2 The sample parameters for data augmentation.

Parameter	**rotation_range**	**width_shift_range**	**height_shift_range**	**zoom_range**	**horizontal_filp**	**fill_mode**	**Random_flip**	**Random rotation**
Value	0.2	0.2	0.2	0.2	True	Nearest	Horizontal	0.2

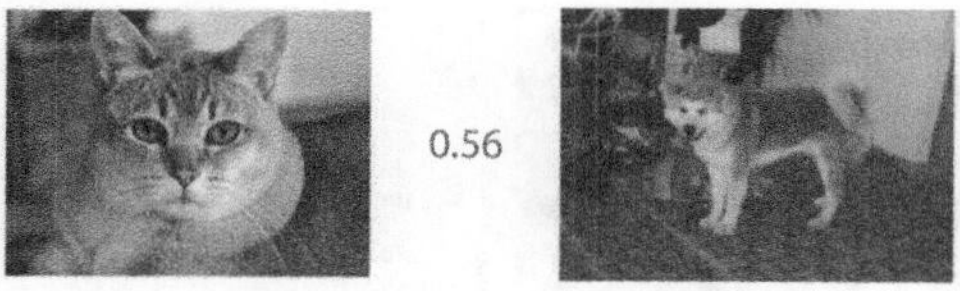

Figure 14.7 Computed similarity between the query image and the image in the dataset.

the feature space $\mathbb{R}^D$ and signify it as $dist(p,q) = \|p-q\|_2$. Let the training set $\{p_1, p_1, \ldots p_n\}$ be a set of features that the sequential search solves nearby features using the following:

$$dist(p,q_i) \leq dist(p,q_{i+1}) \tag{14.4}$$

For instance, for the same feature vectors in Figure 14.7, the computed squared difference between the two features (i.e., $\|p-q\|_2$) is [0.16,0.04,0.36,0.64,0.01] and its sum is equal to 1.21. The computed Euclidean distance is approximately 0.47.

Locality Sensitive Hashing: It is a family of approaches used for nearby neighbor search that maps feature vectors to hash buckets such that identical data fall into the same bucket, while dissimilar data may fall in different buckets [19]. This could be attained by using random projections using $h(x) = floor(x.r+b)/w$, where $h(x)$ denotes the hash code for a given feature vector which holds a dot product, r is a random projection, b is offset, and w is the width of a hash bucket. For a new query, $x \rightarrow h(x) \rightarrow Bucket$, and computes that x be held in a certain slot [20].

14.4 Experimental Results and Analysis

In this section, we have offered a detailed description of the dataset and experimental results achieved using the proposed ICFELSH approach.

14.4.1 Dataset

This paper selects a widely used image retrieval dataset, "Caltech 101." This dataset comprises images from 101 object groups (e.g., "lotus," "chair," and "lamps"), a total of 8677 images. For every image group, there are about 30 to 800 images shown in Figure 14.8, while most groups have about 30

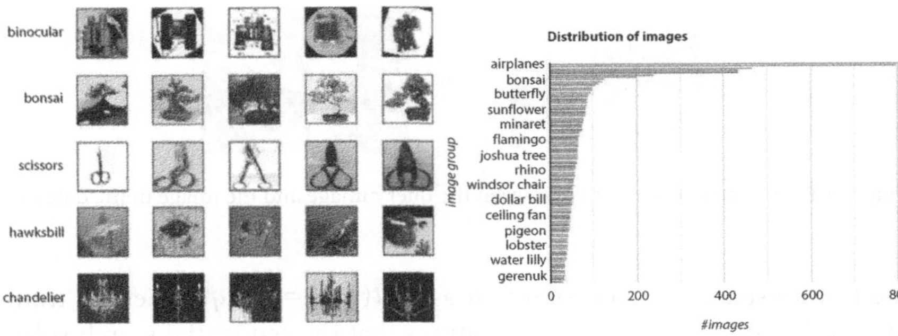

Figure 14.8 Sample group distribution of images in the dataset.

images with a resolution of 300 × 400 pixels. Five samples of five groups are shown in Figure 14.8.

14.4.2 Performance Evolution

Python is used for coding environments. Other libraries used include sklearn, matplotlib, Keras, and TensorFlow. This dataset is split into training and validation images.

The key element in suggesting nearby product images is a feature descriptor that includes image-fetching features to help differentiate identical images from others. To evaluate the quality of our model, use root mean square error (RMSE) and the mean average precision (mAP). The goal would be to minimize this and improve the accuracy of the model. The experiments attempt to reveal that the mAP and RMSE measures decrease when the proposed approach is applied can be figured as follows [21]:

$$mAP = \frac{\#\,relavant\ images\ fetched}{\#\,Total\ images\ fetched} \tag{14.5}$$

$$Recall = \frac{\#\,relavant\ images\ fetched}{\#\,Total\ images\ fetched\ in\ the\ dataset} \tag{14.6}$$

$$RMSE = \sqrt{\frac{\sum_{i=1}^{N}(Predicted_i - Actual_i)}{N}} \tag{14.7}$$

Table 14.3 Sample accuracy per category of different models on the Caltech-101 dataset.

Approach/# images	Airplane	Motorbikes	Faces	Watch	Leopard	Bonsai	Car_side	Ketch	chandelier	hawksbill	grand_piano	brain	butterfly	helicopter	menorah	Average accuracy
Baseline CNN	0.7	0.66	0.67	0.7	0.64	0.67	0.4	0.52	0.52	0.58	0.43	0.55	0.57	0.45	0.67	68
R-Drop CNN	0.8	0.7	0.7	0.8	0.74	0.77	0.4	0.6	0.52	0.68	0.63	0.65	0.67	0.50	0.67	72
ResNet-50 [25]	0.98	0.99	0.97	0.99	0.94	0.97	0.87	0.86	0.92	0.88	0.83	0.95	0.86	0.90	0.74	89
The Proposed ICFELSH	1.0	1.0	1.0	0.99	1.0	0.99	1.0	0.98	0.98	0.98	1.0	0.97	0.95	0.954	0.96	96

We compare the proposed approach with three different current recommender models to prove the efficiency of our approach. The three evaluation methods are Baseline CNN, R-Drop CNN, ResNet-50, and ICFELSH (CNN Resnet-50+LSH). Among the three models, the CNN model combined with the Euclidean and Cosine similarity algorithms can attain fast retrieval of nearby matching images. The R-Drop CNN model uses Regularization and Dropout to prevent complex transformation of training data. The CNN ResNet-50 [22] pre-trained model is an improved model to fetch features and additionally uses different similarity metrics to build a ranking for searching. It is the best choice to combine these models and use the LSH for building an index for searching. We reproduce this in our proposed approach ICFELSH. Table 14.3 shows the changing accuracy of 15 categories of the dataset against all considerable models.

According to Table 14.3, for the same category, the proposed approach is superior to CNN and other models. At the same time, the retrieval time of every category decreases as shown in Table 14.4, without losing mAP. In the considered dataset, the mAP of this work is about 19% higher than that of CNN models. In the same way, the retrieval time of every category of the database is compared with that of other algorithms shown in Table 14.4.

Table 14.4 shows the retrieval time of four approaches on the Caltech-101 dataset. Based on the CNN models, the retrieval time is the longest, and the retrieval time of the proposed approach is knowingly lower than that of R-Drop CNN and RestNet-50 [23]. This significant increase in retrieval

Table 14.4 Sample retrieval time per category of different models on the Caltech-101 dataset.

	Airplane	Motorbikes	Faces	Watch	Leopard	Bonsai	Car_side	Ketch	chandelier	hawksbill	grand_piano	brain	butterfly	helicopter	menorah	Total time
Baseline CNN	10	9	6	5	3	2	1	1	1	1	1	1	0	1	1	44.6
R-Drop CNN	9	9	5	5	2	2	1	1	1	1	1	1	0	1	1	41.7
ResNet-50	7	7	4	4	1	1	1	1	1	1	1	1	0	1	1	35.2
The Proposed ICFELSH	3	3	2	1	1	1	0	1	0	0	0	1	0	1	1	15.8

Table 14.5 Sample accuracy per category of different models on the Caltech-101 dataset.

Approach	Authors in [8]	Baseline CNN [24, 25]	R-Drop CNN	ResNet-50 [19]	The proposed ICFELSH
Accuracy	0.71	0.73	0.76	0.89	0.92
Loss	3.26	3.86	2.21	1.91	1.36
mAP	0.73	0.95	0.863	0.92	0.96
Recall	0.701	0.96	0.775	0.84	0.85
Euclidean mAP (Eq. 14.4) [21]	0.682	0.715	0.817	0.84	0.90
Cosine mAP (Eq. 14.3) [21]	0.701	0.792	0.832	0.89	0.91

Table 14.6 Computed accuracy with different bucket lengths number of hash tables.

Bucket Length & # Hash Tables	g=20 h=20 h=40 h=60	g=40 h=20 h=40 h=60 h=80	g=60 h=20 h=40 h=60 h=80	g=80 h=20 h=40 h=60 h=80 h=100	g=100 h=20 h=40 h=60 h=80 h=100	g=120 h=20 h=40 h=60 h=80 h=100 h=120
mAP	0.46	0.45	0.44	0.43	0.42	0.41

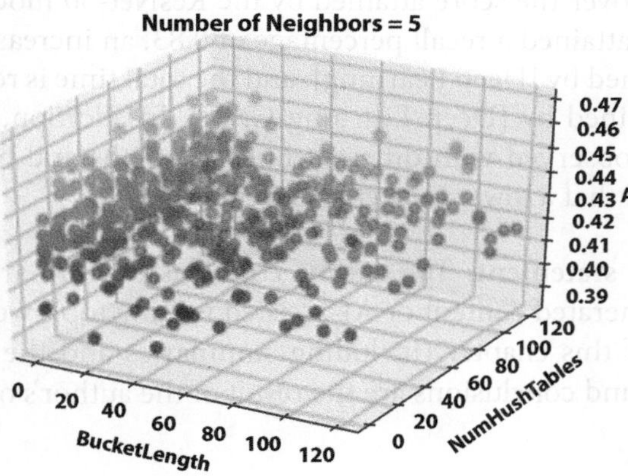

efficiency is the adoption of CNN ResNet-50 for feature extraction and LSH similarity metric. Likewise, we compute the similarity distance between the features extracted from CNN models with the Euclidean and Cosine as shown in Table 14.5.

ICFELSH adopts CNN ResNet-50 to extract features and calculate an LSH search, by varying the Bucket length (g) and Hash table (h) shown in Table 14.6. Moreover, it is interesting that lower bucket values become sparse while increasing the mAP.

14.5 Conclusion

The proposed approach offered a novel approach to recommend nearby images through transfer learning (or embedding), named ICFELSH. This method is based on the incorporation of pre-trained CNN ResNet-50 features to provide a robust, sturdy representation of images. For this purpose, numerous processing methods are employed, including dimensionality reduction, feature normalization, and data augmentation. Later, these features are combined to extract high-dimensional features. In addition, Euclidean, Cosine, and LSH techniques were used as the similarity measure to extract images that are indeed similar to the query image. The proposed approach is relevant to various provisions of RS and specific to the "Accuracy" and the "Recall." The results of experimental results on the Caltech-101 dataset confirm the performance advantage of LSH (while keeping the accuracy high) against traditional Euclidean, Cosine metrics.

On the Caltech 101 dataset, the precision score is 96%, an improvement of around 7% over the score attained by the ResNet-50 model. Moreover, this approach attained a recall percentage of 0.83, an increase of 0.12 over the score attained by [Deep Learning], and the total time is reduced to 15.8 from 44.6 attained by [Deep Learning CNN]. In addition, the precision accuracy was observed with different bucket lengths and hash functions and concluded that a lower bucket is preferable.

AI disclosure statement: The author confirms that no artificial intelligence (AI)-generated content or AI-assisted writing tools were used in the preparation of this chapter (including summaries and the abstract). All text, analysis, and conclusions are the result of the author's original work.

References

1. Tkalcic, M., Kunaver, M., Tasic, J., Košir, A., Personality based user similarity measure for a collaborative recommender system, in: *Proceedings of the 5th Workshop on Emotion in Human-Computer Interaction-Real world challenges*, pp. 30–37, 2009, September.
2. Yang, D., Zhang, J., Wang, S., Zhang, X., A time-aware CNN-based personalized recommender system. *Complexity*, 2019, 1–11, 2019.
3. Jouyandeh, F. and Zadeh, P.M., IPARS: An Image-based Personalized Advertisement Recommendation System on Social Networks. *Procedia Comput. Sci.*, 201, 375–382, 2022.
4. Li, X., Yang, J., Ma, J., Recent developments of content-based image retrieval (CBIR). *Neurocomputing*, 452, 675–689, 2021.
5. Gupta, J., Pathak, S., Kumar, G., Deep learning (CNN) and transfer learning: a review, in: *Journal of Physics: Conference Series*, vol. 2273, IOP Publishing, p. 012029, 2022, May.
6. Chen, L., Yang, F., Yang, H., Image-based product recommendation system with convolutional neural networks, 2017.

7. Bansal, M., Kumar, M., Sachdeva, M., Mittal, A., Transfer learning for image classification using VGG19: Caltech-101 image data set, in: *Journal of ambient intelligence and humanized computing*, pp. 1–12, 2021.
8. Alamdari, P.M., Navimipour, N.J., Hosseinzadeh, M., Safaei, A.A., Darwesh, A., An image-based product recommendation for E-commerce applications using convolutional neural networks. *Acta Informatica Pragensia*, 11, 1, 15–35, 2022.
9. Tuinhof, H., Pirker, C., Haltmeier, M., Image-based fashion product recommendation with deep learning, in: *Machine Learning, Optimization, and Data Science: 4th International Conference, LOD 2018*, Volterra, Italy, September 13-16, 2018, vol. Revised Selected Papers 4, Springer International Publishing, pp. 472–481, 2019.
10. Rizkallah, S., Atiya, A.F., Shaheen, S., New Vector-Space Embeddings for Recommender Systems. *Appl. Sci.*, 11, 14, 64, 2021.
11. Hoang, B.N.M., Vy, H.T.H., Hong, T.G., Hang, V.T.M., Nhung, H.L.T.K., Using Bert Embedding to improve memory-based collaborative filtering recommender systems, in: *2021 RIVF International Conference on Computing and Communication Technologies (RIVF)*, IEEE, pp. 1–6, 2021, August.
12. Almasharawi, M. and Bulut, A., Estimating user response rate using locality sensitive hashing in search marketing. *Electron. Commerce Res.*, 22, 1, 37–51, 2022.
13. Durmaz, O. and Bilge, H.S., Fast image similarity search by distributed locality sensitive hashing. *Pattern Recognit. Lett.*, 128, 361–369, 2019.
14. Samagaio, A.M., Lopes Cardoso, H., Ribeiro, D., Enriching word embeddings with food knowledge for ingredient retrieval, in: *3rd Conference on Language, Data and Knowledge (LDK 2021)*, Schloss Dagstuhl-Leibniz-Zentrum für Informatik, 2021.
15. Nidhya, R., Kalpana, R., Smilarubavathy, G., Keerthana, S.M., Brain Tumor Diagnosis with MCNN-Based MRI Image Analysis, in: *2023 1st International Conference on Optimization Techniques for Learning (ICOTL)*, IEEE, pp. 1–5, 2023, December.
16. Baltescu, P., Chen, H., Pancha, N., Zhai, A., Leskovec, J., Rosenberg, C., ItemSage: Learning product embeddings for shopping recommendations at pinterest, in: *Proceedings of the 28th ACM SIGKDD Conference on Knowledge Discovery and Data Mining*, pp. 2703–2711, 2022 August.
17. Sayed, M.S., Gad-Elrab, A.A., Fathy, K.A., Raslan, K.R., Unsupervised Content Based Image Retrieval Using Pre-Trained CNN and PCNN Features Extractors. *Int. J. Intell. Eng. Syst.*, 16, 1, 2023.
18. Vasudevan, S., Chauhan, N., Sarobin, V., Geetha, S., Image-based recommendation engine using VGG model, in: *International Conference on Advanced Communication and Computational Technology*, pp. 257–265, Springer Nature Singapore, Singapore, 2019, December.

19. Luo, Y., Li, W., Ma, X., Zhang, K., Image Retrieval Algorithm Based on Locality-Sensitive Hash Using Convolutional Neural Network and Attention Mechanism. *Information*, 13, 10, 446, 2022.
20. Zhang, K., Fan, S., Wang, H.J., An efficient recommender system using locality sensitive hashing, 2018.
21. Parola, M., Nannini, A., Poleggi, S., Web image search engine based on LSH index and CNN Resnet50. *arXiv preprint arXiv:2108.13301*, 2021.
22. Sulthana, A.R., Gupta, M., Subramanian, S., Mirza, S., Improvising the performance of image-based recommendation system using convolution neural networks and deep learning. *Soft Comput.*, 24, 19, 14531–14544, 2020.
23. Zangerle, E. and Bauer, C., Evaluating recommender systems: survey and framework. *ACM Comput. Surv.*, 55, 8, 1–38, 2022.
24. Rafidison, M.A., Ramafiarisona, H.M., Randriamitantsoa, P.A., Rafanantenana, S.H.J., Toky, F.M.R., Rakotondrazaka, L.P., Rakotomihamina, A.H., Image Classification Based on Light Convolutional Neural Network Using Pulse Couple Neural Network, in: *Computational Intelligence and Neuroscience*, 20232023.
25. Chauhan, R., Ghanshala, K.K., Joshi, R.C., Convolutional neural network (CNN) for image detection and recognition, in: *2018 First International Conference on Secure Cyber Computing and Communication (ICSCCC)*, IEEE, pp. 278–282, 2018, December.

15

Adversarial Architectures and BERT for Mitigating Gender Bias in Word Embeddings towards Ethical AI Systems

Saraswathi Rangaraju[1]*, P. Lakshmilavanya[2], Karunsagar Kanda[3], Bh. Padma[4], Kothapalli Ramesh Chandra[5] and Jyothi N. M.[6]

[1]*Humanities and Sciences (English), CMR Engineering College, Kandlakoya, Telangana, India*

[2]*Freshman Engineering Department (English), P.V.P. Siddhartha Institute of Technology, Kanuru, Andhra Pradesh, India*

[3]*English Department, Anil Neerukonda Institute of Technology and Sciences, Visakhapatnam, Andhra Pradesh, India*

[4]*Computer Science and Engineering, Gayatri Vidya Parishad College for Degree and PG Courses (Autonomous), Visakhapatnam, Andhra Pradesh, India*

[5]*Electronics and Communication Engineering, Vishnu Institute of Technology, Bhimavaram, Andhra Pradesh, India*

[6]*Computer Science Engineering, Koneru Lakshmaiah Education Foundation, Vaddeswaram, Andhra Pradesh, India*

Abstract

Gender bias in word embeddings poses significant challenges in developing fair and ethical AI systems, as these embeddings influence decision-making processes in applications like recruitment, healthcare, and education. This research aims to mitigate gender bias while preserving the semantic integrity of embeddings by proposing a novel approach that combines adversarial networks with BERT-based contextual embeddings. Traditional methods, such as projection-based techniques, often compromise the usability of embeddings in downstream NLP tasks. In contrast, the proposed framework leverages the dynamic adaptability of BERT and the iterative learning process of adversarial networks to achieve superior bias reduction. The effectiveness of the method is demonstrated through metrics like WEFAT scores, showing significant bias neutralization, and qualitative analyses, such as shifts in word associations. Additionally, the framework ensures scalability

**Corresponding author*: rangaraju.saraswathi@gmail.com

R. Nidhya, A. Dineshkumar, Sheng-Lung Peng, S. Karthik and S. Balamurugan (eds.) Neuro-Symbolic Artificial Intelligence: Concepts & Applications, (291–316) © 2026 Scrivener Publishing LLC

and applicability to real-world NLP scenarios. The results underline the importance of integrating fairness and inclusivity into AI systems, contributing to the development of trustworthy and unbiased technologies.

Keywords: Gender bias, word embeddings, BERT, adversarial networks, ethical AI

15.1 Introduction

Artificial intelligence (AI) has transformed numerous domains, but it has also brought critical ethical challenges, particularly regarding gender bias. Gender bias in AI systems often arises from the word embeddings used in Natural Language Processing (NLP), which encode societal biases present in training data. This bias manifests in real-world applications like recruitment, healthcare, and education, perpetuating harmful stereotypes and leading to unfair decision-making. Static word embeddings, such as Word2Vec and GloVe, are especially prone to such biases due to their fixed representations of relationships between words [13, 14]. Although contextual models like BERT and ELMo dynamically adjust word meanings based on context and have improved NLP performance, studies reveal that they too can inherit biases from training data [5, 6, 15]. Addressing these biases is critical to ensuring fairness and inclusivity in AI systems, especially in applications where ethical considerations are paramount.

Adversarial networks offer a promising solution by iteratively refining embeddings to reduce bias while preserving semantic properties. When combined with BERT's contextual adaptability, adversarial learning provides a robust framework for bias mitigation [16, 17]. This study presents a novel approach that leverages both adversarial networks and BERT to address gender bias in word embeddings, outperforming traditional projection-based techniques that often compromise semantic richness. By integrating quantitative evaluations, such as WEFAT scores, with qualitative analyses, including shifts in word associations, the proposed framework achieves a balance between neutrality and semantic integrity [21, 22]. These contributions support the development of ethical AI systems capable of fair decision-making across diverse NLP applications. This work not only mitigates gender bias but also sets the foundation for building trustworthy and inclusive AI systems.

15.2 Literature Survey

Contextual word embeddings significantly enhance the semantic understanding in NLP tasks by capturing nuanced meanings and relationships between words. The study demonstrates the effectiveness of fine-tuning pre-trained models like BERT and GPT on downstream tasks such as sentiment analysis and question answering. However, the computational complexity and resource requirements of these models remain significant limitations [1]. Explainable AI techniques applied to word embeddings aim to improve interpretability in embedding-driven NLP tasks. This work evaluates models such as Word2Vec, GloVe, and contextual embeddings, proposing a novel framework for embedding transparency. While enhancing interpretability, the challenge of balancing performance with explainability in practical applications remains unresolved [2].

The impact of embedding models such as Word2Vec, GloVe, and fastText on deep learning tasks is extensively reviewed, focusing on their role in text classification, summarization, and machine translation. The paper highlights performance bottlenecks, especially in low-resource languages, and identifies the lack of standardized benchmarks for cross-model comparisons as a key limitation.

An in-depth analysis of Word2Vec embeddings is presented, showcasing the use of negative sampling and hierarchical SoftMax for efficient learning. The study emphasizes the mathematical framework and training methodologies while identifying limitations in handling polysemy and dynamic contexts [4, 17]. Efforts to create large-scale word embeddings for low-resourced languages are discussed, proposing novel methods for scalable and efficient embedding generation. The study highlights improvements in language understanding and task-specific performance but notes the lack of high-quality training data as a persistent challenge [5, 15]. The survey on contextual embeddings outlines advancements in embedding techniques, including BERT, ELMo, and GPT, which capture word meanings in dynamic contexts. These models demonstrate state-of-the-art performance across NLP tasks; however, their interpretability and computational cost remain significant drawbacks [3, 6, 18]. Comparative analysis of word embeddings reveals the strengths and weaknesses of models like GloVe, Word2Vec, and fastText in capturing semantic similarities. While GloVe excels in overall contextual representation, fastText outperforms in morphology-rich languages. Limitations include the static nature of embeddings, which fail to adapt to polysemy [7, 19].

The fusion of contextual word embeddings with concreteness estimation metrics is explored to improve downstream NLP tasks such as machine translation. By combining statistical and contextual methods, the paper achieves improved accuracy; however, scalability to large datasets remains a concern [8, 20]. Advancements in sentiment analysis are facilitated by refined global word embeddings based on sentiment concepts. These embeddings integrate domain-specific features for better task performance but require additional computational resources, making deployment on edge devices challenging [9]. The use of fuzzy logic in enriching word embeddings is investigated to enhance natural language understanding. The paper proposes hybrid embeddings combining statistical and fuzzy representations, leading to improved accuracy in sentiment analysis and classification tasks. Scalability to high-dimensional datasets remains a limitation [10].

Deep contextualized embeddings like ELMo are analyzed for their ability to represent polysemous words dynamically. The study highlights their success in improving question answering and summarization tasks but identifies high computational costs as a significant drawback [11]. FastText embeddings are explored for their capability to encode subword information, enhancing performance in low-resource and morphology-rich languages. The lightweight nature of fastText allows it to operate efficiently, but its limitations in capturing dynamic contexts are noted [12, 21]. The Universal Sentence Encoder is evaluated for its ability to generate task-agnostic sentence embeddings. It demonstrates exceptional performance across classification and similarity tasks, though challenges in fine-tuning for domain-specific tasks are identified [13]. GloVe embeddings are reviewed for their ability to encode word relationships based on co-occurrence statistics. The study emphasizes their efficiency in large-scale training but notes that they fail to capture dynamic contextual nuances effectively [14, 22].

Word2Vec embeddings are analyzed for their scalability and efficiency in generating dense vector representations. The use of skip-gram and continuous bag-of-words models leads to robust embeddings but fails to address polysemy and evolving semantics [16, 23].

The evolution of word embeddings from static models like Word2Vec and GloVe to contextual embeddings such as BERT, ELMo, and GPT has significantly enhanced semantic and syntactic representation in NLP tasks, addressing challenges like polysemy and contextual adaptation. Techniques such as sentiment-specific embeddings, domain-specific fine-tuning, and fuzzy logic integration have further expanded their application to specialized tasks like sentiment analysis and low-resource language processing.

However, their ability to address ethical challenges, such as gender bias, remains underexplored. Bias mitigation methods like projection-based neutralization, which remove gender components from embeddings, often compromise semantic integrity. Adversarial networks offer iterative refinement of embeddings but require careful tuning to avoid overcorrection that distorts semantic properties. While promising, these approaches remain resource-intensive and lack a balance between bias removal and semantic preservation, highlighting the need for more effective solutions.

Current methods for addressing gender bias in embeddings have focused largely on static models like GloVe, leaving contextual models like BERT underexplored. Techniques like projection-based neutralization often compromise semantic richness, reducing the effectiveness of debiased embeddings in real-world tasks. Many approaches rely heavily on metrics like cosine similarity and WEFAT while neglecting qualitative evaluations of word associations and downstream performance. Scalability and the lack of ethical frameworks further limit the adoption of these strategies in diverse domains.

The proposed approach combines adversarial networks and contextual embeddings like BERT to dynamically address gender bias while preserving semantic integrity. It balances bias removal with usability, ensuring that embeddings perform effectively in downstream tasks. By integrating quantitative metrics with qualitative evaluations, the framework provides a comprehensive assessment of its effectiveness. Prioritizing scalability and adaptability, this approach addresses existing limitations and advances ethical, inclusive AI systems.

15.3 Methodology

15.3.1 Dataset Description

The dataset utilized in this study focuses on analyzing gender bias in pretrained GloVe word embeddings. These embeddings, trained on large text corpora such as the 2014 Wikipedia dump and the Gigaword 5 dataset, represent words as high-dimensional vectors based on their co-occurrence patterns. The dataset includes curated lists of male- and female-associated terms, such as names, professions, and adjectives, which are used to evaluate gender associations in the embeddings. Cosine similarity metrics are employed to quantify the extent of alignment between gendered terms and various words, revealing implicit biases embedded in the model.

This dataset provides a benchmark for assessing the inherent gender bias in static word embeddings. Its structured methodology enables systematic identification of biased patterns and serves as a foundation for exploring mitigation strategies. The pre-trained embeddings and word lists make it a valuable resource for experiments aimed at addressing ethical concerns in natural language processing systems.

15.3.2 Pre-Processing

Loading Pre-trained Word Embeddings: The pre-trained GloVe embeddings were loaded from the glove.6B.200d.txt file, which contains 200-dimensional word vectors for a wide range of terms. Pre-trained embeddings provide a rich representation of semantic relationships, enabling the analysis of inherent biases.

Each word w_i in the GloVe embeddings file is represented by a 200-dimensional vector V_{ii}:

$$V_i = \{v_1, v_2, \ldots, v_n\}, v_i \in R^{200} \tag{15.1}$$

where V_i denotes the embedding vector of the i_{th} word and n is the total number of words in the embeddings. Figure 15.1 shows the word embedding.

Normalization of Word Vectors: The embeddings were normalized to have unit length, ensuring consistency in cosine similarity calculations. Normalization focuses comparisons on the angular relationships between vectors, eliminating the influence of vector magnitude and enhancing interpretability. Figure 15.2 shows the sample vector.

$$v_{norm} = v \,/\, ||v|| \tag{15.2}$$

$$||v|| = \sqrt{\sum_{i=1}^{200} v_i^2} \tag{15.3}$$

```
embeddings = {
    "king": [0.215, 0.463, -0.249, ..., 0.145],
    "queen": [0.191, 0.398, -0.225, ..., 0.136],
    "apple": [0.096, -0.032, 0.298, ..., -0.058]
}
```

Figure 15.1 Word embedding.

```
Original Vector (v_doctor): [ 3  4 12]
Magnitude of v_doctor (||v||): 13.0
Normalized Vector (v_doctor_norm): [0.23076923 0.30769231 0.92307692]
```

Figure 15.2 Word vector.

where

v is the original word vector in the embedding space, represented as a 200-dimensional vector from the GloVe embeddings.

v_{norm} is the normalized word vector.

||v|| is the Euclidean norm (magnitude) of the vector v.

Defining Gendered and Non-gendered Terms: Words were categorized into gendered terms (e.g., "he," "she," "man," "woman") and non-gendered terms (e.g., "doctor," "engineer," "teacher"). This categorization allowed the identification of the gender direction, defined as the vector difference between the embeddings of "he" and "she." The gender direction serves as the axis along which gender bias is embedded in the vector space, enabling its quantification and mitigation. Figure 15.3 shows the cosine similarity.

$$\text{Gender direction} \quad g = v_{\text{he}} - v_{\text{she}} \tag{15.4}$$

$$\text{Cosine similarity } cos(\theta) = (v_{\text{term}} \cdot g) / (||v_{\text{term}}|| \, ||g||) \tag{15.5}$$

where

G is the gender direction in the vector space, calculated as the difference between the embeddings of "he" and "she."

v_{he} and v_{she} are the word vectors for the gendered terms "he" and "she."

v_{term} is the vector for a non-gendered term (e.g., "doctor" or "engineer").

cos(θ) is the cosine similarity, measuring the alignment between a non-gendered term and the gender direction.

```
Vector for 'he' (v_he): [2 5 8]
Vector for 'she' (v_she): [1 4 7]
Gender Direction (g): [1 1 1]
Vector for 'doctor' (v_doctor): [ 3  4 12]
Cosine Similarity (cos(theta)): 0.8438196242002224
```

Figure 15.3 Cosine similarity.

The Word Embedding Factual Association Test (WEFAT): It is a method to quantify bias in word embeddings by measuring the difference in alignment between target words and gendered attribute vectors. It identifies how strongly non-gendered terms, such as "doctor" or "nurse," align with male or female directions in the embedding space. In this study, WEFAT was used to compare the bias present in embeddings before and after applying mitigation techniques. The test calculates cosine similarity for each target word with male and female attribute vectors, recording the difference as a numeric score. Higher scores indicate stronger alignment with male terms, while lower scores suggest alignment with female terms. By highlighting changes in WEFAT scores, the results demonstrate the effectiveness of adversarial networks and BERT-based strategies in reducing bias, providing an interpretable and quantitative metric to validate the success of the proposed approach.

Neutralizing Non-gendered Terms: Non-gendered terms were neutralized by projecting them orthogonally to the gender direction, effectively removing their alignment with gendered semantics. The projection-based neutralization ensures that non-gendered terms, such as "doctor" or "nurse," no longer exhibit associations with "he" or "she." This technique preserves other semantic properties of the embeddings, ensuring that they remain useful for tasks unrelated to gender. Figure 15.4 shows the neutralized vector.

$$\text{Neutralized Vector} \qquad v_{\text{neutral}} = v - projg(v) \tag{15.6}$$

$$\text{Projection on the gender direction } projg(v) = ((v \cdot g) / ||g||^2)g \tag{15.7}$$

where

v_{neutral} is the neutralized vector of the non-gendered term, where the gender component is removed.

```
Original Vector for 'doctor' (v_doctor): [ 3  4 12]
Gender Direction (g): [1 1 1]
Projection of 'doctor' onto g (proj_g(v)): [6.33333333 6.33333333 6.33333333]
Neutralized Vector for 'doctor' (v_doctor_neutral): [-3.33333333 -2.33333333  5.66666667]
```

Figure 15.4 Neutralized vector.

```
Vector for 'doctor' (v_doctor): [ 3  4 12]
Vector for 'work' (v_work): [2 6 8]
Cosine Similarity (doctor, work): 0.950408962592738
Semantic Integrity Metric (for 1 term): 0.950408962592738
```

Figure 15.5 Semantic integrity.

$proj_g(v)$ is the projection of the vector v onto the gender direction g. This represents the gender component of the vector.

Semantic Integrity Check: To validate the neutralization process, the semantic integrity of embeddings was assessed. The cosine similarity of non-gendered terms with neutral reference terms (e.g., "work," "knowledge," "intelligence") was computed before and after neutralization. Minimal changes in these similarity scores indicate that the semantic meaning of non-gendered terms was preserved during bias mitigation. The semantic integrity metric provides evidence that embeddings remain robust for downstream tasks after undergoing the neutralization process. Figure 15.5 shows the semantic integrity.

$$S = (1/N)\sum_{(i=1)}^{(N)}((v_i \cdot r)/(||v_i||\,||r||)) \tag{15.8}$$

where

S is the Semantic Integrity Metric.

r is the vector of a reference term (e.g., "work," "knowledge," "intelligence").

15.3.3 BERT Embedding Generation

BERT (Bidirectional Encoder Representations from Transformers) is a pre-trained deep learning model that generates contextual word embeddings. Unlike static embeddings like GloVe, BERT embeddings capture the context of a word based on the sentence it appears in, making them highly effective for tasks involving polysemy or context-dependent word meanings. Figure 15.6(a) shows the BERT architecture, and Figure 15.6(b) shows the word representation.

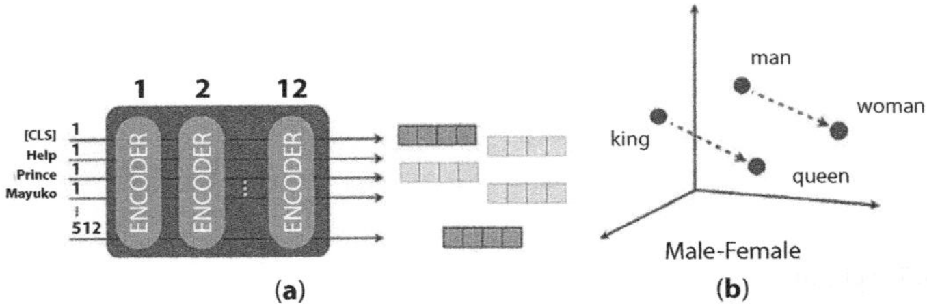

Figure 15.6 (a) BERT architecture. (b) Word representation.

Steps:

1. Tokenize the input text into subwords using the BERT tokenizer, add special tokens [CLS] and [SEP], and ensure that the token sequences are padded or truncated to a fixed length.
2. Load a pre-trained BERT model, such as Bert-base-uncased, along with its corresponding tokenizer.
3. Convert the tokenized input into tensors and pass these tensors through the BERT model to compute embeddings.
4. Extract token-level embeddings from the model's last hidden state or retrieve the [CLS] token embedding for sentence-level tasks.
5. Use the embeddings for word-level analysis, bias detection, or sentence-level tasks, or save them for further processing.

$$\text{Input Tokens} \quad T = \{t_1, t_2, \ldots, t_n\} \tag{15.9}$$

$$\text{Token Embedding } E_t = E_{\text{token}} + E_{\text{seanent}} + E_{\text{position}} \tag{15.10}$$

$$\text{Attention} \qquad Attention(Q, K, V) = Softmax((QK^T) / \sqrt{}(d_k))V \tag{15.11}$$

$$\text{Final Output} \qquad H^L = \{h_{(n)}, h_{t1}, \ldots, h_{tn}, h_{(sep)}\} \tag{15.12}$$

Adversarial Neural Network: Adversarial Networks are composed of two main components: the Generator and the Discriminator. The generator aims to transform embeddings into a bias-free representation, while the discriminator tries to classify the embeddings based on their alignment with the gendered direction. These networks are trained in a competitive manner to achieve bias mitigation. Figure 15.7 shows the architecture of adversarial neural network. Architecture consists of the following:

Generator:
Input: Pre-trained word embeddings.
Layers: Fully connected layers with non-linear activation (e.g., ReLU or Leaky ReLU).
Output: Neutralized embeddings v′.

Discriminator:
Input: Output of the generator v′.
Layers: Fully connected layers with sigmoid activation at the output.
Output: Classification probability p (biased vs. unbiased).

$$\text{Generator } v' = G(v;\theta G) \tag{15.13}$$

$$\text{Discriminator } p = D(v';\theta D) \tag{15.14}$$

$$\text{Discriminator Loss } LD = -Ev[ylog(D(G(v))) + (1-y)\,log(1-D(G(v)))] \tag{15.15}$$

$$\text{Generator Loss} \quad LG = -Ev[log(1-D(G(v)))] \tag{15.16}$$

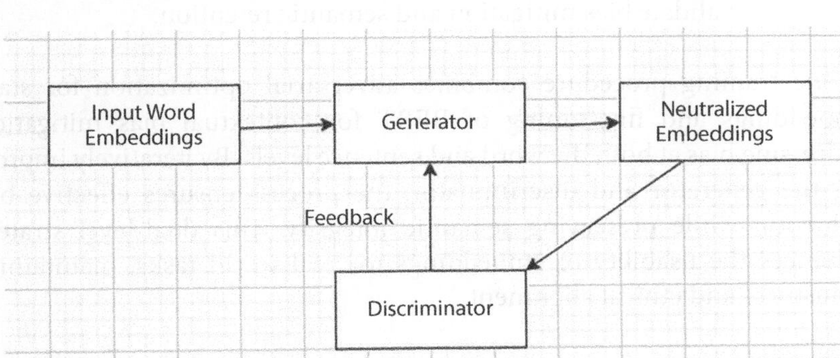

Figure 15.7 Architecture of adversarial neural network.

Training Procedure:

1. Load the GloVe 200-dimensional word embeddings from the Kaggle dataset and normalize them to ensure consistent vector magnitudes.
2. Identify gendered terms (e.g., "he," "she") and non-gendered terms (e.g., "doctor," "nurse") and compute the gender direction by subtracting the vector for "she" from "he."
3. Neutralize the embeddings of non-gendered terms by removing their projection onto the gender direction while retaining other semantic properties.
4. Refine the GloVe embeddings using adversarial networks, iteratively training a generator and discriminator to reduce gender bias while preserving semantic integrity.
5. Prepare a dataset of sentences exhibiting gender bias and tokenize them using the BERT tokenizer, adding [CLS] and [SEP] tokens.
6. Fine-tune a pre-trained BERT model by training it to classify sentences as biased or neutral and, where applicable, predict neutral replacements for gendered terms.
7. Use adversarial learning with BERT embeddings to further reduce context-specific biases, ensuring that the embeddings remain semantically rich.
8. Optimize both models using validation accuracy and loss monitoring, employing learning rate schedulers and dropout techniques to prevent overfitting.
9. Evaluate GloVe and BERT embeddings using metrics like WEFAT, cosine similarity, and qualitative neighbor analysis to validate bias mitigation and semantic retention.

The training procedure combines adversarial optimization for static embeddings and fine-tuning of BERT for contextual bias mitigation, addressing bias at both the word and sentence levels. By iteratively improving the generator and discriminator, the process ensures effective bias reduction while preserving semantic integrity. This dual-level strategy enhances the usability of embeddings for real-world tasks, maintaining robustness and ethical alignment.

15.4 Results

15.4.1 Visualizing Gender Bias in Static Embeddings

Bias Detection in Word Embeddings: This PCA scatter plot shown in Figure 15.8(a) visualizes word embeddings for selected gendered and non-gendered terms. It highlights the clustering of gendered terms such as "he" and "she" close to each other, while non-gendered terms like "engineer" and "nurse" are positioned along directions influenced by gender bias. This indicates the alignment of certain non-gendered terms with gendered directions.

15.4.2 Cosine Similarity Heatmap for Word Embeddings

Semantic Relationships in Word Embeddings: This heatmap in Figure 15.8(b) visualizes the pairwise cosine similarity between selected word embeddings. The diagonal values represent a perfect similarity score of 1, as each word is compared with itself. The varying intensity of colors off the diagonal highlights the relationship between words, revealing clusters of words that are semantically or contextually aligned. This analysis provides insights into the degree of alignment and bias among the selected terms.

15.4.3 PCA Visualization of Word Embeddings (2D)

Dimensionality Reduction for Word Embedding Analysis: This 2D PCA plot shown in Figure 15.9(a) represents the distribution of selected word embeddings in reduced dimensional space. Words are positioned based

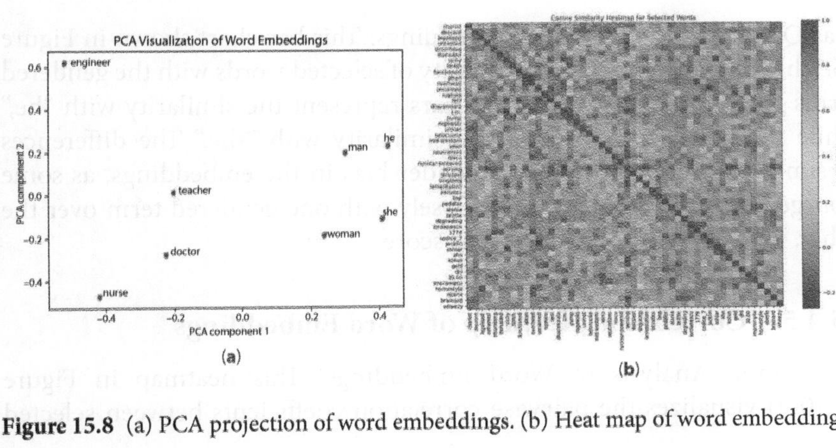

Figure 15.8 (a) PCA projection of word embeddings. (b) Heat map of word embeddings.

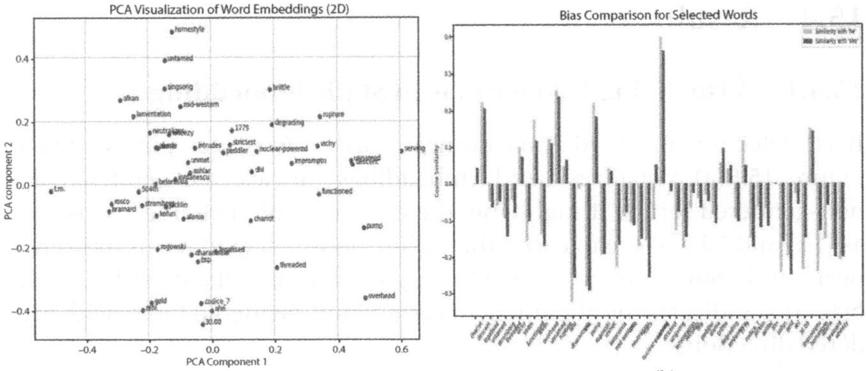

(a) (b)

```
Sample Bias Scores (Top 10):
Word: chariot, Similarity with 'he': 0.0010, Similarity with 'she': 0.0423
Word: descent, Similarity with 'he': 0.2221, Similarity with 'she': 0.2059
Word: legalised, Similarity with 'he': -0.0484, Similarity with 'she': -0.0638
Word: untamed, Similarity with 'he': -0.0593, Similarity with 'she': -0.0485
Word: stromberg, Similarity with 'he': -0.0943, Similarity with 'she': -0.1440
Word: threaded, Similarity with 'he': -0.0416, Similarity with 'she': -0.0793
Word: vichy, Similarity with 'he': 0.1010, Similarity with 'she': 0.0736
Word: 504th, Similarity with 'he': -0.1565, Similarity with 'she': -0.1022
Word: functioned, Similarity with 'he': 0.1748, Similarity with 'she': 0.1160
Word: alkan, Similarity with 'he': -0.1378, Similarity with 'she': -0.1693
```

(c)

Figure 15.9 (a) Dimensionality reduction of word embeddings. (b) Bias comparison. (c) Sample bias score.

on their semantic similarity, with clustering patterns indicating words that share contextual or semantic alignments. The visualization highlights potential relationships or biases embedded in the vector representations.

15.4.4 Bias Comparison for Selected Words

Bias Quantification in Word Embeddings: This bar chart shown in Figure 15.9(b) compares the cosine similarity of selected words with the gendered terms "he" and "she." The orange bars represent the similarity with "he," while the blue bars represent the similarity with "she." The differences in similarity highlight potential gender bias in the embeddings, as some non-gendered terms align more closely with one gendered term over the other. Figure 15.9(c) shows the bias score.

15.4.5 Correlation Heatmap of Word Embeddings

Correlation Analysis of Word Embeddings: This heatmap in Figure 15.10(a) visualizes the pairwise correlation coefficients between selected

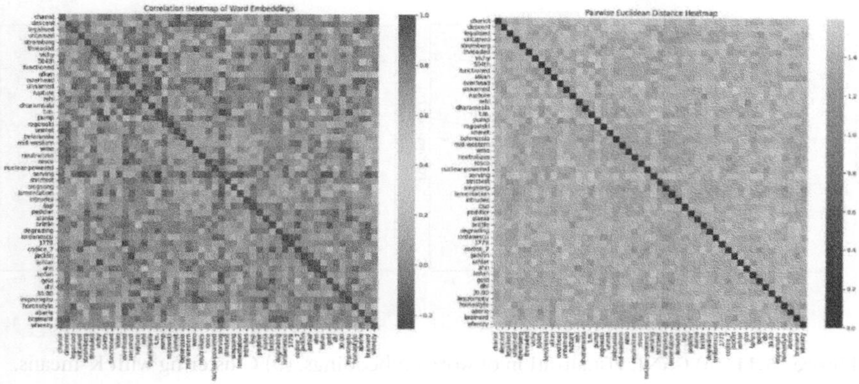

(a) (b)

Figure 15.10 (a) Pairwise correlation of word embeddings. (b) Pairwise Euclidean distance of word embeddings.

word embeddings. The diagonal represents perfect correlations (1.01.01.0) for each word with itself, while the off-diagonal values indicate the level of linear relationship between word pairs. Clusters with high correlations suggest semantic or contextual similarity among terms, which may also reveal patterns of bias.

15.4.6 Pairwise Euclidean Distance Heatmap of Word Embeddings

Distance-Based Analysis of Word Embeddings: This heatmap in Figure 15.10(b) visualizes the pairwise Euclidean distances between selected word embeddings. The diagonal values are zero, indicating no distance between a word and itself, while off-diagonal values represent the magnitude of differences between word pairs in the embedding space. Larger distances indicate less similarity between the embeddings of the respective terms.

15.4.7 t-SNE Visualization of Word Embeddings

Dimensionality Reduction and Clustering of Word Embeddings: This t-SNE plot provides a 2D visualization of high-dimensional word embeddings, capturing the relative similarities and dissimilarities among terms as shown in Figure 15.11(a). Clustering patterns reveal groups of words that share semantic or contextual properties, while dispersed points represent

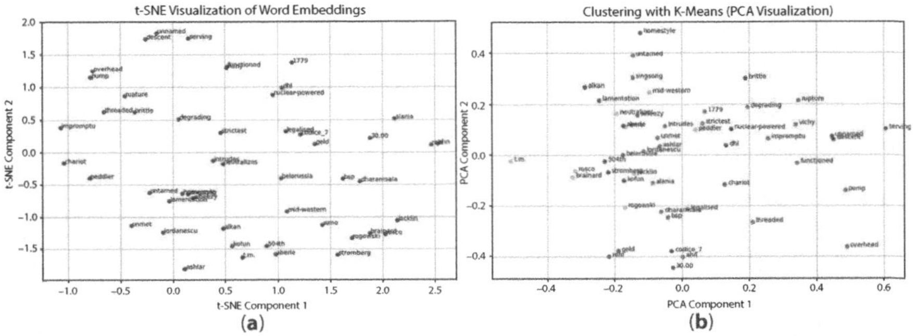

Figure 15.11 (a) t-SNE visualization of word embeddings. (b) Clustering with K-means.

less related terms. This visualization offers insights into how embeddings capture word relationships in reduced-dimensional space.

15.4.8 Clustering with K-Means (PCA Visualization)

Clustering Analysis of Word Embeddings: This PCA scatter plot shown in Figure 15.11(b) visualizes word embeddings grouped into clusters using the K-means algorithm. Each cluster is represented by a different color, highlighting semantic or contextual similarities among words. This clustering demonstrates how words with related meanings or usage tend to form groups in the embedding space after dimensionality reduction.

15.4.9 Gender Bias Identification and Mitigation Results

Impact of Bias Mitigation on Static Word Embeddings: The chart in Figure 15.12(a) visualizes gender bias in word embeddings before neutralization by showing the cosine similarity of selected non-gendered terms with gendered terms like "he" and "she." Positive or negative alignment reflects the degree of bias. The chart in Figure 15.12(b) displays the results after applying the adversarial network for bias mitigation, where cosine similarities are significantly reduced, indicating that the embeddings are more neutral and less biased.

15.4.10 Comparison of Gender Bias Before and After Neutralization (GloVe)

Effectiveness of Bias Mitigation on Static Word Embeddings: This bar chart in Figure 15.13 compares the cosine similarity of non-gendered terms like

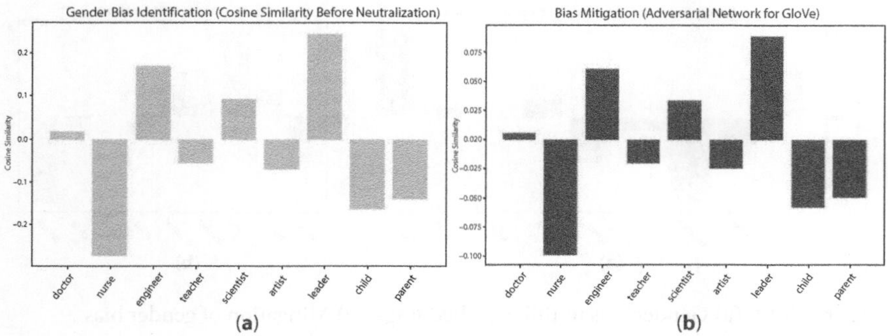

Figure 15.12 (a) Gender bias before neutralization. (b) Gender bias mitigation visualization.

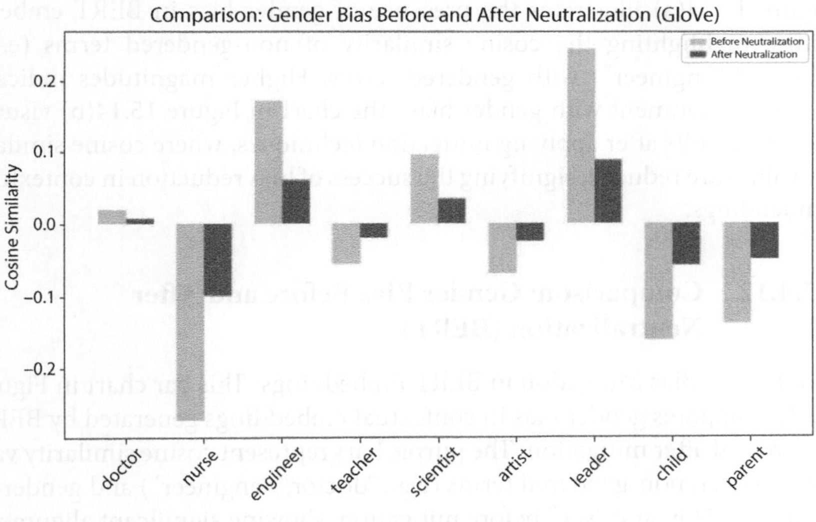

Figure 15.13 Comparison of cosine similarity.

"doctor," "nurse," and "teacher" with gendered terms before and after neutralization. The yellow bars represent cosine similarity values before applying bias mitigation, indicating significant alignment with gendered terms. The blue bars, representing post-neutralization, show reduced alignment, demonstrating the effectiveness of the adversarial network in mitigating gender bias.

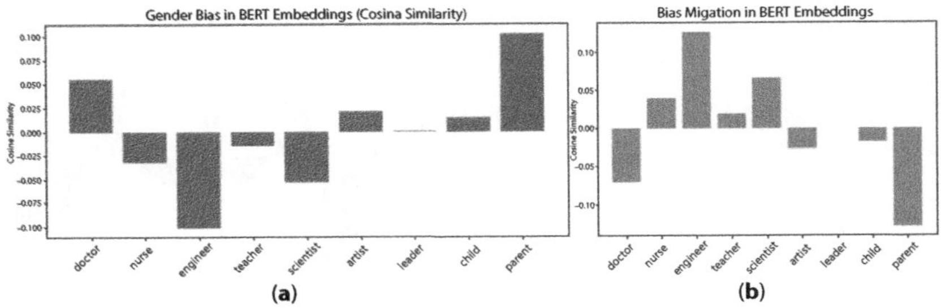

Figure 15.14 (a) Gender bias in BERT embeddings. (b) Mitigation of gender bias.

15.4.11 Bias Analysis and Mitigation in BERT Embeddings

Bias Identification and Mitigation in BERT Embeddings: The chart in Figure 15.14(a) illustrates the presence of gender bias in BERT embeddings, highlighting the cosine similarity of non-gendered terms (e.g., "doctor," "engineer") with gendered terms. Higher magnitudes indicate stronger alignment with gender bias. The chart in Figure 15.14(b) visualizes the results after applying mitigation techniques, where cosine similarity values are reduced, signifying the success of bias reduction in contextual embeddings.

15.4.12 Comparison: Gender Bias Before and After Neutralization (BERT)

Contextual Bias Mitigation in BERT Embeddings: This bar chart in Figure 15.15 compares gender bias in contextual embeddings generated by BERT before and after mitigation. The purple bars represent cosine similarity values between non-gendered terms (e.g., "doctor," "engineer") and gendered terms like "he" and "she" before mitigation, showing significant alignment with gendered terms. The green bars reflect reduced bias after mitigation, indicating the effectiveness of the applied bias-neutralization strategies in BERT embeddings.

15.4.13 GloVe Embeddings Before and After Neutralization (PCA Scatter Plot)

Impact of Neutralization on Static Word Embeddings (GloVe): The left plot in Figure 15.16(a) illustrates the PCA visualization of GloVe embeddings before neutralization, where non-gendered terms like "doctor" and "engineer" align closely with gendered terms. The right plot in Figure 15.16(b)

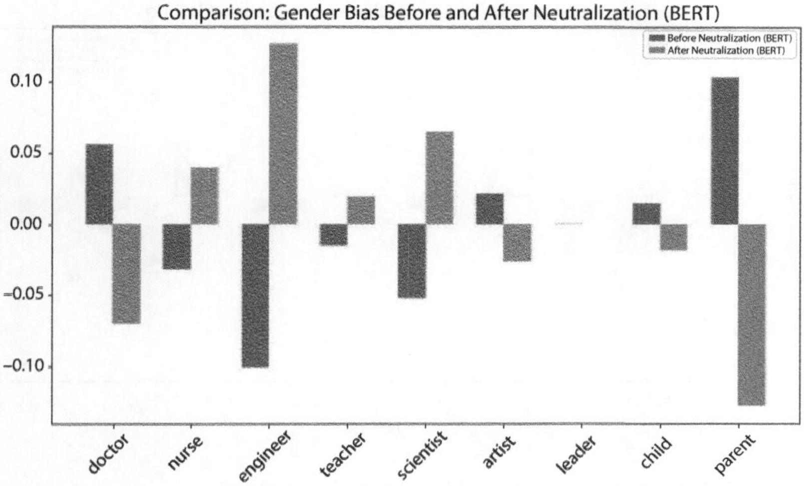

Figure 15.15 Gender bias in contextual embeddings.

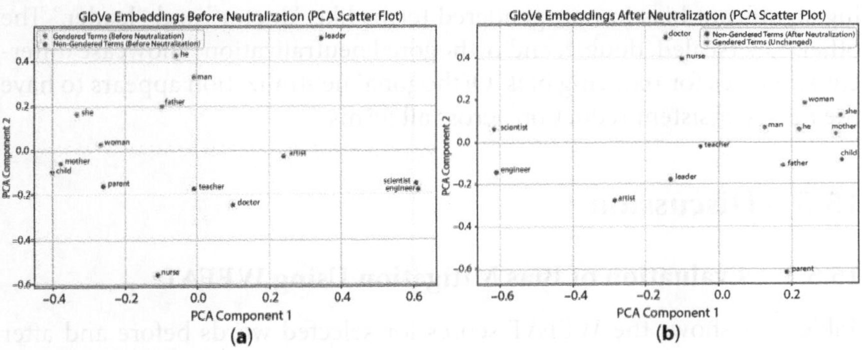

Figure 15.16 (a) PCA visualization of GloVe embeddings before neutralization. (b) PCA visualization of GloVe embeddings after neutralization.

shows the embeddings after neutralization, where non-gendered terms are distributed more neutrally, demonstrating the effectiveness of bias mitigation through adversarial networks.

15.4.14 Comparison of Gender Bias Neutralization Methods

Comparison of Neutralization Techniques in Static Embeddings: This bar chart in Figure 15.17 compares the effectiveness of various gender bias neutralization methods for static embeddings (e.g., GloVe). The yellow

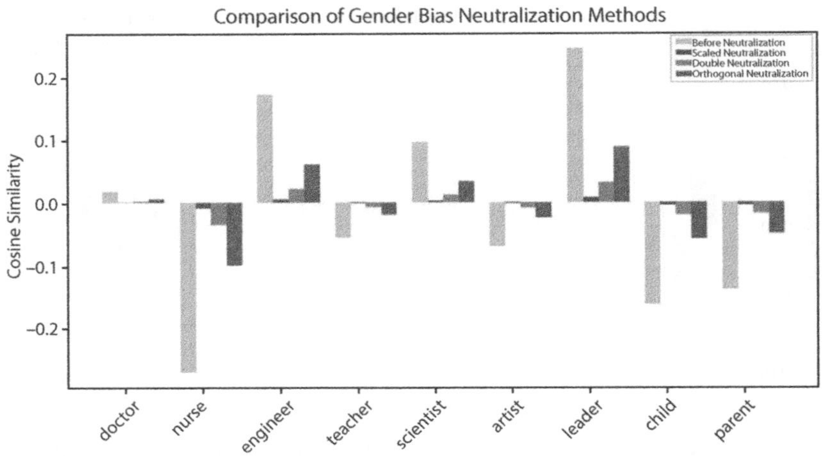

Figure 15.17 Comparison of gender bias from various methods.

bars represent the cosine similarity values before neutralization, indicating significant bias in non-gendered terms like "doctor" and "leader." The other bars (scaled, double, and orthogonal neutralization) showcase different strategies for reducing bias. Orthogonal neutralization appears to have the most consistent reduction across all terms.

15.5 Discussion

15.5.1 Evaluation of Bias Mitigation Using WEFAT

Table 15.1 shows the WEFAT scores for selected words before and after bias mitigation. Positive changes, such as for "scientist" and "doctor," indicate stronger alignment with male terms after mitigation, reflecting semantic preservation. The negative change for "nurse" demonstrates reduced alignment with male terms, indicating effective bias reduction for this term. Overall, the changes validate the impact of the proposed mitigation methods.

15.5.2 Impact of Bias Mitigation on Neighbor Similarities

Table 15.2 compares the nearest neighbors and their similarity scores for selected words before and after applying bias mitigation techniques. For example, "nurse," which was closely associated with "nanny" in the biased embeddings, shifts to "obstetrician" in the debiased embeddings, reflecting

Table 15.1 WEFAT scores for words before and after bias mitigation.

Rank (initial)	Word	WEFAT (initial)	WEFAT (after)	Change
1	Doctor	0.752	0.785	0.033
2	Nurse	0.74	0.708	−0.032
3	Engineer	0.688	0.719	0.031
4	Teacher	0.673	0.681	0.008
5	Scientist	0.68	0.767	0.087
6	Artist	0.659	0.687	0.028
7	Leader	0.649	0.679	0.03

Table 15.2 Biased vs. debiased neighbor table.

Biased neighbor	Similarity (biased)	Debiased neighbor	Similarity (debiased)
maid	0.867	dentist	0.638
dentist	0.857	pharmacist	0.609
woman	0.856	hospital	0.598
nurse	1.012	nurse	0.705
mother	0.861	physician	0.626
fiance	0.862	surgeon	0.63
nanny	0.904	obstetrician	0.687
fiancée	0.87	pediatrician	0.645

a reduction in stereotypical gender associations. Similarly, "fiancée" transitions from "maid" to "pediatrician," demonstrating a shift toward more professional and neutral terms. The reduced similarity scores in the debiased embeddings further indicate the model's success in neutralizing biased alignments while maintaining semantic relevance.

The results of the current study demonstrate the significant advancements achieved through the proposed approach in mitigating gender bias in word embeddings. The use of adversarial networks, combined with BERT's dynamic contextual adaptability, addresses the limitations of traditional projection-based techniques by maintaining both neutrality and semantic integrity. Metrics such as WEFAT scores and qualitative analyses, like neighbor similarity shifts, highlight the robustness and reliability of this approach in creating unbiased representations. By leveraging the strengths of transformer-based models, the study showcases how evolving bias patterns can be effectively mitigated, aligning with findings in recent literature [1, 2]. Additionally, the integration of qualitative insights offers a holistic perspective that surpasses existing frameworks reliant solely on numerical evaluations. These findings affirm the potential of the proposed method to enhance fairness and inclusivity across diverse NLP applications, bridging a critical gap in current research.

15.6 Conclusion

This study demonstrates the effectiveness of adversarial networks and BERT-based contextual embeddings in mitigating gender bias in word embeddings, addressing critical challenges in developing ethical AI systems. The proposed approach achieves a balance between bias neutrality and semantic preservation, validated by reductions in WEFAT scores and qualitative improvements in neighbor relationships. Compared to traditional methods like projection-based techniques, this framework outperforms by dynamically adapting to context while maintaining usability for downstream NLP tasks. These advancements are particularly significant for applications in sensitive domains such as hiring and healthcare, where fairness and inclusivity are paramount. The findings emphasize the importance of integrating ethical considerations into the development of AI systems, ensuring that they align with societal values.

Future work will focus on extending the current method to address other forms of bias, such as racial and intersectional biases, and enhancing its scope and applicability. The exploration of larger and more diverse datasets will further improve the robustness and scalability of the approach. Additionally, refining adversarial architectures to enhance both semantic retention and bias mitigation will remain a priority. By addressing these directions, the framework aims to advance the development of adaptable, inclusive, and trustworthy AI systems capable of fair decision-making across diverse real-world applications.

AI disclosure statement: The author acknowledges the use of AI-based tools for minor language editing or grammatical correction. However, all intellectual contributions, analyses, and conclusions presented in this chapter are entirely the author's own.

References

1. Brown, T.B., *et al.*, Language models are few-shot learners, *arXiv preprint arXiv:2005.14165*, May 2020, doi: https://doi.org/10.48550/arXiv.2005.14165.
2. Boselli, R., D'Amico, S., Nobani, N., eXplainable AI for word embeddings: A survey. *Cognit. Comput.*, 17, Art. 19, 2025, doi: https://doi.org/10.1007/s12559-024-10373-2.
3. Asudani, D.S., Nagwani, N.K., Singh, P., A detailed review on word embedding techniques with emphasis on Word2Vec. *Multimedia Tools Appl.*, 2023, doi: https://link.springer.com/article/10.1007/s11042-023-17007-z.
4. Agüero-Torales, M.M., Abreu Salas, J.I., López-Herrera, A.G., Deep learning and multilingual sentiment analysis on social media data: An overview. *Appl. Soft Comput.*, 107, Art. no. 107373, 2021, doi: https://doi.org/10.1016/j.asoc.2021.107373.
5. Gregory, K.M., Cousijn, H., Groth, P., Scharnhorst, A., Wyatt, S., Understanding data search as a socio-technical practice. *J. Inf. Sci.*, 46, 4, 459–475, 2020, doi: https://doi.org/10.1177/0165551519837182.
6. Zaland, O., Abulaish, M., Fazil, M., A comprehensive empirical evaluation of existing word embedding approaches, *arXiv preprint arXiv:2303.07196*, Mar. 2023, doi: https://doi.org/10.48550/arXiv.2303.07196.
7. Kenyon-Dean, K., Newell, E., Cheung, J.C.K., Deconstructing word embedding algorithms, in: *Proc. 2020 Conf. on Empirical Methods in Natural Language Processing (EMNLP)*, Online, Nov. 2020, pp. 8479–8484, doi: https://doi.org/10.18653/v1/2020.emnlp-main.681.
8. Incitti, F. and Snidaro, L., Fusing contextual word embeddings for concreteness estimation, in: *Proc. 2021 IEEE 24th Int. Conf. on Information Fusion (FUSION)*, Sun City, South Africa, pp. 1–8, 2021, doi: https://doi.org/10.23919/FUSION49465.2021.9626843.
9. Jiao, Q. and Zhang, S., A brief survey of word embedding and its recent development, in: *Proc. 2021 IEEE 5th Advanced Information Technology, Electronic and Automation Control Conf. (IAEAC)*, Chongqing, China, pp. 1697–1701, 2021, doi: https://doi.org/10.1109/IAEAC50856.2021.9390956.
10. Seth, T. and Muhuri, P.K., Enriching word embeddings with fuzzy systems for natural language processing tasks, in: *Proc. 2024 IEEE Int. Conf. on Fuzzy Systems (FUZZ-IEEE)*, Yokohama, Japan, pp. 1–8, 2024, doi: https://doi.org/10.1109/FUZZ-IEEE60900.2024.10611949.

11. Wang, Y., Huang, G., Li, J., Li, H., Zhou, Y., Jiang, H., Refined global word embeddings based on sentiment concept for sentiment analysis. *IEEE Access*, 9, 37075–37085, 2021, doi: https://doi.org/10.1109/ACCESS.2021.3062654.
12. Liu, Y., *et al.*, RoBERTa: A robustly optimized BERT pretraining approach, *arXiv preprint arXiv:1907.11692*, Jul. 2019, doi: https://doi.org/10.48550/arXiv.1907.11692.
13. Liu, Q., *et al.*, A survey on contextual embeddings, *arXiv preprint arXiv:2003.07278*, Mar. 2020, doi: https://doi.org/10.48550/arXiv.2003.07278.
14. Peters, M.E., Neumann, M., Iyyer, M., Gardner, M., Clark, C., Lee, K., Zettlemoyer, L., Deep contextualized word representations, in: *Proc. 2018 Conf. of the North American Chapter of the Association for Computational Linguistics: Human Language Technologies (NAACL-HLT)*, Jun. 2018, vol. 1, Long Papers, New Orleans, LA, USA, pp. 2227–2237, doi: https://doi.org/10.18653/v1/N18-1202.
15. Kuppala, K., Banda, S., Imambi, S.S., Unsupervised image transformation for long wave infrared and visual image matching using two channel convolutional autoencoder network. *Int. J. Comput. Vis. Robot.*, 14, 1, 63–83, 2024, doi: https://www.inderscienceonline.com/doi/abs/10.1504/IJCVR.2024.135132.
16. Kumar, N.S., Deepika, G., Goutham, V., *et al.*, HARNet in deep learning approach—a systematic survey. *Sci. Rep.*, 14, Art. 8363, 2024, doi: https://doi.org/10.1038/s41598-024-58074-y.
17. Mudigonda, Yalavarthi, U.D., Satyanarayana, P., *et al.*, IDEAL: An inventive optimized deep ensemble augmented learning framework for opinion mining and sentiment analysis. *Soc. Netw. Anal. Min.*, 14, Art. 89, 2024, doi: https://doi.org/10.1007/s13278-024-01249-2.
18. Lilhore, U.K., Dalal, S., Varshney, N., *et al.*, Prevalence and risk factors analysis of postpartum depression at early stage using hybrid deep learning model. *Sci. Rep.*, 14, Art. 4533, 2024, doi: https://doi.org/10.1038/s41598-024-54927-8.
19. Kalita, K., Ramesh, J.V.N., Cepova, L., *et al.*, Multi-objective exponential distribution optimizer (MOEDO): A novel math-inspired multi-objective algorithm for global optimization and real-world engineering design problems. *Sci. Rep.*, 14, Art. 1816, 2024, doi: https://doi.org/10.1038/s41598-024-52083-7.
20. Simaiya, S., Lilhore, U.K., Sharma, Y.K., *et al.*, A hybrid cloud load balancing and host utilization prediction method using deep learning and optimization techniques. *Sci. Rep.*, 14, Art. 1337, 2024, doi: https://doi.org/10.1038/s41598-024-51466-0.

21. Saha, Senapati, T., Akram, M., *et al.*, Dual probabilistic linguistic consensus reaching method for group decision-making. *Granular Comput.*, 9, Art. 35, 2024, doi: https://doi.org/10.1007/s41066-024-00458-6.
22. Pradeepa, M., Kumaraperumal, S., Kasat, K., Maguluri, L.P., Shajahan, U.S., Gaikwad, S.M., Digital evolution: Investigating the dynamic interactions of learners with social media. *Entertain. Comput.*, 50, Art. no. 100668, 2024, doi: https://doi.org/10.1016/j.entcom.2024.100668.
23. Berenguer, A., Mazón, J.-N., Tomás, D., Word embeddings for retrieving tabular data from research publications. *Mach. Learn.*, 113, 4, 2227–2248, 2024, doi: https://doi.org/10.1007/s10994-023-06472-0.

16

Exploring Machine Learning in Voice-Based Parkinson's Disease Diagnosis: A Comprehensive Survey

G. Smilarubavathy[1]* and K. Vijayakumar[2]

[1]Department of Computer Science and Engineering, St. Joseph's Institute of Technology, Chennai, India
[2]Department of Information Technology, St. Joseph's Institute of Technology, Chennai, India

Abstract
Parkinson's Disease (PD) is a degenerative condition that impacts the neurological system. Traditional diagnostic methods often detect the disease only at advanced stages. Voice analysis provides a promising non-invasive approach for early detection of PD. It detects small voice alterations such as increased jitter, decreased pitch fluctuation, and aberrant prosody. These features are strongly linked to PD and can be systematically analyzed using computational techniques. Machine learning is playing an important role in improving research in this area. It helps to detect the complex patterns in the analysis of voice data. Traditional methods, such as Support Vector Machines (SVM), have shown good accuracy in detecting PD. Advanced deep learning methods, like Convolutional Neural Networks (CNN), have been successful. These models can effectively distinguish PD from non-PD subjects. This review examines recent developments in ML techniques for voice analysis. It focuses on topics including datasets, feature extraction, and performance indicators. The paper also discusses issues such as dataset limits and ethical considerations. It focuses on the future innovations of the development of explainable AI and real-time diagnostic systems.

Keywords: Parkinson's disease (PD), machine learning (ML), datasets, feature extraction, performance measures

**Corresponding author*: smilarupa@gmail.com

R. Nidhya, A. Dineshkumar, Sheng-Lung Peng, S. Karthik and S. Balamurugan (eds.) Neuro-Symbolic Artificial Intelligence: Concepts & Applications, (317–336) © 2026 Scrivener Publishing LLC

16.1 Introduction

Parkinson's Disease (PD) is a neurodegenerative condition that worsens over time and affects motor and nonmotor functions. Motor symptoms (stiffness, tremors, and slow movement) and non-motor symptoms (speech disturbances and memory decline) are affected by PD [1]. Usually, the traditional method can easily analyze the patient's symptoms. That frequently causes delays in detection. This suggests more accurate and scalable diagnostic tools [2]. Voice analysis can detect increased jitter, shimmer, and reduced pitch fluctuation. It can be combined with the brain motor pathway impairment, making it a promising early detection approach [3]. It is cost-effective and simple to use. Also, it is suitable for large-scale population screening and early PD detection [4].

Machine learning improves PD detection by identifying the patterns in voice data. Traditional ML models containing Random Forest, SVM, and k-nearest Neighbors (k-NN) have shown high classification accuracy [5]. The automatic feature extraction from raw voice recording is done with the help of the CNN and Recurrent Neural Networks (RNNs) [6]. Combining voice analysis with ML not only enhances the accuracy of diagnoses but also tracks the progress of diseases and the effectiveness of treatments [7]. Short datasets and variable recording conditions still restrict clinical implementation [8]. Ethical issues, including privacy and consent, cause the challenges. Establishing a standard process and promoting teamwork are crucial to overcoming these issues. Moreover, using diverse and representative datasets is important for effectively tackling these difficulties [9].

This review examines recent progress in voice-based machine learning methods for PD detection. It discusses challenges, available datasets, and feature extraction methods used in this field. The article also discusses future methods to improve early detection and PD diagnosis.

16.2 Background

Parkinson's Disease (PD) is a chronic neurodegenerative disorder caused by the loss of dopaminergic neurons in the substantia nigra, affecting millions globally [10]. Motor symptoms (tremors, delayed movement (bradykinesia), stiffness, and difficulty balancing) and non-motor symptoms (emotional fluctuations, cognitive impairments, and speech impediments) manifest early as well [11]. These symptoms reduce the quality of life for individuals who are affected. Early diagnosis helps manage symptoms and also helps reduce PD development. However, traditional methods based on clinical observations often fail to detect PD in its early stages [12].

Speech problems are some of the earliest signs of PD and occur due to difficulties in controlling speech-related muscles [13]. Subtle changes (increased jitter, shimmer, reduced pitch variation) and altered speech patterns can be identified through voice analysis [14]. This method is non-invasive, cost-effective, and shows potential for early detection by focusing on vocal biomarkers [15].

ML has transformed PD detection by analyzing complex voice data and discovering patterns in that data. SVMs and Random Forests are good classification models; meanwhile, CNNs and RNNs automatically extract features with high accuracy [16]. However, issues like as irregular recording conditions, tiny datasets, and ethical considerations persist. Solving these problems is essential to fully utilize ML-based voice analysis for scalable and real-time PD detection [17].

16.3 Flowchart

16.3.1 Voice-Based Data in PD Diagnosis

The use of voice-based data is crucial for diagnosing PD using machine learning techniques [18]. Several publicly available datasets have been instrumental in advancing research in this area [19]. These datasets differ in size, language, and the types of information they contain, offering a diverse resource for constructing and verifying diagnostic models [20]. Figure 16.1 shows the flow for voice-based PD diagnosis.

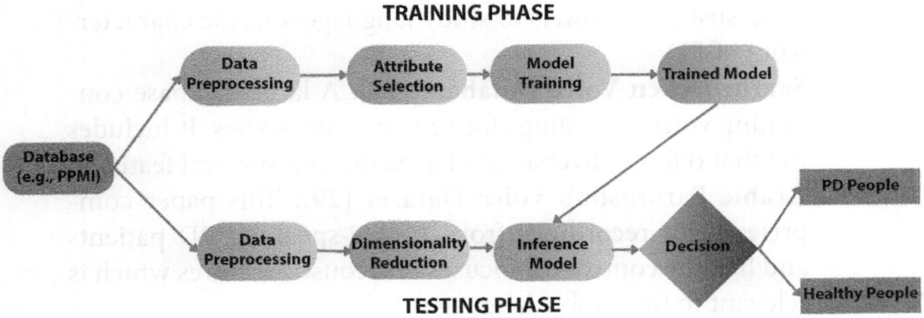

Figure 16.1 Flowchart for voice-based PD diagnosis.

16.3.2 Dataset Overview

1. **UCI Parkinson's Dataset [21]:** One of the most widely used datasets; it contains voice recordings from individuals with and without PD. It includes fundamental frequency measures, Harmonics-to-Noise Ratio (HNR), shimmer, and jitter.
2. **Parkinson's Telemonitoring Dataset [22]:** This dataset contains biomedical voice measures from 42 PD patients, each with several recordings and a variety of properties, like as Mel Frequency Cepstral Coefficients (MFCCs), shimmer, and jitter.
3. **Parkinson's Progression Markers Initiative (PPMI) [23]:** A comprehensive dataset that provides multimodal data that includes voice recordings, from a large cohort. It focuses on the long-term course of PD.
4. **mPower Dataset [24]:** It is sourced from the mobile application study and includes a large collection of voice samples from thousands of people, capturing a wide spectrum of vocal traits in real-world settings.
5. **PC-GITA Dataset [25]:** It contains voice recordings from Spanish-speaking PD patients and healthy controls, which include sustained vowels and speech tasks, with extracted features like MFCCs and pitch variations.
6. **Czech Parkinson's Speech Dataset [26]:** It provides speech recordings from Czech-speaking PD patients and healthy controls. It focused on sustained vowels and sentence readings with extracted features (e.g., jitter and shimmer).
7. **Turkish Parkinson's Dataset [27]:** Includes voice recordings from Turkish-speaking individuals, with features extracted from sustained vowels to study language-specific characteristics of PD.
8. **Saarbruecken Voice Database [28]:** A large database containing voice recordings for various pathologies. It includes PD that offers a diverse set of acoustic and spectral features.
9. **Arabic Parkinson's Voice Dataset [29]:** This paper comprises voice recordings from Arabic-speaking PD patients and healthy controls. It focuses on acoustic features which is relevant to the Arabic language.
10. **Parkinson's Disease Classification Dataset [30]:** Contains a variety of biomedical voice measurements, emphasizing feature diversity to improve classification models.

Table 16.1 Summary of commonly used datasets and features for voice-based PD diagnosis.

Dataset	Description	Number of samples	Features extracted	Access type
UCI Parkinson's Dataset [21]	Speech recordings from 31 individuals (23 with PD).	195 samples	Jitter, shimmer, HNR, MFCC, pitch	Publicly available
Parkinson's Telemonitoring Dataset [22]	Speech data with motor UPDRS and total UPDRS values.	5,875 samples	Jitter, shimmer, NHR, HNR, harmonicity	Publicly available
PPMI Dataset [23]	Multimodal dataset with speech recordings and clinical data.	~500 participants	MFCC, jitter, shimmer, temporal features	Request access (free)
mPower Dataset [24]	Smartphone-recorded speech samples from PD and non-PD individuals.	~9,000 samples	Pitch, formant frequencies, amplitude modulation	Request access (free)
Parkinson's Voice Initiative [31]	Voice recordings collected *via* a smartphone app.	10,000+ samples	Jitter, shimmer, MFCC, ZCR	Publicly available
PC-GITA Dataset [25]	Spanish speech recordings of PD and non-PD individuals.	100 participants	Acoustic features, prosody, spectral contrast	Publicly available
Czech Parkinson's Dataset [26]	Speech recordings of Czech-speaking PD patients.	100 participants	Jitter, shimmer, spectral tilt	Publicly available
Saarbruecken Voice Database [21]	Biomedical voice measurements from 2000 individuals, including sustained vowel phonations.	~60 samples from PD	Jitter, shimmer, HNR, harmonicity	Request Access
Arabic Parkinson's Dataset [29]	Arabic-language dataset with PD and non-PD participants.	~500 samples	Prosodic and phonetic features	Request access (regional studies)
Italian Parkinson's Dataset [32]	Italian speech samples focusing on PD-specific vocal impairments.	160 participants	Acoustic features, formant frequencies	Request access (regional studies)

16.3.3 Key Dataset Description

The Summary of commonly used dataset and its description is shown in Table 16.1

- **UCI Parkinson's Dataset [21]:** It is a foundational dataset in PD speech analysis. It provides a variety of fundamental frequency measures and perturbation features that allow for several studies in the field.
- **Parkinson's Telemonitoring Dataset [22]:** This dataset is valuable for its longitudinal data. It enables researchers to analyze the development of PD by tracking changes in voice over time.
- **PPMI Dataset [23]:** Although access is restricted, it provides important clinical and speech data, making it a useful resource for comprehensive PD studies.
- **mPower Dataset [24]:** Collected *via* a smartphone app. It represents real-world voice data with a large sample size and captures the variability in recording conditions.
- **PC-GITA and Arabic Parkinson's Voice Datasets [25]:** These datasets contribute to understanding language-specific vocal characteristics of PD. It is important for developing global diagnostic tools.

16.3.4 Features Extracted

- **Acoustic Features**: Jitter and shimmer measure frequency and amplitude variations in voice signals that indicate vocal fold stability [33].
- **Spectral Features**: MFCCs represent the short-term power spectrum of sound, which is essential for capturing the timbral features of speech affected by PD [34].
- **Prosodic Features**: Pitch variation, speech pace, and intonation patterns are all important characteristics of speech that represent the rhythm and melody. These features are often changed in PD patients [35].

These datasets contain different samples and attributes needed to create strong PD diagnostic machine-learning models [36]. This allows researchers to validate their models across a variety of demographics, languages, and recording conditions. It makes their results more applicable to other situations [37].

16.3.5 Machine Learning Techniques

Machine learning (ML) is now a key tool for diagnosing PD by analyzing voice data [38]. Advanced algorithms can detect minor vocal changes associated with PD that classic methods may miss [39]. This section examines supervised and deep learning techniques that focus on their applications and performance in this area.

Supervised Learning

Supervised learning models (like SVM and Random Forests (RF)) are commonly used to classify PD [40]. These models analyze labeled data, focusing on features such as Mel-Frequency Cepstral Coefficients (MFCC), shimmer, and jitter [41]. SVMs are particularly good at managing complex, high-dimensional data; meanwhile, RFs are known for their robustness and ease of interpretation [42].

Deep Learning

Deep learning methods (like Recurrent Neural Networks (RNNs) and Convolutional Neural Networks (CNNs)) help to improve PD detection by automating feature extraction [43]. CNNs are well-suited for analyzing spectrograms and image data; however, RNNs effectively analyze sequential voice patterns, capturing temporal dependencies [44].

Feature Engineering

Feature selection and Feature extraction are essential to improve the model accuracy. Recursive Feature Elimination (RFE) and Principal Component Analysis (PCA) are the most important methods that help to identify the most relevant features and also reduce the redundancy and computational costs [45].

16.4 Performance Metrics

ML models are evaluated using metrics that include accuracy, sensitivity, and specificity. Accuracy denotes overall accuracy. Sensitivity assesses the detection of PD instances. Specificity evaluates the identification of non-PD individuals [46]. These metrics collectively guide the development of reliable diagnostic systems. The comparison for model performance metrics is shown in Figure 16.2. Also the Performance Comparison of ML models for PD diagnosis shown in Table 16.2.

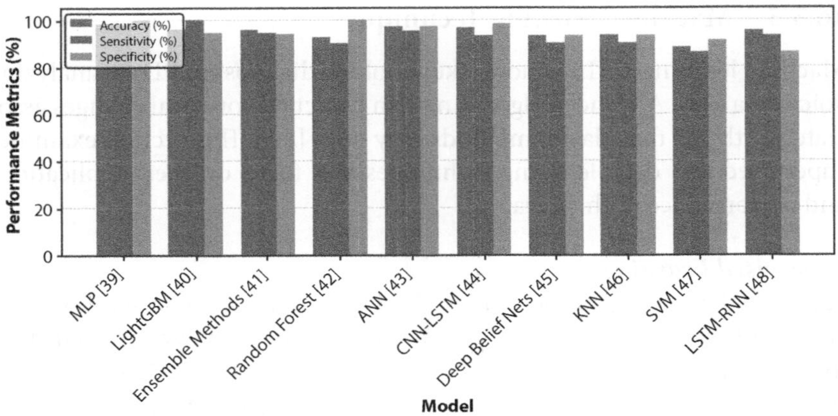

Figure 16.2 Comparison of model performance metrics.

Combining these methods, machine learning-based diagnostics are enabling non-invasive and efficient solutions for detecting Parkinson's Disease (PD). This integration also allows for scalable approaches to PD detection [47].

16.5 Comparative Analysis

Supervised learning models like SVM and RF are commonly used to diagnose PD [58]. These methods examine structured datasets for features including Mel-Frequency Cepstral Coefficients (MFCCs), shimmer, and jitter. They are efficient and easy to interpret, but rely heavily on high-quality feature engineering [59].

Deep learning models such as RNNs and CNNs can automatically detect complicated patterns in raw data. It frequently outperforms classic ML models [60]. CNNs are especially good at analyzing voice spectrograms, while RNNs are very good at analyzing sequential features like prosody and pitch [61]. However, these models need bigger datasets and more computing power, which means they are more likely to overfit when data is limited.

Recent research suggests that combining traditional and deep learning techniques can help to maximize the benefits of both hybrid and ensemble approaches [62]. In PD detection, ensemble techniques like Hard Voting and Gradient Boosting improve generalizability and resilience [63]. Table 16.3 mentioned the strength and weakness of machine learning models. Table 16.3 mentioned the strength and weakness of machine learning models.

Table 16.2 Performance comparison of ML models for PD diagnosis.

Model	Study	Dataset	Features	Accuracy (%)	Sensitivity (%)	Specificity (%)
MLP [48]	Raya Alshammri *et al.*	UCI ML Repository	Jitter, Shimmer, HNR	98.31%	98%	100%
LightGBM [49]	Md Abu Sayed *et al.*	UCI ML Repository	MFCC, HNR, jitter, shimmer, spectral slope	96%	100%	94.43%
Ensemble Methods [50]	Fahmida Khanom *et al.*	UCI Parkinson's Dataset	Optimized voice features	95.6%	94.2%	93.7%
Random Forest [51]	Johnson *et al.*	mPower Dataset	Acoustic Features	92.3%	90%	100%
ANN [52]	Ishu Gupta *et al.*	UCI Parkinson's Dataset	Temporal Features	97%	95%	97%
CNN-LSTM [53]	Nouhaila *et al.*	PC-GITA dataset + Custom Dataset	Acoustic Features	96.55%	93%	98%
Deep Belief Nets [54]	Satvik *et al.*	Custom Dataset (500 subjects)	voice quality, pitch, and fluency	93%	90%	93%
KNN [55]	Mohamed Dahmani *et al.*	Saarbrucken Voice Database	pitch, Formants, Jitter, Mel-Frequency Cepstral Coefficients (MFCC), linear predictive coefficients (LPC)	93.3%	90%	93%
SVM [56]	Gabriel Solana-Lavalle *et al.*	Sakar Datasets (Custom)	vocal fold features, Baseline, wavelet transform-based features, frequency features, MFCC, and TQWT	88%	86%	91%
LSTM-RNN [57]	Yuan *et al.*	Custom Speech Dataset	Speech Signal Features	95%	93%	86%

Table 16.3 Strengths and weaknesses of machine learning models for PD diagnosis.

Author	Scenario	Model	Strengths	Weaknesses
Wenbo Ge *et al.* [64]	Analyzes whether machine learning models are over-promising in the healthcare domain with examples from Parkinson's diagnosis.	Existing models were critically analyzed.	Evaluates machine learning models' effectiveness in Parkinson's diagnosis; highlights the role of clinician-independent diagnosis methods.	There is a lack of specific development metrics for various models.
K.J. Kubota *et al.* [65]	Discusses the application of wearable sensors; Collecting data for PD diagnosis.	SVM and RF models were applied for analyzing wearable sensor data.	Discusses the potential of wearable sensors in data collection and diagnosis accuracy.	High computational cost and dependence on sensor quality.
M.S. Alzubaid *et al.* [66]	Reviews the role of neural networks in detecting PD through speech analysis.	Neural networks were designed to analyze voice signals.	Examines multiple neural network approaches; focuses on speech signal analysis.	Limited to speech data, ignoring multimodal diagnosis approaches.
H.W. Loh, W. Hong *et al.* [67]	Provides a detailed review of deep learning models for automated PD identification from 2011 to 2021.	Models based on deep learning were used for automated diagnosis.	Comprehensive review of deep learning methods; highlights progress in automated identification.	Diverse datasets are difficult to generalize.
M. Pramanik *et al.* [68]	The use of decision trees for effective diagnosis in complex data contexts is the primary focus.	Decision forests for Parkinson's detection.	Presents decision forests' advantages in handling complex features.	The decision-making process is underexplained.

(Continued)

Table 16.3 Strengths and weaknesses of machine learning models for PD diagnosis. (*Continued*)

Author	Scenario	Model	Strengths	Weaknesses
J. Zhang [69]	Integrates imaging and clinical data to improve the accuracy of early stage of PD detection.	Imaging and clinical data are integrated to make predictions.	Integrates imaging and clinical data, which provides a more accurate diagnosis.	Semi-quantitative imaging methods require further validation.
M. Belia *et al.* [70]	Explores AI models and their applications in the diagnosis and assessment of PD.	For diagnostic reasons, hybrid methods like SVM, Decision Trees, and Neural Networks are used.	Explores AI models for diagnostic aid; provides practical use cases.	Overdependence on sensor-derived data.
B.M. Eskofier *et al.* [71]	Concentrates on advances in deep learning algorithms for sensor-based mobility analysis in Parkinson's patients.	Improvements in sensor-based mobility analysis using deep learning.	Concentrates on deep learning advances in mobility analysis.	Analysis confined to sensor-based data.

Despite recent advances, here the dataset variety, real-world application, and ethics remain the unsolved issues.

16.6 Challenges and Limitations

Despite significant progress in using voice-based machine learning for PD diagnosis, there are several challenges that remain. These include (a) limited dataset diversity, (b) uncertainty in recording conditions, and also (c) ethical considerations about data privacy and consent.

Dataset Challenges

Many studies employ publicly available datasets, such as the UCI Parkinson's Dataset, which are frequently limited and lack demographic diversity [72].

Limitations in representation reduce machine learning model generalizability to different populations. Differences in recording settings, such as device type and background noise, are further challenge model robustness [73].

Model Challenges
Overfitting is a common problem with ML models, particularly deep learning algorithms, when trained on short datasets. Generalization to unknown data is a major issue, which limits clinical applicability [74]. Furthermore, the "black-box" nature of deep learning models undermines explainability. It makes it difficult for physicians to trust and interpret predictions [75].

Ethical Concerns
There are serious ethical issues with the collection and use of voice recordings for PD diagnosis. These challenges are clearly depicted in Figure 16.3. To protect the patient's privacy, getting informed consent and securely keeping the sensitive data are critical. Strong data anonymization helps preserve patient privacy [76]. Participants can determine how their data is utilized with dynamic consent models. It promotes transparency and patient autonomy. Data security is enhanced by security assessments and data protection laws. Addressing these problems is critical to establishing public trust and promoting wider adoption of voice-based machine learning diagnostics for PD.

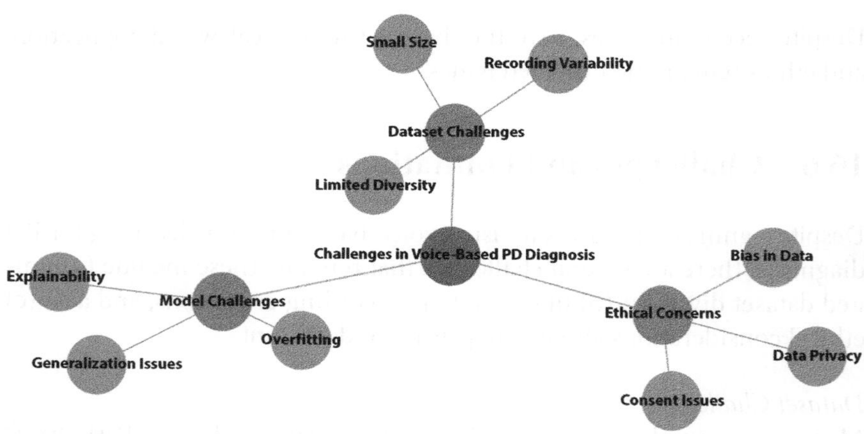

Figure 16.3 Challenges in voice-based PD diagnosis.

16.7 Future Directions

Voice-based machine learning (ML) for the diagnosis of PD presents significant potential, with numerous intriguing directions for future investigation. Explainable AI (XAI) is crucial for increasing confidence, and also, it allows doctors to explain model predictions; hence, it facilitates incorporation into healthcare. Techniques like SHAP or LIME that show how important traits are can make models clearer [77].

Multimodal techniques combine speech data with additional biomarkers that contain handwriting and gait analysis. It provides comprehensive insights into PD, which increases the diagnostic accuracy [78]. Mobile speech monitoring methodologies and other real-time applications could help to diagnose and also manage patients earlier and make technology more accessible.

Developing generalizable models requires larger and more diverse population datasets. Figure 16.4 clearly mentioned the future research in this field. Collaborative initiatives should seek to standardize evaluation frameworks in order to maintain consistency when evaluating ML approaches across research [79]. Data privacy can be addressed with the decentralized model training in emerging fields like federated learning.

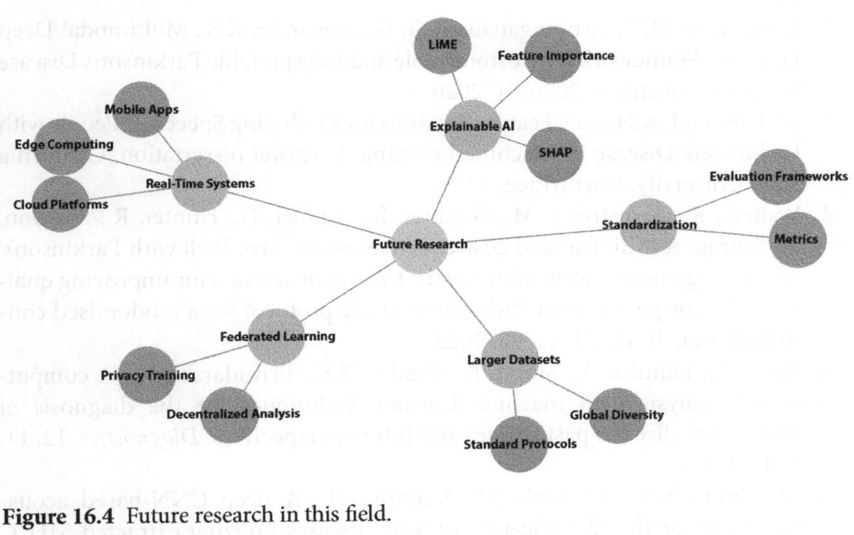

Figure 16.4 Future research in this field.

Conclusion

This review article focused on the enormous potential of machine learning (ML) in increasing PD diagnosis *via* non-invasive voice analysis. ML approaches, including supervised and deep learning models, have shown great accuracy in identifying PD, utilizing crucial voice parameters such as jitter and MFCC. Despite these advancements, challenges such as limited dataset diversity, model generalization, and ethical concerns persist. Addressing these requires collaborative efforts to create larger and more diverse datasets and develop explainable AI models for clinical integration. Future research should focus on real-time diagnostic tools and multimodal approaches. It enhances the reliability and accessibility of PD diagnosis.

AI disclosure statement: The author confirms that no artificial intelligence (AI)-generated content or AI-assisted writing tools were used in the preparation of this chapter (including summaries and the abstract). All text, analysis, and conclusions are the result of the author's original work.

References

1. Rana, A.Q., Ahmed, U. S., Chaudry, Z.M., Vasan, S., Parkinson's disease: a review of non-motor symptoms. *Expert Rev. Neurother.*, 15, 5, 549–562, 2015.
2. Kothari, Sr, M.V., Arumuganainar, Sr, G., Konar, Sr, K.S., Multimodal Deep Learning Framework for Customizable and Interpretable Parkinson's Disease Detection. *medRxiv*, 2026-01, 2026.
3. Mohammad, A.H., Key Feature Analysis for Predicting Speech of People with Parkinson's Disease in Machine Learning, Doctoral dissertation, California State University, Northridge, 2023.
4. Walters, K., Armstrong, M., Gardner, B., Ambler, G., Hunter, R., Maydon, B., Schrag, A., Clinical and cost-effectiveness of 'Live Well with Parkinson's' self-management intervention versus treatment as usual for improving quality of life for people with Parkinson's: study protocol for a randomised controlled trial. *Trials*, 24, 1, 793, 2023.
5. Rana, A., Dumka, A., Singh, R., Panda, M.K., Priyadarshi, N., A computerized analysis with machine learning techniques for the diagnosis of Parkinson's disease: past studies and future perspectives. *Diagnostics*, 12, 11, 2708, 2022.
6. Alghamdi, N.S., Zakariah, M., Karamti, H., A deep CNN-based acoustic model for the identification of lung diseases utilizing extracted MFCC

features from respiratory sounds. *Multimedia Tools Appl.*, 83, 35, 82871–82903, 2024.

7. Pratihar, R. and Sankar, R., Advancements in Parkinson's Disease Diagnosis: A Comprehensive Survey on Biomarker Integration and Machine Learning. *Computers*, 13, Art. no. 11, Nov. 2024, doi: 10.3390/computers13110293.
8. AlMahadin, G., Lotfi, A., Zysk, E., Siena, F.L., Carthy, M.M., Breedon, P., Parkinson's disease: current assessment methods and wearable devices for evaluation of movement disorder motor symptoms-a patient and healthcare professional perspective. *BMC Neurol.*, 20, 1, 419, 2020.
9. Srivastava, A., Sarkar, S., Bose, I., Toward Early Parkinson's Disease Detection: A Novel RL-CNN-Based Approach, in: *Operations Research and Data Analytics: Current Trends and Future Perspectives: Selected Papers from International Conference on Industrial Engineering and Analytics (ICONIEA) 2024*, pp. 177–193, Springer Nature Singapore, Singapore, 2026, January.
10. Kalia, L.V., *et al.*, International Parkinson and Movement Disorder Society Viewpoint on Biological Frameworks of Parkinson's Disease: Current Status and Future Directions. *Mov. Disord.*, 39, 10, 1710–1715, Oct. 2024, doi: 10.1002/mds.30007.
11. Abedinzadeh Torghabeh, F., Ahmadi Moghadam, E., Hosseini, S.A., Houshmand, M., Voice-driven Parkinson's detection using bidirectional long short-term memory and attention on mobile-recorded speech. *Netw. Model. Anal. Health Inform. Bioinform.*, 15, 1, 33, 2026.
12. Silva, A.B.R.L., de Oliveira, R.W.G., Diógenes, G.P., de Castro Aguiar, M.F., Sallem, C.C., Lima, M.P.P., Dos Santos, J.C.C., Premotor, nonmotor and motor symptoms of Parkinson's disease: a new clinical state of the art. *Ageing Res. Rev.*, 84, 101834, 2023.
13. Critchley, E.M., Speech disorders of Parkinsonism: a review. *J. Neurol. Neurosurg. Psychiatry*, 44, 9, 751–758, 1981.
14. Self-supervised learning for early detection of neurodegenerative diseases with small data, NTU Singapore, Accessed: Nov. 28, 2024. [Online]. Available: https://dr.ntu.edu.sg/handle/10356/166402.
15. Sara, J.D.S., Orbelo, D., Maor, E., Lerman, L.O., Lerman, A., Guess What We Can Hear—Novel Voice Biomarkers for the Remote Detection of Disease. *Mayo Clin. Proc.*, 98, 9, 1353–1375, Sep. 2023, doi: 10.1016/j.mayocp.2023.03.007.
16. Keserwani, P.K., Das, S., Sarkar, N., A comparative study: prediction of parkinson's disease using machine learning, deep learning and nature inspired algorithm. *Multimedia Tools Appl.*, 83, 69393–69441, 2024.
17. Reddy, K.P., Satish, M., Prakash, A., Babu, S.M., Kumar, P.P., Devi, B.S., Machine Learning Revolution in Early Disease Detection for Healthcare: Advancements, Challenges, and Future Prospects, in: *2023 IEEE 5th International Conference on Cybernetics, Cognition and Machine Learning Applications (ICCCMLA)*, Oct. 2023, pp. 638–643, doi: 10.1109/ICCCMLA58983.2023.10346963.

18. Ahmed, I., Aljahdali, S., *et al.*, Classification of parkinson disease based on patient's voice signal us. Accessed: Nov. 28, 2024. [Online]. Available: https://zuscholars.zu.ac.ae/works/4673/.
19. Gwinn, K., David, K.K., Swanson-Fischer, C., Albin, R., Hillaire-Clarke, C.S., Sieber, B.A., Rosenthal, L.S., Parkinson's disease biomarkers: perspective from the NINDS Parkinson's Disease Biomarkers Program. *Biomarkers Med.*, 11, 6, 451–473, 2017.
20. Garcia Santa Cruz, B., Husch, A., Hertel, F., Machine learning models for diagnosis and prognosis of Parkinson's disease using brain imaging: general overview, main challenges, and future directions. *Front. Aging Neurosci.*, 15, 1216163, 2023.
21. Parkinsons, UCI Machine Learning Repository, Accessed: Nov. 28, 2024. [Online]. Available: https://archive.ics.uci.edu/dataset/174/parkinsons.
22. Athanasios Tsanas, M.L., Parkinsons Telemonitoring. UCI Machine Learning Repository, 2009, doi: 10.24432/C5ZS3N.
23. Brumm, M.C., Siderowf, A., Simuni, T., Burghardt, E., Choi, S.H., Caspell-Garcia, C., Parkinson's Progression Markers Initiative, Parkinson's progression markers initiative: a milestone-based strategy to monitor Parkinson's disease progression. *J. Parkinsons Dis.*, 13, 6, 899–916, 2023.
24. Bot, B.M., Suver, C., Neto, E.C., Kellen, M., Klein, A., Bare, C., Trister, A.D., The mPower study, Parkinson disease mobile data collected using ResearchKit. *Sci. Data*, 3, 1, 1–9, 2016.
25. Orozco-Arroyave, J.R., Arias-Londoño, J.D., Vargas-Bonilla, J.F., GonzalezRátiva, M.C., Nöth, E., New Spanish speech corpus database for the analysis of people suffering from Parkinson's disease, in: *Lrec*, pp. 342–347, 2014, May.
26. SAMI - Signal Analysis, Modelling, and Interpretation Group, Accessed: Nov. 28, 2024. [Online]. Available: https://sami.fel.cvut.cz/databases.htm.
27. Durmus, H., Gokalp, M.A., Hanagasi, H.A., Prevalence of Parkinson's disease in Baskale, Turkey: a population based study. *Neurol. Sci. Off. J. Ital. Neurol. Soc. Ital. Soc. Clin. Neurophysiol.*, 36, 3, 411–413, Mar. 2015, doi: 10.1007/s10072-014-1988-x.
28. Woldert-Jokisz, B., <bogwol@coli.uni-sb.de>, Saarbruecken Voice Database, http://stimmdatenbank.coli.uni-saarland.de. Accessed: Nov. 29, 2024. [Online]. Available: https://stimmdb.coli.uni-saarland.de/help_en.php4.
29. arabic_speech_corpus, TensorFlow Datasets, TensorFlow, Accessed: Nov. 28, 2024. [Online]. Available: https://www.tensorflow.org/datasets/community_catalog/huggingface/arabic_speech_corpus.
30. Parkinson's Disease (PD) classification, Accessed: Nov. 29, 2024. [Online]. Available: https://www.kaggle.com/datasets/dipayanbiswas/parkinsons-disease- speech-signal-features.
31. Parkinson's Voice Initiative. Accessed: Nov. 28, 2024. [Online]. Available: https://www.parkinsonsvoice.org/.

32. Dimauro, G., Italian Parkinson's Voice and Speech, IEEE, Jun. 11, 2019, Accessed: Nov. 28, 2024. [Online]. Available: https://ieee-dataport.org/open-access/italian-parkinsons-voice-and-speech.
33. Hlavnička, J., Čmejla, R., Klempíř, J., Růžička, E., Rusz, J., Acoustic tracking of pitch, modal, and subharmonic vibrations of vocal folds in Parkinson's disease and parkinsonism. *IEEE Access*, 7, 150339–150354, 2019.
34. Brahmi, Z., Mahyoob, M., Al-Sarem, M., Algaraady, J., Bousselmi, K., Alblwi, A., Exploring the role of machine learning in diagnosing and treating speech disorders: A systematic literature review. *Psychol. Res. Behav. Manag.*, 2205–2232, 2024.
35. Frota, S., Cruz, M., Cardoso, R., Guimarães, I., Ferreira, J.J., Pinto, S., Vigário, M., (Dys) Prosody in Parkinson's disease: effects of medication and disease duration on intonation and prosodic phrasing. *Brain Sci.*, 11, 8, 1100, 2021.
36. Chatterjee, K., *et al.*, PDD-ET: Parkinson's Disease Detection Using ML Ensemble Techniques and Customized Big Dataset. *Information*, 14, Art. no. 9, Sep. 2023, doi: 10.3390/info14090502.
37. Naranjo, L., Perez, C.J., Campos-Roca, Y., Martin, J., Addressing voice recording replications for Parkinson's disease detection. *Expert Syst. Appl.*, 46, 286–292, 2016.
38. Rana, A., Dumka, A., Singh, R., Rashid, M., Ahmad, N., Panda, M.K., An efficient machine learning approach for diagnosing Parkinson's disease by utilizing voice features. *Electronics*, 11, 22, 3782, 2022.
39. Bhambri, P., Soni, R., Tran, T.A., eds. Smart Healthcare Systems: AI and IoT Perspectives. CRC Press, Taylor & Francis Group, 2024.
40. Salari, N., Kazeminia, M., Sagha, H., Daneshkhah, A., Ahmadi, A., Mohammadi, M., The performance of various machine learning methods for Parkinson's disease recognition: a systematic review. *Curr. Psychol.*, 42, 20, 16637–16660, 2023.
41. Parkinson disease prediction using intrinsic mode function based features from speech signal, ScienceDirect, Accessed: Nov. 29, 2024. [Online]. Available: https://www.sciencedirect.com/science/article/abs/pii/S0208521618305564.
42. Xu, X., Li, J., Zhu, Z., Zhao, L., Wang, H., Song, C., Pei, Y., A comprehensive review on synergy of multi-modal data and ai technologies in medical diagnosis. *Bioengineering*, 11, 3, 219, 2024.
43. Shi, X., Wang, T., Wang, L., Liu, H., Yan, N., Hybrid convolutional recurrent neural networks outperform CNN and RNN in task-state EEG detection for Parkinson's disease, in: *2019 Asia-Pacific signal and information processing association annual summit and conference (APSIPA ASC)*, pp. 939–944, IEEE, 2019, November.
44. Tiwari, M. and Verma, D.K., Enhanced text-independent speaker recognition using MFCC, Bi-LSTM, and CNN-based noise removal techniques. *Int. J. Speech Technol.*, 27, 4, 1013–1026, 2024.

45. Zebari, R., Abdulazeez, A., Zeebaree, D., Zebari, D., Saeed, J., A comprehensive review of dimensionality reduction techniques for feature selection and feature extraction. *J. Appl. Sci. Technol. Trends*, 1, 1, 56–70, 2020.
46. Srinivasan, S., Ramadass, P., Mathivanan, S.K., Panneer Selvam, K., Shivahare, B.D., Shah, M.A., Detection of Parkinson disease using multiclass machine learning approach. *Sci. Rep.*, 14, 1, 13813, 2024.
47. Calderone, A., Latella, D., Bonanno, M., Quartarone, A., Mojdehdehbaher, S., Celesti, A., Calabrò, R.S., Towards transforming neurorehabilitation: the impact of artificial intelligence on diagnosis and treatment of neurological disorders. *Biomedicines*, 12, 10, 2415, 2024.
48. Alshammri, R., Alharbi, G., Alharbi, E., Almubark, I., Machine learning approaches to identify Parkinson's disease using voice signal features. *Front. Artif. Intell.*, 6, Mar. 2023, doi: 10.3389/frai.2023.1084001.
49. Sayed, M.A., Tayaba, M., Islam, M.D., Pavel, M.E.U.I., Mia, M.T., Ayon, E.H., ... Ghosh, B.P., Parkinson's disease detection through vocal biomarkers and advanced machine learning algorithms. *J. Comput. Sci. Technol. Stud.*, arXiv preprint arXiv:2311.05435, 2023.
50. Khanom, F., Biswas, S., Uddin, M.S., Mostafiz, R., XEMLPD: an explainable ensemble machine learning approach for Parkinson disease diagnosis with optimized features. *Int. J. Speech Technol.*, Oct. 2024, doi: 10.1007/s10772-024-10152-2.
51. Johnson, S., *et al.*, Wearable Sensor-Based Assessments for Remotely Screening Early-Stage Parkinson's Disease. *Sensors*, 24, Art. no. 17, Jan. 2024, doi: 10.3390/s24175637.
52. Gupta, I., Sharma, V., Kaur, S., Singh, A.K., PCA-RF: An Efficient Parkinson's Disease Prediction Model based on Random Forest Classification, Mar. 21, 2022. *arXiv: arXiv:2203.11287*. doi: 10.48550/arXiv.2203.11287.
53. Boualoulou, N., Drissi, T.B., Nsiri, B., CNN and LSTM for the classification of parkinson's disease based on the GTCC and MFCC. *Appl. Comput. Sci.*, 19, 2, 1–24, 2023.
54. Vats, S. and Mehta, S., The Impact of Deep Belief Networks on the Early Diagnosis of Parkinson's Disease, in: *2024 5th International Conference on Electronics and Sustainable Communication Systems (ICESC)*, pp. 980–984, IEEE, 2024, August.
55. Dahmani, M. and Guerti, M., Glottal signal parameters as features set for neurological voice disorders diagnosis using K-Nearest Neighbors (KNN), in: *2018 2nd international conference on natural language and speech processing (ICNLSP)*, 2018, April, IEEE, pp. 1–5.
56. Solana-Lavalle, G. and Rosas-Romero, R., Analysis of voice as an assisting tool for detection of Parkinson's disease and its subsequent clinical interpretation. *Biomed. Signal Process. Control*, 66, 102415, Apr. 2021, doi: 10.1016/j.bspc.2021.102415.
57. Almasoud, A.S., Eisa, T.A.E., Al-Wesabi, F.N., Elsafi, A., Al Duhayyim, M., Yaseen, I., Motwakel, A., Parkinson's detection using RNN-graph-LSTM

with optimization based on speech signals. *Comput. Mater. Continua*, 72, 872–886, 2022.
58. Amato, F., Voice as the reservoir of valuable clinical information: a diagnosis and monitoring support for speech-affecting diseases.
59. Jovanovic, L., Damaševičius, R., Matic, R., Kabiljo, M., Simic, V., Kunjadic, G., Bacanin, N., Detecting Parkinson's disease from shoe-mounted accelerometer sensors using convolutional neural networks optimized with modified metaheuristics. *PeerJ Comput. Sci.*, 10, e2031, 2024.
60. Noor, M.B.T., Zenia, N.Z., Kaiser, M.S., Mamun, S.A., Mahmud, M., Application of deep learning in detecting neurological disorders from magnetic resonance images: a survey on the detection of Alzheimer's disease, Parkinson's disease and schizophrenia. *Brain Inf.*, 7, 1, 11, 2020.
61. Belabbas, S., Addou, D., Selouani, S.A., Pathological voice classification system based on CNN-BiLSTM network using speech enhancement and multi-stream approach. *Int. J. Speech Technol.*, 27, 2, 483–502, 2024.
62. Rehman, A., Saba, T., Mujahid, M., Alamri, F.S., ElHakim, N., Parkinson's disease detection using hybrid LSTM-GRU deep learning model. *Electronics*, 12, 13, 2856, 2023.
63. Ghaheri, P., Nasiri, H., Shateri, A., Homafar, A., Diagnosis of Parkinson's disease based on voice signals using SHAP and hard voting ensemble method. *Comput. Methods Biomech. Biomed. Eng.*, 27, 13, 1858–1874, Oct. 2024, doi: 10.1080/10255842.2023.2263125.
64. Ge, W., Lueck, C., Suominen, H., Apthorp, D., Has machine learning over-promised in healthcare?: A critical analysis and a proposal for improved evaluation, with evidence from Parkinson's disease. *Artif. Intell. Med.*, 139, 102524, May 2023, doi: 10.1016/j.artmed.2023.102524.
65. Priyadarshi, R., Ranjan, R., Sahana, B.C., Bhandari, A.K., Kankanala, S., A comprehensive overview of smart healthcare technologies in revolutionizing modern rehabilitation practices. *Connect. Sci.*, 38, 1, 2612458, 2026.
66. Alzubaidi, M.S., Shah, U., Dhia Zubaydi, H., Dolaat, K., Abd-Alrazaq, A.A., Ahmed, A., Househ, M., The role of neural network for the detection of Parkinson's disease: a scoping review. *Healthcare*, 9, 6, 740, 2021, June, MDPI.
67. Loh, H.W., Hong, W., Ooi, C.P., Chakraborty, S., Barua, P.D., Deo, R.C., Acharya, U.R., Application of deep learning models for automated identification of Parkinson's disease: a review (2011–2021). *Sensors*, 21, 21, 7034, 2021.
68. Pramanik, M., Pradhan, R., Nandy, P., Bhoi, A.K., Barsocchi, P., Machine learning methods with decision forests for Parkinson's detection. *Appl. Sci.*, 11, 2, 581, 2021.
69. Zhang, J., Mining imaging and clinical data with machine learning approaches for the diagnosis and early detection of Parkinson's disease. *NPJ Parkinsons Dis.*, 8, 1, 13, Jan. 2022, doi: 10.1038/s41531-021-00266-8.
70. Belić, M., Bobić, V., Badža, M., Šolaja, N., Đurić-Jovičić, M., Kostić, V.S., Artificial intelligence for assisting diagnostics and assessment of Parkinson's

disease—A review. *Clin. Neurol. Neurosurg.*, 184, 105442, Sep. 2019, doi: 10.1016/j.clineuro.2019.105442.

71. Eskofier, B.M., *et al.*, Recent machine learning advancements in sensor-based mobility analysis: Deep learning for Parkinson's disease assessment, in: *2016 38th Annual International Conference of the IEEE Engineering in Medicine and Biology Society (EMBC)*, Aug. 2016, IEEE, Orlando, FL, USA, pp. 655–658, doi: 10.1109/EMBC.2016.7590787.
72. Qasim, H.M., Ata, O., Ansari, M.A., Alomary, M.N., Alghamdi, S., Almehmadi, M., Hybrid feature selection framework for the Parkinson imbalanced dataset prediction problem. *Medicina*, 57, 11, 1217, 2021.
73. Sigcha, L., Borzì, L., Amato, F., Rechichi, I., Ramos-Romero, C., Cárdenas, A., Olmo, G., Deep learning and wearable sensors for the diagnosis and monitoring of Parkinson's disease: A systematic review. *Expert Syst. Appl.*, 229, 120541, 2023.
74. Tabashum, T., Snyder, R.C., O'Brien, M.K., Albert, M.V., Machine learning models for parkinson disease: Systematic review. *JMIR Med. Inf.*, 12, 1, e50117, 2024.
75. Priyadharshini, S., Ramkumar, K., Vairavasundaram, S., Narasimhan, K., Venkatesh, S., Amirtharajan, R., Kotecha, K., A comprehensive framework for parkinson's disease diagnosis using explainable artificial intelligence empowered machine learning techniques. *Alexandria Eng. J.*, 107, 568–582, 2024.
76. Ghaffar, W., Anwar, M., Rafiq, M., Masood, S., Nasim, F., Assessing Parkinson's Disease Apps Using Thematic Analysis And Machine Learning Techniques. *J. Comput. Biomed. Inform.*, 6, 02, 463–490, 2024.
77. Magesh, P.R., Myloth, R.D., Tom, R.J., An Explainable Machine Learning Model for Early Detection of Parkinson's Disease using LIME on DaTSCAN Imagery. *Comput. Biol. Med.*, 126, 104041, Nov. 2020, doi: 10.1016/j.compbiomed.2020.104041.
78. Ganesh, S., Vedagiri, S., Srinivas, K.S., Detection of Parkinson's Disease Using Non-invasive Biomarkers, in: *International Conference On Innovative Computing And Communication*, pp. 125–138, Springer Nature Singapore, Singapore, 2024, February.
79. Pavithra, D., Jayanthi, A.N., Nidhya, R., Balamurugan, S., Autism screening tools with machine learning and deep learning methods: a review. *Tele-Healthcare: Applications of Artificial Intelligence and Soft Computing Techniques*, Wiley Online Library, 221-247, 2022.

17

Neuro-AI-Driven Image Augmentation and Data Leak Prevention *via* Automated Classification Agents

S. M. Keerthana[1]* and K. Vijayakumar[2]

[1]*Dept. of Computer Science and Engineering, St. Joseph's Institute of Technology, Chennai, Tamil Nadu, India*

[2]*Dept. of Information Technology, St. Joseph's Institute of Technology, Chennai, Tamil Nadu, India*

Abstract

The advancement of Natural Language Processing (NLP) in Medical Health Records (MHRs) and infrared micro-object detection is constrained by limited access to large, annotated datasets, primarily due to the high cost of annotation and privacy concerns. In parallel, infrared object detection suffers from low signal-to-noise ratios, ambiguous object structures, and insufficient data availability. While Generative Adversarial Networks (GANs) are widely employed for data augmentation, they often produce augmentation leaks—distorted outputs that closely mimic the augmented inputs—thereby compromising data realism and reliability. To address these challenges, we propose a Neuro-AI-inspired Automated Augmentation Classifier Agent (AACA), a lightweight neural module that monitors and regulates augmentation during GAN training. By detecting and filtering augmentation operations, AACA effectively mitigates augmentation leaks and enhances the quality of synthesized data. Achieving an accuracy of 98.57% without increasing training time, AACA offers a high-performance, biologically inspired solution for robust data generation in NLP, medical imaging, and micro-object detection tasks.

Keywords: Augmentation, NLP, synthetic data, neural network

**Corresponding author*: keerthanasmk@gmail.com

R. Nidhya, A. Dineshkumar, Sheng-Lung Peng, S. Karthik and S. Balamurugan (eds.) Neuro-Symbolic Artificial Intelligence: Concepts & Applications, (337–354) © 2026 Scrivener Publishing LLC

17.1 Introduction

In recent years, the exponential rise of computer vision applications requires the use of huge and diverse datasets to properly train deep learning models. Obtaining and classifying massive volumes of data is frequently costly, time-consuming, and in some situations it is impractical. Image augmentation is a technique to increase the volume of a dataset by performing different changes on existing images. It is commonly used in disciplines such as machine learning and computer vision to artificially enlarge training datasets, hence improving model generalization and performance. It has been suggested that synthetic data is a viable substitute for genuine data. In situations where sharing real data is prohibited due to privacy concerns [1], some researchers use fake data to collaborate on common activities. As there are no annotations, the creation of synthetic text by itself is not helpful for training NLP models. A pretrained model or human annotation may have been the source of such in-text annotations. The unique tokens are made explicitly a part of the language modeling goal by being included in the training set. In the business, ensuring that fresh generative models can be consistently built and implemented while maintaining their ability to generalize to new generators is very crucial. Initially, exchanging clinical data with other researchers is prohibited due to privacy concerns. Second, especially at the scale required by contemporary NLP models, annotating data is an expensive and time-consuming procedure that is unfeasible for many businesses. It has been suggested that synthetic data is a viable substitute for genuine data. The privacy problem is addressed by not identifying actual people.

Automated Augmentation: Data augmentation is a learning approach that creates an artificial dataset by applying different changes to the given data. Images can be cropped, rotated, flipped, or have noise added to them. Models are strengthened by augmentation [2], which exposes them to several modified copies of the source data. The word "automated" implies that the AACA controls this procedure without the need for human involvement.

Classifier Agent: In machine learning, a classifier plays the role of classifying incoming data into several classes. Here, "agent" specifies an intermediate that makes judgments on classification tasks on its own (like a neural network model) to enhance the data. The AACA can be in charge of examining enhanced samples to ascertain whether or not they enhance the performance of the classifier.

17.2 Background

Segmenting medical images is a crucial task in medical diagnosis. Medical picture segmentation should properly portray the form of an organ or disease. The shapes that are shown help doctors diagnose patients and keep them from making misdiagnoses. Based on the original images, various augmentation techniques like combining two photos, rotating them, and flipping them horizontally can be achieved [3]; however, medical images cannot be processed using these conventional techniques. Accurate boundaries between the segmented target and backdrop are crucial, yet data augmentation techniques like Gaussian Blur often process the full medical image. This frequently results in the creation of medical images that are inconsistent with the distribution and worsen the diagnosis. Medical image segmentation often lacks efficient data augmentation techniques that are not search-intensive. Most traditional methods involve computationally expensive search-based augmentations, which can be resource-heavy and time-consuming. An alternative is task-aligned augmentation that applies geometric transformations (like rotations, scaling) and intensity variations, tailored to preserve anatomical accuracy. Synthetic data generation using GANs or diffusion models can also enhance diversity without heavy computation. These approaches ensure effective augmentation while being resource-efficient and suitable for medical contexts. By permitting the expansion of a substantial amount of data while preserving the whole boundaries of the segmented target, Keep Mask and KeepMix [4] offer high-performance segmentation results. KeepMix strategy is proposed to generate new images by fusing medical images with and without objects. By disturbing the backdrop, KeepMask may precisely preserve boundaries and multi-segmented targets. Figure 17.1 illustrates the process of image augmentation using GAN architecture, showing how synthetic and real data are differentiated.

Current approaches mostly rely on square or rectangular bounding boxes, which focus on local regions and frequently ignore the discriminative local

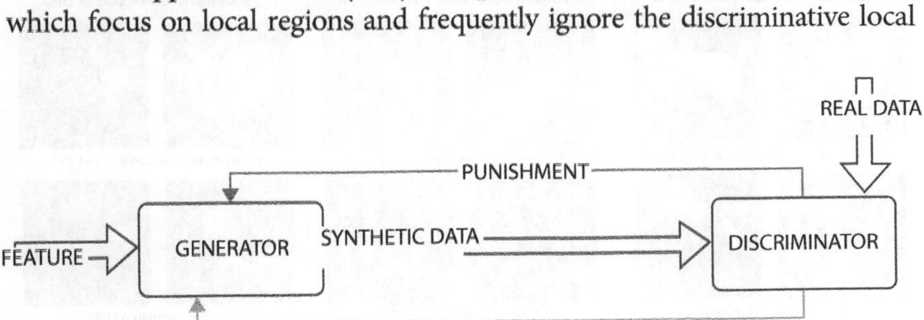

Figure 17.1 Augmentation of images using GAN.

context of the picture, losing entire semantic object parts in the process. A global classification of the fused (augmented) image loss, a superpixel-wise weighted local classification loss, and a superpixel-based weighted contrastive learning loss are employed to train the model. The last two losses are based on the superpixel-aware attentive embeddings. As a consequence, the resulting deep encoder may learn both local and global elements of the images while recording object component local context and information. A brand-new, lightweight convolutional neural network architecture specifically suited for automated exudation identification are intended to reliably and effectively recognize these indicators: domain-specific data additions to improve the generalizability of the model. Within our unique design, they have used a number of regularization approaches to maximize computing efficiency and improve diagnostic accuracy. For convolutional neural networks (CNNs) to operate at their best, there are significant computing requirements for deploying them. Exudates that occur during the non-proliferative stage of diabetic retinopathy (DR) are an important diagnostic sign. Because the integrity of the retinal pericytes is impaired, these lesions increase vascular permeability, which causes plasma components like proteins and lipoproteins to seep out. Figure 17.2 shows examples of medical image augmentation using KeepMix and KeepMask techniques on different datasets.

The significance of image augmentation techniques in optimizing CNN performance for geological image analysis involves in the classification of igneous, metamorphic, and sedimentary rock type images of rock thin sections (RTSs), where they enhance the speed, objectivity, and precision of the classification process. These techniques evaluate how conventional

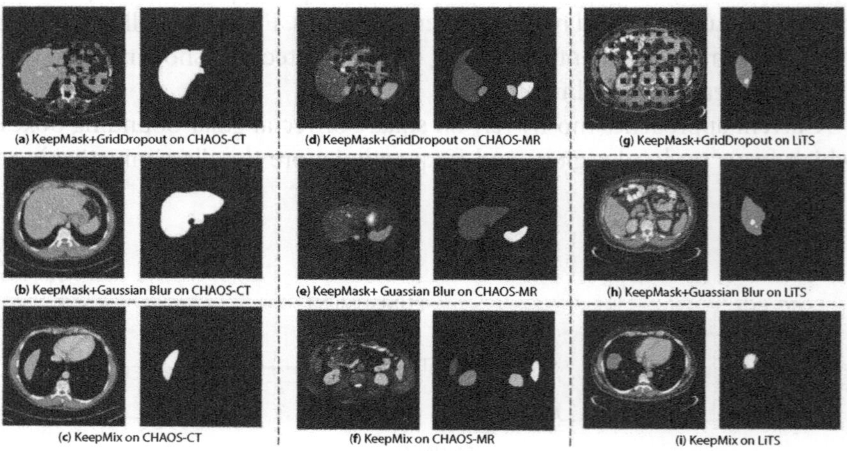

Figure 17.2 Medical Images Augmented using KeepMix and KeepMask techniques [4].

image augmentation techniques affect the accuracy and precision of the model. Augmentation techniques like Equalize significantly enhance the model's classification ability with gain of F_1 scores of 0.9869 for volcanic rocks, 0.9884 for metamorphic rocks, and 0.9929 for sedimentary rocks [6]. Furthermore, the weighted average F_1 score of 0.9886 across all images and techniques indicates as an improvement to this model. However, by producing poorer accuracy and F_1 score (0.949 for volcanic rocks, 0.954 for metamorphic rocks, and 0.9416 for sedimentary rocks), methods like Distort worsen performance compared to the baseline values.

Having a balanced quantity of samples for the different type of diseases is typically a difficult task. These problems hinder the development of machine learning and natural language processing methods for processing data from electronic medical records. A model called the Medical Text Generative Adversarial Network [7] was developed to generate synthetic text from EMRs in order to solve these problems. It is based on the GAN architecture and is trained using the reinforce algorithm. It generates synthetic texts as EMRs for the associated diseases after receiving inputs on the features of the ailment. The model is evaluated at the application level, macro-level, and micro-level using a Chinese EMR text dataset. The model is trained using REINFORCE algorithm to generate synthetic data. It has been suggested to use mtGAN [5] to produce artificial EMR text. In order to meet different research objectives, it is employed to manage the creation process with assigned particular disease traits. The model performance has been evaluated using macro-level, application-level, and micro-level design techniques, and this model performs better than other baseline models. The application-level experiment findings suggest that generated synthetic data can achieve equivalent performance in machine learning tasks compared with the real data, which can be employed as a data augmentation strategy.

Cameras, sensors, and other monitoring tools are widely used in industrial settings for product quality assurance and inspection. Usually, decision trees and other conventional AI models are trained using the data from these cameras and sensors. The majority of these AI models, however, are based on supervised algorithms, which necessitate human-annotated cases, where each instance is given a particular label or class to be taught. One typical application is the automatic detection of faulty items, where the training dataset for the AI model has to have a sufficient number of labeled examples classified as either "good" or "defective." In the industrial setting, creating these datasets poses two major challenges. First, models have difficulty in properly detecting or segmenting the damaged items due to the limited number of training samples. This problem is crucial in many domains, including structural infrastructure monitoring, early defect identification, and segmentation in industrial components. Secondly, time and staffing limitations, particularly in small- or medium-sized businesses, beyond the lack of quality data: there are major challenges in creating the required datasets. The work is made more difficult by the labor-intensive and time-consuming labeling procedure. Table 17.1 lists traditional image augmentation methods and their respective use cases.

An NLP-based transformation is used to convert the high-dimensional eye-tracking data into a learning-suitable representation. Additionally, generative modeling might be applied to the generation of synthetic data. These empirical experiments promote further investigation and development of for NLP-based techniques to generate artificial eye-tracking datasets for a wide range of potential applications. Conventional models typically provide F_1 scores between 0.75 and 0.87, when the model is trained using UMD dataset. For all models, the synthetic data-driven approach [6], which takes social aspects into account, consistently yields F_1 scores of 0.89. Synthetic data creation, which is artificially created data that closely mimics real-world data, offers a workable way to offset the data availability restriction. As it overcomes many of the difficulties associated with gathering and annotating real-world raw data, synthetic data creation may be quite helpful in training the model of machine learning applications.

Table 17.1 Traditional augmentation.

Augmentation methods	Use
Rotation	Rotating the image to different angle.
Flipping	Horizontally or vertically flipping the image.
Scaling	Zooming in or out on the image.
Cropping	Randomly or strategically cropping a portion of the image.
Translation	Shifting the image horizontally or vertically.
Color Jittering	Randomly changing the brightness, contrast, saturation, or hue of the image.
Shearing	Slanting the image along the *x*- or *y*-axis.
Affine Transformation	Combination of scaling, rotation, translation, and shearing.

Traditional Augmentation

- Rotation: Rotating the image by a certain angle (e.g., 90°, 180°). This makes the model invariant to orientation changes.
- Flipping: Horizontally or vertically flipping the image to ensure that the model captures the features in any aspect and non-linearity.
- Scaling: Zooming in or out on the image.
- Cropping: Randomly or strategically cropping a portion of the image.
- Translation: Shifting the image horizontally or vertically.
- Shearing: Slanting the image along the *x*- or *y*-axis.
- Adding Noise: Injecting random noise into the image to make it more challenging for the model.
- Color Jittering: Randomly changing the brightness, contrast, saturation, or hue of the image.
- Gaussian Blur: Applying a blur filter to the image to simulate the effect of an out-of-focus camera.
- Cutout/Masking: Randomly masking out parts of the image by replacing them with black or gray boxes.
- Affine Transformations: Combination of scaling, rotation, translation, and shearing.

Large Language Models in Augmentation Techniques

- LSTM-Based Model: Able to capture long-term dependencies in sequential data, supporting data augmentation through the generation of synthetic sequences. They can be trained on existing datasets in order to create new meaningful text sequences, fill gaps in incomplete data, or even generate variations in text data while still being relevant within context. This feature proves useful in tasks like text generation, paraphrasing, and time-series data augmentation.
  - Sequence Generation: LSTM networks learn very well from patterns of sequential data and thus generate new sequences [7] that closely mimic the original data. For example, in text augmentation, LSTMs can produce plausible sentences or paragraphs to add to the dataset to be used for training language models.
  - Paraphrasing and Variations: LSTM models can be used to paraphrase any given sentence without losing meaning,

thus providing different ways to present the same information; this is very useful when it comes to NLP tasks such as question-answering or summarizing.

- Handling Temporal Data: In time-series data, LSTMs help model trends and generate synthetic data points [8] that mimic those in real-world patterns in order to improve the strength of predictive models in use in weather forecasting or financial market analysis.
- Noise Addition and Removal: Through controlled variation of data *via* LSTM-based generation, models can model noisy environments that would boost generalization for downstream tasks.
- Domain-Specific Augmentation: The models can be fine-tuned on domain-specific data (e.g., medical records or technical documents) to create targeted augmentations that reflect industry-specific language and structure.

- OpenAI's DALL·E and Stable Diffusion.
  - DALL·E, developed by OpenAI, excels at generating high-quality, imaginative, and often surreal images based on detailed textual prompts. It also offers advanced features like inpainting [9], which allows users to edit specific parts of an image by providing a new description. This model is widely used in creative domains such as art, design, and content creation for marketing or storytelling purposes, thanks to its ability to translate complex ideas into visually stunning results.
  - Stable Diffusion is an open-source text-to-image model known for its flexibility and community-driven development. It is designed to work efficiently on consumer-grade hardware, making it accessible to a broader audience. Stable Diffusion provides fine-grained control over image generation, allowing users to create highly detailed and customized visuals. It supports a wide range of applications, including digital art, game design, and prototyping, and is often preferred by developers and artists who value its adaptability and the ability to tweak the underlying model. Both models showcase the transformative potential of AI in creative fields [19], with DALL·E emphasizing ease of use and artistic creativity, while Stable Diffusion offers greater control and

flexibility, particularly for developers and power users. Together, they represent significant advancements in how technology can bridge the gap between language and visual expression.

Application of Augmentation

- Increasing the accuracy of model predictions.
- Enhancing the models with additional training data.
- Avoiding the lack of data to create better models.
- Lowering data over fitting a statistical inaccuracy that occurs when a function matches a small number of data points too closely and introducing data variability improving the models' capacity for generalization, which aids in resolving classification problems, including class imbalance.
- Lowering data collection and labeling costs makes it possible to anticipate unusual events.
- Avoids issues with data privacy.

Challenges of Augmentation
Businesses must develop methods for assessing the quality of enhanced datasets where the quality of the output from data augmentation techniques needs to be evaluated as their use grows. The field of data augmentation must conduct fresh investigation studies to provide novel, synthetic data with cutting-edge uses. For instance, employing GANs to generate high-resolution photos might be difficult, but data that is enhanced from a genuine dataset that has biases in it will also have biases. Determining the best data augmentation approach is crucial in the current scenario. GADT is a brand-new DA-based attack algorithm. Through iterative antagonism, GADT finds appropriate DA parameters and then updates the Artificial Neural Network using posterior estimates based on these values. In order to determine adversarial DA parameters and present a novel loss function as a measure during DA optimization, we exclusively utilize a differentiable DA operation library. This loss term maintains attacks by enhancing adversarial effects while retaining the original image content.

Augmenting Medical Image
Medical image classification is a difficult process that requires accuracy and robustness, particularly in application fields where annotated datasets are few and exhibit significant imbalance across target classes.

Taking into account that gathering data isn't always possible, particularly for underrepresented classes.

Using Variational Autoencoders (VAEs) with Class Specificity: Through latent representation interpolation inside classes, we may produce synthetic pictures that enlarge the feature space and directly solve the issue of class imbalance.
Focused Feature Space Enrichment: By adding realistic synthetic pictures to the feature space [10] where gaps exist, our method increases training efficacy and model sensitivity to crucially important but subtle characteristics for precise classification.
Evidence of Our Method's Adaptability to Different Architectures: The advantages of the augmentation approach are evident in two well-known image classification architectures, ResNet-50 and EfficientNet-V2.

17.3 Methods

17.3.1 Preprocessing and Automatic Annotating

We pseudonymize the genuine data that has been gathered before utilizing it to create the language model. The data is quite similar to that which is utilized in background research publications, and we anticipate findings that are similarly successful. To illustrate the rationale for annotating the original papers, let's assume that the quality is good enough for a preliminary investigation into the feasibility of our synthetic data production technique. Nonetheless, we suggest including the annotations in the language modeling for two reasons. First, a pretrained model, the language models could be able to produce new things. Secondly, annotating the language modeling data is more efficient because it allows us to create synthetic datasets that are several orders of magnitude bigger than the original data.

17.3.2 Architecture

The design approach concentrated on integrating two convolutional blocks to produce a lightweight architecture appropriate for deployment in limited hardware environments. To enable effective feature extraction [11], each block employs a max-pooling layer after a certain number of filters. After that, a ReLU activation function is applied to these feature maps in order to add the required non-linearity to the network. The result of the neural network is a two-layer fully connected (FC) network, where 40 neurons make up the second layer and 100 neurons make up the first. Interestingly, a sparse arrangement of filters is used by the convolutional blocks to reduce processing burden. Although this simplified method simplifies things, it still requires strong feature extraction skills, which is why specific data augmentations are strategically added to improve the approach's capacity for generalization.

Auxiliary Neural Network: In addition to the primary classifier, the AACA may serve as a supplementary neural network model. Its job is to "classify" various methods of augmentation or enhanced data in a way that benefits the main model. Its use might involve evaluating the classifier's performance on the enhanced data and the data distribution [12] to dynamically select the optimal augmentation approach during training.

Intelligent Augmentation Strategy: Rather than implementing augmentations at random, AACA assesses the changes that produce the highest-quality, diversified training data that improves model performance. AACA can optimize the augmentation process by basing this evaluation on input from the primary model, such as accuracy or loss measures.

Self-Learning: As a neural network, AACA may be able to make better augmentation decisions over time as it processes more data and receives feedback from the primary classifier. In order to better suit the requirements of the primary model, the agent would adjust its augmentation tactics through an adaptive process. By automatically figuring out how to create and choose the best augmented data for the primary classification model, the AACA might act as a clever augmentation controller, improving

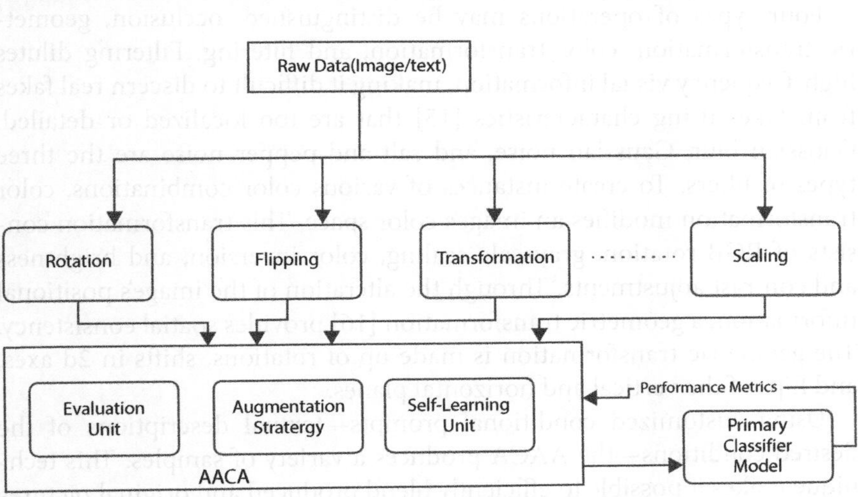

Figure 17.3 Architecture of automated augmentation classifier agent.

the system's overall resilience and generalization. Figure 17.3 presents the architecture of the Automated Augmentation Classifier Agent (AACA), which integrates performance metrics and self-learning for optimization.

First, a description of the used EMR record has been provided, and then, the model is implemented with deep neural networks. In order to guarantee optimal performance [12] for AACA, we test several augmentation techniques and discriminator architectures. We designed micro-, macro-, and application-level studies to assess the efficacy of our model, and the results show that AACA performs better than alternative baselines.

The initial dataset was systematically subjected to horizontal augmentation in order to strengthen the architectural resilience against fluctuations in picture orientation. In order to resolve possible differences that may occur during picture capture, such as variances in image placement or deviations induced by imaging equipment [13], this approach provides controlled adjustments in image orientation. In order to prevent the production of duplicate pictures, which can distort the model's learning process, vertical augmentation was purposefully left out.

Models are exposed to objects of various sizes through the process of rescaling photos. This improves the model's ability to generalize to new data with different object sizes. Rescaling helps the model detect objects at varying distances by simulating the impact of zooming in and out. The model introduces several scales during training [14]. The model is prevented from becoming overly familiar with the training set of objects and from overfitting to it. For neural networks that need fixed-size inputs, rescaling may be required to guarantee that every image in a dataset has the same size.

Four types of operations may be distinguished: occlusion, geometric transformation, color transformation, and filtering. Filtering dilutes high-frequency visual information, making it difficult to discern real fakes from fakes using characteristics [15] that are too localized or detailed. Gaussian blur, Gaussian noise, and salt-and-pepper noise are the three types of filters. To create instances of various color combinations, color transformation modifies an image's color space. This transformation consists of RGB rotation, grayscale scaling, color inversion, and brightness and contrast adjustments. Through the alteration of the image's positional information, a geometric transformation [16] provides spatial consistency. The geometric transformation is made up of rotations, shifts in 2d axes, and flips of the vertical and horizontal planes.

Using customized conditional prompts—textual descriptions of the desired conditions—the AACA produces a variety of samples. This technique makes it possible to efficiently blend produced and original pictures to produce hybrid images, increasing visual diversity while maintaining important semantics. The limitations of utilizing just produced pictures are addressed, which occasionally result in images that don't appear realistic or don't quite match the desired labels. It lowers the possibility of deceiving the training process by combining created material with real photos to guarantee that the augmented images preserve their natural appearance and accurate semantic information. An encoder, a middle block, and a skip-connected decoder are all part of the U-Net. Multiple blocks [7] make up both the encoder and the decoder, with the encoder handling downsampling and the decoder handling upsampling. Additionally, the model design incorporates Vision Transformers (ViTs), which offer processing dependent on attention.

An augmentation operation classifier based on ResNet 101 was used to measure the incidence rate of augmentation leaks and trained it for all augmentation operations [17]. The augmentation operation classifier was then used to identify augmentation leaks using the pictures produced by the GAN model as input. We deemed an augmentation leak to have happened if the chance of any augmentation operation occurring was greater than the criterion.

17.4 Result

A variety of criteria, including as overall accuracy, precision, recall, and F_1 score, were used to evaluate the model's performance and metrics for evaluation. Additionally, the SID performance is assessed across a range of generative models using the classification accuracy (ACC) and average precision (AP). In order to facilitate comparisons, the color scheme is decided by the percent ratio, where 0 and 1 denote the minimum and maximum, respectively, since the label sample sizes fluctuate. Additionally, zero values have been kept blank for easy reading in order to help concentrate attention on samples that were incorrectly categorized. Table 17.2 compares model performance among traditional techniques, machine learning methods, and AACA.

Table 17.2 Model comparison.

Model	Result
Traditional Techniques	86
Machine Learning Techniques	95
AACA	98.75

Two types of images have comparable visual characteristics; there is a propensity in the findings to misclassify igneous samples as metamorphic. On the other hand, the Equalize model shows better agreement between its prediction accuracy in the two datasets. This alignment demonstrates how well-chosen image augmentation methods may improve prediction accuracy [18] and enforce regularization to reduce overfitting.

The average performance of each model is shown by the relationship between the precision and accuracy model metrics for testing. This deviation from the optimal position represents the steady accuracy of the model. Furthermore, a circle with a 98% confidence level that is centered on the average point includes dispersed points, demonstrating steady accuracy. Greater stability is shown by smaller circles. The suggested image augmentation techniques are done with alterations to current SID pipelines [20] as a plug-and-play module because our approach is model-agnostic. The purpose of data augmentation is to improve the detecting object's backdrop. Every time, it takes four pictures from the input and applies random splicing and cropping to them. To acquire a batch size new data, the new photos [21] are constructed and the batch size time is repeated. The first involves training the model as usual, while the second involves sparse training, which induces and updates the weight to make it sparser. The pruning principle is applied while doing sparse training. The third is to compress the model by reducing the weight below the predetermined threshold value. The next step is fine-tuning, which allows the pruned model to be further trained to an ideal state by starting it with the trimmed weight. Table 17.3 presents the accuracy improvement achieved by applying various augmentation techniques.

The unauthorized or accidental exposure, transmission, or disclosure of sensitive, private, or confidential information always leads to a data

Table 17.3 Accuracy comparison based on augmentation techniques.

Augmentation techniques	Accuracy without augmentation	Accuracy with augmentation	Contribution to accuracy improvement
Rotation	78.25	82.25	+4.25
Flipping	73.55	81.65	+8.3
Transformation	81.63	90.77	+9.5
Scaling	79.1	81.52	+2.8
Combined Augmentations	78.17	82.52	+4.6

Table 17.4 Data leak prevention and accuracy achievement.

Metric	Before AACA	After AACA	Improvement
Total Data Leaks	150	15	93.3%
Metadata Exposure	100	13	92.5%
Duplicate Images Generated	30	3	90%
Leak Detection Accuracy	70	95	25%
False Positive Rate	10	2	80%

leak. This information leakage may include personal, financial, intellectual property, or organizational data [22] that is intended to remain protected. Unlike a data breach, where malicious actors intentionally hack systems to steal data, data leaks often occur due to negligence, oversight, or vulnerabilities in systems or processes. Table 17.4 shows the data leak prevention performance and accuracy enhancement achieved after applying AACA.

The leak rate is calculated (17.1),where the number of data leaked is calculated against the total data item. The major objective is to reduce the leakage while augmenting the images and then reduce the data leak using data anonymization to remove the mask or sensitive information before processing the dataset. Figure 17.4 compares model performance among traditional, machine learning, and AACA-based augmentation methods.

$$leakrate = \frac{no.of\ .leaks\ detected}{TotalDataitems} * 100 \tag{17.1}$$

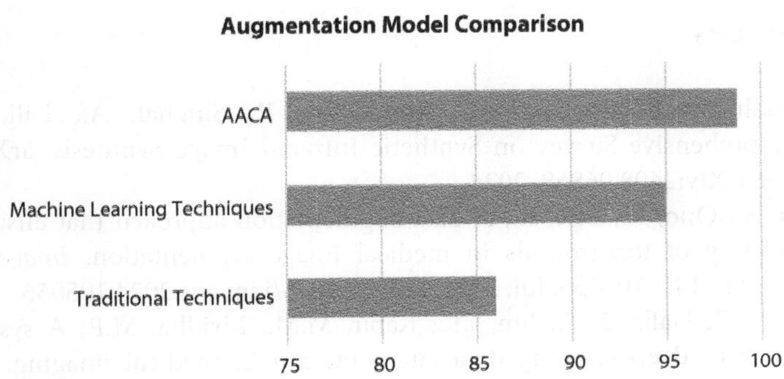

Figure 17.4 Model comparison.

Conclusion

In this research, an automated augmentation Classifier Agent has been implemented that does not require searching for parameters and can identify borders with more accuracy. The classifier technique maintains the segmentation target section with just the background disrupted, preserving more precise bounds. The suggested techniques outperformed the comparison approaches and could be simply implemented into other models without requiring the learning of additional parameters. This validates our method's efficacy, which is especially important for smaller datasets. A ground-breaking approach for contrastive loss and weighted local classification loss combined into a single training framework for a powerful classifier. In the future, we'll start by experimenting with various data augmentation levels or choosing the best data augmentation techniques for various datasets. Using publicly available image datasets, a number of studies have been processed to assess the effectiveness of the AACA. Initially, the datasets and experimental setup have been outlined before going into depth about the actual outcomes. Every experiment was carried out in Python, and it was used to implement every model. The next research is about applying these suggested techniques to a wider variety of activities, such as enhancing classification accuracy by precisely recognizing organ or lesion borders. It will then be expanded to include medical segmentation and self-supervised learning.

AI disclosure statement: The author confirms that no artificial intelligence (AI)-generated content or AI-assisted writing tools were used in the preparation of this chapter (including summaries and the abstract). All text, analysis, and conclusions are the result of the author's original work.

References

1. Upadhyay, A., Sharma, M., Mukherjee, P., Singhal, A., Lall, B., A Comprehensive Survey on Synthetic Infrared Image Synthesis, arXiv preprint arXiv:2408.06868, 2024.
2. Liu, X., Ono, K., Bise, R., A data augmentation approach that ensures the reliability of foregrounds in medical image segmentation. *Image Vision Comput.*, 147, 105056, Jul. 2024, doi: 10.1016/j.imavis.2024.105056.
3. Islam, T., Hafiz, M.S., Jim, J.R., Kabir, M.M., Mridha, M.F., A systematic review of deep learning data augmentation in medical imaging: Recent

advances and future research directions. *Healthc. Anal.*, 5, 100340, Jun. 2024, doi: 10.1016/j.health.2024.100340.
4. Shim, J., Kim, H., Kim, E., Hwang, E., Augmentation leak-prevention scheme using an auxiliary classifier in GAN-based image generation. *J. King Saud Univ. Comput. Inf. Sci.*, 35, 8, 101711, Sep. 2023, doi: 10.1016/j.jksuci.2023.101711.
5. Kou, E. and Curran, N., Enhancing Autonomous Vehicle Perception in Adverse Weather through Image Augmentation during Semantic Segmentation Training.
6. Alif, M.A.R., Enhancing Diabetic Retinopathy Diagnosis: A Lightweight CNN Architecture for Efficient Exudate Detection in Retinal Fundus Images, Aug. 13, 2024, arXiv: arXiv:2408.06784. Accessed: Oct. 27, 2024. [Online]. Available: http://arxiv.org/abs/2408.06784.
7. Chen, H., *et al.*, 3D-Adapter: Geometry-Consistent Multi-View Diffusion for High-Quality 3D Generation. Oct. 24, 2024, arXiv: arXiv:2410.18974. Accessed: Oct. 27, 2024. [Online]. Available: http://arxiv.org/abs/2410.18974.
8. Ghosh, S., *et al.*, DALE: Generative Data Augmentation for Low-Resource Legal NLP. Oct. 24, 2023, arXiv: arXiv:2310.15799. Accessed: Aug. 16, 2024. [Online]. Available: http://arxiv.org/abs/2310.15799.
9. He, X., Nassar, I., Kiros, J., Haffari, G., Norouzi, M., Generate, Annotate, and Learn: NLP with Synthetic Text. *Trans. Assoc. Comput. Linguist.*, 10, 826–842, Aug. 2022, doi: 10.1162/tacl_a_00492.
10. Tatar, A., Haghighi, M., Zeinijahromi, A., Experiments on image data augmentation techniques for geological rock type classification with convolutional neural networks. *J. Rock Mech. Geotech. Eng.*, S167477552400177X, May 2024, doi: 10.1016/j.jrmge.2024.02.015.
11. Guan, J., Li, R., Yu, S., Zhang, X., Generation of Synthetic Electronic Medical Record Text. Dec. 06, 2018, arXiv: arXiv:1812.02793. Accessed: Oct. 27, 2024. [Online]. Available: http://arxiv.org/abs/1812.02793.
12. Li, O., Cai, J., Hao, Y., Jiang, X., Hu, Y., Feng, F., Improving Synthetic Image Detection Towards Generalization: An Image Transformation Perspective. Aug. 13, 2024, arXiv: arXiv:2408.06741. Accessed: Oct. 27, 2024. [Online]. Available: http://arxiv.org/abs/2408.06741.
13. Chen, Z., Geng, A., Jiang, J., Lu, J., Wu, D., Infra-YOLO: Efficient Neural Network Structure with Model Compression for Real-Time Infrared Small Object Detection. Aug. 14, 2024, arXiv: arXiv:2408.07455. Accessed: Oct. 27, 2024. [Online]. Available: http://arxiv.org/abs/2408.07455.
14. microscopic synthe.
15. Ghanadian, H., Nejadgholi, I., Osman, H.A., Socially Aware Synthetic Data Generation for Suicidal Ideation Detection Using Large Language Models. *IEEE Access*, 12, 14350–14363, 2024, doi: 10.1109/ACCESS.2024.3358206.
16. Kim, S., Cho, B., Bae, S., Ahn, S., Yun, S.-Y., VACoDe: Visual Augmented Contrastive Decoding. Jul. 26, 2024, arXiv: arXiv:2408.05337. Accessed: Oct. 27, 2024. [Online]. Available: http://arxiv.org/abs/2408.05337.

17. Ma, Y., Xu, X., Fang, L., Liu, Z., GADT: Enhancing Transferable Adversarial Attacks through Gradient-guided Adversarial Data Transformation. Oct. 24, 2024, arXiv: arXiv:2410.18648. Accessed: Oct. 27, 2024. [Online]. Available: http://arxiv.org/abs/2410.18648.
18. Wang, T., *et al.*, Deep Learning Model Security: Threats and Defenses. Dec. 16, 2024, arXiv: arXiv:2412.08969. doi: 10.48550/arXiv.2412.08969.
19. Mythili, S., Nidhya, R., Kumar, R.A., AI-driven security framework for enhanced threat detection in mobile satellite networks. *ICTACT J. Commun. Technol.*, *16*, 1, 2025.
20. Kabane, S., Impact of Sampling Techniques and Data Leakage on XGBoost Performance in Credit Card Fraud Detection. Dec. 10, 2024, arXiv: arXiv:2412.07437. doi: 10.48550/arXiv.2412.07437.
21. Hamza, A., Lojo, A., Núñez-Marcos, A., Atutxa, A., Ali-AUG: Innovative Approaches to Labeled Data Augmentation using One-Step Diffusion Model, arXiv preprint arXiv:2410.18678, 2024.
22. Choi, Y., Park, J., Byun, J., Lee, J., Leveraging Programmatically Generated Synthetic Data for Differentially Private Diffusion Training. Dec. 13, 2024, arXiv: arXiv:2412.09842. doi: 10.48550/arXiv.2412.09842.

Index

Also of Interest

Check out these published and forthcoming titles in the "Leading-Edge Breakthroughs in Artificial Intelligence" series from Scrivener Publishing

Affective Artificial Intelligence
Fundamentals, Challenges, and Applications
Published 2026. ISBN 978-1-394-42272-2

Platform Engineering
Concepts, Challenges and Applications
Edited by K. Suresh Kumar, S. Sundaresan, R. Prithiviraj, T. Ananth Kumar and S. Balamurugan
Published 2026. ISBN 978-1-394-39588-0

Responsible AI
Principles and Practices
Edited by Manish Kumar, Nitigya Sambyal, Leena Priyadarshini Singh, Ramasamy V. and S. Balamurugan
Published 2026. ISBN 978-1-394-35544-0

Digital Immune System
Principles and Practices
Edited by Sujata Priyambada Dash, Vaibhav Mishra, Bijeta Shaw, Sandeep Kumar Panda and S. Balamurugan
Published 2025. ISBN 978-1-394-38375-7

Adaptive AI
Fundamentals, Challenges, and Applications
Edited by P. Pavan Kumar, G. Suresh Kumar, Ajay Kumar Jena, Sandeep Kumar Panda and S. Balamurugan
Published 2025. ISBN 978-1-394-38904-9

AI Trust, Risk and Security Management
Framework, Principles, and Practices
Edited by R. Karthick Manoj, S. Senthilnathan, S. Arunmozhi Selvi, T. Ananth Kumar and S. Balamurugan
Published 2025. ISBN 978-1-394-39299-5

Forthcoming 2026
Neuro-Symbolic AI: Concepts and Applications
Decision Intelligence: Concepts, Applications, and Case Studies
Human-Centered AI: Frameworks and Applications
Composite AI: Fundamentals, Challenges, and Applications
Visual AI: Fundamentals, Challenges, and Applications
Causal AI: Fundamentals and Applications
Embodied AI: Concepts, Challenges, and Applications
Agentic AI: Concepts, Applications, and Case Studies
Data-Centric AI: Concepts, Applications and Case Studies
Sovereign AI: Frameworks, Principles, and Practices
Accelerated AI: Energy Efficient Computing Systems for Large Language Models (LLMs)
Actionable AI: Powered by Large Action Models (LAMs)
AI-Augmented Software Engineering: Principles and Practices
Ambient Invisible Intelligence: Fundamentals, Challenges, and Applications
Artificial Cognition: Technology, Applications, and Challenges
Artificial General Intelligence: Principles and Practices
Autonomous AI Agents: Foundations and Applications
Principles of Confidential Computing
Disinformation Security for Generative AI Applications: Concepts, Methodologies, and Use Cases
Embedded AI: Concepts, Challenges, and Applications
Graph Neural Networks (GNNs): Concepts and Applications
Industry Cloud Platforms: Fundamentals, Applications, and Case Studies
Multi-Modal Generative AI: Frameworks, Principles, and Practices
Objective-Driven AI: Concepts, Applications, and Case Studies
Physical AI for Robotics and Automation: Concepts, Techniques, and Applications

Predictive AI: Concepts, Applications, and Case Studies
Prescriptive AI: Concepts, Applications, and Case Studies
Shadow AI: Concepts, Applications, and Security
Small Language Models (SLMs) for Compact AI: Architectures, Principles, and Applications

www.scrivenerpublishing.com

Printed and bound by CPI Group (UK) Ltd, Croydon, CR0 4YY
17/09/2026
14964266-0003